The Holy Bible Containing the Old and the New Testaments

by Leicester Ambrose Sawyer

Address:
HardPress
8345 NW 66TH ST #2561
MIAMI FL 33166-2626
USA
Email: info@hardpress.net

THE

HOLY BIBLE,

CONTAINING THE

OLD AND NEW TESTAMENTS.

Translated and Arranged,

WITH NOTES;

BY LEICESTER AMBROSE SAWYER.

VOL. II.

THE LATER PROPHETS.

BOSTON:
WALKER, WISE AND COMPANY,
245 WASHINGTON STREET.
1861.

STEREOTYPED AT THE
BOSTON STEREOTYPE FOUNDRY.

4438

PRINCIPLES OF TRANSLATION.

1. To translate from the most improved texts of the originals. The New Testament follows the text of Tischendorf, and differs essentially from the received text. The text of Tischendorf is formed entirely from ancient authority, embracing the ancient Greek manuscripts, the ancient versions, and the church fathers. The received text is formed from modern manuscripts, with very slight correction, and is in many cases erroneous.

2. To translate as exactly as may be, and as literally as may be, word for word, and particle for particle. Absolute exactness is not possible. The best translation is only an approximation to exactness. Neither is it possible or necessary always to translate to the letter. Some degree of freedom is allowable in respect to idiomatic forms, in order to make the style of a translation agreeable. The present work endeavors to avoid extremes, but is considerably more literal and more exact than the common version.

3. To translate general terms by those equally general, not the more general by the less general, or the less general by the more general. This rule can not be always observed; the imperfection of language and unfavorable associations sometimes require a deviation from it, as in the case of the word which in Rev. 4: 6, etc., is translated beasts in the common version, and cherubs in mine. The corresponding English word is not beast, nor cherub, but animal. The animal intended, however, is the cherub, and I therefore adopt its specific name in the place of its general one. So in a few other cases. The Old Testament is translated from the Hebrew Bible of Hahn.

4. To translate the same words by the same, as far as may be, and different words by different corresponding words. This is a principle of great importance. I have had it continually in view, and

(3)

adhered to it both in the Old Testament and New, to a much greater extent than is done in the common version.   I distinguish between devil and demon, hell and hades, change of mind and repentance, love and friendship, baptism and washing, and many other objects which the common version confounds.

5. To avoid needless indelicacy and vulgarity.   The common version has many needless indelicacies and some vulgarities.   These I avoid.   I do not, however, omit any thing for this purpose.

6. To translate chiefly into the recent improved style of the times in preference to the antiquated style of 250 years ago.   The style of the times is the living English language, in opposition to the partially dead and dying language of a former period.   The inevitable law of change applies to language as it does to other objects. Living languages necessarily change.   When nations improve their language improves, when they decline their language declines.   In the last 250 years the English nation has greatly improved, and its language is proportionably improved.   We have a much better and nobler language than King James had.

7. To continue the use of the words baptize and baptism.   The corresponding Greek words are used by the classic writers to denote common actions ; in the New Testament they are used only to denote religious rites.   These are of the three kinds : 1. The rites prescribed by Moses, Heb. 9 : 10 ; 2. The Jewish traditionary baptisms, Mark 1 : 4 ; and 3. The baptisms of John the Baptist and Christ.

The verb $\beta\alpha\pi\tau i\zeta\omega$ is a derivative from $\beta\acute{\alpha}\pi\tau\omega$, and takes its signification from its primitive, subject to some modifications. $B\acute{\alpha}\pi\tau\omega$ corresponds to the Latin mergo, and English merge or plunge ; $\acute{\epsilon}\mu\beta\acute{\alpha}\pi\tau\omega$ to the Latin [in] *im*mergo, and English [in] *im*merse, plunge in. $Ba\pi\tau i\zeta\omega$ is different from either, and ought not to be confounded with them.   It neither signifies to merge or plunge, nor to *im*merse or plunge *in ;* nor is there any verb in the Latin or English languages to express it perfectly but itself.   The word was Latinized to meet a necessity ; it was also Anglicized for the same purpose, and is as necessary now as it ever has been.   As the primitive means to plunge, the derivative $\beta\alpha\pi\tau i\zeta\omega$ expresses some modification of plunging, and not plunging simply.   This was the use of the verb from the beginning ; for there was no need of forming it to signify the same as its primitive $\beta\acute{\alpha}\pi\tau\omega$, to plunge, or its correlative $\acute{\epsilon}\mu\beta\acute{\alpha}\pi\tau\omega$, to plunge in.   The necessity of it was to express some specific kind or modification of plunging. The classic Greeks never made much use of the word. Why the Greeks formed it at first we can not tell. It was undoubtedly formed to meet an emergency. The Jews found it formed and adapted to their use, and used it to answer their purposes. Christianity took it up, and used it to answer its purposes, and continues to use it still in many different languages. The Greek nouns for baptism are derived from the verb, and have corresponding meanings. A baptism is more than a mersion or *immersion*. It is a cleansing, and was probably administered by the first Christians not in the form of a simple mersion, but of a general washing *in* the water. The mechanical part of baptism corresponds to bathing, and would be more nearly expressed by it, than by any other English word except itself.

8. To preserve Jehovah and Jah as proper names of God. The Septuagint renders the original for this name Lord; and when points representing vowels were added to the Hebrew letters, the Hebrew name for Jehovah received not the points which belonged to it, but those which belonged to the Hebrew word for Lord; and when the Hebrew word for Lord was used with it, the Jewish punctuators gave it the points of the Hebrew word for God. The Jews read the word to this day according to its points, and never according to its letters or consonants. It was probably pronounced in two syllables, Jahveh or Jehveh, and was sometimes contracted to Jah. Its dissyllabic character is conformable to its derivation and the analogy of other Hebrew words, and is demanded by the Hebrew poetry, where its pronunciation in three syllables in many cases injures the measure. Jahveh is derived from the Hebrew verb which signifies to be. It is the imperfect indicative, which combines the present and future of the 3d person singular Was and Will be. The Hebrew God was the Was and Will be, or the Is and the Was and the Is to come. This was expressed by Jahveh, or Jehveh, and is referred to in Rev. 1 : 8. The true name is the shortest and most easily pronounced, but it is impossible to restore it. I therefore take Jehovah as the name which has for many centuries superseded the true one, and is the nearest approximation to it which we have in common use. I also transfer Jah in all cases in which it is found in the original. The common version often changes it to Jehovah. Jah is a contraction of Jahveh, and is used considerably in Psalms. It occurs also in Isa. 26 : 4, 38 : 11, and is the last syllable of many Hebrew names. The formation of one proper name by shortening

1 *

another is in conformity with a general usage of our times, the object of which is increased beauty and convenience.

The other names of God, אֵל, El, the Mighty One, אֱלוֹהַּ, Elöah, and אֱלֹהִים, Elohim, the High One, etc., I translate God, the common title of the Supreme Being in modern times, which denotes him as the Good one. It does not seem expedient to transfer those original titles, nor to attempt to revive the use of them, or to introduce translations of them in competition with a name so beautiful and appropriate as the one in common use.

9. To translate שְׁאוֹל, Sheòl, in the Old Testament, by hades, to allow hades to stand for its corresponding Greek word in the New Testament, and to render γεέννα hell, thus excluding hell from the Old Testament, which contains no allusion to it, and distinguishing it in the New from hades, in conformity with the original. The common version confounds these words. Sheòl is the hades, or under world of the Hebrews, vast, dark, inhabited by the shades of the dead, represented by the poets with gates and bars, with trees and forests, and often as a vast pit, in the sides of which whole nations of shades make their residence. The derivation of the word is from שָׁאַל, Shaal, with a change of ayin to aleph, literally the pit or hole, a derivation similar to that of the English word hell, and the Latin cœlum, heaven. But Hebrew usage does not make this word synonymous with γεέννα, the hell of the New Testament. It therefore ought not to be confounded with it. The word γεέννα, hell of the New Testament is formed from the Hebrew גֵּי הִנֹּם, vale of Hinnom; a valley south of Jerusalem, and extending west, noted for human sacrifices offered to Molech in the time of the Hebrew kings and prophets, and called also Tophet, a place of burning [the dead]. This word appears in the New Testament as synonymous with the Greek Tartarus, or lowest part of hades, where the wicked were supposed to be imprisoned and punished. It contains a lake of fire, and is invested with the greatest conceivable terrors. The New Testament doctrine of punishments in the under world is clearly exhibited in Luke 16 : 22–25. And the rich man died and was buried; and in hades, lifting up his eyes, being in torments, he sees Abraham afar off, and Lazarus on his bosom; and he called and said, Father Abraham, have mercy on me, and send Larazus to plunge the tip of his finger in water and cool my tongue, for I distressed with this flame. That the γεέννα, hell of the New Testament, belongs to the under world, and not to the valley south of

Jerusalem, the name of which is applied to it, is further evident from Luke 12 : 5. But I will show you whom you shall fear ; fear him who, after killing, has power to cast into γεέννα, hell. Men might cast the bodies of dead men into the fires of the vale of Hinnom, but casting into this vale is a prerogative of God. With this agree Mark 9 : 43–48 ; Matt. 18 : 9 ; Jude 5, 13 ; and Jewish Rabbinical usage. It also corresponds to the contemporary doctrine of the Greeks on the subject.

10. To transfer the names of weights, measures, and coins, with expressions of their value in brackets. This is the only possible method of translating these terms correctly. It is adopted in all nations and in all languages, ancient and modern, and is the common approved method of translating such terms in our times. The addition of the value in brackets is the only thing in which I have deviated from the usage of all reputable translators. Shall this method be brought into the Bible, after being carried every where else P or shall the erroneous and unsatisfactory method of King James be perpetuated, making the Bible an exception to all other books P

11. To arrange the books according to their times. The first of the Epistles of Paul is the 1st Epistle to the Thessalonians, A. D. 53 ; then follows the 2d, A. D. 53 ; then the Epistle to the Galatians, A. D. 56 ; then 1st and 2d Corinthians, A. D. 57, 58 ; and 6th in order comes the Epistle to the Romans, A. D. 58 ; and so on. Shall this natural order of the Epistles be observed in the arrangement of these books P or shall we forever discard it ? So in the Old Testament, Jonah, Joel, Amos, Hosea, Micah, and Nahum precede Isaiah, or were contemporary with him in the early part of his life. Shall their books stand before his, or after it P The advantage of a chronological arrangement of the books in both Testaments is very great.

12. To divide the books into chapters and verses according to their natural divisions. There is not another book in Christendom so badly divided as the Bible. A History, Biography, Moral Philosophy, Geography, or miscellaneous work that should be divided as badly as the common Bible, would be the greatest curiosity of the age. The Lord's Sermon on the Mount is commenced in the 5th chapter of Matthew, and continued through the 6th and 7th ; and its subdivisions are 111 verses. Where is there a modern sermon so injured in its publication by improper divisions P No-

where.   Yet this is reported as a single sermon, delivered at one sitting.   In my translation, it is in one chapter, with 14 verses, its natural divisions.   The highest object of divisions is to aid interpretation.   The convenience of references is an after consideration, to which the interests of interpretation can not be sacrificed with propriety, and need not be.   It is high time that an improved system of divisions was inaugurated, at whatever expense may be necessary for that purpose.   The prophets in the Old Testament I do not divide into chapters, but resolve into prophecies and verses, and in a single instance, the last part of Ezekiel, into a prophecy and sections and verses.   The common division of chapters was introduced in Italy, A. D. 1240; Cardinal Hugo adopted it in his Concordance in 1260; and that of verses was first introduced by Robert Stephens in his Greek Testament, in A. D. 1551, and very soon extended to the Old Testament.   Many suppose that these divisions are a finality, and can never be changed.   But this is a mistake.   If the Bible is to be understood, and to retain its hold on the public respect, it must be made as perfect as possible in its text and translations, and also in its arrangements and divisions.   To stop short of this in our labors on it, is to be guilty of culpable negligence.

13. To improve the headings of the chapters, and not to indicate by erroneous headings false modes of interpretation.   This is an error often committed in the common version, both in the Old Testament and New, and the importance of this class of improvements is considerable.   In some cases in the prophets, headings are transferred from the Hebrew text, and printed in Italics, to distinguish them from headings which are supplied, and which are printed in small capitals.

14. To avoid the application of incorrect principles of translation, and allow the sacred writers to mean what they say.

Interpretation is an art.   Its principles are as fixed and settled as those of any other art.   The application of correct principles leads to correct interpretations; that of incorrect principles to incorrect ones.   All violent interpretations are incorrect.   Men do not use words in such a way as to require violence in the interpretation of them.   To interpret the sacred writers contrary to the natural meanings of their words, in conformity with traditionary opinions, or the views of any church, sect, or school of philosophy, is always incorrect.   No external authority whatever should be allowed to have weight against the natural meaning of a writer's words.

Every writer is to be presumed to mean what he says, unless there is evidence that he misapprehended the meaning of his own words. In such a case the known meaning of words may be set aside, and other meanings substituted conformable to the known intention of the writer. Many errors of interpretation are traditionary, many are dogmatic, many arise from interpreting one part of the Scriptures by another, as if, in different stages of the development of religious ideas, men could not be allowed to think differently. The New Testament is not to be interpreted by the Old, nor the Old by the New, except with great allowances for differences of opinion on many subjects. Many of the quotations of the New Testament are applied to express senses the farthest possible from those which they express in the Old Testament. As in Matt. 2 : 15. And he was there till the death of Herod, that the word might be fulfilled which was spoken by the Lord by the prophet, saying, Out of Egypt I called my son. This is here applied to the infant Saviour. In Hosea 11 : 1, the prophet says, in the name of Jehovah, When Israel was a child, then I loved him, and called my son out of Egypt. [As] men called to them, so they went from before them, they sacrificed to Baals, they burned incense to carved images. Here is no allusion whatever to the infant Saviour, but a reference to the Israelites when they came out of Egypt. So in the same chapter, at verses 17, 18. Then was fulfilled that which was spoken by Jeremiah the prophet, saying, A voice was heard in Ramah, weeping and great lamenting, Rachel weeping for her children, and she would not be comforted, because they were not. A reference to the original passage in Jer. 31 : 15, 16, shows that the persons referred to, were the descendants of Rachel who died in Palestine, or went into exile to Babylon. Similar instances might be multiplied, showing that the application of passages in the New Testament is no rule for their interpretation in the Old.

No man can undertsand the common Bible without Commentaries. The reader requires them incessantly, sometimes on account of obscurity, and sometimes on account of errors in the text or translation. He can not depend on the common Bible either for the true text or the true translation. Every man of sense and information knows that some passages are spurious, and some translations erroneous; to learn which they are, he looks to his Commentary. His Commentary, therefore, and not his Bible, is his real authority in respect to the text of the New Testament and its meaning. The common Bible has already lost its authority as a standard, because it is known to be incorrect; and the Commentary supplies its deficiency and supplements it. I propose my version as another supply and another supplement for this purpose, and have endeavored to make it as perfect as possible.

If any imagine that they can much longer sustain the common Bible in credit without admitting the very corrections and improvements which I am making, they are much mistaken. Truth will come to light; it ought to come to light, and men ought to know, and will know, that the studies and labors of seven generations throughout all Christendom, directed to the improvement and interpretation of the sacred text, have not resulted in nothing. They have yielded a rich harvest, and one worth gathering up and appropriating to the benefit of the masses, and of coming ages.

Some imagine that it is not a new translation that is wanted, but a slight revision of the old one. This is a mistake. King James's Bible can not be altered with propriety any more than you can alter Shakspeare or Paradise Lost. It is a great historical monument, representing the knowledge of the times which produced it, and of the times which have adhered to it. It will be the wonder of future ages that it had the sole occupancy of the field so long, not that it was finally obliged to admit a later and more accurate version to be used with it. But when it shall be superseded entirely as the Bible of common use, as it must be; even then it will have a great historical value.

I am laboring for the benefit of no single religious order, to the detriment of others, but for the common good of all. I am thankful to obtain a generous friendship and hearty coöperation from good men in many different connections, and trust, as my work becomes better understood, the number of its friends will be proportionably increased.

All is for God, for his truth, for the good of his creatures, and for the hastening on of those golden ages of bliss, long ago predicted as at hand, by the Hebrew seers, but yet deferred and distanced by human impiety and wickedness. How long, O how long, ere the happy vision will become a glorious reality, and all tears be wiped away from the eyes of the sorrowing by the hand of the Infinite?

CONTENTS.

NOTES.

(11)

1. JONAH.

1 AND the word of Jehovah came to Jonah the son of Amittai, saying, Arise, go to Nineveh, the great city, and cry against it, for their wickedness has come up before me. Then Jonah arose to flee from the presence of Jehovah to Tarshish. And he went down to Joppa, and found a ship there going to Tarshish, and paid his fare, and went down into it, to go with them from the presence of Jehovah to Tarshish.

2 But Jehovah raised up a great wind on the sea, and there was a great tempest on the sea, and the ship was thought to be breaking to pieces. Then the seamen were afraid, and cried every man to his god, and cast the implements which were in the ship into the sea to lighten it; but Jonah went down into the sides of the vessel, and lay down and slept. Then the captain of the ship came to him, and said to him, What do you mean, sleeper? ·Arise, call on your God; perhaps God will think of us, that we perish not.

3 Then they said one to another, Come, let us cast lots, that we may know on whose account this evil is on us. And they cast lots, and the lot fell on Jonah. Then they said to him, Tell us, we pray you, for what this evil is on us; what is your business? whence do you come? what is your land? and from what people are you? Then he said to them, I am a Hebrew, and fear Jehovah, the God of heaven, who made the sea and the dry land. Then the men were greatly afraid, and said to him, What is this which you have done? for the men knew that he was fleeing from the presence of Jehovah, for he told them.

4 Then they said to him, What shall be done to you, that the sea may subside from over us? for the sea raged, and was tempestuous. Then he said, Take me up, and cast me into the sea; and the sea

will subside from over you ; for I know that this great tempest is
against you on my account. But the men struggled to return to
land ; but they could not, for the sea raged, and was tempestuous
against them. Then they called on Jehovah, and said, We beseech
thee, Jehovah, let us not perish for the life of this man, and lay not
innocent blood on us, for thou, Jehovah, hast done as it pleased thee.
Then they took up Jonah and cast him into the sea, and the sea
desisted from its rage. And the men greatly feared Jehovah, and
sacrificed a sacrifice to Jehovah, and vowed vows.

5 Then Jehovah appointed a great fish to swallow Jonah, and
Jonah was in the bowels of the fish three days and three nights.
And Jonah prayed to Jehovah his God from the bowels of the fish,
and said, I cried in my distress to Jehovah, and he answered me ;
from the belly of Hades I cried, and thou heardest my voice. Thou
didst cast me into the deep, into the heart of the seas, and a river
encompassed me ; all thy billows and thy waves passed over me.
Then I said, I am cast out from thy sight, but I will look again to
thy holy temple. The waters came round me to [my] soul, the deep
enclosed me round. Seaweeds were bound about my head ; I went
down to the foundations of the mountains ; the earth and its bars
were around me forever ; but thou, Jehovah my God, didst bring up
my life from the pit ; when my soul fainted within me, I remembered
Jehovah, and my prayer came to thee, to thy holy temple. Those
that serve lying vanities forsake their [own] kindness. But I will
sacrifice to thee with the voice of thanksgiving, I will pay that which
I vowed ; salvation belongs to Jehovah.

6 Then Jehovah commanded the fish, and he vomited up Jonah
on the dry land ; and the word of God came to Jonah a second
time, saying, Arise, go to Nineveh, the great city, and proclaim
against it the proclamation which I will tell you.

7 Then Jonah arose, and went to Nineveh, according to the word
of Jehovah ; and Nineveh was a great city of God, of a journey of
three days. And Jonah began to enter the city a journey of one
day, and cried and said, Yet 40 days and Nineveh shall be destroyed.
And the men of Nineveh believed God, and proclaimed a fast, and
put on sackcloth, from the greatest to the least of them. And word
was brought to the king of Nineveh, and he arose from his throne,
and put off his mantle, and put on sackcloth and sat in ashes. And
he caused it to be proclaimed and commanded in Nineveh, by order
of the king and his nobles, saying, Let neither man nor beast, bird

nor flock, taste of any thing ; let them not feed, nor drink water ; but let man and beast cover themselves with sackcloth, and call mightily on God ; and let them turn every one from his evil way, and from the violence which is in their hands. Who knows that God will not turn, and change his mind, and turn from his fierce anger, and we perish not?

8 And God saw their works, that they turned from their evil way ; and God changed his mind concerning the evil which he said he would do them, and did it not.

9 Then Jonah was greatly displeased and angry. And he prayed to Jehovah, and said, I beseech thee, Jehovah, was not this what I said when I was in my land? Therefore I formerly fled to Tarshish, for I knew that thou art gracious and merciful, slow to anger and of great kindness, and one that changes his mind in respect to evil. And now, Jehovah, take, I pray thee, my life from me, for death is better for me than life. Then Jehovah said, Is it right for you to be angry?

10 But Jonah went out of the city, and sat down on the east side of the city, and made him a booth, and sat under it in the shade, that he might see what would happen to the city. And Jehovah God appointed a ricinus [a tall biennial plant of elegant appearance] and brought it up over Jonah to be a shade for his head, to deliver him from his trouble ; and Jonah was greatly pleased with the ricinus.

11 Then God appointed a worm when the morning rose on the next day, and it killed the ricinus, and it was dried up. And when the sun rose, God appointed a sultry east wind, and the sun struck the head of Jonah, and he was faint and begged for his life, that he might die, for he said, Death is better for me than life.

12 Then God said to Jonah, Is it right for you to be angry on account of the ricinus? And he said, It is right for me to be angry, even to death. Then Jehovah said, You pitied the ricinus, for which you labored not, nor caused it to grow ; which was the product of a night, and in a night perished ; and should not I pity Nineveh, that great city, which has in it more than 120,000 human beings [infants] who cannot distinguish their right hand from their left, and many beasts?

2. JOEL.

The word of Jehovah which came to Joel the son of Pethuel,
[plague of locusts.]

1 HEAR this, elders ; attend, all the inhabitants of the land.   Has
this been in your days ? or even in the days of your fathers ?   Tell
it to your sons, and your sons to their sons, and their sons to
another generation.   What the creeping locust left, the winged locust has eaten ; and what the winged locust left, the hairy locust
has eaten ; and what the hairy locust left, the voracious locust has
eaten.

2 Awake, drunkards, and weep ; and lament, all who drink wine
for the new wine, for it is cut off from your mouth.   For a nation
has come up on my land strong and without number ; its teeth are
the teeth of a lion, and it has the jaw-teeth of a lioness.   It has
made my vine a waste, and broken down my fig-tree ; it has stripped
off the bark and cast it away ; its branches are white.

3 Lament like a young woman girded with sackcloth for the husband of her youth : the bread-offering and libation are cut off from
the house of Jehovah ; the priests, the ministers of Jehovah, mourn ;
the country is destroyed ; the field mourns, for the grain is destroyed ;
the new wine is dried up, the oil languishes.   The husbandmen are
ashamed, the vine-dressers lament for the wheat and for the barley,
for the harvest of the field has perished.   The vine is dried up, the
fig-tree languishes, the pomegranate, also the palm-tree and apple-
tree, all the trees of the field are dried up ; for joy is dried up from
the sons of men.

4 Gird yourselves and lament, priests, ministers of the altar ; go,
lodge in sackcloth, ministers of my God ; for the bread-offering and
libation are withheld from the house of your God.   Appoint a fast,
call an assembly, assemble the elders [and] all the inhabitants of
the land to the house of Jehovah your God, and cry to Jehovah,
Alas for the day, for the day is at hand, the day of Jehovah ; it shall
come like destruction from the Almighty.   Is not our food cut off
before our eyes ? joy and gladness from the house of our God ?   The

sowings have died under their clods, the treasure-houses are destroyed, the store-houses are torn down, for the grain is dried up. How do the beasts groan ! the herds of cattle are perplexed, for they have no pasture; flocks of sheep also perish. To thee, Jehovah, will I cry, for fire has consumed the pastures of the wilderness, and a flame destroyed all the trees of the field. The cattle of the field also look up to thee, for the channels of water are dry, and fire has consumed the pastures of the wilderness.

5 Blow a trumpet in Zion, cry aloud in my holy mountain; let all the inhabitants of the land tremble, for the day of Jehovah has come, for it is at hand; a day of darkness and thick darkness, a day of clouds and dark clouds; a great and strong people like morning breaking on the mountains; there has been none like it from of old, and there shall not be again after it, to the years of many generations. Before it a fire consumes, and after it a flame burns; the earth is like the garden of Eden before it, after it, a desolate wilderness, and none shall escape.

6 Their appearance is like the appearance of horses, and like horsemen so they run. They leap on the tops of the mountains like the sound of chariots, like the sound of a flame of fire consuming the stubble, like a strong people arrayed for battle. Before them peoples tremble; all faces collect paleness; they run like mighty men; they ascend a wall like men of war; they go each one his ways, and change not their paths. They crowd not one another; they go every one in his way; and if they fall in the midst of weapons, they are not wounded. They run about in the city; they run on the wall; they ascend the houses; they come in at the windows like a thief. Before them the earth trembles, the heavens shake, the sun and moon are darkened, and the stars withdraw their light. And Jehovah utters his voice before his host, for his camp is large exceedingly; for strong is he that performs his word; for great is the day of Jehovah, and greatly to be feared, and who can endure it?

7 And now also, says Jehovah, Turn to me with all your heart, and with fasting, and weeping, and lamentation, and rend your heart and not your garments, and turn to Jehovah your God; for he is gracious and merciful, slow to anger, and of great kindness, and he changes his mind concerning evil. Who knows that he will not turn and change his mind, and leave behind him a blessing, a bread-offering and libation for Jehovah your God?

8 Blow a trumpet in Zion, appoint a fast, call an assembly, col-

3 *

lect the people, appoint a convention, assemble the elders, collect the children and those that suck the breasts ; let the bridegroom go forth from his chamber, and the bride from her bridal bed ; let the priests, the ministers of Jehovah, weep between the porch and the altar, and let them say, Jehovah, spare thy people, and give not thy inheritance to reproach, that the nations should rule over them. Why should they say among the peoples, Where is your God ?

9 Then will Jehovah be jealous for his land, and pity his people. And Jehovah will answer, and say to his people, Behold, I send you grain, new wine, and oil, and you shall be satisfied with it, and I will not make you any more a reproach among the nations. And I will remove far away from you my northern [host], and will drive it to a dry and desolate land, and its face shall be toward the eastern sea, and its rear toward the western sea, and its scent shall come up, and its stench ascend, for it did great things.

10 Fear not, land ; be glad and rejoice ; for Jehovah has done great things. Fear not, beasts of the field ; for the pastures of the wilderness have become green, for the tree bears its fruit, the fig-tree and the vine give their strength. Be glad, sons of Zion, and rejoice in Jehovah your God ; for he has given you the autumnal rain kindly, and he will cause showers to come down on you, the autumnal rain and the vernal rain as formerly ; and the threshing floors shall be filled with wheat, and the vats overflow with new wine and oil. And I will restore you the grass which the winged locust has eaten, the hairy locust, the voracious locust, and the creeping locust, my great host, which I sent on you ; and you shall eat and be satisfied, and praise the name of Jehovah your God, who has done wonderful things for you, and my people shall never be ashamed.

11 And afterwards I will pour out my Spirit on all flesh ; and your sons and your daughters shall prophesy, and your young men shall dream dreams, and your elders shall see visions ; and also on my man-servants and female-servants in those days will I pour out my Spirit ; and I will show prodigies in the heavens and in the earth, blood and fire and columns of smoke, and the sun shall be turned into darkness, and the moon into blood, before the coming of the great and terrible day of Jehovah. And every one that shall call on the name of Jehovah shall be delivered, for in Mount Zion and Jerusalem shall be deliverance, according as Jehovah has said, and for the remnant whom Jehovah shall call.

12 For behold, in those days and at that time when I shall restore the captives of Judah and of Jerusalem, then I will gather all nations, and bring them down to the valley of Jehoshaphat, and contend with them there for my people, and for my inheritance, Israel, whom they scattered among the nations, and divided my land. They even cast lots for my people, and gave a boy for a harlot, and sold a girl for wine, that they might drink.

13 And now what will you give me, Tyre and Zidon, and all the regions of Palestine ? Will you give me a compensation ? But if you compensate me most speedily, I will put your compensations on your head. Because you took my silver and my gold, and brought my choice goods to your palaces, and sold the sons of Judah and the sons of Jerusalem to the sons of the Ionians, that they might be far off from their border ; behold, I will raise them up from the place to which you sold them, and return your recompense on your head. And I will sell your sons and your daughters into the hand of the sons of Judah, and they shall sell you to the Sabeans, to a nation far off, for Jehovah has said it.

14 Proclaim this among the nations, declare war, rouse up the mighty men, let all the men of war approach, let them come up. Beat your plowshares into swords, and your pruning knives into lances ; let the weak say, I am strong. Hasten and come, all nations from every side, and gather yourselves together ; there shall Jehovah prostrate your mighty ones. The nations shall arise, and go up to the valley of Jehoshaphat, for there will I sit to judge all the nations from every side.

15 Send the sickle, for the harvest is ripe ; go, tread, for the press is full, the vats overflow ; for great is their wickedness. Multitudes, multitudes, in the valley of judgment, for the day of Jehovah is at hand in the valley of judgment. The sun and moon shall be darkened, and the stars withdraw their light ; and Jehovah shall roar from Zion, and utter his voice from Jerusalem, and the heavens and earth shall shake, but Jehovah shall be the refuge of his people, and the defense of the sons of Israel ; and you shall know that I am Jehovah your God, who dwells in Zion, my holy mountain ; and Jerusalem shall be holy, nor strangers pass through it any more.

16 In that day the mountains shall drop down new wine, and the hills flow with milk, and all the streams of Judah shall flow with water, and a fountain shall go out from the house of Jehovah, and water the vale of the Acacias. Egypt shall be a desolation, and

Edom shall be a desolate wilderness, for violence against the sons
of Judah, because they shed innocent blood in their land ; but
Judah shall be inhabited forever, and Jerusalem from generation to
generation ; and I will avenge their blood which I have not avenged,
for Jehovah dwells in Zion.

3. AMOS.

*Words of Amos who was among the shepherds of Tekoa, which he
saw concerning Israel in the days of Uzziah king of Judah,
and in the days of Jeroboam son of Joash king of Israel, two
years before the earthquake.*

PROPHECY I. [1, 2.

THE JUDGMENTS OF SEVERAL NATIONS.

1 AND he said, Jehovah will roar from Zion, and utter his voice
from Jerusalem, and the habitations of the shepherds shall mourn,
and the top of Carmel be dried up.

2 Thus says Jehovah, For three transgressions of Damascus,
and for four, — I will not recall it, — because they threshed Gilead
with iron threshing drays, but I will send a fire on the house of
Hazael, and it shall consume the palaces of Ben-hadad. And I
will break down the bar [prince] of Damascus, and cut off the
inhabitant of the valley of Aven, and the scepter bearer from the
house of Eden, and the people of Syria shall go into captivity to
Kir, says Jehovah.

3 Thus says Jehovah, For three transgressions of Gaza, and
for four, — I will not recall it, — because they carried away the captives entire, to deliver them over to Edom, therefore I will send a fire
on the wall of Gaza, and it shall consume her palaces. And I will
cut off the inhabitant from Ashdod, and the scepter bearer from Ash-
kelon, and I will return my hand on Ekron, and the remnant of the
Philistines shall perish, says the Lord Jehovah.

4 Thus says Jehovah, For three transgressions of Tyre, and for
four, — I will not recall it, —because they delivered over the captives

entire to Edom, and remembered not the covenant of brothers, therefore I will send a fire on the wall of Tyre, and it shall consume her palaces.

5. Thus says Jehovah, For three transgressions of Edom, and for four, — I will not recall it, — because he pursued his brother with the sword, and cast off his mercies, and his anger tore continually, and his wrath kept on forever, therefore will I send a fire on Teman, and it shall consume the palaces of Bozrah.

6 Thus says Jehovah, For three transgressions of the sons of Ammon, and for four, — I will not recall it, — because they cut open women with child in Gilead, that they might enlarge their border, therefore will I kindle a fire on the wall of Rabbah, and it shall consume her palaces, amid shouting in the day of battle, and with a whirlwind in a stormy day ; and their king shall go into captivity, he and his princes together, says Jehovah.

7 Thus says Jehovah, For three transgressions of Moab, and for four, — I will not recall it, — because he burnt the bones of the king of Edom to lime, therefore will I send a fire on Moab, and it shall consume the palaces of Kerioth ; and Moab shall die amid shouting and the sound of the trumpet ; and I will cut off the judge from the midst of her, and kill all her princes with him, says Jehovah.

8 Thus says Jehovah, For three transgressions of Judah, and for four, — I will not recall it, — because they rejected the law of Jehovah, and kept not his ordinances, and their lies have caused them to err, after which their fathers walked, therefore will I send a fire on Judah, and it shall consume the palaces of Jerusalem.

9 Thus says Jehovah, For three transgressions of Israel, and for four, — I will not recall it, — because they sold a righteous man for silver, and the poor for a pair of shoes ; panting for the dust of the earth on the head of the weak ; — and they turn aside the way of the meek; a man and his father go to a girl, that they may profane my holy name ; and they lie down on pledged garments, by the side of every altar, and drink the wine of the oppressed in the house of their gods. But I destroyed the Amorite from before you, whose height was like the height of the cedars, and his strength like oaks ; but I destroyed his fruit above, and his roots below ; and brought you up out of the land of Egypt, and led you in the wilderness 40 years, to possess the land of the Amorite. And I

took of your sons for prophets, and of your young men for Nazarites.　Have I not indeed [done] this, sons of Israel, says Jehovah?
But you made my Nazarites drink wine, and commanded my
prophets, saying, Prophesy not.　Behold, I am pressed under you,
as a cart is oppressed, which is full of sheaves, and refuge shall
perish from the swift, and the strong shall not prevail with his
strength, nor the mighty man save his life, nor he that handles the
bow stand, nor the swift of foot be delivered, nor he that rides the
horse save his life; and he that is of great courage among the
mighty shall flee away naked in that day, says Jehovah.

PROPHECY II.　　　　　　　　　　[3, 4.

ISRAEL ADMONISHED.

1 HEAR this word which Jehovah has spoken against you, sons of
Israel, against all the family which I brought up out of the land of
Egypt, saying, Only you have I known of all the families of the
earth; therefore I will punish you for all your wickedness.　Can two
walk together unless they meet together?　Will a lion roar in
the forest when he has no prey?　Will a young lion utter
his voice from his den when he has taken nothing?　Will a bird
fall into a net on the earth when no snare [is set] for it?　Will a
net spring up from the earth, and not take any thing?　Shall a
trumpet be blown in the city, and the people not fear?　Shall there
be evil in the city, and Jehovah has not done it?　But the Lord
Jehovah will do nothing, unless he reveals his secret to his servants
the prophets.　A lion has roared, who will not fear?　The Lord
Jehovah has spoken, who will not prophesy?

2 Publish to the palaces of Ashdod, and to the palaces of the
land of Egypt, and say, Gather yourselves together against the
mountains of Samaria, and see the great tumults in the midst of it,
and the oppressions in the midst of it.　For they know not how to
do right, says Jehovah, treasuring up violence and destruction in
their palaces.　Therefore thus says the Lord Jehovah, An adversary
shall come and encompass the land, and your strength shall be
brought down from you, and your palaces be plundered.　Thus
says Jehovah, As a shepherd delivers from the mouth of a lion two
legs, or a piece of an ear, so shall the sons of Israel be delivered
who dwell in Samaria on the side of a bed, and in Damascus on a

couch. Hear and testify to the house of Jacob, says the Lord Jehovah, the God of hosts : for in the day on which I visit the sins of Israel on them, I will also visit them on the altars of Bethel ; and the horns of the altar shall be cut off, and fall to the earth : and I will smite the winter-house with the summer-house, and the houses of ivory shall be destroyed, and many houses shall be destroyed, says Jehovah.

3 Hear this word, heifers [women] of Bashan, who on the mountain of Samaria oppress the weak, who crush the poor, who say to their masters [husbands], Bring [wine] that we may drink. The Lord Jehovah has sworn by his holiness, Behold, the days shall come on you, in which he will take you with hooks, and those who come after you with fish-hooks, and you shall go out at breaches every woman directly forward, and you shall be cast into a fortress, says Jehovah. Go to Bethel and transgress ; at Gilgal multiply transgression ; bring your sacrifices every morning, and your tithes every three years ; offer a thank-offering with leaven, and proclaim voluntary offerings, [and] publish [them], for so you love to do, sons of Israel, says the Lord Jehovah. And I also gave you cleanness of teeth in all your cities, and want of bread in all your places, but you turned not to me, says Jehovah. And I also withheld from you the rain three months before the harvest, and rained on one city and rained not on another, and one field received rain, and the field which received no rain was dried up, and two [and] three cities went to one city to drink water, and were not satisfied ; but you turned not to me, says Jehovah.

4 I smote you with blasting and paleness ; your large gardens and your vineyards, and your fig-trees and your olives, the creeping locust devoured ; but you turned not to me, says Jehovah. I sent on you pestilence in the manner of Egypt ; I killed your young men with the sword, with the capture of your horses, and brought up the stench of your camp in your nostrils ; but you turned not to me, says Jehovah. I overthrew you, as God overthrew Sodom and Gomorrah, and you became like a firebrand plucked out of the burning fire ; but you turned not to me, says Jehovah.

5 Therefore I will do thus to you, Israel ; but because I will do this to you, prepare to meet your God, Israel. For behold, he forms the mountains and creates the winds, and declares to man what his thought is, making the morning dark, and walking on the high places of the earth. Jehovah, the God of hosts, is his name.

PROPHECY III.   [5, 6.

A LAMENTATION FOR ISRAEL.

1 HEAR this word which I take up against you, a lamentation,
house of Israel. The virgin of Israel has fallen, she shall no more
rise; she is cast down on her land, there is none to raise her up.
For thus says the Lord Jehovah, The city that went out a thousand
shall be left a hundred, and the city that went out a hundred shall
be left ten, of the house of Israel. For thus says the Lord to the
house of Israel, Seek me and live but seek not Bethel, and go not to
Gilgal, pass not over to Beersheba; for Gilgal shall certainly go
into exile, and Bethel shall come to nought. Seek Jehovah and
live, lest he fall like lightning on the house of Joseph, and consume
it, and there be none to extinguish it in Bethel. You that turn
judgment to wormwood, and cast righteousness to the ground, he
makes the seven stars and Orion, and turns the shade of death to
morning, and changes day into night; he calls the waters of the
sea, and pours them out on the face of the earth: Jehovah is his
name. He flashes destruction on the mighty, and destruction comes
on the fortress.

2 They hate him that reproves in the gate, and abhor him that
speaks uprightly. Therefore, because you tread down the weak, and
take from him loads of wheat, you shall build houses of cut stone,
but shall not inhabit them; you shall plant desirable vineyards, but
shall not drink their wine. For I know your many transgressions
and your mighty sins, afflicting the righteous with taking bribes;
and they thrust away the needy in the gate. Therefore the wise
man will be silent at that time, for it is an evil time. Seek good,
and not evil, that you may live, and Jehovah, the God of hosts, will
be just with you, as you have said. Hate evil and love good, establish justice in the gate. It may be that Jehovah, the God of hosts,
will be gracious to the remnant of Joseph.

3 Therefore thus says Jehovah, the God of hosts the Lord, There
shall be lamentation in all the streets and in all places without;
they shall say, Alas, alas! and they shall call the husbandman to
mourning, and those that know how to lament to lamentation, and
there shall be lamentation in all the vineyards; for I will pass through
the midst of you, says Jehovah.

4 Woe to you who desire the day of Jehovah. What is the day of Jehovah to you ? It is darkness, and not light. As if a man fled from before a lion, and a bear met him, or went to his house and put his hand on the wall, and a serpent bit him. Is not the day of Jehovah darkness, and not light ? and thick darkness, and no light in it ?

5 I have hated and rejected your feasts, and will not smell in your assemblies. When you offer me burnt offerings and bread offerings I will not be pleased, nor look on the peace offerings of your fat beasts. Take away from me the noise of your songs, for I will not hear the music of your nabliums, but let justice flow like water, and righteousness like a mighty river. Did you bring me sacrifices and bread offerings in the wilderness forty years, house of Israel ? But you took up the tabernacles of your king and of Chiun, your images, the star of your god, which you made for you ; and I will carry you away captive beyond Damascus, says Jehovah ; the God of hosts is his name.

6 Woe to those who are at ease in Zion, and to those who trust in the mountain of Samaria, called the chief of the nations, to whom the house of Israel came ! Pass over to Calneh and see, and thence to Hamath the great, and go down to Gath of the Philistines, are they better than these kingdoms ? Is their boundary greater than your boundary, you who put far off the evil day, and cause the seat of violence to approach, who lie on beds of ivory, and are stretched on your couches, and eat lambs from the flock and calves from the stall, who prate to the mouth of the nablium, [and] like David, invent for themselves instruments of music, who drink wine in bowls, and anoint themselves with the best of oils, but they have not inherited the ruin of Joseph. Therefore they shall now be made captives with the first that are made captives, and the shouting of the loungers shall depart.

7 Jehovah has sworn by himself, Jehovah the God of hosts says, I hate the pride of Jacob, and I hate his palaces, and will deliver up the city and all it contains ; and if ten men shall be left in one house they shall die. And when a man's friend, or he that burns him, shall take him up, to carry out the bodies from the house, then he shall say to those in the sides of the house, Are there yet any more with you ? and one shall say, No. Then shall he say, Be still, for we are not allowed to mention the name of Jehovah. For behold, Jehovah will command, and smite the great house with breaches,

and the small house with clefts. Will horses run on a rock? will one plow with oxen [there]? But you have turned justice to the poppy and the fruit of righteousness to wormwood. You rejoice in a thing of no account, and say, Have we not by our strength taken to ourselves horns? But behold, house of Israel, says Jehovah the God of hosts, I will raise up a nation against you, and they shall oppress you from the entrance of Hamath to the brook of Arabah [the desert].

PROPHECY IV. [7, 8.

VISION OF THE LOCUSTS AND PLUMB LINE.

1 Thus the Lord Jehovah showed me; and behold, he formed locusts in the beginning of the coming up of the latter grass. And behold it was the latter grass after the king's mowing. And when he had finished devouring the herbage of the earth, then I said, Lord Jehovah, forgive now: who will raise up Jacob? for he is small. Jehovah changed his mind concerning this: It shall not be, said Jehovah.

2 Then the Lord Jehovah showed me; and behold, Jehovah called fire to contend [with his people]. And it consumed the great deep, and consumed the portion [of Israel]. Then I said, Lord Jehovah, cease now: who shall raise up Jacob? for he is small. Jehovah changed his mind concerning this: This also shall not be, said the Lord Jehovah.

3 Thus he showed me; and behold, the Lord stood on a plumb line wall, and a plumb line was in his hand. And Jehovah said to me, What do you see, Amos? And I said, A plumb line. Then said the Lord, Behold, I will put a plumb line in the midst of my people Israel, and will not pass through them again any more. The high places of Isaac shall be made desolate, and the sanctuaries of Israel destroyed, and I will rise up against the house of Jeroboam with the sword.

4 Then sent Amaziah the priest of Bethel to Jeroboam king of Israel, saying, Amos has conspired against you in the midst of the house of Israel; the land is not able to bear all his words: for thus says Amos, Jeroboam shall die by the sword, and Israel shall certainly go into captivity from their land.

5 Then said Amaziah to Amos the seer, Go, flee to the land of

Judah, and eat bread there, and there prophesy, for you can no longer prophesy at Bethel, for it is the king's sanctuary, and the house of the kingdom.

6 Then answered Amos, and said to Amaziah, I was not a prophet, nor the son of a prophet; but I was a herdman and a cultivator of sycamore [fruits]; and Jehovah took me from following the flock, and Jehovah said to me, Go, prophesy to my people Israel. And now hear the word of Jehovah, you who say, Prophesy not against Israel, and drop not a word against the house of Isaac. Therefore thus says Jehovah, Your wife shall commit adultery in the city, and your sons and your daughters shall fall by the sword, and your land shall be divided with a line, and you shall die in an impure land, and Israel shall certainly go into captivity from off his land.

7 Thus the Lord Jehovah showed me; and behold, a basket of fruits. And he said, What do you see, Amos? And I said, A basket of fruits. And Jehovah said to me, The end has come to my people Israel; I will pass through them again no more. In that day the songs of the palace shall lament, says the Lord Jehovah. Many dead bodies shall be in every place; cast [them] out; be still.

8 Hear this, you that pant for the needy, and cause the poor of the earth to cease, saying, When will the new moon be gone, that we may sell grain! and the sabbath, that we may open the wheat! who make the ephah [1.25 bushels] small, and the shekel [56 cents] large, and falsify the deceitful scales, to buy the weak for silver and the needy for a pair of shoes, and [who say], We will sell the refuse of the grain.

9 Jehovah has sworn by the excellency of Jacob, Surely I will never forget their works. Shall not the earth tremble for this? and all who inhabit it, mourn? And will it not all rise up like a river, and be driven off and overflowed, as by the river of Egypt? And in that day, says the Lord Jehovah, I will cause the sun to go down at noon, and make the earth dark in the daytime. And I will turn your feasts into mourning, and all your songs into lamentation, and I will bring up sackcloth on all loins, and on all heads baldness; and I will make it like a mourning for an only son, and its latter end shall be like a bitter day.

10 Behold, the days come, says the Lord Jehovah, in which I will send a famine on the earth; not a famine of bread, nor a thirst for water, but for hearing the word of Jehovah. And

they shall go from sea to sea, and shall run about from the north
to the east, to seek the word of Jehovah, and shall not find it. In
that day shall the fair virgins and young men faint from thirst.
Those who have sworn by the sin of Samaria, and said, Thy god,
Dan, lives, and the way of Beersheba lives, shall both fall, and not
rise again.

PROPHECY V.   [9.

THE DESTRUCTION AND RESTORATION OF ISRAEL.

1 I saw the Lord standing by the altar, and he said, Smite the
capitals, till the sills shall shake, and break them all on the head ;
and the rest of them I will kill with the sword, and he that flees of
them shall not escape, and he that escapes of them shall not be
delivered. If they dig into Hades, thence shall my hand take them ;
and if they ascend to heaven, thence will I bring them down ; and if
they hide themselves in the top of Carmel, thence will I search and
take them ; and if they are concealed from my sight at the bottom
of the sea, there will I command the serpent, and he shall bite
them ; and if they go into captivity before their enemies, there will
I command the sword, and it shall kill them ; and I will set my eyes
on them for evil, and not for good. For the Lord Jehovah of hosts
touches the earth, and it melts, and all its inhabitants mourn, and it
all comes up like a river, and is overflowed as by the river of Egypt.
He builds his chambers in the heavens, and founds his arch on the
earth, and calls for the waters of the sea, and pours them out on
the face of the earth : Jehovah is his name.

2 Are you not like the sons of the Ethiopians to me, sons of Israel,
says Jehovah ? Did I not bring up Israel from the land of Egypt,
and the Philistines from Caphtor, and the Assyrians from Kir ?
Behold, the eyes of the Lord Jehovah are on the sinful kingdom,
and I will destroy it from the face of the earth. But I will not entirely destroy the house of Jacob, says Jehovah, for behold, I will
command and sift the house of Israel in all nations, as one sifts
with a sieve, and not a bundle shall fall to the earth. But all the
sinners of my people who say, Evil shall not approach nor anticipate
us, shall die by the sword.

3 In that day I will set up the booth of David, which has fallen
down, and close up their breaches, and set up his ruins, and build
up [the city] as in the days of old, that they may possess the rem-

nant of Edom, and all nations which are called by my name, says Jehovah who does this.

4 Behold, the days come, says Jehovah, when the plowman shall overtake the reaper, and he that treads the grapes him that sows the seed ; and the mountains shall drop new wine, and all the hills be melted. Then I will restore the captives of my people Israel, and they shall build the desolate cities and dwell [in them], and plant vineyards and drink their wine, and make gardens and eat their fruit. And I will plant them in their land, and they shall not be plucked up any more from their land which I gave them, says Jehovah your God.

---

4. HOSEA.

The word of Jehovah which came to Hosea, the son of Beeri, in the days of Uzziah, Jotham, Ahaz, [and] Hezekiah, kings of Judah, and in the days of Jeroboam the son of Joash, king of Israel.

PROPHECY I.   [1, 2.

The beginning of the word of Jehovah by Hosea. [The prophet's wife a type of Israel.]

1 AND Jehovah said to Hosea, Go, and take you a lewd wife, and have children of lewdness, for the land has committed fornication in departing from Jehovah. Then he went and took Gomer, the daughter of Diblaim, and she became with child, and bore him a son. And Jehovah said to him, Call his name Jezreel, for yet a little while and I will visit the blood of Jezreel on the house of Jehu, and put an end to the kingdom of the house of Israel ; and in that day I will break the bow of Israel in the valley of Jezreel.

2 And she became with child again, and bore a daughter. And he said to him, Call her name Not pitied, for I will not again pity the house of Israel, but will certainly take them away. But the house of Judah I will pity, and will save them by Jehovah their God ; but I will not save them with bow, or sword, or war, or horses, or horsemen.

3 Then she weaned Not pitied, and became with child, and bore

3 *

a son. And he said, Call his name Not my people, for you are not my people, and I will not be your [God]. But the number of the sons of Israel shall be as the sands of the sea, which can not be measured nor numbered, and in the place where it was said to them, You are not my people, they shall be called sons of the living God; and the sons of Judah and the sons of Israel shall be gathered together, and appoint themselves one head, and come up from the land, for great shall be the day of Jezreel. Call your brothers My people, and your sisters Pitied; contend with your mother, contend, for she is not my wife, and I am not her husband. But let her put away her fornications from before her, and her adulteries from between her breasts, lest I strip her naked, and set her as in the day in which she was born, and make her like a wilderness, and set her like a dry land, and kill her with thirst. And I will not pity her sons, for they are sons of fornications, for their mother committed fornication, and she that received them was put to shame. For she said, I will go after my lovers who give me my bread and my water, my wool and my flax, my oil and my wine. Therefore, behold, I will hedge up your way with thorns, and make a wall, and she shall not find her paths. And she shall pursue her lovers, but shall not overtake them, and seek them, but not find them, and shall say, I will return again to my first husband, for it was better with me then than now; for she knew not that I gave her grain and wine and oil, and multiplied to her silver and gold, [which] they gave to Baal. Therefore I will return and take away my grain in its time, and my wine in its season, and will take away my wool and my flax to cover her nakedness; and now I will uncover her shame in the sight of her lovers, and no man shall deliver her from my hand. And I will put an end to all the joy of her feasts, her new moons and her sabbaths, and all her assemblies. And I will destroy her vines and her fig trees, of which she said, They are my reward which my lovers gave me, and will make them a forest, and the beasts of the field shall devour them. And I will visit on her the days of the Baals, to which she has burned incense, and adorned herself with her ear-rings and her jewels, and gone after her lovers, and forgotten me, says Jehovah.

4 Therefore behold, I will persuade her, and lead her in the wilderness, and speak kindly to her. And I will give her her vineyards thence, and the valley of Achor for a door of hope, and she shall sing there, as in the days of her youth, and as in the day in which

she came up out of the land of Egypt. And in that day, says Jehovah, you shall call me My husband, and shall not call me any
longer My Baal, and I will put away the names of Baals from her
mouth, and they shall no more be mentioned by their names.   And
I will make a covenant for them on that day with the beasts of the
field, and with the birds of heaven and reptiles of the earth, and
bow and sword and war will I destroy from the earth, and will cause
them to lie down in security.   And I will betroth you to me forever,
and betroth you to me in righteousness and justice, and kindness
and mercies, and betroth you to me in truth, and you shall know
Jehovah.   And in that day I will answer, says Jehovah, I will
answer [from] the heavens, and they shall answer [from] the
earth, and the earth shall answer with grain and wine and oil, and
they shall answer Jezreel.   And I will sow her in the earth and
pity Not pitied, and will say to Not my people, You are my people,
and they shall say, My God.

PROPHECY II.   [3.

THE PROPHET'S SECOND WIFE.

AND Jehovah said to me, Go again, [and] love a woman that is
loved by her friend, and is an adulteress, as Jehovah loves the sons
of Israel, and they turn to other gods, and love raisin cakes.   Then
I bought her for me for 15 shekels of silver [$8.50] and a homer
and a lethek [17.25 bushels] of barley, and said to her, Live with
me many days, and commit not adultery, nor be with a man, and I
also will be true to you ; for the sons of Israel shall live many days
with no king, nor prince, nor sacrifice, nor idol, nor ephod, nor do-
mestic gods.   Afterwards the sons of Israel shall return and seek
Jehovah their God, and David their king, and fear Jehovah and his
goodness in the latter days.

PROPHECY III.   [4, 5, 6.

GOD'S CONTROVERSY WITH JUDAH AND ISRAEL.

1 HEAR the words of Jehovah, sons of Israel, for Jehovah has a
controversy with the inhabitants of the land, because there is no
truth, nor kindness, nor knowledge of God in the land.   Cursing,

and lying, and murder, and stealing, and adultery have broken out, and blood reaches to blood. For this cause the land mourns, and all that live in it languish, with the beasts of the field and the birds of heaven ; and the fishes of the sea also are destroyed. Yet let no man contend, nor give reproof, for your people are like those that contend with the priest, and you shall stumble by day, and the prophet also shall stumble with you by night, and I will destroy your people.

2 My people are destroyed for lack of knowledge : because you have rejected knowledge, I will reject you from being a priest to me ; because you have forgotten the law of your God, I also will forget your sons, even I. According to their greatness, they sinned against me ; according to their glory will I make their shame. They shall eat the sins of my people, and on their wickedness they shall set their souls ; and it shall be, as with the people, so with the priest, and I will visit their ways on them, and return to them their doings. And they shall eat and not be satisfied, and commit fornication and not be multiplied, because they have forsaken the service of Jehovah. Fornication and wine and new wine have taken away [their] mind. My people ask of the wood, and their staff tells them ; for the spirit of fornication causes them to err, and they have departed wickedly from their God. They sacrifice on the tops of the mountains, and burn incense on the hills, under the oak, and the poplar and the terebinth, because their shade is good ; therefore your daughters shall commit fornication, and your wives adultery. I will not punish your daughters when they commit fornication, nor your wives when they commit adultery, when they go aside with harlots, and when they sacrifice with prostitutes, and a people that will not understand shall fall.

3 If you, Israel, commit fornication, let not Judah offend. And come not to Gilgal, go not up to Bethaven, nor swear, As Jehovah lives ; for Israel is refractory, like a refractory heifer. Now Jehovah will feed them like a young sheep in a wide place. Ephraim is joined to his idols ; let him alone. When their strong drink departs, they commit fornication, her shields love shame, the wind has bound her up with its wings, they shall be ashamed of their sacrifices.

4 Hear this, priests, and attend, house of Israel, and, house of the king, attend, for the judgment is for you. For you have been a snare to Mizpeh, and a net spread out on Tabor. The transgressors have plunged deep in slaughter, and I will chastise them all. I know

Ephraim, and Israel is not hid from me ; for you have committed fornication, Ephraim, and Israel is defiled. They will not give up their works to turn to their God, for a spirit of fornication is in the midst of them, and they know not Jehovah. Therefore the excellency of Israel shall be humbled before him, and Israel and Ephraim shall fall in their wickedness, and Judah shall fall with them. They shall go with their flocks and herds to seek Jehovah, and shall not find [him] ; he shall pass away from them. They have dealt treacherously with Jehovah ; for they have borne sons that are strangers, now the new moon shall consume them with their possessions.

5 Blow the horn in Gibeah, the trumpet in Ramah ; cry aloud, Bethaven ; [look not] behind you, Benjamin. Ephraim shall be a desolation in the day of rebuke ; I make known to the tribes of Israel what is sure. Judah's princes are like those that remove the boundary ; I will pour out on them my wrath like water. Ephraim is oppressed, justice is trodden down, because he consented and went after the commandment. And I was as a moth to Ephraim, and like rottenness to the house of Judah ; and when Ephraim saw his sickness and Judah his wound, Ephraim went to Assyria, and sent to king Jarib, and he was not able to heal you, nor to remove from you the wound. For I am as a lion to Ephraim, and as a young lion to the house of Judah. I, I will take the prey, and go [and] carry [it off], and none shall deliver. I will go and return to my place, till they become sensible of their fault, and seek my face ; in their distress they will seek me early.

6 Come, and let us return to Jehovah, for he has torn, and he will heal us ; he has smitten, and he will bind us up ; after two days he will revive us ; on the third day he will raise us up, and we shall live before him ; and we shall know, if we follow on to know Jehovah, that his coming is sure as the morning, and he will come on us like the rain ; he will water the earth like vernal showers.

7 What shall I do to you, Ephraim ? what shall I do to you, Judah ? for your kindness is like the morning cloud, and it passes away like the early dew. Therefore have I cut [them] down with prophets, and killed them with the word of my mouth ; and your judgments have gone forth [like] light. For I delight in kindness, and not a sacrifice, and in knowledge of God more than burnt offerings. But they, like Adam, have transgressed the covenant ; then they dealt treacherously with me. Gilead is a city of those that commit wickedness ; it is tracked with blood ; the company

of priests wait for a man like the waiting of troops ; they murder in the way to Shechem ; for they commit wickedness. I have seen horrible deeds in the house of Israel ; there is the fornication of Ephraim, and Israel is defiled. Judah, he has also set a harvest for you, when I restore the captives of my people. When I healed Israel, then was the wickedness of Ephraim discovered, and the evil doing of Samaria. For they practice deceit, and the thief comes, and the troop plunders without, but they think not that I remember all their evil doing. Now their doings shall encompass them ; they shall be before my face. They make glad the king with their evil doing, and with their lies the princes. All of them are adulterers ; they are like an oven heated by the baker, he desists from stirring [the fire] after kneading the dough, till it is leavened. On the day of our king the princes are sick with the heat of wine, and he joins his hand with scoffers. For they bring near their heart like an oven when they lie in wait ; their baker sleeps all night ; in the morning he burns like a flame of fire. They are all hot as an oven, and devour their judges ; all their kings have fallen ; none among them calls on me.

8 Ephraim has mixed himself with the peoples ; Ephraim is a cake not turned ; strangers devour his strength, and he knows it not ; gray hairs also are sprinkled on him, and he knows it not ; the excellency of Israel is humbled before him, but they turn not to Jehovah, their God, nor seek him, for all this. Ephraim is like a silly dove, which has no mind ; they call to Egypt, they go to Assyria. When they go, I will spread my net over them, I will bring them down like a bird of heaven, I will chasten them according to the hearing of their congregation. Woe to them, for they have wandered from me ; destruction to them, for they have transgressed against me. For I redeemed them, but they have spoken lies against me ; neither have they cried to me with their heart when they lament on their beds for the grain, and gather themselves together for new wine, and depart from me. But I admonished [them] ; I strengthened their arms, yet they devise evil against me. They return not to the yoke ; they are like a deceitful bow. Their princes shall fall by the sword, from the wrath of their tongues ; this shall be their reproach in the land of Egypt.

9 The trumpet to your mouth ; one comes like an eagle against the house of Jehovah, because they have transgressed my command ; they have sinned against my law. They shall cry to me,

My God, we know thee; [we are] Israel. Israel has rejected good; an enemy shall pursue him. They set up kings, but not by me; they made princes, and I knew it not. They made themselves idols of their silver and gold, that they may be cut off. Your calf, Samaria, is loathsome; my anger is kindled against them. How long will it be ere they will be able to be pure? For it came from Israel; the workman made it, and it is not God; for they shall sow the wind and reap the whirlwind. He shall have no standing grain; the stalk shall bear no increase; if by chance it shall bear, strangers shall eat it.

10 Israel is destroyed; now has he become among the nations as a vessel in which there is no pleasure. For they went up to Assyria; he is a wild ass alone for himself; Ephraim hires lovers. But though they are given up to the nations, now I will assemble them, and they shall rest a little while from the burden of king and princes. For Ephraim has built many altars to sin; therefore altars shall be his sin. I wrote him the great things of my law; they were regarded like a stranger. They sacrifice voluntary sacrifices, and eat flesh; Jehovah shall not delight in them. Now shall their wickedness be remembered, and their sin punished, [and] they shall return to Egypt. For Israel has forgotten his Maker, and built palaces; and Judah has multiplied fortified cities; but I will send a fire on his cities, and it shall consume her palaces.

PROPHECY V. [9, 10.

PUNISHMENT THREATENED.

1 REJOICE not, Israel, with joy, like [other] peoples; for you have committed fornication against your God; you have loved harlot-hire on all grain floors. The floor and the vat shall not feed them, and the new wine shall fail her. They shall not dwell in Jehovah's land; but Ephraim shall return to Egypt, and eat things defiled in Assyria. They shall not pour out wine to Jehovah, nor shall their sacrifices be sweet to him. Their sacrifices are like the bread of mourners; all that eat them are defiled; for their bread shall be for themselves, it shall not come to the house of Jehovah.

2 What will you do in the day of the assembly, and in the day of the feast of Jehovah? For behold, they shall go forth from violence; Egypt shall gather them; Memphis shall bury them;

nettles shall possess the desirable objects of their silver; thorn bushes shall be in their tents. Days of visitation shall come; days of retribution shall come. Israel shall know that the prophet was a fool, [and] the man of the spirit mad; for the greatness of your wickedness your destruction shall be also great.

3 Ephraim waits [a response] with my God; the prophet is a snare of the fowler in all his ways, a destruction in the house of his God. They are deeply corrupt, as in the days of Gibeah; he will remember their wickedness; he will punish their sins.

4 I found Israel like grapes in the wilderness; like the early fig on the fig tree in its first bearing. I saw your fathers; they went after Baal Peor, and devoted themselves to shame, and became abominations according as they loved them. As for Ephraim, their glory flew away like a bird from being hatched, even from birth and from conception; but if they bring up their sons, I will deprive them of men, for woe to them also when I depart from them.

5 Ephraim, as I saw in respect to Tyre, was planted in a pasture; but Ephraim shall bring forth his sons to a slaughterer. Give them, Jehovah, what wilt thou give them? a miscarrying womb and dry breasts. All their wickedness is in Gilgal, for there I hated them; for the evil of their doings I will drive them from my house; I will love them no more; all their princes are rebellious. Ephraim is smitten; their root is dried up; they shall not bear fruit, and I will kill the desirable fruit of their womb. My God will reject them, because they have not obeyed him; and they shall be wanderers among the nations.

6 Israel is a spreading vine; he puts forth for himself fruit. He multiplies altars according to the abundance of his fruit; according to the goodness of his land he makes good images. He flatters himself; now they shall offend; one shall break down their altars and destroy their images; for now they shall say, We will have no king, for we fear not Jehovah: and as for a king, what can he do for us?

7 They have spoken false oaths in making a covenant; and judgment blossoms like poppies in the furrows of the field. The inhabitant of Samaria shall fear for the calves of Bethaven, for his people shall mourn for him, and his idol priests shall tremble for him, for his glory, because it has departed from him into captivity; and it shall be carried to Assyria a present to king Jarib. Ephraim shall be put to shame, and Israel shall be ashamed of his counsel. Samaria shall be deprived of her king; she shall be like splinters

on the waters; and the high places of Aven, the sin of Israel, shall
be destroyed; the thorn bush and thistle shall come up on their
altars, and they shall say to the mountains, Cover us, and to the
hills, Fall on us.

8 You have sinned, Israel, from the days of Gibeah; there they
stood; the battle in Gibeah reached not the sons of wickedness. I
will chastise them according to my pleasure, and the peoples shall
be assembled against them, when I have bound them for their two
sins. For Ephraim is a trained heifer; I love to thresh, and will
put the yoke on her neck, and cause Ephraim to ride, that Judah
may plow, [and] Jacob harrow for him. Sow in righteousness, reap
in kindness; break up for yourselves fallow ground, for it is time
to seek Jehovah, till he come and rain righteousness on you.
You have plowed wickedness and harvested transgression; you
have eaten the fruit of lies, for you have trusted in your way, in
the multitude of your mighty men. A tumult shall arise among
your people; all your fortresses shall be destroyed, as Shalman
destroyed Betharbel in the day of battle, and mother was dashed to
pieces on her sons. Thus shall Bethel do to you, on account of
your great wickedness. The king of Israel shall be cut off in the
morning.

PROPHECY VI.   [11, 12, 7.

GOD'S LOVE TO ISRAEL.

1 WHEN Israel was a child, then I loved him, and out of Egypt I
called my son. [As others] called them, so they went forward.
They sacrificed to Baals; they burnt incense to carved images. But
I taught Ephraim to walk, taking him by his arms; but they knew
not that I healed them. I drew them with the cords of a man, with
bands of love, and became to them as one that takes off the
yoke from their jaws; I went softly to him, and caused him to eat.
He shall not return to the land of Egypt, but Assyria, shall be
his king; for they have refused to return; therefore a sword shall
afflict his cities and consume his bars, on account of their counsels.
For my people are bent on defection; when they call them to the
Most High, none will extol [him]. How shall I give you up,
Ephraim? how shall I give you up, Israel? how shall I make you
as Admah? how shall I set you as Zeboim? My heart is turned
against me; my compassions are kindled together. I will not exe-

cute my fierce anger; I will not again destroy Ephraim; for I am God, and not man, the Holy One in the midst of you, and I will not come to the city [in anger].

2 They shall walk after Jehovah; he shall roar like a lion when he roars, and the sons of the sea shall tremble. They shall tremble like a bird from Egypt, and like a dove from the land of Assyria, and I will cause them to dwell in their houses [to keep within doors], says Jehovah.

3 Ephraim has encompassed me with lies, and the house of Israel with deceit; but Judah yet walks with God, and is faithful to the holy ones. Ephraim feeds on wind, and pursues the east wind; all the day he multiplies lying and violence; they have both made a covenant with Assyria, and oil is carried to Egypt; but Jehovah will contend with Judah, and punish Jacob according to his ways, and requite him according to his doings. He circumvented his brother in the womb, and with his strength he contended with God. He contended with the angel and prevailed; he wept and made supplication to him; he found him at Bethel, and there he spoke with him; for Jehovah is the God of hosts; Jehovah is his name. And now turn to your God; do kindness and justice, and wait on your God continually.

PROPHECY VII.   [12, 8; 13, 14.

ISRAEL REPROVED.

1 EPHRAIM is a merchant; he has in his hands false scales; he loves to oppress, and he says, Certainly I am rich, I have found wealth for myself; as to all my labors, they shall not find wickedness which is sin. But I Jehovah was your God from the land of Egypt till I caused you to dwell in tents as on festal days; and spoke by the prophets, and multiplied visions, and used similitudes by the hand of the prophets.

2 Since Gilead is a vanity, they are certainly vain; they sacrifice oxen in Gilgal, their altars also are like heaps in the furrows of the field. But Jacob fled to the land of Syria, and Israel served for a wife, for a wife kept [flocks]. But by a prophet Jehovah brought up Israel out of Egypt, and by a prophet he was kept. Ephraim has committed bitter provocation, and his Lord will cast his blood on him, and return his reproach to him.

3 When Ephraim spoke, there was terror ; he was exalted in
Israel ; but he sinned by Baal, and died.　And now they sin more
and more ; they make themselves cast images of their silver by their
knowledge, images all of which are the work of workmen.　They
say to them, Let the men that sacrifice, kiss the calves ; therefore
they shall be like the morning cloud, and shall go away like the
early dew, as a whirlwind drives chaff from a threshing floor, and like
smoke from a chimney.　But I am Jehovah your God from the land
of Egypt, and you shall know no God besides me, nor any Saviour.
　4 I knew you in the wilderness, in a land of thirst.　According
as they were fed they were satisfied ; they were filled, and their heart
became elated so that they forgot me.　But I was to them like a
lion ; like a leopard I watched the way ; I met them like a bear
bereaved, and rent the caul of their heart, and then I devoured
them like a lioness ; the beast of the field tore them.　You have
destroyed yourself Israel, but in me is your help.　I was your king ;
[where is your king] now, that he may save you in all your cities ?
[and] your judges, of whom you said, Give me a king and princes ?
I gave you a king in my anger, and took him away in my wrath.
　5 Ephraim is a bundle of wickedness ; his sin is laid up.　The
pains of a woman in childbirth have come on him ; he is not a wise
son, for it is no time to stop in the breaking forth of sons.　I will
redeem them from the hand of Hades, and save them from death.
I will be your destruction, death ; I will be your destruction, Hades ;
compassion shall be hid from my eyes.　Though he is fruitful
among the brothers, an east wind of Jehovah shall come up from
the wilderness, and his spring become dry, and his fountain be
dried up, and the treasury of all his precious things be destroyed.
Samaria is guilty because she has rebelled against her God ; their
children shall fall by the sword, they shall be dashed to pieces, and
women with child shall be cut open.
　6 Turn, Israel, to Jehovah your God, for you have fallen by your
wickedness.　Take with you words, and turn to Jehovah, say to him,
Forgive all wickedness, and receive [us] kindly, and we will render
up the calves of our lips.　Assyria shall not save us, we will not
ride on horses, neither will we say any more to the work of our
hands, Ye are our gods ; for by thee is the fatherless pitied.　I
will heal their defections, I will love them freely, for my anger has
turned away from him.　I will be like dew to Israel ; he shall blossom like the lily, and strike his roots like Lebanon.　His sprouts

shall grow, and his beauty be like the olive, and his smell like Lebanon. Those who dwell in his shade shall return; they shall revive like the grain, and flourish like the vine; its remembrance shall be like the wine of Lebanon. Ephraim [shall say], What have I to do any more with idols? I have afflicted and I will look after him; [he shall be] like a green cypress; from me is your fruit found.

7 Who is a wise man? and he shall understand these things; intelligent? and he shall know them; for the ways of Jehovah are right, and the righteous shall walk in them, but sinners shall fall in them.

---

5. MICAH.

The word of Jehovah which came to Micah the Morashthite, in the days of Jotham, Ahaz, [and] Hezekiah, kings of Judah, which he saw concerning Samaria and Jerusalem.

PROPHECY I.   [1, 2, 3, 8.

ISRAEL AND JUDAH THREATENED WITH GREAT JUDGMENTS.

1 HEAR, peoples, all of you; attend, earth, and all it contains; for the Lord Jehovah is a witness among you, the Lord from his holy temple. For behold, Jehovah comes out of his place, and comes down; he walks on the high places of the earth, and the mountains melt under him, and the valleys are opened like wax before the fire, like water poured down a declivity. All this is for the wickedness of Jacob, and for the sins of the house of Israel. What is the wickedness of Jacob? Is it not Samaria? And what are the high places of Judah? Are they not Jerusalem? But I will make Samaria ruins of the field, for the planting of vineyards, and pour down her stones in the valley, and her foundations will I uncover. And all her carved images shall be broken to pieces, and all her harlot-hire shall they burn with fire, and I will make all her idols desolate, for she gathered [them] from harlot-hire, and to a harlot's hire shall they return.

2 For this I will mourn and lament, I will go stripped and naked,
I will make a lamentation like jackals, and a mourning like the
daughters of the ostrich, for her wound is mortal, for it extends
to Judah, it reaches to the gate of my people, to Jerusalem.
Tell it not in Gath, weep not at all in Bethophra, roll yourself in
dust. Pass on, inhabitant of Shaphir naked to [your] shame; the
inhabitant of Zaanan goes not out, its station shall receive from you
the lamentation of Bethazel, for the inhabitant of Maroth is in pain
for Tob, for evil shall come down from Jehovah to the gate of
Jerusalem.

3 Bind the chariot to the steed, inhabitant of Lachish; she was
the beginning of sin to the daughter of Zion, for in you were found
the transgressions of Israel. Therefore you shall abandon your
possessions to Moreshath of Gath, the houses of Achzib shall be a
lie to the kings of Israel. I will yet bring you a possessor, inhabitant of Mareshah; the glory of Israel shall go to Adullam. Make
yourself bald, cut off [your locks] for the sons of your delights,
enlarge your baldness like an eagle, for they have gone from you
into captivity.

4 Woe to those who devise wickedness and do evil on their beds;
in the light of the morning they do it, because it is in the power of
their hand. And they desire fields and take them by violence, and
houses and take [them,] and they oppress a man and his house,
and a man and his inheritance. Therefore thus says Jehovah: Behold, I devise evil against this family, from which you shall not
remove your necks, nor go loftily, for it is an evil time. In that
day shall one take up a song concerning you, and wail a wailing.
He shall say, We [once] were; we are entirely destroyed; he has
changed the portion of his people; how has it gone from me? he
has divided our fields to an apostate. Therefore you shall have
none to cast a line by lot in the congregation of Jehovah. Prophesy
not, [they say] to them that prophesy; let them not prophesy to
them, that they be not put to shame.

5 You that are called the house of Jacob, is the Spirit of Jehovah
restricted? Are these his works? Are not my words good to him
that walks uprightly? But long since have my people risen up
against me for an enemy. You strip off the mantle before the robe
of travelers who pass securely along, returning from war. The
women of my people you cast out of the house of their pleasures,
from their children you take away my glory forever. Arise and go,

4 *

for this is not a rest, for it is defiled, it shall be destroyed, and its
destruction shall be severe.   If a man follows wind and invents a
lie, [and says,] I will prophesy to you of wine and strong drink,
even he shall be a prophet of this people.

6 But [hereafter] I will certainly gather all of you, Jacob, I will
collect the remnant of Israel, I will put them together like sheep of
Bozrah, like a flock in its fold, and they shall be tumultuous with
men.   A breaker shall go up before them, and they shall break
down, and pass through the gate; they shall go forth by it, and their
king shall pass on before them, and Jehovah shall be their head.

7 Then I said : Hear, I pray you, heads of Jacob, and rulers of the
house of Israel : Is it not for you to know justice, you haters of
of good and lovers of evil, plundering men's skin off from them,
and their flesh off from their bones, and who eat the flesh of my
people, and strip their skin off from them, and break up their bones
and divide them as for a pot, and as flesh in a kettle ?   Then they
shall cry to Jehovah, but he will not answer them, and he will hide
his face from them at that time, according as they are evil in their
doings.

8 Thus says Jehovah concerning the prophets who cause my
people to err, who bite with their teeth, and proclaim peace ; and
who, if one is not given to their mouth, even declare war against
him : Therefore a night shall come on you without a vision, and
darkness without a divination, and the sun shall go down on the
prophets, and the day shall be dark over them.   Then the seers
shall be ashamed, and the diviners confounded, and they shall
cover their lips, all of them, for there shall be no answer from God.
But on the contrary, I am full of the power of the Spirit of Jehovah, and of judgment and might to declare to Jacob his
transgression and to Israel his sin.

PROPHECY II.   [3, 9 ; 4, 5.

JERUSALEM TO BE DESTROYED AND RESTORED.   THE FUTURE
KINGDOM OF GOD.

1 HEAR this, I pray you, heads of the house of Jacob, and rulers
of the house of Israel, who hate justice, and pervert every right
way.   They build up Zion with blood and Jerusalem with wickedness.   Her heads judge for a reward, and her priests teach for pay,

and her prophets divine for money, and they lean on Jehovah, saying, Is not Jehovah in the midst of us ? No evil shall come on us. Therefore on your account shall Zion be plowed as a field, and Jerusalem be heaps, and the mountain of the house, high places of the forest.

2 But in the latter days the mountain of the house of Jehovah shall be established on the top of the mountains, and exalted above the hills, and the peoples shall flow to it. And many nations shall go and say, Come and let us go up to the mountain of Jehovah, and to the house of the God of Jacob, and he will teach us of his ways, and we will walk in his paths, for the law shall go forth from Zion, and the word of Jehovah from Jerusalem. And he shall judge between many peoples, and rebuke strong nations, even the distant ; and they shall beat their swords into plowshares, and their spears into pruning knives, and shall not lift up sword, nation against nation, nor learn war any more. But they shall sit every man under his vine, and under his fig-tree, and none shall make them afraid, for the mouth of Jehovah of hosts has spoken it. For all peoples shall walk every one by the name of his God, and we will walk by the name of Jehovah our God forever and ever.

3 In that day, says Jehovah, I will gather the lame and assemble the outcasts and those whom I afflicted ; and I will make the lame a remnant, and the distant one a strong nation, and Jehovah shall reign over them in mount Zion henceforth and forever. And, you tower of the flock, hill of the daughter of Zion, to you shall certainly come the former dominion, the kingdom of the daughter of Jerusalem.

4 Now why do you cry on account of evil ? Is there no king in you ? Have your counselors perished, that pain has seized you as a woman in childbirth ? Be in pain, and be in anguish, daughter of Zion, as a woman in childbirth, for now you shall go forth from the city and live in the country, and go even to Babylon ; there shall you be delivered ; there shall Jehovah redeem you from the hand of your enemies.

5 But now many nations are gathered together against you, saying, Let her be defiled, and let our eyes look on Zion. But they know not the thoughts of Jehovah, nor understand his counsel, for he shall gather them as sheaves of a threshing floor. Arise, thresh, daughter of Zion ; for I will make your horn iron, and your hoofs brass ; and you shall break in pieces many peoples, and I will devote their

plunder to Jehovah, and their wealth to the Lord of the whole earth. Gather yourselves together now, daughter of a troop ; they have set a garrison against you, they have smitten the judge on the cheek, the judge of Israel.

6 And you, Bethlehem Ephratah, little to be among the thousands of Judah, out of you shall come one to be ruler of Israel, and his descent is from of old, from ancient days. Therefore [God] shall give them up, till one with child shall bear, and the rest of his brothers return to the sons of Israel. Then one shall stand up and rule with the strength of Jehovah, with the majesty of the name of Jehovah his God, and they shall dwell [in safety], for now he shall be great to the ends of the earth. And he shall be the peace of Assyria when he shall come into our land, and tread down our palaces. For we will appoint against him seven shepherds, and eight principal men, and they shall feed the land of Assyria with the sword, and the land of Nimrod [shall remain] within her gates, and he shall deliver [us] from Assyria, when he comes into our land, and when he treads down our border.

7 And the remnant of Jacob shall be in the midst of many peoples, as dew from Jehovah, as rain-drops on the grass, which stay not for man, nor wait for the sons of man. And the remnant of Jacob shall be among the nations, in the midst of many peoples, as a lion among the beasts of the forest, as a young lion in flocks of sheep, who, if he passes through, both treads down and tears, and none can deliver. Your hand shall be lifted up over your adversaries, and all your enemies shall be cut off.

8 And in that day, says Jehovah, I will cut off your horses from the midst of you, and destroy your chariots. And I will cut off the enemies of your land, and destroy all your fortresses ; and I will cut off the magi from your land, and you shall have no sorcerers ; and I will cut off your carved images and your statues from the midst of you, and you shall no more worship the work of your hands. And I will cast down your Asheras from the midst of you, and will destroy your enemies. And I will execute judgment in anger and indignation on the nations which obey not.

PROPHECY III. [6, 7, 8.

GOD INSISTS ON RIGHTEOUSNESS.   HIS JUDGMENTS AND KINGDOM.

1 HEAR now what Jehovah says : Arise, contend before the mountains, and let the hills hear your voice.   Hear, mountains, the controversy of Jehovah, and you strong foundations of the earth, for Jehovah has a controversy with his people, and will contend with Israel.   My people, what have I done to you? and in what have I wearied you?   Answer me.   For I brought you up out of the land of Egypt, and redeemed you from the house of servants; and I sent before you Moses and Aaron and Miriam.   My people, remember now what counsel Balak king of Moab took, and what Balaam the son of Beor answered him from the Acacias to Gilgal, that you may know the righteousness of Jehovah.

2 With what shall I come before Jehovah, and bow myself before the most high God?   Shall I come before him with burnt offerings of bullocks a year old?   Will Jehovah be pleased with thousands of rams? and ten thousand rivers of oil?   Shall I give my first born for my transgression? the fruit of my body for the sin of my soul?   He has showed you, man, what is good; and what does Jehovah require of you, but to do justice, and to love kindness, and to walk humbly with your God?   The voice of Jehovah calls to the city, and is the help of those that fear thy name.   Hear the rod, and [him] who has appointed it.   Are not the treasures of wickedness a fire in the house of the wicked? and [is not] the scant ephah [a cause of] indignation?   Shall I account [men] pure with false scales, and with a bag of false weights?   And her rich men also are full of violence, and her inhabitants speak lies, and their tongue is deceitful in their mouth.

3 And I also will make you sick; I will smite you to make [you] desolate, for your sins.   You shall eat and not be satisfied, and your emptiness shall be within you; and you shall turn back, and not escape; and him that is delivered will I give to the sword. You shall sow, and not reap; you shall tread the olive, and not anoint yourself with oil; and [you shall make] new wine, and not drink wine.   For you have kept the ordinances of Omri, and all the works of the house of Ahab, and walked in their counsels, that I should make you a desolation, and your inhabitants a hissing, and you shall bear the reproach of my people.

4 Alas for me ! For I am like the gathering of the fruit harvest, like the gleaning of the vintage. There is not a cluster to eat, and my soul craves the first ripe fruits. The pious man has perished from the earth, and there is not a just man among men. All of them lie in wait for blood ; they hunt each one his brother with a net. Their hands are expert for mischief ; the prince and the judge ask for a reward ; the great man speaks the desire of his soul, and they are perverse. Their good [man] is like a thorn bush, and the just sharper than a thorn hedge. The day of your watch-towers, of your visitation, has come ; now shall be their perplexity. Believe not a neighbor, trust not in a friend ; keep the doors of your mouth from her that lies in your bosom. For the son despises the father, the daughter rises up against her mother, [and] the daughter-in-law against her mother-in-law. A man's enemies are the men of his house. But I will watch for Jehovah ; I will wait on the God of my salvation ; my God will hear me. Rejoice not over me, my enemy, for when I fall I shall arise, when I sit in dark-ness Jehovah shall be my light. I will bear the indignation of Jehovah, because I have sinned against him, till he pleads my cause and executes my judgment. He will bring me to the light ; I shall see his righteousness ; my enemy shall see it, and shame shall cover her. She said to me, Where is Jehovah, your God ? My eyes shall see her ; now shall she be trodden down, like the mire of the streets.

5 The day of building your walls, — in that day shall the task be put far away. In that day shall they come to you from Assyria and the cities of Egypt, and [you shall extend] from Egypt to the Euphrates, and from sea to sea, and from mountain to mountain ; for the land is made a desolation on account of its inhabitants, because of their doings.

6 Feed thy people with thy rod, the flock of thy inheritance living solitary in the forest ; let them feed in the midst of Carmel, Bashan, and Gilead, as in days of old. I will show you wonders, as in the days when you went out of the land of Egypt. Nations shall see and be ashamed of all their power ; they shall put their hand on their mouth ; their ears shall be deaf. They shall lick the dust like a serpent, and tremble like reptiles of the earth, from their strong-holds. They shall tremble at Jehovah our God, and fear him.

7 Who is a God like thee ? forgiving wickedness, passing over transgression to the remnant of his inheritance, that keeps not his

anger forever, for he delights in kindness. He will again have mercy on us ; he will tread under foot our wickedness, and cast all our sins into the depths of the sea. Thou wilt give truth to Jacob, [and] kindness to Abraham, as thou didst swear to our fathers from ancient times.

6. NAHUM.

Burden of Nineveh. Book of the vision of Nahum the Elkoshite.

1 JEHOVAH is a jealous God, and an avenger ; Jehovah is an avenger, and Lord of indignation ; Jehovah executes vengeance on his adversaries, and keeps [his anger] for his enemies. Jehovah is slow to anger, and of great power, but will by no means acquit [the guilty]. Jehovah's way is in the whirlwind and in the storm, and clouds are the dust of his feet. He rebukes the sea, and dries it up, and dries up all the rivers. Bashan languishes, and Carmel, and the verdure of Lebanon languishes. The mountains shake before him, and the hills are dissolved ; the earth rises up before him, and the world and all its inhabitants. Before his indignation who can stand ? And who can withstand his fierce anger ? His indignation is poured out like fire, and the rocks are cast down by it.

2 Jehovah is a good fortress in a day of distress, and he knows those that trust in him. But he will destroy [Nineveh] with an overflowing torrent, and make her place [desolate] ; and darkness shall pursue his enemies. What do you devise against Jehovah ? He finishes [the work] which he does ; distress shall not rise up a second time. For while they are entangled with thorn bushes, and drunk as with wine, they shall be consumed like chaff that is fully dry.

3 One went forth from you, devising evil against Jehovah, [and] taking wicked counsel. Thus says Jehovah, Though they are sound and so many, they shall both be cut down and pass away ; and I will afflict you, I will not afflict you again ; for now I will break his yoke off from you, and burst your bands. For Jehovah has commanded concerning you, that nothing of your name shall be sown any more. I will cut off [says God] the carved image and the cast image from the house of your God ; I will make your grave, for you have become small.

4 Behold on the mountains the feet of him that brings good news, that publishes peace. Celebrate, Judah, your feasts, perform your vows, for the destruction shall pass through you no more ; for it is entirely cut off. A war club has come up against your face, [Nineveh ;] guard the fortress, watch the way, gird the loins, strengthen yourselves greatly. For Jehovah has restored the excellency of Jacob, like the excellency of Israel, for desolators desolated them, and destroyed their branches. The shields of his mighty men are red ; men of war are clothed in crimson ; chariots are with flashing blades in the day of his preparation ; and the lances tremble. In the streets the chariots shall rage, and run about in the ways. Their appearance is like torches, and they shall run like lightnings. He shall review his nobles ; they shall stumble on their march ; they shall hasten to the wall and to the prepared covert. The gates of the rivers shall be opened, and the palace dissolved. She shall be set up ; she shall be made naked ; she shall go up, and her maids shall sigh like the voice of doves, beating on their breasts. Though Nineveh was like a pool of waters from the days of old, yet they said to the fleeing, Stand, stand ; but none turned. Plunder the silver ; plunder the gold ; there is no end of the costly furniture ; there is an abundance of all precious vessels.

5 She is poured out and emptied ; her heart melts, and her knees smite together ; trembling is in all loins, and the faces of all contract paleness. Where now is the habitation of lions, and the pasture of young lions, where the lion and the young lion walked, and the lion's whelp, and none made them afraid ? The lion tore in pieces for his whelps, and strangled for his young lions, and filled his den with booty, and his habitation with prey. Behold, I am against you, says Jehovah of hosts, and will burn your chariots with fire ; and the sword shall devour your young lions, and I will cut off your prey from the land ; and the sound of your work shall be heard no more.

6 Woe to the city which is all blood ; it is full of lies and violence ; it withdraws not from plunder. The noise of the whip, and the noise of the rumbling of the wheel, and the horse whirling, and the chariot leaping ! The horseman lifts up both the flaming sword and the glittering spear ; and there is a multitude of killed, and a multitude of dead bodies, and no end to bodies ; they stumble on their bodies. From the multitude of the fornications of the

harlot, beautiful, graceful, mistress of enchantments, who sold
nations for her fornications, and families for her enchantments,
behold, I am against you, says Jehovah of hosts, and will lift your
skirt over your face, and show the nations your nakedness, and
the kingdoms your shame. And I will cast on you abominable things,
and dishonor you, and make you a gazing stock; and all who see
you shall flee from you, and say, Nineveh is destroyed; who will
pity her? Whence shall we seek comforters for you?

7 Are you better than Thebes, that dwelt on the rivers? waters
were around her; her intrenchment was the sea, and her wall from
the sea. Ethiopia and Egypt were her strength, and it was without
end; Phut and the Lybians were your help. But she went an
exile into captivity, and her children were dashed to pieces at the
head of all the streets; and they cast lots for her honorable men,
and all her great men were bound in chains. You also shall be
drunk; you shall be covered, and you shall seek a refuge from the
enemy. All your fortresses shall be fig trees with the first ripe
figs; when they are shaken, they shall fall into the mouth of the
consumer.

8 Behold, your people shall be women in the midst of you; the
gates of your land shall be opened wide to your enemies; a fire
shall consume your bars. Draw for yourself water for the siege;
strengthen your fortifications; go to the clay and tread mortar;
enlarge the brick-kilns. There shall the fire devour you; the sword
shall cut you off; it shall consume you like the winged locust,
though you multiply yourself like the winged locust, though you
multiply yourself like the migratory locust. You have multiplied
your merchants like the stars of heaven; the winged locust shall
strip them and fly away. Your princes are like the migratory
locusts, and your military governors like swarms of locusts which
encamp on the hedges in a cold day; the sun rises, and they flee
away, and their place is not known where they were. Your shepherds have fallen asleep, king of Assyria; your nobles have lain
down; your people are scattered on the mountains, and none gathers
[them]. Your bruise is incurable; your wound is mortal; all that
hear the report of you shall clap their hands over you; for on whom
has not your wickedness continually passed?

7 . ISAIAH.

*Vision of Isaiah the son of Amoz, which he saw concerning Judah
and Jerusalem, in the days of Uzziah, Jotham, Ahaz, [and]
Hezekiah, kings of Judah.*

PROPHECY I.   [1.

SIN REBUKED, AND RIGHTEOUSNESS ENCOURAGED.

1 HEAR, heavens, and attend, earth ; for Jehovah has spoken.
I nourished and brought up sons, and they have rebelled against
me.   An ox knows his owner, and an ass his master's crib ; Israel
does not know ; my people do not consider.   Alas, sinful nation !
a people loaded with wickedness, children of evil doers, sons of
destroyers ! they have forsaken Jehovah ; they have despised the
Holy One of Israel ; they have gone away backward.   Why should
you be smitten any more ?   You will revolt more and more.   The
whole head is sick, and the whole heart faint ; from the sole of
the foot to the head, there is no soundness in it ; a wound, a bruise,
and a fresh wound ; they have not been pressed, nor bound up, nor
softened with oil.

2 Your land is a desolation ; your cities are burnt with fire ;
strangers devour your country before you, and it is desolate, as over-
turned by strangers.   And the daughter of Zion is left like a booth
in a vineyard ; like a lodge in a field of cucumbers ; like a besieged
city.   Unless Jehovah of hosts had left us a very small remnant,
we should have been like Sodom, and should have resembled
Gomorrah.

3 Hear the word of Jehovah, rulers of Sodom ; attend to the
law of your God, people of Gomorrah.   Of what use to me is the
abundance of your sacrifices ? says Jehovah.   I am sated with burnt
offerings of rams, and the fat of fatted beasts, and delight not in
the blood of bullocks, and young sheep, and goats.   When you
come to appear before me, who has required this of your hand, to
tread down my courts ?   Bring no more vain bread offering ; in-

cense is an abomination to me ; new moon and sabbath, calling the
assembly ; I cannot bear wickedness and an assembly.　Your new
moons and your appointed feasts my soul hates ; they are a trouble
to me ; I am weary of bearing them.　When you spread out your
hands, I· will hide my eyes from you ; and when you make many
prayers, I will not hear.　Your hands are full of blood.　Wash,
make yourselves pure ; put away the evil of your doings from before my eyes ; cease to do evil, learn to do well, seek justice,
right the oppressed, judge the fatherless, plead the cause of the
widow.　Come, I pray you, let us reason together, says Jehovah :
Though your sins are as crimson, they shall be white as snow ;
though they be red as worm crimson, they shall be like wool.　If
you consent and obey, you shall eat the good of the land ; but if
you refuse and rebel, you shall be devoured by the sword, for the
mouth of Jehovah has said it.

4 How has a faithful city become a harlot ?　I made [it] full of
justice ; righteousness lodged in it ; but now murderers.　Your
silver has become dross ; your wine is mixed with water ; your
princes are rebellious, and companions of thieves ; every one loves
a gift, and seeks rewards ; they judge not the fatherless, nor does
the widow's cause come before them.　Therefore, says the Lord
Jehovah of hosts, the Mighty One of Israel, I will be comforted
from my adversaries, and I will be avenged on my enemies ; and I
will turn my hand on you, and melt away your dross as with an
alkali, and separate all your tin ; and I will restore your judges as
at first, and your counselors as at the beginning.　Afterwards you
shall be called City of Righteousness, The Faithful City.　Zion shall
be redeemed with justice, and her captives with righteousness ; but
the destruction of transgressors and sinners shall be together, and
they that forsake Jehovah shall be consumed.　For they shall be
ashamed of the oaks which you have desired, and be confounded
at the gardens which you have chosen.　For you shall be like an
oak whose foliage has fallen off, and like a garden which has no
water.　And the strong shall be tow, and his work a spark ; and
they two shall burn together, and none shall extinguish them.

PROPHECY II.   [2, 3, 4.

The word which Isaiah son of Amoz, saw concerning Judah and
Jerusalem.   [The latter day glory; Israel exhorted and
threatened.]

1 AND in the latter days, the mountain of Jehovah's house shall
be established on the top of the mountains, and elevated above the
hills, and all nations shall flow to it.   And many peoples shall go
and say, Come, and let us go up to the mountain of Jehovah, to
the house of the God of Jacob, that he may teach us of his ways,
and we may walk in his paths ; for the law shall go forth from Zion,
and the word of Jehovah from Jerusalem ; and he shall judge
among nations, and rebuke many peoples ; and they shall beat their
swords into plowshares, and their lances into pruning knives; nation shall not lift up sword against nation, neither shall they learn
war any more.
    2 Come, house of Jacob, and let us walk in the light of Jehovah.
But thou [Jehovah] hast rejected thy people, the house of Jacob ;
for they are filled from the east, and practice sorcery like the Philistines, and form compacts with the children of strangers.   And their
land is full of silver and gold, and there is no end of their treasures ; and their land is full of horses, and there is no end of their
chariots ; and their land is full of idols ; they worship each one the
work of his hands, which his fingers made.   Therefore let the man
of low degree be abased, and the man of high degree cast down,
and forgive them not.
    3 Go to the rock, and hide yourself in the earth, from the fear
of Jehovah, and from the splendor of his majesty.   For the high
looks of the man of low degree shall be abased, and the dignity of
the man of high degree shall be brought low ; and Jehovah alone
shall be exalted in that day.   For the day of Jehovah of hosts shall
come on every one that is high and exalted, and on every one that
is lifted up, and he shall be brought low, and on all cedars of
Lebanon that are high and exalted, and on all oaks of Bashan, and
on all high mountains, and on all high hills, and on every high
tower, and on every fortified wall, and on all ships of Tarshish [large
ships], and on all desirable flags; and the pride of the man of low
degree shall be humbled, and the dignity of men of high degree
shall be brought low ; and Jehovah alone shall be exalted in that

day. And the idols shall entirely pass away, and go into the caves of the rocks, and into the holes of the earth, from the fear of Jehovah, and from the splendor of his majesty, when he arises to terrify the earth.

4 In that day a man shall cast away his idols of silver, and his idols of gold, which he made for himself to worship, to the moles and to the bats ; to go into the clefts of the rocks, and into the fissures of the great rocks, from fear of Jehovah, and from the splendor of his majesty, when he arises to terrify the earth. Cease from man, whose breath is in his nostril, for what account is to be made of him ? For behold, the Lord Jehovah of hosts will remove from Jerusalem and Judah the staff and support ; all the staff of bread, and all the support of water ; the mighty man and the man of war ; the judge and the prophet ; and the diviner and the elder ; the captain of fifty and the honorable man ; and the counselor and the skillful mechanic and the skillful diviner ; and I will make boys their princes, and children shall rule over them ; and the people shall oppress every one his fellow, and every one his neighbor ; and the boy shall behave proudly against the elder, and the vile against the honorable. For a man shall take hold of his brother of the house of his father [saying], You have clothes ; be a ruler over us, and let this ruin be under your hand. In that day he shall lift up [his hand], saying, I will not be a ruler ; in my house there is neither bread nor clothing ; make me not a ruler of the people. For Jerusalem has stumbled, and Judah fallen, because their tongue and their doings were against Jehovah, to provoke the eyes of his glory.

5 A regarding of their persons testifies against them, and they declare their sin as Sodom ; they conceal it not. Woe to their souls, for they have procured evil for themselves. Say to the righteous, that [he shall enjoy] good ; for they shall eat the fruit of their doings ; woe to the wicked, [he shall experience] evil ; for the reward of his hands shall be given him. As for my people, children are their oppressors, and women rule over them. My people, your guides cause [you] to err, and your paths have lost the way.

6 Jehovah stands up to enter into judgment, and he stands to judge the peoples. Jehovah will enter into judgment with the elders of his people, and their princes. For you have consumed the vineyard ; the plunder of the poor is in your house. What, do you mean to crush my people, and grind the faces of the poor, says the Lord Jehovah of hosts ?

5 *

7 And Jehovah says, Because the daughters of Zion are haughty, and walk with outstretched neck and wanton eyes, walking and mincing as they go, and make a tinkling with their feet, therefore will the Lord make the heads of the daughters of Zion bald, and Jehovah will expose their nakedness. In that day will the Lord remove the ornaments of the anklets, and the caps of network, and the crescents, the earrings, and the chains, and the vails, the turbans, and the slip chains, and the belts, and the smelling bottles, and the amulets, the finger rings, and the nose jewels, the festive garments, and the mantles, and the cloaks, and the purses, the mirrors, and the shifts, and the tiaras, and the vails ; and instead of an aromatic odor, there shall be putridity ; and instead of a girdle, a cord ; and instead of artificial curls, baldness ; and instead of an embroidered garment, a girdle of sackcloth ; [and] a scar from burning, instead of beauty. Your men shall fall by the sword, and your power in battle. The gates [of Zion] shall be made empty, and mourn ; and she shall be desolate, and sit on the ground.

8 And in that day seven women shall take hold of one man, saying, We will eat our bread and wear our clothes ; only let us be called by your name, to take away our reproach. In that day a branch of Jehovah shall be excellent and glorious, and a fruit of the earth shall be majestic and beautiful to the escaped of Israel. And he that remains in Zion, and he that is left in Jerusalem, shall be called holy, every one that is written with the living in Jerusalem, when the Lord has washed away the filth of the daughters of Zion, and banished the blood of Jerusalem from the midst of it, by the spirit of judgment and the spirit of burning. And Jehovah will create on every dwelling of mount Zion, and on her assemblies, a cloud by day, and a smoke and the brightness of a flame of fire by night ; for over all the glory shall be a covering and a booth, for a shade by day from heat, and a refuge and shelter from the storm and rain.

PROPHECY III. [5.

THE PARABLE OF THE VINEYARD.

1 I WILL sing now to my beloved a song of my friend respecting his vineyard. My beloved had a vineyard on a hill of great fertility ; and he dug it up, and cleared it of stones, and planted it with a choice vine. And he built a tower in it, and also cut a wine

vat in it, and waited for it to bear grapes ; and it bore wild grapes.
And now, inhabitants of Jerusalem and men of Judah, judge, I
pray you, between me and my vineyard. What could I have done
more for my vineyard which I did not do ? Why, when I waited
for it to bear grapes, did it bear wild grapes ? And now I will tell
you what I will do to my vineyard : I will take away its hedge,
and it shall be eaten up ; I will break down its wall, and it shall be
trodden down ; and I will make it waste ; it shall not be pruned nor
dug, but shall grow up with briers and thorn bushes. And I will
command the clouds, and they shall rain no rain on it ; for the
house of Israel is the vineyard of Jehovah of hosts, and the men of
Judah are his pleasant plant ; and he looked for justice, and behold murder : and for righteousness, and behold a cry [of the
oppressed].

2 Woe to those who join house to house, who add field to field,
till there is no place, and you dwell alone in the land. Jehovah of
hosts [said] in my hearing, Surely many great and good houses
shall be desolate, without inhabitant. For 10 acres of vineyard shall
yield one bath [1.11 bushels], and the seed of a homer [10.11
bushels] shall yield an ephah [the same as bath 1.11 bushels]. Woe
to those who rise early in the morning to pursue strong drink,
who continue late at night till wine inflames them ; and the harp
and the nablim [an instrument resembling a harp], the timbrel
and the pipe, and wine, are at their feasts ; but they do not regard the work of Jehovah, nor consider the work of his hands.

3 Therefore my people are carried away captive, because they
have no knowledge ; and their glory is famished men, and their
multitude is parched with thirst. Therefore Hades enlarges herself, and opens her mouth without measure ; and our excellency
and riches, and tumult and exultation, have gone down into it ;
and the man of low degree is abased, and the man of high degree is
brought low, and the eyes of the haughty are humbled ; but Jehovah of hosts shall be exalted in judgment, and God that is holy
shall be hallowed in righteousness ; and lambs shall feed in their
manner, and strangers eat the desolations of the rich.

4 Woe to them that draw wickedness with cords of vanity, and
sin with cart ropes ; that say, Let him hasten and come speedily,
that we may see his work, and let the counsel of the Holy One of
Israel draw near and come, that we may know it. Woe to them
that call evil good, and good evil ; that put darkness for light, and

light for darkness; that put bitter for sweet, and sweet for bitter. Woe to them that are wise in their own eyes, and intelligent in their own sight. Woe to them that are mighty to drink wine, and valiant to mix strong drink; that justify the wicked for a reward, and take away the righteousness of the righteous from him.

5 Therefore, as a flame of fire consumes the stubble, and as the burning hay sinks down, their root shall be like rottenness, and their fruit go up like dust; for they have rejected the law of Jehovah of hosts, and despise the words of the Holy One of Israel. Therefore the anger of Jehovah is kindled against his people, and he will stretch out his hand against them and smite them; and the mountains shall tremble, and their dead bodies shall be like dust in the streets. For all this, his anger has not turned away, but his hand is stretched out still.

6 And he shall lift up a standard to the nations from afar, and hiss for one, to the end of the earth; and behold, it shall come swiftly; it shall not faint nor stumble; it shall not slumber nor sleep; neither shall the girdle of its loins be loosed, nor a string of its shoes be broken; its arrows shall be sharp, and all its bows bent; the hoofs of its horses shall be accounted like flint, and its wheels like a whirlwind; its roaring shall be like a lion, and it shall roar like a young lion; it shall roar and seize the prey, and bear it away, and none shall deliver. But in that day [Jehovah] shall roar against [it], like the roaring of the sea, and [men] shall look on the earth, and behold darkness and distress; and the light shall be darkened in the heavens.

PROPHECY IV.   [6.

VISION OF JEHOVAH.

1 IN the year that king Uzziah died, I saw the Lord sitting on a throne high and exalted, and his skirts filled the temple. And seraphs stood over him; each had six wings; with two he covered his face, and with two he covered his feet, and with two he flew. And one cried to another and said, Holy, holy, holy is Jehovah of hosts; the whole earth is full of his glory.

2 And the foundations of the thresholds were moved at the voice of him that cried, and the house was filled with smoke. Then I said, Woe is me, for I am cut off; for I am a man of impure lips,

and I live among a people of impure lips; for my eyes have seen the King, Jehovah of hosts.

3 Then flew to me one of the seraphs, with a stone in his hand, which he took with the tongs from the altar; and he touched my mouth, and said, Behold, this has touched your lips, and your wickedness has departed, and your sin is forgiven.

4 Then I heard the voice of the Lord, saying, Whom shall I send? and who will go for us? Then I said, Behold, here am I; send me. And he said, Go, and say to this people, Hear indeed, but understand not; and see indeed, but perceive not. Make fat the heart of this people, and make its ears heavy, and shut its eyes; lest it see with its eyes, and hear with its ears, and understand with its heart [mind], and turn and be healed.

5 Then I said, How long, Lord? And he said, Till the cities are wasted without inhabitant, and houses without man, and the land is made entirely desolate, and Jehovah has removed man far away, and there is a great ruin in the midst of the land. But as yet a tenth part shall remain in the land; and this shall again be consumed, like a terebinth, and like an oak, which leave a stump when cast down; its stump shall be a holy race.

PROPHECY V.   [7.

THE ISRAELITES AND SYRIANS AGAINST JUDAH; THEIR DESTRUCTION PREDICTED.

1 AND in the days of Ahaz, the son of Jotham, son of Uzziah, king of Judah, came up Rezin, king of Syria, and Pekah, the son of Remaliah, king of Israel, to Jerusalem, to fight against it, and were not able to fight against it. And it was told the house of David, saying, Syria has encamped in Ephraim; and his heart was moved, and the heart of his people, as the trees of a forest are moved before a wind.

2 Then Jehovah said to Isaiah, Go now to meet Ahaz, you and Shearjashub [remnant shall return], your son, at the end of the aqueduct of the upper pool, on the highway of the fuller's field, and say to him, Take heed to yourself, and be quiet; fear not, nor let your heart be faint on account of the two tails of these smoking firebrands, on account of the fierce anger of Rezin and Syria, and Remaliah's son; because Syria, Ephraim, and Remaliah's son have

devised evil against you, saying, Let us go up against Judah, and
terrify it, and make a breach in it, and anoint a king in it, the son
of Tabael.

3 Thus says the Lord Jehovah, It shall not stand, it shall not be ;
for the head of Syria is Damascus, and the head of Damascus, Rezin ; and yet 65 years and Ephraim shall be destroyed from being
a people ; and the head of Ephraim is Samaria, and the head of
Samaria, Remaliah's son ; if you will not believe, surely you shall
not be confirmed.

4 And Jehovah spoke again to Ahaz, saying, Ask of me a sign
from Jehovah your God ; let the request be in the depths, or in
the heights above. But Ahaz said, I will not ask, neither will I
try Jehovah.   Then he said, Hear now, house of David ; Is it too
little for you to weary men, but will you weary my God also ?
Therefore the Lord shall give you a sign.   Behold, the young woman shall be with child, and bear a son, and you shall call his name
Immanuel [God is with us].   Curdled milk and honey shall he eat,
till he knows how to refuse evil and choose good ; but before the
child shall know how to refuse evil and choose good [be 3 years
old], the land which you abhor shall be forsaken before her two
kings.

5 Jehovah shall bring on you, and on your people, and on the
house of your father, days that have not come, from the day of the
departing of Ephraim from Judah ; the king of Assyria.   And in
that day Jehovah shall hiss to the fly which is at the extremities of
the rivers of Egypt, and to the bee which is in the land of Assyria,
and they shall come and light all of them on the clefts of the rocks,
and on all thickets, and on all pastures.

6 In that day the Lord will shave with a hired razor from beyond
the Euphrates, the king of Assyria, the head and the hair of the
feet, and it shall also shave the chin.   And in that day a man shall
keep a young cow and two sheep, and from the abundance of milk
shall eat curdled milk ; for curdled milk and honey shall every one
eat that is left in the land.   And in that day every place where
there were a thousand vines, worth 1000 [shekels] of silver [$560],
shall be for briers and thorn bushes.   And one shall go there with
bow and arrows, for briers and thorn bushes shall be in all the
land.   And as to all the mountains which are dug up with a hoe,
there shall not come there the fear of brier and thorn bush [the
hoe], but it shall be a pasture for oxen, and a range for sheep.

PROPHECY VI.   [8, 9, 6.

THE PROPHET'S SON A SIGN.

1 AND Jehovah said to me, Take a great roll, and write on it with a man's pen, concerning Mahar-shalal-hash-baz [Hastening to the spoil, he rushes to the prey]. Then I took faithful witnesses, Uriah the priest, and Zechariah the son of Berechiah, and I went in to the prophetess, and she became with child, and bore a son. And Jehovah said to me, Call his name Mahar-shalal-hash-baz [Hastening to the spoil, he rushes to the prey]; for before the child shall know how to call, My father, and, My mother, the riches of Damascus and the plunder of Samaria shall be carried away before the king of Assyria.

2 And Jehovah spoke to me again, saying, Because this people refuse the waters of Shiloh, which flow gently, and rejoice in Rezin and Remaliah's son, therefore, behold, the Lord will bring on them the waters of the Euphrates, strong and many; the king of Assyria, and all his glory; and he shall come up over all his channels, and overflow all his banks, and pass through Judah; he shall overflow and pass over; he shall reach to the neck, and his outstretched wings shall fill the breadth of your land, Immanuel.

3 Cry, peoples, and be confounded; attend, all you distant lands; gird yourselves, and be confounded; gird yourselves, and be confounded. Take counsel, and it shall be broken off; speak a word, but it shall not stand; for God is with us. For thus said Jehovah to me with a strong hand, and instructed me not to walk in the way of this people, saying, Call not a conspiracy all which this people call a conspiracy, and fear not their fear, nor be afraid. Sanctify Jehovah of hosts, and let him be your fear and your dread; and he shall be a sanctuary; but he shall be a stone of stumbling and rock of offense to the two houses of Israel, a trap and snare to the inhabitants of Jerusalem; and many of them shall stumble and fall, and be broken, and ensnared, and taken.

4 Bind up the testimony; seal up the oracle for my disciples; and I will wait for Jehovah, who hides his face from the house of Jacob, and will look for him. Behold, I and the children which Jehovah has given me are for signs and prodigies in Israel, from Jehovah of hosts, who dwells in mount Zion. And when they say

to you, Seek the necromancers and the wizards, those that peep
and those that mutter ; should not a people seek its God ?　[Should
they seek of] the dead for the living ?　To the oracle and the testimony : if they speak not according to this word, he [that does so]
shall have no morning.　But he shall pass through [the land]
oppressed and hungry ; and when he is hungry, he shall be offended,
and curse his king and his God, and look up.　And he shall look to
the earth and behold distress and darkness, oppressive darkness,
and outer darkness.　For the affliction shall not be such as that with
which he afflicted her at the time when he first abased the lands of
Zebulun and Naphtali, and afterward honored the way of the
lake, beyond the Jordan, the circuit of the nations.

5 The people that walk in darkness have seen a great light ; on
those sitting in the land of the shade of death has light shone.
Thou hast multiplied the nation ; thou hast increased its joy ; they
rejoice before thee like the joy in harvest, as [men] rejoice when
they divide the spoil.　For thou hast broken the yoke of his burden,
and the rod for his shoulder, the staff of the oppressor, as in
the day of Midian.　For every shoe of the warrior [who was] in
the tumult, and garment rolled in blood shall be even for burning,
fuel for the fire.　For a child is born to us, a son is given us, and
the government shall be on his shoulder, and [men] shall call his name
Wonderful, Counselor, Mighty God, Eternal Father, Prince of
Peace.　Of the increase of government and power, there shall
be no end on the throne of David, and over his kingdom, to establish
it, and to found it with justice and righteousness, from henceforth
and forever.　The zeal of Jehovah of hosts will do this.

PROPHECY VII.　　　　　[9, 7, 10, 4.

ISRAEL THREATENED.

1 JEHOVAH sent a word on Jacob, and it fell on Israel ; and all
the people shall know, Ephraim and the inhabitant of Samaria, who
say in pride and haughtiness, The bricks have fallen down, but we
will build with cut stone ; the sycamores are cut down, but we will
replace cedars.　Jehovah will raise up the adversaries of Rezin
against him, and will arm his enemies ; Syria before, and the Philistines behind ; and they shall devour Israel with open mouth.　For
all this his anger has not turned away ; but his hand is stretched
out still.

2 The people turned not to him that smote them, and sought not Jehovah of hosts ; therefore Jehovah will cut off from Israel head and tail, palm branch and bulrush, in one day. The elder and the honorable man is the head, and the prophet that teaches lies is the tail ; for the guides of this people cause them to err, and those led by them are destroyed. Therefore the Lord will take no pleasure in their young men, nor pity their fatherless ones, nor their widows ; for all of them are profane and evil doers ; every mouth speaks folly. For all this his anger has not turned away, but his hand is stretched out still.

3 For wickedness burns like fire ; it shall consume the briers and thorn bushes, and be kindled in the thickets of the forest, and they shall roll themselves up like the rising of smoke. By the wrath of Jehovah of hosts the land shall be consumed, and the people become like fuel for the fire ; none shall spare one another. One shall snatch on the right hand, and be hungry and eat on the left hand, and not be satisfied ; they shall eat, each one, the flesh of his arm : Manasseh against Ephraim, and Ephraim against Manasseh, [and] they together against Judah. For all this his anger has not turned away ; but his hand is stretched out still.

4 Woe to those who make unjust decrees, and write the wickedness which they have prescribed, to turn away the weak from judgment, and to rob the poor of my people of justice, that widows may be their spoil, and that they may rob the fatherless. But what will you do in the day of visitation and of destruction that shall come from far ? To whom will you flee for help, and where will you leave your glory ? Without me they shall bow down under the prisoner, and shall fall under the killed. For all this his anger has not turned away, but his hand is stretched out still.

PROPHECY VIII. [10, 5, 11, 12.

ASSYRIA TO BE ABASED, AND ISRAEL RESTORED AND EXALTED UNDER A BRANCH OF JESSE.

1 Woe to Assyria : the rod of my anger and my indignation is a staff in their hand. I will send it against a hypocritical nation, and will command it against the people of my wrath, to take the spoil and seize the prey, and to tread [men] down like the mire of the streets. But he [the king of Assyria] shall not purpose this ;

neither does his mind intend it; but it shall be his intention to destroy and cut off nations not few. For he says, Are not my princes altogether kings? Is not Calno like Carchemish? Is not Hamath like Arpad? Is not Samaria like Damascus? As my hand found the kingdoms of idols, whose carved images were more than those of Jerusalem and Samaria, shall I not, as I did to Samaria and her idols, do also to Jerusalem and her idols?

2 But when the Lord has accomplished all his work on mount Zion and Jerusalem, I will punish [says he] the fruit of the stout heart of the king of Assyria, and the beauty of his proud face. For he says, I did this by the strength of my hand, and by my wisdom, for I am intelligent; and I removed the bounds of peoples, plundered their treasures, and brought down, like a mighty man, the inhabitants. My hand found, like a nest, the riches of the peoples; and as one gathers eggs that are left, I gathered all the earth; and there was none that moved the wing, or opened the mouth, or peeped. Shall the axe glorify itself against him that cuts with it? or the saw magnify itself against him that moves it? As if a rod should move against him that lifts it up; as if a staff could lift itself up, [and] was not wood.

3 Therefore the Lord, the Lord of hosts, shall send on his fat ones leanness; and under his glory he shall kindle a burning, like the burning of fire. And the light of Israel shall be a fire, and his Holy One a flame; and it shall burn and consume their thorn bushes and briers in one day; and it shall consume the glory of his forest, and of his fruitful field, soul and body; and he shall be like a sick man who faints away; and the rest of the trees of his forest shall be few, so that a child can take account of them.

4 And in that day the remnant of Israel, and the escaped of the house of Jacob, shall no more lean on him that smites them, but shall lean on Jehovah, the Holy One of Israel, in truth. A remnant shall return a remnant of Jacob to the mighty God; for though your people Israel be as the sand of the sea, a remnant of them [only] shall return; a destruction is decreed, overflowing [with] righteousness; for a destruction and a decreed [visitation] will the Lord Jehovah of hosts execute in all the earth.

5 Therefore thus says the Lord Jehovah of hosts, Fear not, my people who dwell in Zion, on account of Assyria; it shall smite with a rod, and its staff be lifted up against you, in the manner of Egypt; but yet a very little while, and my indignant anger shall be

quieted in their destruction. For Jehovah of hosts will raise up a scourge against him, as he smote Midian at the rock Oreb ; and his rod shall be on the sea, and he shall lift it up in the manner of Egypt. And in that day his burden shall be removed from your shoulder, and his yoke from your neck ; and the yoke shall be broken by fatness.

6 He came to Aiath ; he passed through Migron ; at Michmash he laid up his baggage ; they passed over the ford ; Geba [he says] is our place of encampment. Ramah is greatly afraid ; Gibeah of Saul has fled. Lift up your voice, daughter of Gallim ; attend, Laish, and poor Anathoth. Madmena has fled ; the inhabitants of Gebim have betaken themselves to hasty flight. He is yet to stop a day at Nob ; he will shake his hand against the mountain of the daughter of Zion, the hill of Jerusalem.

7 Behold, the Lord Jehovah of hosts will cut off the green bough with sudden violence, and the high ones shall be cut down, and the proud brought low ; and he will cut down the thickets of the forest with an axe, and Lebanon shall fall by a mighty one ; but there shall come forth a shoot from the stock of Jesse, and a sprout shall grow from his roots, and the Spirit of Jehovah shall rest on him, a spirit of wisdom and understanding, a spirit of counsel and might, a spirit of knowledge and the fear of Jehovah. And his delight shall be in the fear of Jehovah ; and he shall not judge according to the sight of his eyes, nor reprove according to the hearing of his ears ; but he shall judge the weak with righteousness, and reprove with equity the meek of the earth ; and he shall smite the earth with the rod of his mouth, and kill the wicked with the breath of his lips. And righteousness shall be the girdle of his loins, and truth the girdle of his waist ; and the wolf shall dwell with the lamb, and the leopard shall lie down with the kid ; and the calf and the lion, and the fat creature together ; and a little child shall lead them. And the cow and the bear shall feed, their young shall lie down together, and the lion shall eat straw like the ox. The nursing child shall admire the hole of the asp, and the weaned child put its hand on the viper's den ; they shall not hurt nor destroy in all my holy mountain ; for the earth shall be full of the knowledge of Jehovah, as water covers the sea.

8 And in that day there shall be a sprout of Jesse, which shall stand for a standard of the peoples, and him shall the nations seek, and his rest shall be [in] glory. And in that day the Lord will

stretch out his hand a second time, to gather the remnant of his people, who remain from Assyria, and from Egypt, and from Pathros, and from Ethiopia, and from Elam, and from Shinar, and from Hamath, and from the islands of the sea; and he shall set up a standard for the nations, and assemble the outcasts of Israel, and collect the dispersed of Judah from the four quarters of the earth. And the envy of Ephraim shall depart, and the adversaries of Judah be cut off; and Ephraim shall not envy Judah, nor Judah distress Ephraim. And they shall fly on the shoulders of the Philistines; they shall plunder the sons of the east together; Edom and Moab shall be the prey of their hand, and the sons of Ammon obey them. And Jehovah will entirely destroy the tongue of the Egyptian sea, and shake his hand over the Euphrates with his mighty wind, and smite it in its seven streams, and cause [men] to go over in their shoes. And there shall be a highway for those that remain of his people, who shall remain from Assyria, as there was for Israel in the day that he brought him up out of the land of Egypt.

9 In that day you shall say, I will praise thee, Jehovah, for thou wast angry with me, and thy anger is turned away, and thou hast comforted me. Behold, God is my salvation; I will trust and not be afraid; for Jah Jehovah is my strength and my song, and he has become my salvation; and you shall draw water with joy from the wells of salvation, and say in that day, Praise Jehovah, call on his name, make known among the peoples his doings, cause it to be remembered that his name is exalted. Sing of Jehovah, for he has done great things; let this be known in all the earth. Cry aloud and shout, inhabitant of Zion, for great is the Holy One of Israel in the midst of you.

PROPHECY IX. [13, 14, 27.

Burden of Babylon which Isaiah the son of Amoz saw.

1 ON a bare mountain lift up a standard; raise a voice to them; wave the hand, that they may enter the gates of princes. I have commanded my consecrated ones, and called my mighty ones, for my anger, my proudly exulting warriors. There is a voice of a multitude on the mountains, an appearance of a great people, a noise of the tumult of kingdoms, of nations assembled together; Jehovah of hosts musters his host for war. They come from a

distant country, from the end of heaven, Jehovah and the instruments of his indignation, to bind fast all the earth.

2 Lament, for the day of Jehovah is at hand; it shall come like destruction from the Almighty; therefore all hands shall be feeble, and every heart of mortal shall melt, and they shall be confounded; pain and anguish shall seize them; they shall be in pain like a woman in childbirth; they shall be astonished one at another; their faces shall be flames, before the day of Jehovah which comes cruel both with wrath and fierce anger, to make the earth a desolation, and its sins he shall destroy out of it.

3 For the stars of heaven and their orions [great constellations] shall not give their light; the sun shall be darkened when he goes forth, and the moon shall not cause her light to shine; and I will bring evil on the world, and on transgressors their wickedness, and will cause the arrogance of proud ones to cease, and bring down the haughtiness of tyrants. I will make a mortal more scarce than fine gold, a man than the fine gold of Ophir. Therefore I will make the heavens tremble, and the earth shall be shaken from its place by the wrath of Jehovah of hosts, and in the day of his fierce anger. And [men] shall be like a chased antelope, and like a flock which no man gathers; they shall turn each one to his people, and flee each one to his land; every one that is found shall be thrust through, and every one that is scraped together shall fall by the sword; and their children shall be dashed to pieces before their eyes, their houses plundered, and their women ravished. Behold, I will raise up against them the Medes, who shall not regard silver nor delight in gold. Their bows shall strike down the young men, and they shall not pity the fruit of the womb, neither shall their eyes spare sons. And Babylon, the glory of kingdoms, the excellent beauty of the Chaldeans, shall be like God's overthrow of Sodom and Gomorrah. It shall not be inhabited forever, nor dwelt in from generation to generation; neither shall the Arab pitch his tent there, nor shepherds keep their flocks there. Beasts of the desert shall lie down there, and their houses shall be full of owls; and the daughters of the ostrich shall dwell there, and wood demons dance there; and jackals shall howl in its palaces, and wolves in its pleasant edifices; and the time is near to come, and its days shall not be prolonged.

4 For Jehovah will have mercy on Jacob, and yet choose Israel, and cause them to rest in their land, and strangers shall be joined

6 *

to them and annexed to the house of Jacob. And the peoples shall take them and bring them to their place ; and the house of Israel shall possess themselves of them in the land of Jehovah, for men servants and female servants, and those who captured them, shall be their captives, and they shall rule over their oppressors. And in that day Jehovah shall give you rest from your sorrow, and from your fear, and from the hard service with which you were made to serve ; and you shall take up this song against the king of Babylon, and say ; —

5 How has the exacter ceased! the golden city ceased! Jehovah has broken the rod of the wicked, the staff of the rulers. He smote the peoples in wrath with a blow that turns not away, he trampled down nations in anger with unrestrained dominion. All the earth rests, [and] is quiet ; they break forth into singing ; the cypress trees also rejoice over you ; the cedars of Lebanon [say], From the time that you lay down, no feller has come up against us. Hades from below is moved for you, to meet you at your coming ; it raises up for you the shades ; it causes all the mighty ones of the earth to stand up from their thrones, all the kings of nations.

6 All of them shall answer and say to you, Have you become weak as we ? Are you made to resemble us ? Your splendor is brought down to Hades, the noise of your nabliums [species of harps] ; worms are spread under you, and crimson worms cover you. How have you fallen from heaven, Lucifer, son of the morning ! [How] are you cut down to the earth, you that overthrew the nations !

7 For you said in your heart, I will ascend to heaven ; I will exalt my throne above the stars of God ; I will sit on the mountain of the congregation, on the sides of the north. I will ascend above the high places of the clouds ; I will make myself like the Most High. But you are brought down to Hades, to the sides of the pit.

8 Those that see you shall look at you ; they shall consider, Is this the man that caused the earth to tremble ? that shook kingdoms ? that made the world like a wilderness, and destroyed cities ? that dismissed not his prisoners to [their] homes ? All the kings of nations, all of them lie in glory, each in his house ; but you are cast out of your grave as a detested branch, covered with the killed, the smitten with the sword, who go down to the stones of the pit ; like a dead body trodden down. You shall not be joined with them in burial, for you destroyed your land, you killed your people : the

posterity of evil doers shall never be renowned. **Prepare slaughter for his children**; for the wickedness of their fathers they shall not rise up nor inherit the earth, nor fill the world with cities; but I will rise up against them, says Jehovah of hosts, and cut off from Babylon name and remnant, offspring and descendant, says Jehovah. And I will make it a possession of the porcupine and pools of water, and I will sweep it with the besom of destruction, says Jehovah of hosts.

9 Jehovah of hosts has sworn, saying, Surely according as I have purposed, so shall it be, and as I have determined, it shall stand, to break Assyria on my land and on my mountain. I will trample him down, and his yoke shall depart from being on you, and his burden shall depart from your shoulder. This is the purpose which is formed against all the earth, and this is the hand stretched out over all nations. For Jehovah of hosts has purposed; and who shall break it off? and his hand is stretched out, and who shall turn it back?

PROPHECY X.   [14, 28, 15, 16.

PHILISTIA AND MOAB.

1 IN the year in which king Ahaz died [B. C. 725], was this burden: Rejoice not, Philistia, all of you, for the rod that smote you is broken; but from the root of the serpent shall come forth a viper, and his fruit shall be a fiery flying serpent. And the weakest shall feed, and the poor shall lie down in safety; but I will cause your root to die with famine, and it shall kill your remnant. Lament, gate; cry, city; all Philistia is dissolved; for a cloud has come from the north, and none shall be alone in their hosts. And what shall one answer the messengers of the nation? That Jehovah founded Zion, and the poor of his people shall find refuge in it.

2 *Burden of Moab.* Surely in a night Ar of Moab is destroyed, it is cut off; surely in a night Kir of Moab is destroyed, it is cut off. He went up to the house, and to Dibon, the high places, to weep; Moab shall lament, for Nebo and for Medeba; baldness shall be on all heads; every beard shall be cut off. Those without gird themselves with sackcloth on her housetops, and in her streets the whole city laments; it flows down with weeping. And Heshbon and Elealeh shall cry; their voice is heard to Jahaz; therefore the

armed soldiers of Moab shall cry aloud ; their life shall be a burden to them.

3 My heart shall cry for Moab, for her fugitives are at Zoar, a three years old heifer ; for they ascend the heights of Luhim with weeping ; for in the way to Horonaim they raise a cry of destruction ; for the waters of Nimrim are desolate, for the grass is dried up, the herbage is consumed, there is not a green thing ; therefore the riches which they have gained, and their store, they shall carry to the brook of willows, for a cry surrounds the boundary of Moab, her lamentation reaches to Eglaim, and her wailing to Beerelim ; for the waters of Dimon are full of blood, for I will put on Dimon additional evils ; I will be a lion to the escaped of Moab, and to the remnant of the land.

4 Send the lamb of the ruler of the land, from Sela of the wilderness, to the mountain of the daughter of Zion. But the daughters of Moab shall be like a wandering bird, [like] a forsaken nest at the fords of the Arnon. Give counsel, do right, make your shade like night in the midst of noon ; conceal the outcasts, betray not the fugitives. Let my outcasts, Moab, dwell with you ; be a covert to them from the destroyers, for the violent man shall cease, the plunderer shall be consumed, [and] the oppressor destroyed from the earth ; and a throne shall be established with kindness, and one shall sit on it with truth in the tabernacle of David, judging, and seeking justice, and hastening righteousness.

5 We have heard of the pride of Moab ; he is very proud ; and his haughtiness, and his pride, and his wrath, and his vain boasting. Therefore Moab shall lament for Moab ; every one shall lament ; you shall mourn, even crushed, for the foundations of Kir Haresheth. For the fields of Heshbon languish ; as for the vine of Sibmah, the lords of the nations have broken down her choice vines ; they reached to Jazar, they wandered to the wilderness ; her branches were extended abroad, they passed over the sea. Therefore I will weep with the weeping of Jazar, for the vine of Sibmah : I will water you with my tears, Heshbon and Elealeh ; for the battle shout has fallen on your fruits and on your harvest.

6 Gladness and joy are taken away from the fruitful field, and there shall be no singing nor shouting in the vineyards ; he that treads shall not tread out wine in the vats ; I will make the shouting to cease. Therefore my bowels shall sound like a harp for Moab, and my soul for Kir Heres. And when it is seen how Moab

is wearied on the high places, and goes to his sanctuary to pray, and prevails not, this is the song which Jehovah will speak concerning Moab at that time. And now Jehovah has spoken, saying, Three years, like the years of a hired man, and the glory of Moab shall be despised, with all his. great multitude, and the remnant shall be very small ; it shall not be mighty.

PROPHECY XI. [17, 18.

Burden of Damascus.

1 BEHOLD, Damascus is removed from cities ; it shall be a heap of ruins. The cities of Aroer are forsaken, they shall be for flocks ; and they shall lie down, and none make them afraid. The fortress shall cease from Ephraim, and the kingdom from Damascus ; and the remains of Syria shall be like the glory of the sons of Israel, says Jehovah of hosts.

2 And in that day the glory of Jacob shall be brought low, and the fatness of his flesh shall become lean, and he shall be as when the harvester cuts the standing grain, and harvests the heads with his arm ; and he shall be as when one gathers the heads of grain in the valley of Rephaim. But gleanings shall be left of them, as in the shaking of the olive, two [or] three berries on the top of the bough, four [or] five on its fruitful branches, says Jehovah, the God of Israel.

3 In that day a man shall look to his Maker, and his eyes shall see the Holy One of Israel ; and he shall not look to altars, the work of his hands, nor see what his fingers have made, either the Asheras or Hammons [objects of idolatrous worship].

4 In that day his fortified cities shall be like a forsaken forest, and like a mountain top, which they shall leave before the sons of Israel, and it shall be a desolation. For you forgot God, your salvation, and remembered not the rock of your strength ; therefore you shall plant beautiful plants, and set foreign shoots ; in the day of your planting you shall enclose ; in the morning you shall cause your plants to blossom ; [but] your harvest shall flee away in the day of possession, and hopeless sorrow [shall come].

5 Alas ! the tumult of many peoples ; they shall rage like the raging of seas, and the noise of peoples ; they shall lift up [the voice] like the noise of mighty waters. And [God] shall rebuke him, and

he shall flee from afar, and be driven like chaff on the mountains before the wind, like stubble before a whirlwind. At the time of evening, and behold terror ; before morning, they are not. This shall be the portion of those that pillage us, and the lot of those that plunder us.

6 Alas for the land of whizzing wings, which is beyond the river of Ethiopia, that sends messengers on the sea, in skiffs of papyrus on the face of the waters ; [saying], Go, swift messengers, to a nation tall and naked, to a people feared from the first and till now, a most mighty nation, and one that treads down [its enemies], whose land the rivers rend. All you inhabitants of the world, and all you who dwell on the earth, when the standard is lifted up on the mountains, look ; and when the trumpet is sounded, hear.

7 For thus said Jehovah to me, I will be still and look on from my place, like a clear heat before the sun, like a cloud of dew in the heat of harvest ; for before the harvest, when the blossom is perfected and the flower has become a ripe grape, then he will cut off the shoots with prunning knives, and the branches he will remove and cast down; [and] they shall be left together to the rapacious birds of the mountains, and to the beasts of the field. And the rapacious birds shall summer on them, and every beast of the field shall winter on them.

8 At that time gifts shall be brought to Jehovah of hosts from a people tall and naked, and from a people feared from the first till now, a most mighty nation, and one that treads down [its enemies], whose land the rivers rend, to the place of the name of Jehovah of hosts, to mount Zion.

PROPHECY XII.   [19.

Burden of Egypt.

1 BEHOLD, Jehovah rides on a swift cloud, and goes to Egypt, and the idols of the Egyptians are moved before him, and the heart of Egypt melts within him ; and I will arouse [says God] the Egyptians against the Egyptians ; every man against his brother, and every man against his neighbor ; city against city, and kingdom against kingdom ; and the spirit of Egypt shall be emptied out from within him ; and I will destroy his counsel, and they shall seek the idols,

and the whisperers, and the necromancers, and the wizards ; and
I will deliver Egypt into the hand of hard masters, and a mighty
king shall rule over them, says the Lord Jehovah of hosts.

2 And the water shall fail from the sea, and the Nile shall be
dried up and become dry, and the streams shall become putrid, and
the rivers of Egypt shall become small and dried up, and the reeds
and bulrushes shall die. The meadows by the Nile, by the mouth
of the Nile, and every grain field of the Nile, shall be dried up, and
driven away, and destroyed ; and the fishermen shall mourn ; and
all who cast hooks in the river shall mourn ; and those that spread
nets on the face of the waters shall languish.

3 And those that work the hatcheled flax, and those that weave
the white linens, shall be ashamed ; and her pillars shall be broken
down ; and all who work for wages shall be of a sorrowful mind.
Certainly the princes of Zoan are fools, and counsel is destroyed
from the counselors of Pharaoh. How do you say to Pharaoh, I am a
son of the wise, a son of ancient kings ? Where now are your wise
men ? Let them tell, I pray you, and make known what Jehovah
of hosts has purposed against Egypt. The princes of Zoan are
fools ; the princes of Noph are deceived ; and the corner stones of
her tribes have caused Egypt to err. Jehovah has mixed in the
midst of her a spirit of perverseness, and they have caused Egypt
to err in all his work as a drunkard wanders about in his vomit.
And there shall be no more work which shall be done by head or
tail, palm branch or bulrush.

4 In that day Egypt shall be like a woman, and shall tremble and
be afraid, on account of the waving of the hand of Jehovah of
hosts, which he shall wave against it. And the land of Judah shall
be a terror to Egypt ; all that mention it to [Egypt] shall be afraid,
on account of the purpose of Jehovah of hosts, which he has purposed against it. In that day there shall be five cities in the land
of Egypt, speaking the language of Canaan, and swearing by
Jehovah of hosts. One shall be called the city of the sun
[Heliopolis].

5 In that day there shall be an altar to Jehovah in the midst of
the land, and an altar to Jehovah by its boundary. And it shall be
for a sign and witness to Jehovah of hosts in the land of Egypt,
that they cried to Jehovah on account of their oppressors, and he
sent them a deliverer, and a great man, and delivered them. And
Jehovah shall be known to the Egyptians, and the Egyptians shall

know Jehovah in that day, and offer sacrifices and bread offerings, and vow vows to Jehovah, and perform them. And Jehovah shall smite Egypt; he shall smite and heal [it]; and they shall turn to Jehovah, and he shall be entreated of for them, and heal them.

6 In that day there shall be a highway from Egypt to Assyria, and Assyria shall go to Egypt, and Egypt to Assyria; and Egypt shall serve Assyria. In that day Israel shall be a third with Egypt and Assyria, a blessing in the midst of the earth, which Jehovah of hosts shall bless, saying, Blessed is my people Egypt, and Assyria the work of my hand, and Israel my inheritance.

PROPHECY XIII. [20, 21.

EGYPT AND ETHIOPIA.

1 In the year that Tartan came to Ashdod, when Sargon, king of Assyria, sent him, he fought against Ashdod, and took it. At that time Jehovah spoke by Isaiah the son of Amoz, saying, Go and loose the sackcloth from your loins, and put off your shoes from your feet; and he did so, walking naked and barefoot. And Jehovah said, As my servant Isaiah has walked naked and barefoot three years, a sign and token concerning Egypt and concerning Ethiopia, so shall the king of Assyria lead the captives of Egypt and the captives of Ethiopia, boys and old men, naked and barefoot, and uncovered as to their hind parts, to the shame of Egypt. And they shall be confounded and ashamed of Ethiopia their confidence, and of Egypt their glory. And the inhabitants of the seacoast shall say in that day, Behold, thus it is with those in whom we trusted, to whom we fled for help to be delivered from the king of Assyria; and how are we delivered!

2 *Burden of the wilderness of the sea.* He comes from a fearful land like storms in the south, which rush from the wilderness. A grievous vision was told me: a plunderer plunders, and a destroyer destroys. Go up, Elam; besiege, Media; I will make all sighing to cease. Therefore my loins are full of pain; pains have seized me, like the pains of a woman in childbirth. I am convulsed, so that I can not hear; I am confused, so that I can not see. My mind reels, terrors make me afraid; the night of my desire he has changed into my dread. Spread a table, set a watch, eat, drink; rise, princes, anoint the shield; for thus said the Lord to me: Go set a watch,

that he may see, [and] report.   And he saw a troop, pairs of horsemen, a troop of asses, [and] a troop of camels ; and he attended with great attention, and cried, A lion : I stand on the watch, my Lord, continually during the day, and I am set on my charge all nights ; and behold, there comes a troop of men, pairs of horsemen.   Then he answered and said, Babylon has fallen, has fallen ; all the carved images of her gods has she broken on the earth. My threshing and the grain of my floor ; I have declared to you what I heard of Jehovah of hosts, the God of Israel.

3 *Burden of Dumah.*   One calls to me from Seir, Watchman, what of the night ?   Watchman, what of the night ?   And the watchman said, The morning comes, and also the night ; if you will inquire, inquire ; come again.

4. *Burden of Arabia.*   You shall lodge in the forest of Arabia, travelers of Dedanim.   The inhabitants of the land of Teman brought water to meet the thirsty, they anticipated the wanderer with bread ; for they wandered away from swords, from the sword stretched out, and from the bow bent, and from the violence of war.   For thus said the Lord to me, Yet a year, according to the years of a hired man, and all the glory of Kedar shall be consumed.   And the remnant of the archers of the mighty men, the sons of Kedar, shall be made few in number, for Jehovah the God of Israel has said it.

5 *Burden of the valley of vision.*   What ails you now, that you have all gone up on the house tops ?   It was full of clamor, a city of noise, an exulting city ; your killed were not those killed with the sword, nor those who died in battle.   All your rulers have fled together ; they are bound by the bow ; all that are found in you are bound together ; they flee from afar.   Therefore I said, Look away from me ; I will weep bitterly ; hasten not to comfort me, for the destruction of the daughter of my people.   For it is a day of tumult, and treading down, and perplexity, from the Lord Jehovah of hosts in the valley of vision, undermining the wall, and crying to the mountain.

6 And Elam bears a quiver with chariots of horsemen, and Kir uncovers the shield ; and your choice valleys are full of chariots ; and horsemen occupy the gate.   And one shall remove the vail of Judah, and he shall look in that day to the armory of the house of the forest ; and you shall see the breaches of the city of David, for they shall be many ; and you shall gather yourselves to the waters of the lower pool, and count the houses of Jeru-

salem, and break down houses to strengthen the wall, and make a
reservoir between the walls for the waters of the old pool ; but you
will not look to him that does this, nor see him that performs it
from afar.

7 On that day the Lord Jehovah of hosts will call [you] to weeping and lamentation, and to baldness and girding with sackcloth.
And behold, joy and gladness, killing cattle and slaughtering sheep,
eating meat and drinking wine, [saying,] Let us eat and drink, for
to-morrow we die.   And it has been revealed in my ear by Jehovah
of hosts, Surely this sin shall not be forgiven you till you die, says
the Lord Jehovah of hosts.

8 Thus said the Lord Jehovah of hosts, Go, go to this friend, to
Shebna, who is over the house, [and say,] What have you here ?
and whom have you here ? that you cut for yourself here a tomb, as
one cuts his tomb on high, excavating a dwelling for himself in the
rock ?   Behold, Jehovah will cast you down with the fall of a man,
and wholly wrap you up.   He will fully wind you up like a ball in
a broad land ; there shall you die, and there shall the chariots of
your glory be the contempt of your master's house.   I will thrust
you down from your pillar, and one shall destroy you from your
standing place.

9 And in that day I will call my servant Eliakim, son of Hilkiah,
and clothe him with your coat, and bind him with your girdle, and
give your dominion into his hands, and he shall be a father to the
inhabitants of Jerusalem and the house of Judah.   And I will put
the key of the house of David on his shoulder ; and he shall open,
and none shall shut ; and he shall shut, and none shall open ; and
I will drive him like a pin in a sure place ; and he shall be a throne
of glory to his father's house ; and on him shall hang all the glory
of his father's house, the offshoots and the excrescences, [and] all
small vessels, from basins to bottles.   In that day, says Jehovah of
hosts, the pin fastened in the sure place shall be removed and
cut down, and fall ; and the burden which is on it shall be cut
down, for Jehovah has said it.

PROPHECY XIV.　　　　　　[23.

Burden of Tyre.　　　　・

1 LAMENT, ships of Tarshish, for [Tyre] is destroyed without a house to enter. He was discovered to them from the land of the Cyprians. Be silent, inhabitants of the sea coast; the merchant of Zidon, the traveler on the sea, filled you; the grain of Shihor [a title of the Nile], the harvest of the river [the Nile], was her revenue, and she became the emporium of the nations. Be ashamed, Zidon, for the sea has spoken, the fortress of the sea, saying, I am not with child, neither do I bear children, nor bring up young men, nor rear young women. When it shall be heard in Egypt, they shall be in pain at the report of Tyre.

2 Pass over to Tarshish; lament, inhabitants of the sea coast. Is this your exulting city, whose antiquity is from the days of old? Her feet shall carry her far off to dwell as a stranger. Who formed this purpose against Tyre, the bestower of crowns, whose merchants were princes, and her traders the honorable of the earth? Jehovah of hosts formed the purpose, to wound the pride of all glory, and to make contemptible all the honorable of the earth.

3 Pass through your land like a river, daughter of Tarshish; the bond is no more. He stretched out his hand over the sea, and made kingdoms tremble. Jehovah commanded concerning the merchant [city] to destroy her fortresses, and said, You shall no more exult, oppressed young woman, daughter of Zidon. Arise, go to Cyprus; there also you shall not rest. Behold, the land of the Chaldeans; they were not a people, the Assyrian founded it for inhabitants of the desert. They set up watch towers, and raised up her palaces; this [nation] has made her a ruin. Lament, ships of Tarshish; your fortress is destroyed.

4 And in that day Tyre shall be forgotten 70 years, according to the days of one king. At the end of 70 years, it shall be with Tyre like the singing of a harlot. Take a harp, go about the city, forgotten harlot; play well, sing many songs, that you may be remembered. And at the end of 70 years, Jehovah will visit Tyre, and she shall return to her hire, and have commerce with all the kingdoms of the earth on the face of the world; and her merchandise and her hire shall be holy to Jehovah; it shall not be treasured up

nor hoarded up ; but her merchandise shall be for those who dwell
before Jehovah, that they may eat and be satisfied, and for splendid vestments.

PROPHECY XV.   [24, 25, 26, 27.

THE WORLD TO BE DESTROYED AND RENEWED ; THE LATTER
DAY GLORY.

1 BEHOLD, Jehovah empties out the earth, and makes it empty ;
he turns it upside down, and scatters its inhabitants ; and it shall
be with the priest as with the people, with his master as with the
man servant, with her mistress as with the female servant, with the
buyer as with the seller, with the lender as with the borrower of
him.   The earth shall be entirely emptied and entirely plundered,
for Jehovah has spoken this word.   The earth shall mourn and be
dried up ; the world shall languish and fade away ; the high ones
of the people of the earth shall languish.   For the earth is defiled
under its inhabitants ; for they have transgressed the laws, they
have changed the ordinance, they have broken the eternal covenant.
Therefore the oath has consumed the earth, and the inhabitants
shall be found guilty of it ; therefore the inhabitants of the earth
are burned up, and few mortals left in it.   The new wine mourns, the
vine languishes, all those of a joyful heart sigh.   The delight of
tabrets has ceased, the noise of revelers has ceased, the joy of the
harp rests.   They shall not drink wine with singing ; strong drink
shall be bitter to him that drinks it.

2 The city of desolation is broken down ; every house is shut up
without entrance ; there is a cry for wine in the streets ; all joy is
dried up, and the delight of the earth has gone.   Desolation remains
in the city, and the gate is smitten with ruins.   When it shall be
thus in the midst of the earth among the peoples, [it shall be] like
the shaking of the olive, like the gleaning when the harvest is
finished.   They shall lift up their voice and sing, they shall shout
from the sea for the majesty of Jehovah.   Therefore glorify Jehovah in the east, [and] the name of Jehovah, the God of Israel, in
the islands of the sea.

3 From the end of the earth we hear singing, Glory to the
righteous ; but I cry, My leanness, my leanness ; woe is me ! the
plunderers have plundered ; yes, the plunderers have taken the plunder.   Fear, and a pit, and a snare are on you, inhabitant of the

earth. He that flees from the noise of the fear shall fall into the
pit ; and he that comes up from the midst of the pit shall be taken
by the snare ; for the windows shall be opened from on high, and
the foundations of the earth shall shake. The earth is entirely
broken to pieces ; the earth is rent to fragments ; the earth is
greatly shaken ; the earth reels like a drunken man ; it moves
hither and thither like a [traveler's] hammock [suspended from the
trees] ; its transgression is heavy on it, and it has fallen to rise no
more.

4 And in that day shall Jehovah punish the host of high [ones]
on high [beings in the spiritual world], and the kings of the earth
on the earth, and they shall be gathered together in an assembly,
and I will cast them off into a pit, and they shall be shut up in prison,
and be punished many days. And the moon shall be confounded,
and the sun ashamed ; for Jehovah of hosts shall reign [as king] in
mount Zion and in Jerusalem, and [his] glory [shall be] before his
elders.

5 Jehovah, thou art my God. I will extol thee ; I will praise
thy name, for thou hast done wonders ; thy counsels from afar are
faithfulness and truth. For thou hast made a city a heap, a strong
city a ruin, a palace of strangers to be no city ; it shall never be
built. Therefore a mighty people shall glorify thee, the cities of
terrible nations shall fear thee ; for thou art the fortress of the
weak, the fortress of the needy in his distress, a refuge from the
storm, a shade from the heat, when the breath of the terrible is like
a storm prostrating walls. Thou wilt bring down the noise of
strangers like heat in a dry place, [like] heat with the shade of a
cloud, and the songs of tyrants shall be brought low.

6 For Jehovah of hosts has prepared for all peoples in this mountain a feast of fat creatures, a feast of old wines, a feast of fat
creatures with the marrows unremoved, old wines refined. And he
will cause the covering which covers the face of all peoples, and the
canopy which is poured out over all nations [the sky], to disappear,
and he will destroy death forever ; and the Lord Jehovah shall wipe
away tears from all faces, and put away the reproach of his people
from all the earth, for Jehovah has said it.

7 And one shall say in that day, Behold, this is our God ; we
waited for him, and he will save us : this is Jehovah ; we waited for
him, and we will be glad and rejoice in his salvation. For the
hand of Jehovah shall rest on this mountain, and Moab shall be

7 *

trodden down in his place, as straw is trodden down in a dung pool.
And he shall stretch out his hands in the midst of it, as a swimmer
stretches out his hands to swim ; and he shall abase his pride with
the plots of his hands, and the high fortification of your walls shall
be cast down, and laid low, and razed to the ground, even to the dust.

8 In that day shall this song be sung in the land of Judah: We
have a strong city ; it has set salvation for walls and ramparts.
Open the gates, that the righteous nation which keeps [its] pledges
may come in ; of a stable purpose it shall retain abundant peace,
because it trusts in thee. Trust in Jehovah forever, for Jah Jehovah is the rock of ages. For he abases those that dwell on high ;
as for the high city, he brings it down to the earth, he razes it to
the dust. The foot shall tread on it, the feet of the poor and the
steps of the needy. The path of the righteous man is plain ; thou,
just one, wilt make plain the way of the righteous. We have
waited also for thee in the way of thy judgments ; the desire of
[our] soul is for thy name, and the remembrance of thee. My soul
desires thee by night, my spirit also in the midst of me seeks thee
earnestly ; for according to thy judgments for the earth do the
inhabitants of the world learn righteousness. [When] a wicked
man is favored, he learns not righteousness ; in a land of uprightness he will do wickedly, and will not see the majesty of Jehovah.
Thy hand, Jehovah, is lifted up ; they will not see ; but they shall
see, and be ashamed ; the wrath of the people, the fierce anger of
thy adversaries, shall consume them.

9 Jehovah, thou wilt give us peace ; for all our works thou hast
wrought for us. Jehovah, our God, lords besides thee have ruled
over us ; we will mention only thee [and] thy name. The dead
shall not live ; the shades shall not rise up ; therefore thou hast
visited and thou hast destroyed them, and caused all remembrance
of them to perish. Thou hast increased the nation, Jehovah, thou
hast increased the nation ; thou hast glorified thyself ; thou hast
put far off all the ends of the earth.

10 Jehovah, in distress they cried to thee ; they poured out
prayers when thy correction was on them. As a woman with child,
when she approaches her delivery, is in pain, and cries out in her
pains, so have we been before thee, Jehovah. We have been with
child, we have been in pain, we have, as it were, borne wind. We
have not wrought a deliverance of the earth, and the inhabitants of
the world have not fallen. Your dead ones shall arise with my dead

body ; they shall awake and sing that dwell [sleep] in the dust ; for thy dew is the dew of plants, and the earth shall yield up the shades.

11 Come, my people, go into your private rooms, and shut your doors on you ; hide a little while till the indignation shall pass by. For behold, Jehovah goes out of his place to visit on the inhabitants of the earth their wickedness ; and the earth shall disclose her blood, and no more cover her killed.

12 In that day Jehovah shall punish with his sword, well tempered, and great, and strong, the dragon the fleeing serpent, and the dragon the tortuous serpent, and kill the sea monster which is in the sea. In that day sing to her, A vineyard of red wine ; I Jehovah keep it ; I will watch it every moment ; lest any one injure it, I will keep it night and day. Anger is not for me ; who will set briers and thorn bushes against me in battle ? I would rush on them, I would burn them together. Or else, let one lay hold of my refuge, that he may make peace with me, [and] he shall make peace with me.

13 In days to come [God] will cause Jacob to take root, and Israel shall blossom and bear fruit, and they shall fill the face of the world with the increase. Did he smite him according to the smiting of him that smote him ? or does he slaughter him, [as he does] those that slaughter him. When thou puttest forth [thy hand], thou contendest moderately with [Zion] ; [them] he takes away with his strong wind in the day of his east wind. Therefore by this is the wickedness of Jacob expiated, and this is all the fruit, to take away his sin. When he sets him up, all the stones of the altar shall be scattered like lime-stones, and the Asheras and Hammons [objects of idolatrous worship] shall stand up no more. For the strong city is left solitary, and the dwelling [of men] abandoned and forsaken, like a wilderness. The calf shall feed there, and there lie down, and consume its green branches. And when her boughs are dry, they shall be broken off, [and] women shall come to burn them ; for this is not a people of intelligence ; therefore he that made them shall not pity them, nor he that formed them, favor them.

14 And in that day Jehovah shall beat off [fruits] from the channels of the Euphrates to the river of Egypt, and you shall be gathered one by one, sons of Israel. And in that day a great trumpet shall be blown, and the perished shall come from the land of Assyria, and the banished from the land of Egypt, and shall worship Jehovah in [his] holy mountain in Jerusalem.

PROPHECY XVI.   [28.

1 WOE to the proud crown of the drunkards of Ephraim, and
the glorious beauty of his fading flower, which is on the top of the
fat valley of those overcome with wine. Behold, a strong and
mighty one of the Lord shall lay his hand on the earth, like a hail-
storm, like a destroying tempest, like a flood of mighty waters overflowing; and the proud crown of the drunkards of Ephraim shall
be trodden under foot; and the fading flower of his glorious beauty,
which is on the top of the fat valley, shall be like the first ripe fruit
before the fruit harvest; while the observer sees it yet in his hand,
he eats it up.

2 In that day Jehovah of hosts shall be a beautiful crown and a
glorious diadem to the remnant of his people, and a spirit of judgment to him that sits in judgment, and of might to those who
return war to the gate. And these also stagger with wine, they go
astray with strong drink; the priest and the prophet stagger with
strong drink, they are consumed with wine, they go astray with
strong drink, they err in vision, they waver in judgment; for all
tables are full of filthy vomit, with no place [clean].

3 Whom shall he teach knowledge? and whom shall he cause to
understand a report? Those weaned from milk, and those taken
from the breasts. For command must be on command, command
on command; law on law, law on law; here a little, there a little;
for with stammering lips and a foreign tongue he spoke to this people,
who said to them, This is not the rest with which they caused the
weary to rest, but this is the rest; but they would not hear. And
the word of Jehovah was to them command on command, command
on command; law on law, law on law; here a little, there a little;
that they might go and fall backwards, and be broken, and be
ensnared and taken.

4 Therefore hear the word of Jehovah, mockers who rule this
people which is in Jerusalem.. For you say, We have made a covenant with death, and a compact with Hades. The overflowing
scourge, when it passes through, shall not come to us; for we have
made lies our refuge, and have concealed ourselves with falsehood.
Therefore thus says the Lord Jehovah: Behold, I lay in Zion a

stone, a tried stone, a precious corner stone, a strong foundation ; he that believes shall not make haste.   And I will put justice for the line, and righteousness for the plummet, and hail shall sweep away the refuge of lies, and water overflow the hiding place ; and your covenant with death shall be broken off, and your compact with Hades shall not stand ; for the overflowing scourge shall pass through, and you shall be trodden down.   As often as it passes it shall take you ; for it shall pass through every morning, by day and by night ; and only to understand the report shall produce terror.

5 For the bed is too short for a man to stretch himself on, and the covering too narrow to wrap himself with.   For Jehovah will rise up as in mount Perazim ; he will be angry, as in the valley of Gibeon, to do his work, his strange work, and to perform his service, his strange service.   And now scoff not, lest your bands be made strong, for I have heard a destruction, and one that is decreed from the Lord Jehovah of hosts on all the earth.   Listen and hear my voice, attend and hear my words : Will the plowman plow all day to sow ?   Will he open and break the ground ?   When he has made its surface smooth, will he not scatter the negilla [black cumin], and sow the cumin, and set the wheat in rows, and the barley in its appointed place, and the spelt in its border ?   For his God has instructed him in judgment [and] taught him.   For the negilla is not threshed with a threshing dray, nor is the wheel of the dray rolled on the cumin ; but he beats the negilla with a rod, and the cumin with a staff.   Bread is threshed, but one will not thresh it forever.   He drives the wheel of his dray, and his horsemen do not bruise it.   This also comes from Jehovah of hosts, who makes wonderful his counsel and great his wisdom.

PROPHECY XVII.   [29.

JERUSALEM WARNED AND DESTRUCTION THREATENED.

1 Woe to Ariel, to Ariel, [Lion of God, Jerusalem,] the city where David dwelt ; add year to year ; go round with the feasts. But I will distress Ariel, and there shall be mourning and sorrow ; and she shall be to me like a lion of God.   And I will encamp about you, and besiege you with a garrison, and raise up mounds against you, and you shall be brought low, and speak from the ground, and whisper your words from the dust ; and your voice

shall be like that of a necromancer, and you shall mutter your words from the ground.

2 And the multitude of your adversaries shall be like the fine dust ; and the multitude of oppressors like flying chaff ; and [destruction] shall come in a moment suddenly. You shall be punished from Jehovah of hosts with thunder, and an earthquake, and a great noise, a storm and wind, and a flame of devouring fire. And the multitude of all nations that fight against Ariel, and all that fight against her and her fortress, and distress her, shall be like a dream, a vision of the night ; as when a hungry man dreams, and behold, he eats ; but he awakes, and his soul is empty ; and as when a thirsty man dreams, and behold, he drinks ; but he awakes, and behold, he is faint, and his soul is empty ; so shall the multitude of all nations be, that fight against mount Zion.

3 Delay and linger ; look on each other with astonishment, and look for help ; be drunk, but not with wine ; stagger, but not with strong drink ; for Jehovah has poured out on you a spirit of stupor, and closed your eyes, [and] those of your prophets, and covered your heads, the seers. Every-vision shall be to you as the words of a sealed letter ; they give it to one that knows how to read, saying, Read this, I pray you ; and he says, I can not read it, for it is sealed ; then the letter is given to one that knows not how to read, saying, Read this, I pray you ; and he says, I know not how to read.

4 And the Lord said, Because this people draws nigh to me with their mouth, and honors me with their lips, and their heart is far from me, and their fear of me is according to the commandments of men which are taught, therefore, behold, I will again perform on this people a wonder and an astonishment, and the wisdom of its wise men shall perish, and the understanding of its prudent men disappear.

5 Woe to those who go deep to hide counsel from Jehovah, and their works are in darkness ; and they say, Who sees us ? and who knows us ? Your perverseness ! Shall the potter be considered like the clay ? Shall the work say of the workman, He made me not ? and the thing formed say of him that formed it, He understands not ? Is it not a very little while, and Lebanon shall be like Carmel, and Carmel be considered a forest ? And in that day the deaf shall hear the words of the book, and out of obscurity and darkness the eyes of the blind shall see, the meek shall receive joy in Jehovah, and the needy among men shall exult in the Holy

One of Israel. For the oppressor shall cease, the scoffer shall perish, and all who watch to do evil shall be cut off; that made a man an offender for a word, that laid snares for him that rebuked in the gate, that turned aside the righteous to emptiness.

6 Therefore thus says Jehovah, who redeemed Abraham, concerning the house of Jacob : Jacob shall not now be ashamed, nor his face become pale [with confusion], for when his children see the work of my hands in the midst of them, they shall hallow my name, and glorify the Holy One of Jacob, and fear the God of Israel ; then the erring in judgment shall understand knowledge, and the rebellious shall learn doctrine.

PROPHECY XVIII.   [30, 31.

NO ALLIANCE ALLOWED WITH EGYPT.

1 WOE to rebellious sons, says Jehovah, who take counsel, but not from me, and pour out a libation, but not of my Spirit, that they may add sin to sin ; who take journeys to go down to Egypt, but inquire not [at home] at my mouth ; who flee for refuge to the fortress of Pharaoh, and seek protection in the shade of Egypt. But the fortress of Egypt shall be your shame, and protection in the shade of Egypt your confusion ; for his princes were at Zoan, and his embassadors went to Hanes. All are ashamed of a people that can not profit them ; they shall not be a help nor a profit, but a shame and reproach.

2 *The burden of the beasts of the south.* In a land of distress and affliction, of the lioness and the lion, among which are the viper and the fiery flying serpent, they shall carry their wealth on the shoulders of young asses, and their treasures on the bunches of camels, to a people that can not profit, and Egypt shall help in vain, and to no purpose ; therefore have I called this [power], Their pride is to rest.

3 Go now, write it on a tablet before them, and inscribe it in a book, that it may be for after times, forever and ever. For this people is rebellious ; they are sons that lie, sons that will not obey the law of Jehovah ; that say to the seers, See not ; and to the prophets, Prophesy not to us right things, speak to us flatteries, prophesy deceptions, depart from the way, incline from the path, cause the Holy One of Israel to cease from before us.

4 Therefore thus says the Holy One of Israel : Because you reject this word, and trust in oppression and perverseness, and lean on it, therefore this wickedness shall be to you like a falling mass, which breaks out in a high wall; the ruin which it produces shall come suddenly in an instant; and he has broken her to pieces, like the breaking of an earthen bottle ; which being broken one will not spare, neither shall there be found among its fragments a broken piece with which to take up fire from a burning [mass], or to dip water from a cistern.

5 For thus said the Lord Jehovah, the Holy One of Israel : By conversion and rest you shall be saved, and in quietness and confidence shall be your strength ; but you would not [hear].   And you said, No, but we will flee on horses, and ride on swift beasts ; therefore you shall flee ; therefore they shall be swift that pursue you ; a thousand shall flee from the rebuke of one, and you shall flee from the rebuke of five, till you are left like a signal pole on a mountain top, and a standard on a hill.   But nevertheless, Jehovah shall wait to favor you; but nevertheless, he shall rise up to have mercy on you ; for Jehovah is a God of justice ; blessed are all that wait for him.

6 Therefore, people of Zion, who dwell at Jerusalem, weep not very bitterly ; he will certainly favor the voice of your cry; when he hears it, he will answer you.   For the Lord has given you the bread of affliction and the water of distress ; but your teachers shall be taken from you no more, and your eyes shall see your teachers, and your ears shall hear a word behind you, saying, This is the way, walk in it, when you turn to the right hand or to the left.

7 Then you shall defile the silver covering of your carved images, and the gold covering of your cast images ; you shall cast them away like a detestable thing, [and] say to them, Go.   And he will give rain for your seed which you shall sow in the ground, and bread, the produce of the land ; and it shall be rich and nourishing. And he will feed your cattle in that day in a large pasture ; and the oxen and asses which till the ground shall eat salted provender, which is cleaned with a winnowing fork and shovel.   And on every lofty mountain and on every high hill shall be brooks flowing with water in the day of great slaughter, when the towers fall.   And the light of the moon shall be as the light of the sun, and the light of the sun shall be sevenfold, as the light of seven days, in the day

on which God shall bind up the bruise of his people, and heal the wound with which he had smitten them.

8 Behold, the name of Jehovah comes from afar, burning with his anger, and the burden is great; his lips are full of indignation, and his tongue devours like fire ; and his breath is like an overflowing torrent; it divides even to the neck, to sift the nations with the sieve of destruction ; and [he has] a bridle causing to err, for the jaws of the peoples. You shall have song, as on a night when one keeps a feast, and joy of heart, as when one goes with the pipe to the mountain of Jehovah, to the rock of Israel. And Jehovah will cause his glorious voice to be heard ; and the coming down of his arm shall be seen, with fierce anger and a flame of devouring fire, storms, and showers, and hail stones. For Assyria shall come down by the voice of Jehovah ; he shall smite with his rod ; and at every passage of the appointed rod, which Jehovah shall bring on him, it shall be with tabrets and harps ; and with tumultuous battles will he fight with him. For Tophet [a place of burial or burning] was long since prepared ; it is also made ready for the king ; he has made the pile of fire deep and large, and has provided much wood ; the breath of Jehovah, like a stream of sulphur, shall kindle it.

9 Woe to those that go down to Egypt for help, that are carried on horses, and trust in chariots because they are many, and in horsemen because they are of great power, and look not to the Holy One of Israel, nor seek Jehovah. And he also is wise, and will bring evil, and will not turn away his words, but will arise against all the house of evil doers, and against the help of those that do wickedness. The Egyptians are men, and not God ; and their horses are flesh, and not spirit ; and Jehovah will stretch out his hand, and the helper shall stumble, and the helped fall, and all of them shall be consumed together. For thus said Jehovah to me : As when a lion or young lion growls over his prey, when a multitude of shepherds is called forth, he is not terrified by their noise, nor disheartened by their multitude, so Jehovah of hosts will come down to fight on mount Zion, and on its hill. As birds cover their young, so will Jehovah of hosts protect Jerusalem ; he will defend and deliver, he will pass over and save it.

10 Turn to him from whom the sons of Israel have greatly revolted ; for in that day they shall cast away every one his idols of silver and his idols of gold, which your hands made for you to sin

with ; and Assyria shall fall by the sword not of man, and a sword
not of man shall destroy him.   And he shall flee before the sword,
and his young men be under tribute.   And he shall pass by his
fortress through terror, and his princes shall be driven from the
standard, says Jehovah, whose fire is in Zion, and his furnace in
Jerusalem.

PROPHECY XIX.   [32, 33.

A RIGHTEOUS KING TO ARISE ; SINNERS REBUKED.

1 BEHOLD, a king shall reign with righteousness, and princes
hall rule with justice.   And the man [the king] shall be like a
hiding place from the wind, and a covert from the storm; like
streams of water in a dry land; like the shadow of a great rock in
a weary land.   The eyes of those that see shall not be blinded, and
the ears of those that hear shall attend, and the mind of the hasty
shall understand knowledge, and the tongue of the stammering
shall speak rapidly and plainly.   The fool shall no more be called
liberal, nor the deceitful rich.   For the fool will speak folly, and
his mind will do wickedness to commit impiety, and to speak wickedness against Jehovah, to make the hungry soul empty, and to
cause the thirsty to want drink.   As for the deceitful man, his instruments are evil, he devises mischiefs to destroy the poor with
lies, even when he pronounces the judgment of the needy.   But a
liberal man devises liberal things, and by liberal things shall he
stand.

2 Women that are at ease, arise, hear my voice ; daughters who
are secure, attend to my words.   The days of a year, [and] you
who are secure shall tremble ; for the vintage is finished, and the
harvest shall not come.   Be afraid, women that are at ease ; let
trembling [seize] the secure.   Strip, make bare, and gird [sack-
cloth] on [your] loins, you that mourn for the pleasant fields, for
the fruitful vines.

3 Briers and thorn bushes shall come up on the land of my
people, for [they shall be] on all the houses of joy in the exulting
city.   For the palace shall be thrown down, the multitude of the city
shall be forsaken, and the hill and the watch tower shall be amid
dens forever, a joy of wild asses, and a pasture of flocks, till the
Spirit shall be poured out on us from on high, and the wilderness
become a fruitful field, and the fruitful field be accounted a forest.

Then justice shall dwell in the wilderness, and righteousness inhabit the fruitful field, and the work of righteousness shall be peace, and the service of righteousness quietness and assurance forever. And my people shall dwell in a peaceful habitation, and in secure dwellings, and in quiet resting places; but it shall hail, to bring down the forest, and the city thou shalt bring low in the plain. Blessed are you that sow by all waters, who send forth the feet of the ox and the ass.

4 Woe to you that destroyed and you were not destroyed, and plundered and they did not plunder you: when you shall finish destroying, you shall be destroyed; and when you shall desist from plundering, they shall plunder you. Jehovah, be gracious to us; we have waited for thee; be our arm every morning, and our salvation in time of distress. At the noise of the tumult, peoples fled; at the lifting up of yourself, nations were scattered; and your spoil is gathered, like the gathering of the devouring locust; they shall run about like the running of locusts.

5 Jehovah is exalted, for he dwells on high, he fills Zion with justice and righteousness. Riches, salvation, wisdom, and knowledge shall be the security of your times, [and] the fear of Jehovah one's treasure.

6 Behold, their heroes cry without; the embassadors that ask for peace shall weep bitterly. The highways are deserted, the traveler ceases from the path. He has broken the covenant, he despises cities, he regards not mortal. The earth mourns [and] languishes; he has put Lebanon to shame, [and] it pines away; Sharon is like a desert, Bashan and Carmel are made bare. Now I will arise, says Jehovah, now I will lift myself up, now I will be exalted. You shall conceive chaff, and bring forth stubble; your breath like a fire shall consume you. Peoples shall be burnt to lime, they shall be thorn bushes cut up and consumed with fire. Hear, the far off, what I have done, and, the near, know my might. Sinners in Zion are afraid, trembling has seized the hypocrites. Who of us can dwell with devouring fire? Who of us can dwell with eternal burnings? He that walks righteously and speaks rightly, that refuses the gain of oppressions, that shakes his hand from holding bribes, that stops his ear from hearing of blood, and closes his eyes from seeing evil, he shall dwell on high; the fortresses of rocks shall be his refuge, bread shall be given him, and his water shall be sure. Your eyes shall see the king in his glory; they shall

see the land of the far off. Your mind shall meditate on terrors.
Where [you shall say] is the scribe [overseer] ? where the weigher
[of taxes] ? where the scribe of the towers [secretary of war] ? You
shall not see a strong people, a people of difficult language, which
you can not understand, and of barbarous tongue, which you do not
know. You shall see Zion, the city of our solemnities, and your
eyes shall see Jerusalem, a quiet habitation, a tent that shall never
remove, nor its pins be taken up, nor any of its cords broken. For
there the mighty Jehovah shall be to us a place of rivers and broad
streams, in which no ship with oars shall sail, nor large ship shall
pass through it. For Jehovah is our judge, Jehovah is our law-
giver, he is our king ; he will save us. Your tacklings are cast
down, they can not hold the base of their mast, they can not spread
the standard ; then a great spoil shall be divided, [and] the lame
shall take the prey ; but no inhabitant shall say, I am sick ; the
people who live in that [age] shall be forgiven their wickedness.

PROPHECY XX.   [34, 35.

THE ENEMIES OF THE JEWS TO BE DESTROYED, AND THE JEWS
RESTORED TO THEIR LAND.

1 NATIONS, come near to hear, and peoples, attend ; hear, earth
and all it contains, the world and all its products. For the anger
of Jehovah is against all nations, and his indignation against all their
hosts ; he has cursed them, he has given them to slaughter. Their
killed shall be cast out, and the scent of their carcasses ascend,
and the mountains be soaked with their blood. All the host of
heaven shall be dissolved, the heavens shall be rolled up like roll ;
and all their host fall, like the falling of a leaf from a vine, and as
a [fig] falls from a fig tree. For my sword shall be bathed in
heaven ; behold, it shall descend on Edom, and on the people of
my curse for judgment. The sword of Jehovah is full of blood, it
is made fat with fat, with the blood of young sheep and goats, with
the fat of the kidneys of rams, for Jehovah has a sacrifice in Bozrah
and a great slaughter in the land of Edom. The buffaloes shall
come down with them, and the bullocks with the bulls, and their
lands shall be soaked with blood, and their dust made rich with fat.
2 For it is the day of Jehovah's vengeance, and the year of
recompenses for the cause of Zion ; and her streams shall be

turned into pitch, and her dust into sulphur, and her land shall become burning pitch. It shall not be extinguished night nor day; its smoke shall ascend forever; it shall be desolate from generation to generation; none shall pass through it forever and ever. The pelican and the porcupine shall possess it, the heron and the raven shall dwell in it, and he shall stretch on it the line of emptiness and stones of confusion. They shall call her nobles to the kingdom, and none shall be there, and all her princes shall be [brought to] nothing. Her palaces shall be overgrown with briers, the thistle and the thorn bush shall be in her fortresses, and she shall become a habitation of jackals, a court of the daughters of the ostrich; and jackals shall attack jackals, and the wood demon cry to his fellow; there also shall the night specter light and find herself a rest. There the arrow snake shall make her nest, and lay and hatch, and brood her young in its shade; there also shall kites be assembled, every one with her mate. Search in the book of Jehovah and read: Not one of them shall be wanting, nor shall any one seek his mate, for the mouth [of Jehovah] shall command and his Spirit shall gather them; and he shall cast lots for them, and his hand shall give them an inheritance by line; they shall possess it forever, they shall dwell in it to all generations.

3 The wilderness and the dry [land] shall be glad with them, and the desert shall rejoice and blossom like the meadow saffron. It shall blossom abundantly, and rejoice, and shall have joy and singing. The glory of Lebanon shall be given it, the excellency of Carmel and Sharon, they shall see the glory of Jehovah, the excellency of our God. Strengthen the weak hands and confirm the feeble knees; say to the faint-hearted, Be strong, fear not; behold, your God will come [with] vengeance, God with a recompense; he will come and save you.

4 Then shall the eyes of the blind be opened, and the ears of the deaf unstopped; then shall the lame leap like a hart, and the tongue of the dumb sing; for waters shall break out in the wilderness, and streams in the desert. The mirage shall become a pool, and the dry land springs of water; in the habitation of jackals, where each lay shall be a court for reeds and bulrushes.

5 And there shall be a highway, and a way, and it shall be called, The way of holiness. The impure shall not pass through it, but it shall be for them; the traveler, and even the fool, shall not miss their way. No lion shall be there, nor shall a ravenous beast go up on it

8 *

[or] be found there; but the redeemed shall walk [there]; and the redeemed of Jehovah shall return and come to Zion with singing, and eternal joy on their heads; they shall attain joy and gladness, and sorrow and sighing shall flee away.

PROPHECY XXI. [36, 37.

THE INVASION OF SENNACHERIB.

1 AND in the fourteenth year of king Hezekiah came up Senna-cherib, king of Assyria, against all the fortified cities of Judah, and took them. And the king of Assyria sent Rabshakeh from Lachish to Jerusalem, to king Hezekiah, with a great army. And he stood at the channel of the upper pool, in the highway of the fuller's field; and there went out to him Eliakim, the son of Hilkiah, who was over the house, and Shebna the scribe, and Joah, the son of Asaph, the recorder. · And Rabshakeh said to them, Say, I pray you, to Hezekiah, Thus says the great king, the king of Assyria, What confidence is this in which you trust? I say [say you], Cer-tainly it is a word of the lips; — there is counsel and strength for war. Now, in whom do you trust, that you rebel against me? Behold, you trust on that staff of a broken reed, on Egypt, which, if a man leans on it, will even enter into his hand, and pierce it through; so is Pharaoh king of Egypt to every one that trusts in him.

2 But you will tell me, We trust in Jehovah our God. Is not this he whose high places and altars Hezekiah took away, and said to Judah and Jerusalem, Worship before this altar? And now make an arrangement, I pray you, with my master the king of Assyria, and I will give you a thousand horses, if you for your part can put riders on them. How then can you turn away the face of the least of the captains of the servants of my master? But you trust in Egypt for chariots and horsemen; and now have I come up against this land without Jehovah to destroy it? Jehovah said to me, Go up against this land and destroy it.

3 Then said Eliakim, and Shebna, and Joah to Rabshakeh, Speak, we pray you, to your servants in Syriac, for we understand, and speak not to us in Hebrew, in the hearing of the people who are on the wall. Then Rabshakeh said, Has my master sent me to your master, and to you, to speak these words, and not to the men who sit

on the wall, to eat their dung and drink their urine with you ?
Then Rabshakeh stood and cried with a loud voice in Hebrew, and
said, Hear the words of the great king, the king of Assyria. Thus
says the king : Let not Hezekiah deceive you, for he will not be able
to deliver you. Let not Hezekiah make you trust in Jehovah, saying, Jehovah will deliver us ; this city shall not be given up into the
hand of the king of Assyria. Hear not Hezekiah ; for thus says
the king of Assyria : Make me a present, and come out to me, and
eat every man of his vine, and every man of his fig tree, and drink
every man water from his cistern, till I come and take you away to
a land like your land, a land of grain and wine, a land of bread
and vineyards, lest Hezekiah deceive you, saying, Jehovah will deliver us. Have the gods of the nations delivered any one his land
from the hand of the king of Assyria ? Where are the gods of
Hamath and Arpad ? Where are the gods of Sepharvaim ? But
did they even deliver Samaria from my hand ? Who are there, of
all the gods of these lands, who have delivered their land from my
hand, that Jehovah should deliver Jerusalem from my hand ?

4 Then they were silent, and answered him not a word ; for that
was the command of the king, saying, Answer him not. Then
came Eliakim the son of Hilkiah, who was over the house, and
Shebna the scribe, and Joah, the son of Asaph, the recorder, to
Hezekiah, with their clothes rent, and told him the words of Rabshakeh.

5 And when king Hezekiah heard, he rent his clothes, and covered himself with sackcloth, and went to the house of Jehovah.
And he sent Eliakim, who was over the house, and Shebna the
scribe, and the elders of the priests, they having covered themselves
with sackcloth, to Isaiah, son of Amoz the prophet. And they said
to him, Thus says Hezekiah : This day is a day of distress, and rebuke, and reproach, for sons have come to the breaking forth, and
there is no strength to bear. Perhaps Jehovah your God will hear
the words of Rabshakeh, whom his master, the king of Assyria,
has sent to reproach the living God, and to revile him with the
words which Jehovah your God has heard ; and do you lift up prayer
for the remnant that is found.

6 Then the servants of king Hezekiah went to Isaiah, and Isaiah
said to them, Say thus to your master : Thus says Jehovah : Fear
not on account of the words with which you have heard the servants
of the king of Assyria reproach me. Behold, I give him breath,

and he shall hear a report and return to his land, and I will cause
him to fall by the sword in his land.

7 And Rabshakeh returned, and found the king of Assyria fighting against Libnah; for he heard that he had removed his camp
from Lachish. And he heard concerning Tirhakah king of Ethiopia, saying, He has come out to fight with you. When he heard
[this] he sent messengers to Hezekiah, saying, Thus say to Hezekiah king of Judah: Let not your God in whom you trust deceive
you, saying, Jerusalem shall not be delivered into the hand of the
king of Assyria. Behold, you have heard what the kings of Assyria
did to all lands to utterly destroy them, and shall you be delivered?
Did the gods of the nations which my father destroyed deliver
them? Gozan and Haran? and Rezeph, the sons of Eden who
were in Talassar? Where is the king of Hamath, and the king of
Arpad? and the king of the city of Sepharvaim, Hena and Iva?

8 Then Hezekiah took the letter from the hand of the messengers, and read it, and went up to the house of Jehovah; and
Hezekiah spread it before Jehovah. And Hezekiah prayed to
Jehovah, saying, Jehovah of hosts, God of Israel, who sittest on
the cherubs, thou alone art the God of all the kingdoms of the
earth; thou madest the heavens and the earth. Incline, Jehovah,
thy ear and hear; open, Jehovah, thy eyes and see; and hear all
the words of Sennacherib, which he has sent to reproach the living
God. Truly, Jehovah, the kings of Assyria have destroyed all coun-
tries and their lands, and cast their gods into the fire; for they were
not gods, but the work of men's hands, wood and stone; and they
destroyed them. And now, Jehovah our God, save us from his
hand, that all kingdoms of the earth may know that thou art
Jehovah alone.

9 Then sent Isaiah the son of Amoz to Hezekiah, saying, Thus
says Jehovah the God of Israel: Because you have prayed to me
concerning Sennacherib, king of Assyria, this is the word which
Jehovah has spoken concerning him. The virgin daughter of Zion
has laughed you to scorn, the daughter of Jerusalem has shaken
her head at you. Whom have you blasphemed and reproached?
Against whom have you lifted up your voice and raised your eyes
on high? Against the Holy One of Israel. By your servants you
have reproached the Lord, and you have said, I have come up with
a multitude of chariots to the heights of the mountains, to the sides
of Lebanon; and I will cut down the highest of its cedars, and the

choice of its cypresses ; and I will go to its highest summit, to its
forest Carmel.   I have dug and drunk waters, and I will dry up
with the soles of my feet all the rivers of Egypt.

10 Have you not heard from a distant time that I did it ; from
former days also I purposed it ; now I have brought it forth, to
make fortified cities desolate ruins.   Therefore their inhabitants
were weak-handed, they were confounded and put to shame, they
were grass of the field and a green herb, grass on the house tops,
and a blight was on the grain.   I know both your sitting down,
and your going out and your coming in, and your rage against me.
Because your rage against me and your arrogance have come up
into my ears, therefore I will put my hook in your nose, and my
bridle in your jaws, and will turn you back by the way by which
you came.

11 And you shall have this sign : To eat this year what is self-
sown, and the second year what grows of itself ; and the third year
sow, and reap, and plant vineyards, and eat the fruit of them.   And
the escaped of the house of Judah that remain shall add roots below, and bear fruit above ; for a remnant shall go forth from Jerusalem, and those escaped from mount Zion ; the zeal of Jehovah
of hosts will do this.

12 Therefore thus says Jehovah concerning the king of Assyria :
He shall not come to this city, nor shoot an arrow there, nor display
a shield before it, nor cast up a mound against it.   By the way that
he came, by that shall he return, and shall not come to this city,
says Jehovah.   For I will defend this city and save it, for my sake,
and for my servant David's sake.

13 And then went forth an angel of Jehovah, and smote the
camp of Assyria 185,000 ; and they arose in the morning, and behold they were all dead men.   Then Sennacherib, king of Assyria,
broke up his camp, and went and returned to Nineveh.   And he
was worshiping in the house of Nisroch his god, and Adrammelech
and Sharezer his sons smote him with the sword ; and they escaped
to the land of Ararat ; and Esarhaddon his son reigned in his
stead.

PROPHECY XXII.   [38, 39.

HEZEKIAH'S SICKNESS.

1 IN those days Hezekiah was sick and about to die ; and Isaiah, the son of Amoz the prophet, came to him and said, Thus says Jehovah : Give charge to your house, for you shall die, and not live. Then Hezekiah turned his face to the wall [the temple], and prayed to Jehovah ; and he said, I beseech thee, Jehovah, remember now how I have walked before thee in truth and with a perfect heart, and have done good in thy sight ; and Hezekiah wept bitterly.

2 Then came the word of Jehovah to Isaiah, saying, Go and say to Hezekiah, Thus says Jehovah, the God of David your father : I have heard your prayer, I have seen your tears ; behold, I will add to your days 15 years ; and I will deliver you and this city from the hand of the king of Assyria, and will defend this city. And this shall be a sign to you from Jehovah that Jehovah will do this thing which he has said : behold, I will cause the shadow of the degrees, which has gone down on the degrees of Ahaz with the sun, to turn back 10 degrees. And the sun turned back 10 degrees of the degrees which it had gone down.

3 *Song of Hezekiah, king of Judah, when he was sick, and had recovered from his sickness.*
I said, in the quiet of my days, I shall go down to the gates of Hades ; I am deprived of the rest of my years. I said, I shall not see Jah, Jah in the land of the living ; I shall behold man no more among the inhabitants of Hades ; my habitation is taken down, and carried away from me, like a shepherd's tent ; I have rolled together like a weaver my life ; he will cut me [like a web] from the thrums ; from day to night thou wilt make an end of me. I composed myself for the morning, like a lion, so will he break all my bones ; like a twittering swallow will I chirp ; I will mourn like a dove ; my eyes have become weary with looking up ; Jehovah, I am in distress ; protect me.

4 What shall I say ? For he spoke to me and did it. I will walk softly all my years on account of the bitterness of my soul. Lord, beyond these shall [men] live, and for all these years is the life of my spirit ; for thou hast healed me and caused me to live. Behold, for peace I had great bitterness, but in love to my soul thou didst deliver me from the pit of destruction ; for thou hast cast all

my sins behind thy back ; for Hades can not give thee thanks ; death can not praise thee ; those who go down to the pit can not hope in thy truth. The living, the living, he shall give thee thanks, as I do this day ; fathers to sons shall make known thy truth. Jehovah has restored me ; therefore will we play on my stringed instruments all the days of our life, for the house of Jehovah.

5 For Isaiah said, Let them take a cake of figs, and lay them softened on the ulcer, and he shall live. And Hezekiah said, What is the sign that I shall go up to the house of Jehovah ?

6 At that time sent Merodach Baladan, son of Baladan, letters and a present to Hezekiah, because he heard that he was sick, and had recovered. And Hezekiah was pleased with them, and showed them the house of treasures of silver and of gold, and of spices, and of excellent oil, and all his armory, and all that was found in his treasures. There was not a thing which Hezekiah did not show them, either in his house or in all his kingdom.

7 Then came Isaiah the prophet to king Hezekiah, and said to him, What said these men ? and whence did they come to you ? And Hezekiah said, They came to me from a distant land, from Babylon. And he said, What did they see in your house ? And Hezekiah said, They saw all that is in my house ; there was not a thing which I did not show them in my treasures.

8 Then said Isaiah to Hezekiah, Hear the word of Jehovah of hosts : Behold, the days come when all that is in your house, and that your fathers laid up, to this day, shall be carried to Babylon. There shall not be left a thing, says Jehovah. And he shall take of your sons who shall proceed from you, who shall be born, and they shall be eunuchs in the palace of the king of Babylon.

9 Then said Hezekiah to Isaiah, Good is the word of the Jehovah which you have spoken ; but he said, Yet let there be peace and truth in my days.

PROPHECY XXIII. [40.

THE RETURN FROM THE BABYLONIAN EXILE PROCLAIMED ; GOD COMES TO DELIVER HIS PEOPLE ; HIS MAJESTY, AND THE VANITY OF IDOLS.

1 COMFORT, comfort my people, says your God. Speak kindly to Jerusalem, and cry to her that her warfare is accomplished, that her wickedness is forgiven, for she has received at Jehovah's hand double for all her sins.

2 A voice cries in the wilderness, Prepare the way of Jehovah, make straight in the desert a highway for our God. Every valley shall be raised up, and every mountain and hill be cut down; and the hill shall be made a plain, and the rough places a valley, and the glory of Jehovah shall be revealed, and all flesh shall see it together, for the mouth of Jehovah has spoken it.

3 A voice said, Cry. And I said, What shall I cry? All flesh is grass, and all its beauty like the flower of the field; the grass withers, the flower fades; for the breath of Jehovah breathes on it. Certainly the people are grass; the grass withers, the flower fades; but the word of our God shall stand forever.

4 Get yourself up on a high mountain, bearer of good news to Zion; lift up your voice with strength, bearer of good news to Jerusalem; lift up, fear not; say to the cities of Judah, Behold your God. Behold, the Lord Jehovah will come with strength, and his arm shall rule for him; behold, his reward is with him, and his work before him. He shall feed his flock like a shepherd, he shall gather the lambs with his arm, and carry them in his bosom, and shall lead the ewes.

5 Who measured the waters in the hollow of his hand, and proved the heavens with a span, and took up the dust of the earth in a shalish [.37 of a bushel], and weighed the mountains in a balance, and the hills in scales? Who measured the Spirit of Jehovah, and being his counselor, taught him? With whom took he counsel? and [who] made him understand, and taught him the way of justice, and taught him knowledge, and made him know the way of understanding? Behold, the nations are as a drop from a bucket, they are accounted as the fine dust of the scales; behold, he takes up the islands as an atom; Lebanon is not sufficient to burn, nor its beasts sufficient for a burnt offering. All nations are as nothing before him; they are accounted by him less than nothing and vanity. To whom then will you liken God? and what similitude will you make of him?

6 The workman casts an image, and the goldsmith covers it with gold, and makes chains of silver. One that is impoverished by a gift chooses a tree that will not rot; he seeks a skillful workman to make an image that can not be moved. Have you not known? have you not heard? has it not been told you from the beginning? have you not understood from the foundations of the earth? He sits above the circle of the earth, and its inhabitants are as locusts. He stretches out the heavens like a curtain, and spreads them out

like a tent to dwell in. He brings princes to nothing, and the judges of the earth he makes like nothing. Indeed, they shall not be planted ; indeed, they shall not be sown ; indeed, their stem shall not take root in the earth ; and he also blows on them, and they wither, and a storm shall bear them away like straw.

7 To whom then will you compare me, and whom shall I be like, says the Holy One ? Lift up your eyes on high, and see who made these things, brings out by number their hosts, calls all of them by name, by the greatness of his power, for he is mighty in power ; not one fails. Why do you say, Jacob, and declare, Israel, My way is hid from Jehovah, my judgment has passed over from my God ? Have you not known ? Have you not heard, that the eternal God, Jehovah, the creator of the ends of the earth, faints not, nor is weary ? There is no searching of his understanding. He gives strength to the faint, and to those who have no power he increases strength. Youth faint and are weary, and young men stumble and fall ; but those that wait on Jehovah shall increase in strength ; they shall mount up on wings as eagles, they shall run and not be weary, they shall walk and not faint.

PROPHECY XXIV. [41, 1-20.

GOD ASSERTS HIS SUPREMACY AND INTEREST IN HIS PEOPLE, AND ENCOURAGES THEM.

1 BE silent before me, islands, and let the peoples renew [their] strength ; let them approach ; then, let them speak, let them speak together ; let us draw near for judgment. Who raised up righteousness from the east ? called him to his foot ? gave nations before him ? and he subdued kings, and their swords were made like dust, and their bows scattered like chaff. He pursued them, and passed on safely by a path in which he had not gone with his feet. Who attempted and accomplished calling the generations from the beginning ? I Jehovah, the first and the last, I am he. The islands saw and were afraid ; the ends of the earth feared ; they drew near and came.

2 [Look at idol gods]. They help each one his neighbor, and each one says to his brother, Be strong. And the carpenter encourages the goldsmith, and he that smooths with the hammer him that smites on the anvil, saying, It is ready for the soldering ; and they fasten it with nails, that it may not be moved.

3 But you, Israel, are my servant; you are the Jacob whom I choose, the children of Abraham my friend, whom I took from the ends of the earth, and called you from its sides, and said to you, You are my servant; I have chosen you, and not rejected you. Fear not, for I am with you; be not dismayed, for I am your God. I will strengthen you; indeed, I will help you; indeed, I will uphold you with my righteous right hand. Behold, all that are angry with you shall be ashamed and confounded; they shall be as nothing; and the men that contend with you shall perish. You shall seek the men that contend with you, and shall not find them, and the men that fight with you shall be as nothing and vanity. For I am Jehovah your God, holding your right hand, saying to you, Fear not, I am your help.

4 Fear not, worm Jacob, [and] men of Israel, I am your help, says Jehovah, and your redeemer, the Holy One of Israel. Behold, I will make you a new sharp threshing dray having teeth, [and] you shall thresh the mountains, and beat them to powder, and make the hills like chaff; [and] you shall winnow them, and the wind shall bear them away, and a whirlwind scatter them; but you shall rejoice in Jehovah, you shall praise the Holy One of Israel.

5 When the poor and needy seek for water, and there is none, and their tongue is dried up with thirst, I Jehovah will answer them, [I] the God of Israel will not forsake them; I will open rivers on the hills, and fountains in the valleys; I will make the wilderness pools of water, and the dry land springs of water; I will set in the wilderness the cedar, the acacia, and the myrtle, [and] the olive; I will put in the desert the cypress, the oak, and the sherbin cedar, that they may see, and know, and consider, and understand together, that the hand of Jehovah did it, and the Holy One of Israel created it.

PROPHECY XXV.   [41, 21, 42, 43.

GOD RAISES UP CYRUS; REPROVES IDOLATERS, AND ENCOURAGES HIS WORSHIPERS.

1 BRING forward your cause, says Jehovah, present your strong [evidences], says the King of Jacob; let them come forward and show us what shall happen; tell us former things, what has happened hitherto, that we may attend and know their latter end; or inform us of things to come. Tell what shall come to pass hereafter, that

we may know that you are gods; indeed, do good or do evil, that we may be astonished and fear together. Behold, you are nothing, and your work is nothing; he that chooses you is an abomination.

2 I have raised up one from the north [Cyrus], and he shall come from the rising of the sun; he shall call on my name; and he shall come on princes like mortar, and as a potter treads the clay. Who declared [this] from the beginning that we may know? and from a former period, that we may say, He is righteous? Indeed, none declared [it], indeed, none published [it], indeed, none heard your words; I first gave to Zion, Behold! Behold! and to Jerusalem a bearer of good news. For I saw, and there was no man, and [looked] among them, but there was no counselor, that I might ask them, and they give me an answer. Behold, all of them are vanity, and their works are nothing; their cast images are wind and emptiness.

3 Behold my servant, whom I will uphold, my chosen, with whom my soul is well pleased. I have put my Spirit on him; he shall bring forth justice to the nations. He shall not cry nor lift up his voice, nor cause it to be heard in the streets; a bruised reed he shall not break, nor extinguish the smoking flax, till he brings forth justice to truth. He shall not faint nor run, till he has set justice in the earth, and the islands shall wait for his law.

4 Thus says God, Jehovah, who created the heavens and stretched them out, and spread out the earth and the things which proceed from it; who gives breath to the people, and life to those that walk on it; I Jehovah have called you in righteousness, and I will strengthen your hand, and will keep you and give you for a covenant of the people, for a light of the nations, to open the eyes of the blind, to bring out of prison the prisoner, and from the dungeon those that sit in darkness. I am Jehovah; that is my name; and my glory I will not give to another, nor my praise to carved images. Behold, the former things have come to pass, and I declare new things; before they spring up, I tell you of them.

5 Sing a new song to Jehovah, [and] his praise in the ends of the earth, you that go down to the sea, and all it contains, the islands and their inhabitants. Let the wilderness and its cities, the villages which Kedar inhabits, lift up [the voice]; let the inhabitants of Selah [the rock] sing; let them shout from the tops of the mountains; let them give glory to Jehovah, and declare his praise in the islands. Jehovah shall go forth like a mighty man; [his] indigna-

tion shall be excited like a man of war ; he shall cry aloud ; yes, he shall shout, he shall prevail against his enemies.

6 [He shall say], I was silent from of old ; I have been still and restrained myself ; [now] I will cry out like one in childbirth : I will be astonished and enraged together : I will lay waste the mountains and hills, and dry up all their herbage ; and I will make the rivers islands, and dry up the pools. And I will lead the blind by a way which they know not, and in paths which they know not will I direct them ; I will make darkness light before them, and crooked ways plain ; these things will I do, and will not forsake them. They shall turn back and be ashamed, that trust in a carved image, that say to cast images, You are our gods.

7 Hear, you deaf, and look, you blind, to see. Who is blind but my servant ? and deaf as my messenger whom I send ? Who is as blind as a friend, and as blind as Jehovah's servant ? You see many things, but observe not ; he opens the ears [of others], but hears not. Jehovah is pleased-on account of his righteousness ; he will magnify the law and make it honorable. But this people is plundered and destroyed, all of them are ensnared in holes and hid in dungeons ; they are a prey, and none delivers ; a spoil, and none says, Restore.

8 Who of you will listen to this ? will attend and hear for the time to come ? Who gave Jacob to the spoiler, and Israel to plunderers ? Did not Jehovah, he against whom we have sinned ? and they would not walk in his ways nor obey his law. Therefore he poured out on them his fierce anger, and the strength of war, and it set them on fire on every side, and they knew it not ; and it burned them, yet they laid it not to heart.

9 And now, thus says Jehováh that created you, Jacob, and formed you, Israel : Fear not, for I am your Redeemer ; I have called you by name ; you are mine. When you pass through the water, I will be with you, and through the rivers, they shall not overflow you. When you go through the fire you shall not be burned, neither shall the flame consume you. For I, Jehovah, am your God, the Holy One of Israel, your Saviour. I gave Egypt for your ransom, Ethiopia and Seba for you. Since you were precious in my sight, you have been honored, and I have loved you ; and I will give men for you, and peoples for your life.

10 Fear not, for I am with you ; I will bring your children from the east, and will gather you from the west ; I will say to the north,

Give up ; and to the south, Keep not back ; bring my sons from afar, and my daughters from the end of the earth, every one that is called by my name ; for I have created him for my glory ; I have formed him, yes, I have made him. Bring out the people who are blind, but have eyes, and deaf, but have ears ; let all nations be gathered together, and let the peoples be assembled. Who among you declared this, and published to us the former things ? let them produce their witnesses and be justified, and let them hear and say, It is true. You are my witnesses, says Jehovah, and my servant whom I have chosen, that you may know and believe me, and understand that I am he ; before me there was no God formed, nor shall there be any after me.

11 I, I am Jehovah, and besides me there is no Saviour. I have declared, and saved, and made known, when there was no strange god among you. You are my witnesses, says Jehovah, that I am God. Even before the day, I am he, and none can deliver out of my hand. I will work, and who shall turn it back ? Thus says Jehovah your Redeemer, the Holy One of Israel : For your sakes have I sent to Babylon and brought down the princes, all of them, and the Chaldeans, whose cry is in the ships. I am Jehovah, your Holy One, the Creator of Israel, your King.

12 Thus says Jehovah, who makes a way in the sea, and a path in mighty waters ; who brings out chariot and horse, army and mighty man ; they shall lie down together ; they shall not rise ; they are crushed, they are extinguished like flax. Remember not the former things, neither consider things of old. Behold, I do a new thing ; now shall it spring up ; will you not know it ? I will even make a way in the wilderness, and rivers in the desert. The beasts of the field shall honor me, the jackals and the daughters of the ostrich, for I will put waters in the wilderness, [and] rivers in the desert, to give drink to my people, my chosen.

13 This is a people which I formed for myself, that they should declare my praise. But you did not call on me, Jacob, but you were tired of me, Israel ; you brought me not the sheep of your burnt offerings, nor honored me with your sacrifices. I did not cause you to serve with a bread offering, nor weary you with frankincense ; you bought me no sweet cane with your money, neither did you supply me abundantly with the fat of your sacrifices. Indeed, you made me to serve with your sins, and wearied me with your wickedness. I, I am he that blots out your transgressions

9 *

for my sake ; and I will not remember your sins.   Put me in mind ;
let us reason together ; declare [your case], that you may be justified.   Your first father sinned, and your interpreters transgressed
against me.   Therefore I profaned the princes of the sanctuary, and
gave Jacob to the curse, and Israel to reproaches.

PROPHECY XXVI.   [44, 45, 7.

GOD TO BE SERVED; IDOLS TO BE DESPISED.

1 AND now hear, Jacob my servant, and Israel, whom I have
chosen : Thus says Jehovah, that made you, and formed you from
birth, and helped you : Fear not, my servant Jacob, and Jeshurun
[little saint], for I will pour out water on the thirsty, and streams on
the dry land.   I will pour out my Spirit on your children, and my
blessing on your offspring ; and they shall grow up as willows by
streams of water.   One shall say, I am Jehovah's, and another shall
call himself by the name of Jacob, and another shall subscribe with
his hand to Jehovah, and speak kindly the name of Israel.

2 Thus says Jehovah the King of Israel, and his Redeemer Jehovah of hosts : I am the first, and I the last, and besides me
there is no God.   And who like me can call, and declare, and set
it in order for me, since I made the people of the world ? and let
them declare to [men] things to come which shall also come to pass.
Fear not, neither be afraid ; have I not published and declared from
of old ? Indeed I declared, and you are my witnesses.   There is no
God besides me, nor any rock ; I know not any.

3 The makers of carved images are all of them emptiness, and
their desirable works can not profit ; and they are their witnesses ;
they see not, neither know, that they may be ashamed.   Who
forms a god and casts an image that can not profit ?   Behold, all
his companions are ashamed ; the mechanics themselves are of men ;
they all of them gather themselves together, they stand still, they
are afraid, they are ashamed together.   One makes an axe of iron,
and works on the coals, and forms it with hammers ; he makes it
with his strong arm.   He is also hungry, and has no strength; he
drinks no water, and is thirsty.

4 A carpenter stretches out the line [to make an image] ; he
marks its form with an awl, he forms it with chisels, and marks it
with a compass, and makes it according to the likeness of a man,

according to the beauty of a man, to stand at home. He cuts down cedars for himself, then he takes a maple and an oak and strengthens it with the trees of the forest. He plants a pine, and the rain makes it grow, and it is for a man to burn; and he takes some of it and warms himself, and he sets it on fire, and bakes bread; he also makes a god, and worships it, a carved image, and falls down to it. Half of it he burns with fire; with half of it he eats meat; he roasts roasted meat, and is satisfied; he also warms himself, then he says, Aha, I am warm; I have seen the fire. Then with the rest he makes a god, his carved image; he bows down to it, and worships it, and prays to it, and says, Deliver me, for thou art my god.

5 They know not now nor understand, for he has covered their eyes, that they can not see, nor understand with their mind; neither will one apply his mind, nor has he any knowledge or understanding to say, Half of it I burned with the fire, and I also baked bread on its coals; I roasted meat and eat; and shall I make the rest of it an abomination? Shall I bow down to the trunk of a tree? He feeds on ashes; a perverted heart has caused him to err, and he can not deliver his soul, nor say, Is there not a lie in my right hand?

6 Remember these things, Jacob and Israel, for you are my servant; I formed you, you are my servant. Israel, you shall not be forgotten by me; I have blotted out as a cloud your transgressions, and as a thick cloud your sins; return to me, for I have redeemed you.

7 Sing, heavens, for Jehovah has done it; shout, lower parts of the earth; mountains, break forth into singing, the forest, and all the trees in it, for Jehovah has redeemed Jacob, and will glorify himself in Israel. Thus says Jehovah your Redeemer, and your Creator from birth: I am Jehovah, that made all things; I stretch out the heavens by myself; I spread out the earth like water under me. He frustrates the tokens of liars [conjurers], and makes diviners mad; he turns the wise back, and their knowledge becomes a burden; he establishes the word of his servant, and performs the counsel of his messengers; he says to Jerusalem, You shall be inhabited, and to the cities of Judah, You shall be built; and I will set up her wastes. He says to the deep, Be dry, and I will dry up your rivers; he says of Cyrus, He is my shepherd, and shall do all my pleasure and say to Jerusalem, You shall be built, and the walls shall be founded.

8 Thus says Jehovah concerning his anointed, concerning Cyrus, whom I have taken by the right hand to subdue nations before him ; and I will loosen the loins of kings to open before him the folding doors, and the gates shall not be shut.   I will go before you, and the raised places will I make plain, the gates of brass will I break, and the bars of iron will I cut in two ; and I will give you the treasures of darkness, and the concealed treasures of secret places, that you may know that I Jehovah call you by name, the God of Israel.   For the sake of Jacob my servant, and of Israel my chosen, I will both call you by name and address you kindly, though you have not known me.   I am Jehovah, and there is none besides me, no God.   I will gird you, though you have not known me, that they may know, from the rising of the sun and from the west, that there is none besides me.   I am Jehovah, and there is none else. I form light and create darkness ; I make peace and create evil.   I Jehovah do all these things.

PROPHECY XXVII.   [45, 8, 46.

THE FOLLY OF CONTENDING WITH GOD ; HIS DIRECTION OF CYRUS.

1 DROP down, heavens, from above, and let the skies pour down righteousness ; let the earth open, and let [the fields] bear salvation, and let righteousness spring up together.   I Jehovah have created it.   Woe to him that contends with his Maker.   Let fragments of earthen ware contend with fragments of the earth.   Shall the clay say to him that forms it, What do you make? or your work, He has no hands ?   Woe to him that says to a father, What do you beget ? or to the woman, What do you bear ?   Thus says Jehovah, the Holy One of Israel, his Creator : Do you ask me of things to come ? and concerning my sons and the work of my hands do you command me ?   I made the earth, and created man on it ; I created, [and] my hand stretched out the heavens, and I commanded all their host.   I have raised him up [Cyrus] in righteousness, and all his ways will I direct ; he shall build my city, he shall send back my captives, not for price nor reward, says Jehovah of hosts.

2 Thus says Jehovah : The labor of Egypt, and the merchandise of Ethiopia, and of the Sabeans, men of stature, shall come to you, and they shall be yours.   They shall pass along in chains, they

shall fall down to you, they shall even supplicate you. Indeed
[shall they say] God is among you, and there is no God [besides].
Truly thou art a God that hidest thyself, God of Israel, the Saviour.
They shall be ashamed and confounded, all of them ; they shall go
to confusion together that are the makers of idols. Israel is saved
by Jehovah with eternal salvations ; you shall not be ashamed nor
confounded forever. For thus says Jehovah, who created the
heavens : God, who formed the earth and made it, he made it firm,
he created it not in vain, he formed it to dwell in ; I am Jehovah,
and there is none else. I have not spoken in secret, in a dark place
of the earth ; I said not to the children of Jacob, Seek me in vain.
I am Jehovah, who speaks righteousness, who declares things that
are right.

3 Gather yourselves together and come ; draw near, escaped of
the nations. They know not who lift up [their voice] to the wood
of their carved image, and pray to a god that can not save. Declare, and let them come near ; yes, let them take counsel together.
Who has declared this from of old, to tell it from an ancient time ?
Have not I Jehovah ? and there is no God besides me ; a righteous
God and a Saviour, and there is none besides me. I have sworn
by myself ; the word has gone out of my mouth in righteousness ;
it shall not return : That to me every knee shall bow, and every
tongue swear. Only by Jehovah shall [men] say, have I righteousness and strength ; to him shall they come, and all who are displeased with him shall be ashamed, all the children of Israel be
justified, and glory in Jehovah.

4 Bel bows down, Nebo falls ; their images are on the beasts
and on the cattle ; your loads were bound, a burden to the weary
[beast]. They bent, they bowed down together ; they were not able
to deliver the burden, and went into captivity themselves. Hear
me, house of Jacob, and all the remnant of the house of Israel carried
by me from infancy, and borne from birth ; even to old age I am
he, and to gray hairs I will carry you ; I have done it, and I will
bear, and carry, and deliver you.

5 To whom will you liken me, and make me equal, and compare
me that I may be like ? [Men] pour gold out of a bag, and weigh
silver in a balance ; they hire a goldsmith, and he makes a god ;
they fall down also and worship it ; they bear it on the shoulder ;
they carry it and put it in its place, and it stands in its place, and
is not moved. Yes, one cries to it, and it can not answer, it can
not save him from his distress.

6 Remember this, and show yourselves men ; think, transgressors, remember the former things from of old, for I am God, and there is none else ; God, and there is none besides me ; declaring the end from the beginning, and from ancient times things which are not yet done, saying, My counsel shall stand, and I will do all my pleasure ; calling the bird of prey [Cyrus] from the east, from a distant land the man of my counsel ; indeed, I have said it, I will also bring it to pass ; I have purposed it, I will also do it. Hear me, stout hearted, who are far from righteousness. I have brought my righteousness near ; it shall not be far off ; and my salvation shall not be deferred, for I have put salvation in Zion for Israel my glory.

PROPHECY XXVIII   [47, 48.

BABYLON TO BE DESTROYED BY CYRUS ; THE PEOPLE OF GOD CALLED TO FLEE FROM IT.

1 COME down, sit in the dust, virgin daughter of Babylon ; sit on the ground ; there is no throne, daughter of the Chaldeans, for you shall no more be called tender and delicate. Take millstones and grind meal, remove your vail, take off your skirt, uncover your leg, pass through the rivers. Your nakedness shall be uncovered, and your shame also be seen ; I will take vengeance, I will not strike [as] a man.

2 As for our Redeemer, Jehovah of hosts is his name, the Holy One of Israel. Sit in silence, and go into darkness, daughter of the Chaldeans, for you shall no more be called mistress of kingdoms. I was angry with my people, I profaned my inheritance, and gave them into your hand ; you showed them no mercy, you made your yoke exceedingly heavy on the elder ; for you said, I shall be a lady forever ; so that you did not apply your mind to these things, nor remember your latter end.

3 And now hear this, delicate one, living in security, saying in her heart, I am, and there is none besides me ; I shall not sit a widow, nor know the loss of children : these two things shall come on you suddenly in one day, loss of children and widowhood ; they shall come on you in their perfection, notwithstanding the multitude of your magic arts, and the great abundance of your enchantments. For you have trusted in your wickedness ; you said, None sees me ; your wisdom and knowledge have perverted you. You said in your

heart, I am, and there is none else ; therefore evil has come on you, and you shall not know its morning ; destruction has fallen on you, and you shall not be able to avert it ; and desolation shall come on you suddenly, you shall not know it.

4 Stand now with your enchantments, and with the multitude of your magic arts, on which you have labored from your youth ; perhaps you will be able to profit, perhaps you may inspire terror ; you are wearied with the multitude of your counsels. Let those in league with the heavens, the observers of the stars, those who discern times, stand up now and save you from the things which shall come on you. Behold, they are like stubble ; a fire shall consume them ; they can not deliver themselves from the power of the flame ; there is not a coal to warm them, [nor] a spark, that they may sit before it. Thus shall these things be to you, for which you have labored, your riches from your youth ; they shall wander off, every man his own way ; none shall save you.

5 Hear this, house of Jacob, called by the name of Israel ; and they proceed from the waters of Judah, swearing by the name of Jehovah, and mentioning the God of Israel, but not in truth nor in righteousness ; but they call themselves from the holy city, and lean on the God of Israel ; Jehovah of hosts is his name.

6 I declared the former things from of old, before they came to pass ; I made them known, I performed them suddenly, and they came to pass. Because I knew that you were stubborn ; your neck is an iron sinew, and your forehead brass ; therefore I told you from of old, before it came to pass I informed you, lest you should say, My image did them, and my carved image and my cast image commanded them. You have heard, you have seen it all, and will you not declare it ? From this time I will inform you of new things, and things concealed, and which you have not known. They are created now, and not from of old ; and at the present time, and you have not heard of them ; lest you should say, Behold, I knew them.

7 Indeed, you have not heard ; indeed, you have not known ; indeed, from of old your ear was not opened, for I knew that you were most false, and that you were called a transgressor from birth. For my name's sake I will defer my anger, and for my praise I will restrain myself [from] you, that I may not cut you off. Behold, I have tried you, but not with silver ; I have chosen you in the furnace of affliction. For my sake entirely will I do it ; for how

should [my name] be profaned? and I will not give my glory to
another.

8 Hear me, Jacob, and Israel, my called: I am he, I am the first,
I also am the last; my hand also founded the earth, and my right
hand spanned the heavens; I called them, and they stood together.
Gather yourselves together, all of you, and hear; who of them has
declared these things? He whom Jehovah loves will do his pleasure on Babylon, and his arm shall be on the Chaldeans. I, I have
spoken; I also called and brought him [Cyrus], and made his way
to prosper.

9 Draw near to me, hear this: I spoke not in secret; from the
time when it occurred I was there; and now the Lord Jehovah and
his Spirit have sent me. Thus says Jehovah your Redeemer, the
Holy One of Israel: I am Jehovah your God, that teach you to
profit, that lead you in the way in which you should go. O that
you would attend to my commandments; then should your peace be
as a river, and your righteousness like the waves of the sea; and
your children should be like the sand, and the offspring of your
bowels like the offspring of the sea, which shall not be cut off, nor
their name destroyed from before me.

10 Go out from Babylon, flee from the Chaldeans with the voice
of singing, declare, publish this; carry it to the ends of the earth;
say, Jehovah has redeemed his servant Jacob, and they thirsted not
in the desert through which he led them; he caused water to flow
from the rock for them; he cleft the rock, and the waters flowed.
There is no peace, says Jehovah, to the wicked.

PROPHECY XXIX.   [49, 50.

GOD CALLS AND ENDOWS HIS SERVANT TO SAVE BOTH JEWS
AND GENTILES; HIS SALVATION.

1 HEAR me, islands, and attend, peoples from afar; Jehovah
called me from birth, from the bowels of my mother he mentioned
my name; he made my mouth like a sharp sword; in the shadow
of his hand he hid me, and he made me a polished shaft; in his
quiver he concealed me; and he said to me, You are my servant
Israel; I will be glorified in you. Then I said, I have labored in
vain, I have spent my strength for emptiness and vanity; but my
judgment is with Jehovah, and my work with my God.

2 And now, says Jehovah, that formed me from birth to be his servant, to restore Jacob to him, Though Israel be not gathered, yet I shall be glorious in the sight of Jehovah, and my God shall be my strength. But he said, It is too little that you should be my servant to set up the tribes of Jacob, and to restore the preserved of Israel ; but I will make you a light of the nations, to be my salvation to the ends of the earth.

3 Thus says Jehovah, the Redeemer of Israel, and his Holy One, to the despised of men, and the abhorred of the nation, to the servant of rulers : Kings shall see and rise up, princes also shall bow down, because of Jehovah, who is faithful, the Holy One of Israel, for he shall choose you. Thus says Jehovah : In an acceptable time have I answered you, and in a time of salvation have I helped you ; and I will keep you, and give you for a covenant of the people, to raise up the earth, and to cause the desolate inheritances to be inherited ; to say to the prisoners, Go forth ; and to those in darkness, Come to the light ; that they may feed in the highways, and their pastures be on all high places.

4 They shall not hunger nor thirst, and the mirage shall not smite them, nor the sun ; for he that has mercy on them shall lead them, and conduct them to fountains of water. And I will make all my mountains a way, and my highways shall be exalted. Behold, these shall come from afar, and behold, those from the north and from the sea, and those from the land of Sinim. Sing, heavens, and rejoice, earth, and break forth, mountains, into singing, for Jehovah has comforted his people, and will have mercy on his poor.

5 But Zion said, Jehovah has forsaken me, and my Lord has forgotten me. Can a woman forget her sucking child, not to pity the son of her womb ? Even these may forget, but I will not forget you. Behold, I have inscribed you on the palms of my hands, your walls are continually before me ; your sons shall hasten [to you], and those that destroyed and wasted you shall go away from you. Lift up your eyes round about, and see ; all of them are gathered together ; they come to you. As I live, says Jehovah, surely you shall clothe yourself with all of them, and bind them on as a bride does. For your waste and desolate places, and the land of your destruction, shall now be too confined for the inhabitants, and your destroyers shall be far away. The sons of your bereavement shall yet say in your ears, The place is too confined ; give me room, that I may dwell. Then you shall say in your heart, Who bore me

these? for I was bereaved and barren, a captive and an exile; but these, — who brought them up? I was left alone; as for these, whence are they?

6 Thus says the Lord Jehovah: Behold, I will lift up my hand to the nations, and raise my standard to the peoples, and they shall bring your sons in their bosom, and your daughters shall be borne on their shoulders; and kings shall be your nursing fathers, and their princesses your nursing mothers. They shall worship you with their faces to the earth, and lick the dust of your feet; and you shall know that I am Jehovah, and that those who trust in me shall not be ashamed.

7 Shall the prey be taken from the mighty, and the lawful captive delivered? For thus says Jehovah: Even the captive shall be taken from the mighty, and the prey of the terrible be delivered; for I will contend with those that contend with you, and will save your sons. And I will cause your oppressors to eat their flesh; and they shall drink their blood as sweet wine; and all flesh shall know that I am Jehovah your Saviour and your Redeemer, the mighty one of Jacob.

8 Thus says Jehovah: Where is the bill of your mother's divorcement, whom I put away? or which of my creditors is it to whom I sold you? Behold, you have been sold for your wickedness; and for your transgressions was your mother put away. Why did I come, and there was no man? and I call, and none answers? Is my hand cut entirely off that it can not redeem? And have I no strength to deliver? Behold, with my rebuke I dry up the sea, and make the rivers a desert. Their fish become putrid without water, and die with thirst. I clothe the heavens with blackness, and put on sackcloth for their covering.

9 The Lord Jehovah gave me the tongue of the learned, that I might know how to help the weary with a word. He wakes me every morning; he wakes my ear to hear like the taught. The Lord Jehovah opened my ear, and I was not rebellious; I turned not away; my back I gave to the smiters, and my cheeks to them that plucked [the beard]; I hid not my face from shame and spitting.

10 But the Lord Jehovah will help me; therefore I shall not be confounded; therefore I have set my face like a flint, and I know that I shall not be ashamed. He that justifies me is near; who is he that will contend with me? Let us stand up together: who is lord of my judgment? let him come near to me. Behold, the Lord

Jehovah will help me ; who is he that will condemn me ? Behold, all of them shall become old like a garment, a moth shall eat them.

11 Who is there among you that fears Jehovah, [and] obeys the voice of his servant, that walks in darkness, and has no light ? let him trust in the name of Jehovah, and lean on his God. Behold, all of you who kindle a fire, who compass yourselves with sparks, walk in the light of your fire, and in the sparks which you have kindled ; from my hand you shall have this, that you shall lie down in sorrow.

PROPHECY XXX. [51, 52, 12.

GOD COMFORTS HIS PEOPLE, AND ENCOURAGES THEM TO RETURN FROM THE BABYLONIAN EXILE.

1 HEAR me, you that follow after righteousness, that seek Jehovah : look at the rock from which you were cut, and at the hole of the pit from which you were dug. Look at Abraham, and at Sarah who bore you ; for I called him alone, and I blessed and multiplied him. For Jehovah will comfort Zion ; he will comfort all her waste places, and will make her wilderness like Eden, and her desert like the garden of Jehovah ; joy and gladness shall be found in it, thanksgiving and the voice of song.

2 Attend to me, peoples, and, nations, listen to me ; for a law shall proceed from me, and I will set my justice for a light of the peoples. My righteousness is near, my salvation has gone forth, and my arms shall judge the peoples. The islands shall wait for me, and in my arm shall they hope. Lift up your eyes to the heavens, and look at the earth below, for the heavens shall vanish away like smoke, and the earth become worn out like a garment ; and its inhabitants in like manner shall die ; but my salvation shall be forever, and my justice shall not be destroyed.

3 Hear me, you that know righteousness ; people in whose heart is my law, fear not the reproach of man, nor be dismayed by their revilings ; for a moth shall eat them like a garment, and an insect shall consume them like wool ; but my justice shall be forever, and my salvation to all generations.

4 Awake, awake, put on strength, arm of Jehovah ; awake as in days of old, the ancient generations. Art thou not he that cut down the sea monster, and wounded the crocodile ? Art thou not he that dried up the sea, the waters of the great deep ? that made

the depths of the sea a way for the redeemed to pass over? But the redeemed of Jehovah shall return and come to Zion, with singing and joy eternal on their heads. They shall obtain joy and gladness, [and] sorrow and sighing shall flee away.

5 I, I am he that comforts you; who are you, that you are afraid of a mortal that shall die, and of a son of man that shall be made as grass, and forget Jehovah your Maker, who stretched out the heavens, and founded the earth? and you tremble continually all the day before the wrath of the oppressor, as one aiming to destroy; but where is the wrath of the oppressor? The bent captive hastens to be released, that he may not die in the pit, nor his bread fail. For I am Jehovah your God, who make the sea afraid, and its waves roar; Jehovah of hosts is his name; and I will put my words in your mouth, and with the shade of my hand will I cover you to plant the heavens, and found the earth, and say to Zion, You are my people.

6 Awake, awake, arise, Jerusalem, who have drunk from the hand of Jehovah the cup of his indignation. You have drunk the goblet-cup of intoxication, and sucked it out. There was none to comfort her of all the sons she bore, and none to take her by the hand of all the sons she brought up. Behold, I have brought these two things on you; who shall comfort you? Destruction and ruin, and famine and sword, how can I comfort you? Your sons have fainted; they lie at the head of all the streets, like an antelope in a net; they are full of the wrath of Jehovah, the rebuke of your God. Therefore hear now this, afflicted one, and drunken, but not with wine; thus says your Lord Jehovah, and your God that defends his people: Behold, I will take from your hand the cup of intoxication and the goblet-cup of my wrath, and you shall not drink it any more. And I will put it into the hand of those that troubled you; who said to you, Lie down, that we may pass over; and you made your back like the earth, and like the street, for them that passed over.

7 Awake, awake, put on your strength, put on your beautiful garments, Jerusalem, holy city; for there shall no more come to you the uncircumcised or the impure. Shake yourself from the dust; arise, sit up, Jerusalem; loose the bands of your neck, captive daughter of Zion. For thus says Jehovah: You have been sold for nothing, and you shall be redeemed without money. For thus says the Lord Jehovah: Formerly my people went down to Egypt to live there, and latterly Assyria oppressed them. And now what have I

here? says Jehovah. For my people are taken for nothing, their rulers lament, says Jehovah, and my name is continually every day despised. Therefore my people shall know my name indeed in that day, for I am he that speaks; behold, it is I.

8 How beautiful on the mountains are the feet of him that brings good news, that publishes peace, that brings good news of good, that publishes salvation, that says to Zion, Your God reigns! Your watchmen shall lift up the voice; they shall sing together, for they shall see eye to eye when Jehovah brings again Zion. Break forth, sing together, wastes of Jerusalem, for Jehovah has comforted his people, he has redeemed Jerusalem. Jehovah has made bare his holy arm in the sight of all nations, and all the ends of the earth have seen the salvation of our God.

9 Depart, depart, go out from thence; touch not the impure; go out from the midst of her; be pure, you that bear the vessels of Jehovah. For you shall not go out with haste, neither shall you go out by flight, for Jehovah shall go before you, and the God of Israel shall bring up your rear.

PROPHECY XXXI. [52, 13, 53.

GOD'S SERVANT; HIS HUMILIATION, SUFFERINGS, ACHIEVEMENTS, AND REWARDS.

1 BEHOLD, my servant shall conduct himself wisely; he shall be raised up and set on high, and shall be highly exalted. As many nations were astonished at you, so of the destroyed one; his appearance was more than man, and his form than the sons of man. Thus shall he sprinkle many nations, [and] kings shall shut their mouths before him; for what was not told them they shall see, and what they had not heard they shall consider.

2 Who has believed our report? and to whom is the arm of Jehovah revealed? For he shall grow up like a sprout before him, and like a sprout from a dry ground; he has no form, that we should look on him, nor [pleasant] appearance, that we should desire him. And he is despised and forsaken by men; a man of sorrows, and acquainted with grief; and we hid, as it were, our faces from him; he was despised, and we esteemed him not. And he bore our sicknesses, and carried our sorrows; but we esteemed him struck by [divine judgment], smitten by God, and afflicted [on his own account].

10 *

3 But he was wounded for our transgressions, he was bruised for our sins ; the chastisement of our peace was on him, that by his stripes we may be healed. All of us, like sheep, went astray ; we turned each one to his own way ; and Jehovah laid on him the wickedness of us all. He was oppressed and afflicted, but he opened not his mouth. He was brought for slaughter, and as a ewe before her shearers is dumb, so he opened not his mouth. He was taken from prison and from justice, and who can think of his generation [the men that killed him] ? for he was cut off from the land of the living, for the transgression of my people was he smitten.

4 And he made his grave with the wicked, and was with the rich in his death, although he did no violence, and there was no deceit in his mouth ; but Jehovah was pleased to crush him with grief. When thou shalt make his soul a sacrifice, he shall see [his] children, he shall prolong [his] days, and the pleasure of Jehovah shall prosper in his hand. He shall see of the labor of his soul, he shall be satisfied with his knowledge ; my righteous servant shall justify many, and bear their wickedness. Therefore will I assign him a portion with the great, and he shall divide the spoil of the mighty ; instead of which he poured out his soul to death, and was numbered with transgressors, and bore the sin of many, and interceded for transgressors.

PROPHECY XXXII.　　　[54.

GOD ENCOURAGES HIS PEOPLE WITH THE PROMISE OF A GLORIOUS FUTURE.

1 SING, barren one, that did not bear ; break forth into singing and shout, you that were not sick, for the sons of the desolate are more than those of the woman with a husband, says Jehovah. Enlarge the place of your tent, and let them extend the curtains of your habitation ; hold not back, lengthen your cords, and strengthen your pins, for you shall break forth on the right hand and on the left, and your children shall inherit the nations, and cause the destroyed cities to be inhabited.

2 Fear not, for you shall not be ashamed ; and be not confounded, for you shall not be put to shame ; for you shall forget the shame of your youth, and the reproach of your widowhood you shall remember no more. For your Maker is your husband ; Jehovah of hosts is his name ; and your Redeemer, the Holy One of Israel, shall

be called the God of all the earth. For Jehovah called you like a woman forsaken, and grieved in spirit, and a youthful wife, but you were rejected, says your God. For a small moment I forsook you, but with great mercies will I gather you ; in an outpouring of anger I hid my face from you for a moment ; with eternal kindness will I have mercy on you, says your Redeemer, Jehovah. For this shall be to me like the waters of Noah, of which I swore that the waters of Noah should no more overflow the earth ; so have I sworn that I will not be angry with you, nor rebuke you. For the mountains shall depart, and the hills be removed, but my kindness shall not depart from you, nor the covenant of my peace be shaken, says Jehovah, that has mercy on you.

3 Afflicted, tempest-beaten, [and] not comforted, behold, I will lay your stones with eyepaint [cement of the most brilliant kind], and your foundations with sapphires ; and I will make your battlements rubies, and your gates sparkling gems, and all your bounds precious stones. And all your sons shall be taught by Jehovah, and great shall be the peace of your sons. You shall be established with righteousness, you shall be far from oppression, for you shall not fear ; and from war, for it shall not come nigh you. If any shall gather themselves together, it shall not be from me, [and] those that gather themselves together against you shall fall.

4 Behold, I create the smith that blows the fire of coals, and brings forth the instrument for his work ; and I create the destroyer to destroy. No weapon formed against you shall prosper, and every tongue which shall rise up against you in judgment, you shall condemn. This is the inheritance of the servants of Jehovah, and their righteousness [happiness] from me, says Jehovah.

PROPHECY XXXIII. [55.

GOD CALLS JEWS AND GENTILES TO HIS SERVICE, AND TO THE ATTAINMENT OF ITS BLESSINGS.

1 Ho, every one that thirsts, come to the waters ; and he that has no money, come, buy and eat ; and come, buy wine and milk without money and without price. Why do you spend your money for that which is not bread ? and your labor for that which satisfies not? Hear diligently to me, and eat that which is good, and let your soul delight itself with fatness. Incline your ear and come to

me ; hear, and your soul shall live ; and I will make with you an eternal covenant, the sure kindness of David. Behold, I have appointed him [David] a witness to the peoples, a ruler and a commander to the peoples. Behold, you shall call a nation which you know not ; and nations which knew not you shall run to you, on account of Jehovah your God, and of the Holy One of Israel ; for he has glorified you.

2 Seek Jehovah while he may be found ; call on him while he is near ; let the wicked man forsake his way, and the evil man his thoughts ; and let him turn to Jehovah, and he will have mercy on him ; and to our God, for he will abundantly pardon. For your thoughts are not my thoughts, neither are your ways my ways, says Jehovah ; for as high as the heavens are above the earth, so much are my ways higher than your ways, and my thoughts than your thoughts. For as the rain comes down, and the snow from heaven, and returns not thither, but waters the earth, and causes it to bear and to send forth shoots, that it may give seed to the sower, and bread for food, so shall my word be, that goes forth out of my mouth ; it shall not return to me empty, but it shall accomplish that which I please, and shall prosper in that for which I send it. For you shall go forth with joy, and be led with peace ; the mountains and hills shall break out before you into singing, and all the trees of the field shall clap [their] hands. Instead of the thorn bush shall come up the cypress ; and it shall be to Jehovah for a name, for an eternal sign, that shall not be cut off.

3 Thus says Jehovah : Keep justice, and do righteousness, for my salvation is near to come, and my righteousness to be revealed. Blessed is the man that does this ; and the son of man that holds it fast, keeping the Sabbath from profaning it, and keeping his hand from doing any evil. And let not the son of the stranger that cleaves to Jehovah say, Jehovah has separated me entirely from his people ; nor let the eunuch say, I am a dry tree ; for thus says Jehovah to the eunuchs, Who keep my Sabbaths, and choose that in which I delight, and adhere to my covenant, I will surely give them, in my house and within my walls, a place and name better than sons and daughters ; I will give them an eternal name, which shall not be cut off.

4 And as for the sons of the stranger, who adhere to Jehovah, to minister to him, and love the name of Jehovah, to be to him for servants, every one that keeps the Sabbath from profaning it, and

those who adhere strongly to my covenant, them will I bring to my
holy mountain, and make them glad in my house of prayer ; their
burnt offerings and their sacrifices shall be acceptable on my altar ;
for my house shall be called a house of prayer for all peoples.
[Thus] says the Lord Jehovah, who gathers together the outcasts
of Israel : I will yet gather [the nations] to him for his gathered ones.

PROPHECY XXXIV.   [56, 9, 57.

GOD REPROVES THE WICKEDNESS OF THE JEWS, THREATENS THEM
WITH A GREAT DESTRUCTION, BUT BLESSES THE HUMBLE.

1 COME to eat, all beasts of the field, all beasts of the forest ;
his watchmen are all of them blind, they know nothing ; they are
all of them dumb dogs, they can not bark ; dreaming, lying down,
loving to slumber ; and they are greedy dogs, they can not be
satisfied ; and the shepherds can not understand ; they have all
turned to their own way, every man to his gain from his quarter.
Come [they say], let us take wine, let us drink to excess of strong
drink, for to-morrow shall be as this day, [and] the abundance is
very great.

2 The righteous man perishes, and none lays it to heart ; and
men of kindness are taken away, none considering that the righteous is taken from evil. He enters into peace ; they rest on their
beds [in death] each one that walks uprightly. But now come hither,
sons of the enchantress, children of the adulterer and the harlot.
Whom do you mock ? against whom do you enlarge the mouth and
run out the tongue ? Are you not children of transgression, a
lying race ? inflamed with gods under every green tree, slaughtering
children in the valleys, under the clefts of the rocks ? With the
smooth [stones] of the brook is your portion ; they, they are your
lot. To them also you pour out a libation, you offer up a bread
offering. Shall I have compassion on these ?

3 On the high and lofty mountain you have set your bed ; there
also you have gone up to sacrifice a sacrifice. And behind the door
and the door-post you set your memorial ; for you have departed from me, and gone up and enlarged your bed, and made
an agreement with them, and loved their bed wherever you saw it.
You have gone to the king with oil, and multiplied your perfumes,
and sent your messengers to distant parts, and abased yourself to

Hades. You were wearied by the length of your way, [but] you said not, There is no hope; you found the life of your hand, therefore you were not discouraged. About whom are you anxious and afraid, that you lie to me, and remember me not, nor think [of me]? Have I not been silent from of old, and you fear me not? I will declare your righteousness and your works, and they shall not profit you. When you cry, let your throngs [of idols] deliver you; but the wind shall carry them all away, a breath shall take them off; but he that trusts in me shall inherit the land, shall possess my holy mountain.

4 Then he said, Cast up, cast up; prepare the way, take up the stumbling blocks out of the way of my people. For thus says the high and lofty One who inhabits eternity, and whose name is Holy: I inhabit the high and holy [world], and him that is of a contrite and humble spirit, to revive the spirit of the humble, and to revive the heart of the contrite. For I will not contend forever, nor will I forever be angry; for spirits would fail before me, and the souls which I have made. I was angry at his unjust gain, and covered [my face and] smote him; and I will be angry when he goes on perversely in the way of his heart; but I have seen his ways, and will heal him, and lead him, and impart consolations to him and his mourners. I create [make] the fruit of the lips; peace to the far off and to the near, says Jehovah; and I will heal him. But the wicked are like a troubled sea when it can not rest, and its waters cast up mire and dirt. There is no peace, says my God, to the wicked.

PROPHECY XXXV.   [58.

GOD DENOUNCES FASTING WITHOUT HOLINESS, AND REQUIRES BENEFICENCE AND THE OBSERVANCE OF THE SABBATH.

1 CRY aloud, spare not; lift up your voice like a trumpet; tell my people their transgressions, and the house of Jacob their sins. Yet they seek me daily, and delight to know my ways, as a nation which did righteousness, and forsook not the law of its God. They ask of me righteous judgments; they delight in drawing nigh to God. Why do we fast [say they], and thou seest not? We afflict our souls, and thou dost not notice it. Behold, in the day of your fast you find pleasure, and exact all your labors; behold, you fast for strife and contention, and you smite with a wicked fist; you

shall not fast as you do this day, to cause your voice to be heard on high. Is this the fast which I have chosen? a day for a man to afflict his soul? Is [this] to bow down his head like a bulrush, and to spread sackcloth and ashes under him? Will you call this a fast? a day pleasing to Jehovah?

2 Is not this the fast which I choose, to loose the tightly-drawn cords of wickedness, to shake off the bands of the yoke, to send the oppressed away freed, and to break every yoke? Is it not to break your bread to the hungry, and to bring home the wandering poor; when you see the naked, to clothe him; and to hide not yourself from your own flesh [relations]? Then shall your light break forth like the morning, and your healing spring up speedily, and your righteousness go before you, and the glory of Jehovah bring up your rear. Then shall you call, and Jehovah will answer; you shall cry, and he shall say, Behold, I am here, if you put away from the midst of you the yoke, the putting forth of the finger, and speaking vanity.

3 If you give your soul to the hungry, and satisfy the afflicted soul, then shall your light arise in darkness, and your thick darkness be as noon. And Jehovah shall lead you continually, and satisfy your soul in drouth, and make strong your bones; and you shall be like a well-watered garden, and like a spring whose waters fail not. And your children shall build the old wastes, and you shall set up the foundations of many generations; and men shall call you, The repairer of breaches, The restorer of paths to inhabit. If you turn away your foot from the Sabbath, from doing your pleasure on my holy day, and call the Sabbath a delight, the holy [day] of Jehovah, honorable, and honor it, not pursuing your ways, nor finding your pleasure, but speaking the word; then shall you have delight in Jehovah, and I will cause you to ride on the high places of the earth; and I will cause you to enjoy the inheritance of Jacob, your father; for the mouth of Jehovah has said it.

PROPHECY XXXVI.

GOD'S BENEFITS DEFERRED ON ACCOUNT OF MEN'S WICKEDNESS; HE WILL CERTAINLY SAVE HIS PEOPLE.

1 BEHOLD, Jehovah's hand is not cut off, that he can not save; neither is his ear heavy, that he can not hear; but your wickedness has separated between you and your God, and your sins have hid his face from you, that he does not hear. For your hands are defiled with blood, and your fingers with wickedness; your lips have spoken lies, and your tongues muttered perverseness. None calls for righteousness, nor does any judge with truth; they trust in emptiness, and speak lies; they conceive [with] anguish, and bring forth vanity; they break [for use] a viper's eggs, and weave spider's webs. He that eats of their eggs dies, and the crushed [egg] breaks out a viper. Their webs shall not become a garment, neither shall they cover themselves with their works. Their works are works of vanity, and deeds of violence are in their hands; their feet run to evil, and make haste to shed the blood of the innocent. Their thoughts are vain thoughts; violence and destruction are in their ways. The way of peace have they not known; there is no justice in their steps; they have made crooked paths for themselves; none that walks in them shall know peace.

2 Therefore justice is far from us, and righteousness overtakes us not; we wait for light, and behold darkness; for brightness, and walk in thick darkness. We grope like the blind along the wall; we grope like those who have no eyes; we stumble at noon as in the evening; we are anointed like the dead. We all of us groan like bears; we mourn sadly like doves; we wait for justice, and there is none; for deliverance, and it is far from us. For our transgressions are multiplied before thee, and our sins answer against us; for our transgressions are with us, and we know our wickedness; transgressing and lying against Jehovah, and turning back from our God; speaking oppression and revolt; conceiving and uttering from the heart words of falsehood. And justice is turned back, and righteousness stands afar off; for truth has fallen in the streets, and equity is not able to enter. And truth is eradicated, and he that departs from evil makes himself a prey.

3 Then Jehovah saw, and it was evil in his sight, that there was no justice. And he saw that there was no man [to right things], and wondered that there was none to interpose. Then his arm wrought salvation for him, and his righteousness upheld him. He put on righteousness like a cuirass, and a helmet of salvation on his head; and he put on garments of vengeance for clothing, and covered himself with zeal as a cloak. According to their deeds, so will he render wrath to his adversaries, retribution to his enemies; to the islands will render retribution.

4 Then those from the west shall see the name of Jehovah, and those from the rising of the sun his glory; for he shall come like an impetuous river which the breath of Jehovah impels. And a Redeemer shall come to Zion, and to those that turn back transgression in Jacob, says Jehovah. And as for me, this is the covenant which I will make with them, says Jehovah: My Spirit which is on you, and my words which I have put in your mouth, shall not depart from your mouth, nor from the mouth of your children, nor from the mouth of your children's children, from this time henceforth and forever.

PROPHECY XXXVII. [60.

GOD THE LIGHT AND GLORY OF HIS PEOPLE; HE PROMISES THEM GREAT PROSPERITY AND HAPPINESS.

1 ARISE, shine, for your light has come, and the glory of Jehovah has risen on you. For behold, darkness shall cover the earth, and thick darkness the peoples; but Jehovah shall rise on you, and his glory be seen on you; and nations shall come to your light, and kings to the brightness of your rising. Lift up your eyes around and see; all of them are gathered together; they come to you; your sons shall come from afar, and your daughters be carried at [your] side. Then you shall see and rejoice, and your heart swell, for the abundance of the sea shall be turned to you; the riches of the nations shall come to you. A multitude of camels shall cover you, young camels from Midian and Ephah; all of them from Sheba shall come. They shall bring gold and frankincense, and tell the good news of the praises of Jehovah.

2 All the sheep of Kedar shall be gathered to you, the rams of Nebaioth shall minister to you; they shall come up with acceptance on my altar, and I will glorify the house of my glory.

3 Who are these that fly like a cloud, and like doves to their windows? For the islands shall wait for me, and the ships of Tarshish foremost to bring your sons from afar, and their silver and their gold with them, to the name of Jehovah your God, and to the Holy One of Israel, for he has glorified you. The sons of the stranger shall build your walls, and their kings shall serve you; for in my wrath I smote you, but with my favor will I have mercy on you.

4 And your gates shall be open continually, they shall not be shut day nor night, to bring to you the riches of the nations; and their kings shall be led to you. For the nation and kingdom that will not serve you shall perish, and the nations shall be entirely destroyed. The glory of Lebanon shall come to you, the cypress, the holm, and the Sherbin cedar together, to beautify the place of my sanctuary, and I will make the place of my feet glorious.

5 The sons of your oppressors shall come bending to you, and all that despised you shall worship the soles of your feet, and call you the city of Jehovah, the Zion of the Holy One of Israel. Instead of being forsaken and hated, and none passing by, I will make you an eternal excellency, a joy of many generations. And you shall suck the milk of the nations, and suck the breasts of kings; and you shall know that I am Jehovah your Saviour, and your Redeemer, the Mighty One of Jacob. Instead of brass, I will bring gold; and instead of iron, I will bring silver; and instead of trees, brass; and instead of stones, iron; and I will make your government peace, and your rulers righteousness.

6 Violence shall no more be heard in your land, wasting nor destruction in your bounds; you shall call your walls Salvation, and your gates Praise. The sun shall no more be your light by day, nor shall the brightness of the moon shine on you; for Jehovah shall be your eternal light, and your God your glory. Your sun shall no more go down, nor your moon be taken away, for Jehovah shall be your eternal light, and the days of your mourning shall be ended. And all your people shall be righteous; they shall possess the earth forever, a sprout of my planting, a work of my hands, that I may be glorified. A little one shall become a thousand, and a small one a mighty nation. I Jehovah will hasten it in its time.

PROPHECY XXXVIII.

GOD SENDS GOOD NEWS; HE WILL RESTORE AND MULTIPLY HIS
PEOPLE, AND GREATLY EXALT THEM.

1 THE Spirit of the Lord Jehovah is upon me, because Jehovah
has anointed me to tell good news to the oppressed, to bind up the
broken hearted, to proclaim liberty to the captives, and deliverance
to the bound ; to proclaim the year of the grace of Jehovah, and the
day of the vengeance of our God; to comfort all that mourn, to
appoint for mourners in Zion ; to give them beauty for ashes, the oil
of joy for mourning, [and] the garment of praise for a spirit of
heaviness ; and [men] shall call them terebinths of righteousness, a
plantation which Jehovah will glorify.   And they shall build the old
wastes, they shall set up the former desolations, and repair the destroyed cities, the desolations of many generations.   And strangers
shall stand and feed your flocks, and the sons of the stranger shall
be your plowmen and vine-dressers.   But you shall be called priests
of Jehovah, ministers of our God shall you be called ; you shall eat
the riches of the nations, and substitute yourselves in their glory.
Instead of your shame, you shall have a double [reward], and [in-
stead of] reproach, they shall sing in their portion ; therefore in
their land they shall possess double, they shall have eternal rejoicing.
2 For I Jehovah love justice, I hate robbery for burnt offering ;
and I have appointed their work in truth, and will make an eternal
covenant with them.   Their children shall be known among the
nations, and their offspring in the midst of the peoples ; all who see
them shall know them, that they are a race which Jehovah has
blessed.
3 I will greatly rejoice in Jehovah, my soul shalt exult in my
God ; for he has clothed me with garments of salvation, he has
covered me with a robe of righteousness, as a bridegroom decks
himself with a turban, and as a bride adorns herself with her jewels.
For as the earth causes its sprout to grow, and as a garden causes
the seed sown in it to spring up, so will the Lord Jehovah cause
righteousness and praise to spring up before all nations.
4 For Zion's sake I will not rest, for Jerusalem's sake I will not
be still, till her righteousness goes forth like brightness, and her
salvation burns like a lamp.   For the nations shall see your right-

eousness, and all kings your glory; and they shall call you by a new name, which the mouth of Jehovah shall name. For you shall be a crown of glory in the hand of Jehovah, and a royal diadem in the hand of your God. You shall no more be called The Forsaken, nor your land The Desolation, but you shall be called Hepzibah [My delight is in her], and your land Beulah [Bridal Land], for Jehovah will delight in you, and your land shall be married. For as a young man marries a virgin, so shall your sons marry you; and as a bridegroom rejoices over a bride, so shall your God rejoice over you.

5 I have set watchmen on your walls, Jerusalem, who shall never be still day nor night. You that celebrate Jehovah, keep not silence, and give him no rest till he establish, till he make Jerusalem a praise in the earth. Jehovah has sworn by his right hand, and by his strong arm, Surely I will no more give your grain to be food for your enemies, nor shall the sons of the stranger drink your new wine, for which you have labored; but they that gather it shall eat it, and praise Jehovah; and they that collect it shall drink it in my holy courts.

6 Go through, go through the gates, prepare the way of the people, cast up, cast up the highway, take away the stones, raise up a standard for the peoples; behold, Jehovah publishes to the ends of the earth: Say to the daughter of Zion, Behold, your salvation comes; his reward is with him, and his work before him. And they shall call them The holy people, The redeemed of Jehovah, and they shall be called A city sought for, not forsaken.

PROPHECY XXXIX.   [63, 64.

GOD PUNISHES EDOM; A PRAYER IN BEHALF OF THE JEWS IN THE BABYLONIAN EXILE.

1 WHO is this that comes from Edom, in gorgeous robes from Bozrah? this that is glorious in his apparel, moving majestic in the greatness of his strength? I that speak in righteousness, mighty to save. Why is your clothing red, and your garments like one that treads in a wine press? I have trodden the wine press alone; and of the peoples there was none with me; and I will tread them down in my anger, and trample them down in my indignation, and their blood shall sprinkle my clothing, and I will stain all my garments.

For the day of vengeance is in my heart, and the year of my redeemed came. And I looked, and there was no helper; and I was
astonished that none upheld; then my arm saved me, and my indignation upheld me. Then I trod down the peoples in my anger,
and made them drunk in my indignation, and brought down their
blood to the ground.

2 *The kindness of Jehovah.* I will celebrate the praises of Jehovah, according to all the good which Jehovah has done to us,
and his great goodness to the house of Israel, which he has done
to them, according to his mercies and his great kindness. For he
said, Surely they are my people, sons that will not lie; and he became their Saviour. In all their affliction he was not an adversary,
and the angel of his presence saved them. In his love and in his
pity he redeemed them, and bore them, and carried them all the
days of old. But they rebelled, and grieved his Holy Spirit, and
he was turned to be their enemy, [and] he fought against them.
Then he remembered the days of old, Moses and his people. Where
is he that brought them up from the sea, the shepherd of his flock?
Where is he that put his Holy Spirit in him? that led Moses by
the right hand with his glorious arm? that divided the sea before
them, to make for himself an eternal name? that led them through
the deep like a horse in a wilderness, [and] they did not stumble?
The Spirit of Jehovah caused them to rest, like a beast in a valley.
Thus thou leddest thy people to make to thyself a glorious name.

3 Look from heaven and see, from thy holy and glorious habitation. Where is thy zeal, and thy power, the sounding of thy
bowels, and thy compassions for me? Are they restrained? For
thou art our Father, though Abraham knows us not, and Israel
acknowledges us not; thou, Jehovah, art our Father; our Redeemer
from of old is thy name. Why, Jehovah, hast thou caused us to
err from thy ways? Thou hast hardened our heart from thy fear.
Return, for thy servants' sake, the tribes of thy inheritance. For a
little while they possess thy holy people; our adversaries have plundered thy sanctuary. We are [thine] from of old; thou didst not
rule over them; they are not called by thy name.

4 O that thou wouldst rend the heavens and come down, that the
mountains might flow down before thee, as fire kindles the brush-
wood, [as] fire causes water to boil, to make known thy name to
thy adversaries, that the nations may tremble before thee! When
thou didst terrible things which we looked not for, thou camest

11 *

down ; the mountains flowed down at thy presence.   But from of old [men] have not heard nor understood, nor has eye seen, besides thee, what God will do for him that waits for him.   Thou meetest him that rejoices and does righteousness, those who remember thee in thy ways.

5 Behold, thou wast angry, and we have sinned with those of old, and are saved.   But we are all like an impure thing, and all our righteousness is a filthy rag ; and we all of us fade like a leaf, and our wickedness, like the wind, has carried us away.   And none calls on thy name, nor awakes to take hold of thee ; for thou hast hid thy face from us, and caused us to melt away by our wickedness.

6 But now, Jehovah, thou art our Father ; we are the clay, and thou art our potter ; we are all the work of thy hands.   Be not very angry, Jehovah, and remember not our wickedness forever ; behold, look now, all of us are thy people ; our holy cities are a wilderness ; Zion is a wilderness, Jerusalem is a desolation.   Our holy and glorious house, in which our fathers praised thee, is consumed with fire, and all our desirable things are destroyed.   Wilt thou restrain thyself, Jehovah, for these things ?   Wilt thou be silent, and afflict us exceedingly ?

PROPHECY XL.   [65.

GOD'S PATIENCE ; HE PUNISHES THE GUILTY, BUT WILL SAVE A
PIOUS REMNANT ; THE NEW HEAVEN AND EARTH.

1 [ANSWER.] I am sought by those that asked not for me ; I am found by those that sought me not ; I said, Behold me, behold me, to a nation not called by my name ; [but] I have stretched out my hand all the day to a rebellious people, which walks in a way that is not good, after their thoughts ; a people that provoke me to my face continually, sacrificing in gardens, and burning incense on bricks ; sitting in tombs, and lodging in guarded places ; eating swine's flesh, and the broth of abominable things is in their vessels ; that say, Stand by yourself, approach not me, for I am holier than you ; these are a smoke in my nose, a fire burning all the day. Behold, it is written before me, I will not keep silence, but will repay, and repay in your bosom, your wickedness and the wickedness of your fathers together, says Jehovah, because you have burned incense on the mountains, and reproached me on the hills ; therefore I will measure your former works into your bosom.

2 Thus says Jehovah, As when new wine is found in the cluster, and one says, Destroy it not, for a blessing is in it, so will I do for the sake of my servants, that I may not destroy all. And I will bring out of Jacob a descendant, and out of Judah a possessor of my mountain; and my chosen shall possess it, and my servants shall dwell there. And Sharon shall be a pasture for flocks, and the valley of Achor a resting place for cattle, for my people who shall seek me.

3 And now, you that forsake Jehovah and forget my holy mountain, who set a table for Gad and pour out your libation to Meni [objects of idolatrous worship], I will even appoint you for the sword, and all of you shall bow down to the slaughter; because I called, and you did not answer; I commanded, and you did not obey, but did evil in my sight, and chose that in which I delighted not. Therefore thus says the Lord Jehovah : Behold, my servants shall eat, but you shall be hungry; behold, my servants shall drink, but you shall be thirsty; behold, my servants shall rejoice, but you shall be ashamed; behold, my servants shall sing for joy of heart, but you shall cry for distress of heart, and lament for brokenness of spirit; and you shall leave your names for a curse to my chosen, and the Lord Jehovah will kill you, and call his servants by another name. He that blesses himself in the earth shall bless himself in the God of truth; and he that swears in the earth shall swear by the God of truth; because the former troubles shall be forgotten, and because they shall be hid from my eyes.

4 For behold, I create a new heaven and a new earth, and the former shall not be remembered nor come into mind. But rejoice and exult forever in that which I create; for behold, I create Jerusalem a gladness, and my people a joy. And I will exult in Jerusalem, and rejoice in my people; and there shall not be heard in [Jerusalem] any more the voice of weeping, nor the voice of crying; there shall not be from thence any more an infant of days, nor an old man who has not filled his days; for the child shall die 100 years old, and the sinner of 100 years shall be cursed.

5 And they shall build houses and inhabit [them], and plant vineyards and eat their fruit; they shall not build and another inhabit, nor [one] plant and another eat; for the days of my people shall be like the days of a tree, and my chosen shall long enjoy the work of their hands. They shall not labor in vain, nor bring forth for sudden destruction; for they are the children of the blessed of

Jehovah, and their offspring with them. And before they call I will answer, and while they are speaking I will hear. The wolf and lamb shall feed alike, and the lion shall eat straw like the ox, and dust shall be the serpent's food; they shall not hurt nor destroy in all my holy mountain, says Jehovah.

PROPHECY XLI. [66.

GOD'S PEOPLE HIS TEMPLES; HIS COMING TO JUDGE AND PUNISH THE WICKED OF ALL NATIONS, AND TO BLESS THE RIGHTEOUS.

1 THUS says Jehovah: Heaven is my throne, and the earth my footstool; where is the house that you will build me? and where is this place of my rest? For all these things has my hand made, and all these have been, says Jehovah. But to this man will I look, that is poor and of a contrite spirit, and trembles at my word. One kills an ox, smites a man, slaughters a sheep, breaks a dog's neck, offers a bread offering of swine's blood, burns incense, blesses an idol. They have also chosen their ways, and their soul delights in their abominations; therefore, I also will choose their calamities, and will bring their fear on them, because I called and none answered; I commanded and they did not hear, but did evil in my sight, and chose that in which I delighted not.

2 Hear the word of Jehovah, you that tremble at his word: Your brothers who hate you, and drive you out on account of my name, said, Let Jehovah be glorified; but we shall see your joy, and they shall be ashamed. There is a voice of noise from the city, a voice from the temple, a voice of Jehovah rendering recompense to his enemies. Before she was sick, she brought forth; before her pains came on her, she was delivered of a male child. Who has heard of such a thing? Who has seen such things? Shall a land be born in one day? Shall a nation be born at once? for as soon as Zion was sick she bore her sons. Shall I cause to break forth, and not cause to be fully born, says Jehovah? Shall I cause to be born, and shut up [the womb], says your God?

3 Rejoice with Jerusalem, and exult with her, all that love her; be very joyful with her, all that mourn for her, that you may suck and be satisfied from the breast of her consolations; that you may press out and be delighted with the abundance of her glory. For thus says Jehovah: Behold, I will extend to her peace like a river,

and you shall suck the glory of the nations like an overflowing stream ; you shall be carried at her side and caressed on her knees. As one whom his mother comforts, so will I comfort you, and you shall be comforted in Jerusalem.   And you shall see, and your heart rejoice, and your bones flourish like grass ; and the hand of Jehovah shall be known to his servants, and indignation to his enemies.

4 For behold, Jehovah will come with fire, and his chariot is like a whirlwind, to render his anger with indignation, and his rebuke with flames of fire.   For Jehovah will judge all flesh with fire, and with his sword, and the killed by Jehovah shall be many.   Those who sanctify themselves, and those who purify themselves in gardens after one [who directs them] in the midst, who eat swine's flesh, and the abomination, and the mouse, together shall be destroyed, says Jehovah ; for I [know] their works and their thoughts ; [the time] shall come to assemble all nations and tongues, and they shall come and see my glory.

5 And I will put a sign on them, and will send some of them that escape to the nations, to Tarshish, Pul, and Lud, who bend the bow, to Jubal and Ionia, to the distant islands, which have not heard a report of me, nor seen my glory ; and they shall declare my glory to the nations.

6 And they shall bring all your brothers from all nations, a bread offering to Jehovah, on horses, and in chariots, and in litters, and on mules and dromedaries, to my holy mountain, to Jerusalem, says Jehovah, as the sons of Israel bring a bread offering in a pure vessel to the house of Jehovah.

7 And I will also take of them for priests and Levites, says Jehovah.   For as the new heaven and the new earth which I make shall continue before me, says Jehovah, so shall your children and your name continue.   And from new moon to new moon, and from Sabbath to Sabbath, all flesh shall come to worship before me, says Jehovah ; and they shall go forth and see the bodies of the men that transgressed against me ; for their worm shall not die, nor their fire be extinguished, and they shall be an abhorrence of all flesh.

8. ZEPHANIAH.

The word of Jehovah which came to Zephaniah, the son of Cushi, son of Gedaliah, son of Amariah, son of Hezekiah, in the days of Josiah, the son of Amon, king of Judah.

PROPHECY I.   [1, 2.

GOD WILL DESTROY THE WHOLE WORLD, AND EXECUTE JUDGMENTS ON THE JEWS AND OTHER NATIONS.

1 I WILL entirely destroy all things from the face of the earth, says Jehovah ; I will destroy man and beast ; I will destroy the birds of heaven and the fishes of the sea, and the stumbling blocks with the wicked ; and I will destroy man from the face of the earth, says Jehovah ; and I will stretch out my hand over Judah, and over the inhabitants of Jerusalem, and will cut off from this place the remnant of Baal, the name of the idol priests with the priests, and those that worship on the house tops the host of heaven, and those that worship [and] swear by Jehovah, and those that swear by their king, and those that turn back from following Jehovah, and inquire not for Jehovah, nor seek him.

2 Be silent before the Lord Jehovah, for the day of Jehovah is at hand ; for Jehovah has appointed a sacrifice, he has sanctified his called. And in the day of the sacrifice, Jehovah will punish the princes and the sons of the king, and all who wear foreign garments ; and I will punish every one that leaps over the threshold in that day, [and] those that fill the houses of their masters with violence and deceit, [unfaithful servants.]

3 And in that day, says Jehovah, there shall be the sound of a cry from the fish gate, and lamentation from the second gate, and great destruction from the hills. Lament, inhabitants of Maktesh, for all the merchants are destroyed, all that carry silver are cut off.

4 And at that time I will search Jerusalem with lamps, and punish the men that settle on their lees [sit in the Oriental luxurious style], that say in their hearts, Jehovah will not do good, neither

will he do evil; and their property shall become a prey, and their houses a desolation; and they shall build houses, but not inhabit them; and plant vineyards, but not drink wine from them.

5 The day of Jehovah is at hand; the great day is at hand, and hastens on exceedingly; at the sound of the day of Jehovah the mighty man shall cry there bitterly. That day is a day of wrath; it is a day of distress and oppression, a day of noise and tumult, a day of darkness and thick darkness, a day of clouds and dark clouds, a day of the trumpet and war shout against the fortified cities, and against the high towers. And I will distress men, and they shall go like the blind, because they have sinned against Jehovah. And their blood shall be poured out like dust, and their flesh like dung; and they shall not be able to deliver their silver, nor their gold, in the day of the wrath of Jehovah; and all the earth shall be consumed by the fire of his jealousy; for he will execute a speedy destruction of all the inhabitants of the earth.

6 Gather yourselves together, and be gathered together, nation not ashamed, before the bringing forth of the decree, when the day shall pass away like chaff, while yet the fierce anger of Jehovah shall not come on you, while yet the day of the anger of Jehovah shall not come on you. Seek Jehovah, all you meek of the earth who do justice, seek righteousness, seek humility; perhaps you may be hid in the day of Jehovah's anger; for Gaza shall be forsaken, Ascalon a desolation, Ashdod they shall drive out at noon, and Ekron shall be destroyed.

7 Woe to the inhabitants of the region of the sea, the Cherethites. The word of Jehovah is against you, Canaan, land of the Philistines; and I will destroy you [says Jehovah], without inhabitant; and the region of the sea shall be-pastures full of shepherds' cisterns, and folds for flocks. And that region shall be for the remnant of the house of Judah; they shall feed on it, they shall lie down in the houses of Ascalon in the evening; for Jehovah their God shall visit them, and restore their captives.

8 I have heard the reproach of Moab, and the revilings of the sons of Ammon, with which they reviled my people, and acted proudly against their bounds. Therefore, as I live, says Jehovah of hosts, the God of Israel, Surely Moab shall be like Sodom, and the sons of Ammon like Gomorrah, a possession of the thorn bush, and a pit of salt, and a desolation forever; the remnant of my people shall plunder them, and the remnant of my nation possess them.

They shall have this for their pride, because they reproached the people of Jehovah of hosts, and magnified themselves against them. Jehovah will be feared against them; for he will make lean all the gods of the earth, and all the islands of the nations each man from his places shall worship him.

9 And as for you, Ethiopians, you shall be killed with the sword; and he will stretch out his hand over the north, and destroy Assyria, and make Nineveh a desolation, a dry land, like a wilderness; flocks shall lie down in the midst of it; all the beasts of the nations, both the pelican and the porcupine, shall lodge in her capitals [the capitals of her pillars]; a voice shall sing in the windows, desolation shall be on the thresholds; for her cedar [work] shall be laid bare. This is the exulting city that dwelt securely, that said in her heart, I am, and there is none besides me; how has she become a desolation, a resting place of beasts? every one that passes by her, hisses and waves his hand.

PROPHECY II.   [3.

JERUSALEM WARNED; GOD TO BE WAITED FOR TILL THE DAY OF JUDGMENT; ZION TO BE REFORMED AND GLORIFIED.

1 WOE to her that is rebellious and defiled, an oppressive city. She listens to no voice, she receives not correction, she trusts not in Jehovah, she draws not nigh her God. Her princes in the midst of her are roaring lions, her judges are evening wolves; they reserve nothing for the morning. Her prophets are vainglorious, treacherous men; her priests defile the sanctuary, they violate the law.

2 Jehovah the righteous is in the midst of her; he will not commit wickedness; from morning to morning he will bring his justice to light, he will not fail; but the evil man knows not shame. 1 have cut off nations [says God]; their turrets are destroyed; I have made their streets desolate, with none passing through them; their cities are laid waste without man, without inhabitant. I said, Surely you will fear me, you will receive instruction. [I desired] that her habitation might not be cut off; of all which I informed her, but they earnestly corrupted all their doings.

3 Therefore wait for me, says Jehovah, till the day in which I rise up to the prey; for my determination is to assemble the

nations, to gather together the kingdoms, to pour out on them my
indignation, all my fierce anger; for by the fire of my anger shall
all the earth be consumed.   But then I will change to peoples of a
pure lip, to call all of them by the name of Jehovah, to serve him
with one heart; [and] from beyond the rivers of Ethiopia my suppliants, the daughter of my dispersed, shall bring my bread offering.

4 In that day you shall not be ashamed of all your doings, by
which you transgress against me; for then I will remove from the
midst of you your proud exulters, and you shall no more exercise
pride in my holy mountain.   And I will cause a poor and weak
people to remain in the midst of you, and they shall trust in the
name of Jehovah; and the remnant of Israel shall not do wickedness, nor speak falsehood, nor shall a deceitful tongue be found in
their mouth; but they shall feed and lie down, and none shall make
them afraid.

5 Sing, daughter of Zion; shout, Israel; rejoice and exult with
all [your] heart, daughter of Jerusalem; Jehovah has removed your
judgments, the King of Israel has turned away your enemies; Jehovah is in the midst of you; you shall no more see evil.

6 In that day it shall be said to Jerusalem, Fear not; and to
Zion, Let not your hands hang down; Jehovah your God will be in
the midst of you; the Mighty One will save [you]; he will rejoice
over you with joy; he will be silent in his love; he will rejoice over
you with singing.   And I will gather those who grieved you [by
being away] from the assembly; they were far from you, [and]
reproach was a burden on them.   Behold, at that time I will execute
[judgments] on all that afflict you, and save her that is lame, and
gather her that is cast out, and make them a praise and a name in
the land of their shame.

7 At that time I will bring you back, and at that time I will
gather you; for I will make you a name and a praise among all the
peoples of the earth, when I restore your captives to your eyes,
says Jehovah.

9. HABAKKUK.

The burden which Habakkuk the prophet saw [concerning the Jews and Chaldeans.]

1 How long, Jehovah, shall I cry to thee concerning violence, and thou wilt not hear? Why dost thou show me vanity, and cause me to see trouble, and plunder and violence are before me, and there is contention, and strife rises up? Therefore the law is relaxed, and judgment never goes forth; for the wicked circumvents the righteous; therefore a wrong judgment goes forth.

2 See [says God] the nations, look, and wonder, and be astonished; for I will perform a work in your days which you shall not believe when it is told you. For behold, I will raise up the Chaldeans, that bitter and impetuous nation, which goes through the breadth of the earth to possess habitations not his. He is fearful and terrible; his judgment and his majesty proceed from himself; and his horses are swifter than leopards, and fiercer than evening wolves; and his horsemen move proudly, and his horsemen come from afar, and fly as an eagle hastens to devour. He shall come entire for violence; the faces of the host shall [look] forward, and he shall collect captives like sand; and he shall scoff at kings, and princes shall be his laughing stock; he shall laugh at every fortress, and heap up earth and take it. Then his spirit shall pass on, and he shall transgress and be guilty; his strength is his god.

3 Art not thou from of old, Jehovah, my holy God? Let us not die. Jehovah, thou hast set him for judgment; rock [of ages], thou hast established him for reproof; thou art of purer eyes than to behold evil, and canst not look on trouble; why wilt thou look on plunderers? Thou art silent when the wicked devours the more righteous than he; and thou hast made men like the fishes of the sea, like reptiles which have no ruler. He takes them up with his hook entire; he draws them away with his net, and collects them with his drag-net; therefore he rejoices and is glad. Therefore he sacrifices to his net, and burns incense to his drag-net; for by them is his portion rich and his food fat. Shall he therefore

empty his net, and continually kill the nations, and not spare? I will stand on my post, I will set myself on the fortress, and watch to see what he will say to me, and what answer I shall have returned to my argument.

4 Then Jehovah answered me, and said, Write the vision, and inscribe it on tablets, that he may run that reads it; for the vision is yet for an appointed time; and at the end it will hasten, and not fail; if it tarries, wait for it; for it will certainly come; it will not be deferred.

5 Behold the proud one, his soul is not just; but the righteous shall live by his faith; and moreover he offends with wine; he is a proud man, and will not rest; he enlarges his desire like Hades, and he is like death, and can not be satisfied; and he assembles to himself all nations, and gathers to himself all peoples. Will not these, all of them, take up a proverb and a song of derision against him, and say, Woe to him that increases what is not his! how long? and loads himself with goods taken in pledge? Will they not rise up suddenly that shall bite you? and will they not wake [suddenly] that shall vex you, and you become their prey? For you have plundered many nations; all the remnant of the peoples shall plunder you for the blood of men, and. violence committed against the earth, the city, and all who live in it.

6 Woe to him that procures unjust gain for his house, to set his nest on high, and to deliver himself from the fear of evil! You have consulted for shame to your house; in cutting off many peoples you have also lost your life. For the stone from the wall cries out, and the cross-beam of wood answers it. Woe to him that builds a city with blood, and founds a town with wickedness. Behold, is it not from Jehovah of hosts that peoples labor for the fire, and nations labor for nothing? For the earth shall be filled with the knowledge of the glory of Jehovah, as water covers the sea.

7 Woe to him that gives his neighbor drink; you pour out your glowing [wine], you also produce drunkenness, that you may look on their nakedness; you are filled with shame instead of glory; do you drink also, and show yourself uncircumcised; the cup in the right hand of Jehovah shall come round to you, and shame shall be on all your glory. For the violence done to Lebanon shall cover you, and the destruction of beasts which terrifies them, on account of the blood of men, and the violence done to the earth, the city, and all who live in it.

8 What can the carved image profit, that its maker carves it; the cast image and the teacher of lies, that he who forms it trusts in his work, and makes dumb idols ?   Woe to him that says to the wood, Awake, and to the dumb stone, Arise, he shall teach.   Behold, it is overlaid with gold and silver, and there is no breath in it ; but Jehovah is in his holy temple; be silent before him, all the earth.

Prayer of Habakkuk the prophet, after the manner of the hymns.

9 Jehovah, I heard a report of thee, [and] I was afraid.   Jehovah, revive thy work in the midst of years, in the midst of years make known ; in wrath remember mercy.   God came from Teman, and the Holy One from mount Paran.   Pause.   His glory covered the heavens, and his praise filled the earth, and his brightness was like the light, and he had two horns from his hand, and there was the hiding of his strength.   Before him went Pestilence, and a consuming fire went forth at his feet ; he stood and surveyed the earth ; he saw and made the nations tremble ; the everlasting mountains were broken to fragments ; the eternal hills bowed down ; his goings [works] are [those] of old.

10 I saw the tents of Cushan [Eastern Arabia] in trouble ; the curtains of the land of Midian trembled.   Was Jehovah indignant at the rivers ?   Was thy anger against the rivers ?   Was thy wrath against the sea, that thou didst ride on thy horses, thy chariots of salvation ?   Thy bow was stripped bare, the rods of speech were oaths.   Pause.   Thou didst cleave the earth with rivers ; the mountains saw thee [and] trembled ; a shower of rain passed by ; the deep uttered his voice ; the height lifted up his hands ; the sun and moon stood still [in their] habitation ; thy arrows went forth for light, for brightness the gleam of thy spear ; thou didst march through the earth in indignation ; thou didst thresh the nations in anger ; thou wentest for the salvation of thy people, for the salvation of thy anointed.   Thou didst smite the head from the house of the wicked, thou laidest bare the foundation to the neck.   Pause.   Thou didst pierce with his staff the head of the chief, when they came like a whirlwind to scatter me.   Their exultation was like those who devour the poor in secret.   Thou wentest through the sea with thy horses, the foam of many waters ; [they perished.]

11 I heard, my soul trembled, my lips quivered at the sound ; decay entered my bones ; I trembled to my feet, that I might rest in the day of trouble.   At the coming up of the people, they shall invade

us ; [but] though the fig tree shall not blossom, and there be no fruit on the vines, the labor of the olive shall fail, and the fields yield no food, the sheep be cut off from the fold, and there be no cattle in the stalls, yet will I rejoice in Jehovah, I will be glad in the God of my salvation.   The Lord Jehovah is my strength, and he will make my feet like the hind's, and lead me on my high places.

For the chorister on neginas [a species of musical instruments like the harp].

10. JEREMIAH.

The words of Jeremiah the son of Hilkiah, of the priests who were in Anathoth, in the land of Benjamin, to whom the word of Jehovah came in the days of Josiah the son of Amon, king of Judah, in the 13th year of his reign; and it also came in the days of Jehoiakim the son of Josiah, king of Judah, to the 11th year of Zedekiah the son of Josiah, king of Judah, to the capture of Jerusalem, in the fifth month; [and subsequently.]

PROPHECY I.   [1.

JEREMIAH CALLED TO THE PROPHETIC OFFICE.

1 AND the word of Jehovah came to me, saying, Before I formed you in the womb, I knew you; and before you were born, I sanctified you; I appointed you a prophet to the nations.   Then I said, Ah, Lord Jehovah, behold, I know not how to speak, for I am a child.   Then Jehovah said to me, Say not, I am a child; but against all to whom I shall send you, go; and all which I shall command you, say.   Fear not their faces; for I am with you to deliver you, says Jehovah.

2 Then Jehovah put forth his hand and laid it on my mouth, and Jehovah said to me, Behold, I have put my words in your mouth; see, I set you this day over the nations, and over the kingdoms, to pluck up and to pull down, and to destroy and to overthrow, to build and to plant.

3 And the word of Jehovah came to me, saying, What do you

see, Jeremiah? Then I said, I see a rod of an almond tree. And Jehovah said to me, You see well, for I will watch over my word to perform it.

4 And the word of Jehovah came to me a second time, saying, What do you see? Then I said, I see a pot [with a fire] blown [under it], and its face is north. Then Jehovah said to me, From the north shall evil be opened against all the inhabitants of the land. For behold, I will call all the families of the kingdoms of the north, says Jehovah; and they shall come and set every man his seat at the entrance of the gates of Jerusalem, and against all her walls on every side, and against all the cities of Judah; and I will pronounce my judgments against them for all their wickedness, because they have forsaken me, and burned incense to other gods, and worshiped the work of their hands.

5 And gird up your loins, and stand and speak to them all that I shall command you; be not dismayed before them, lest I confound you before them. For behold, I have made you this day a fortified city, an iron pillar, and walls of brass against all the land, against the kings of Judah, her princes, her priests, and all the people of the land. And they shall fight against you, but shall not prevail; for I am with you to deliver you.

PROPHECY II.   [2, 3, 5.

JEREMIAH CONTENDS AGAINST IDOLATRY AND DEFECTION FROM JEHOVAH.

1 AND the word of Jehovah came to me, saying, Go and cry in the ears of Jerusalem, saying, Thus says Jehovah: I remember you, the kindness of your youth, the love of your bridal state, your going after me in the wilderness, in a land not sown. Israel was holiness to Jehovah, and his increase the first fruits. All that devoured him offended; evil came on them, says Jehovah.

2 Hear the word of Jehovah, house of Jacob, and all the families of the house of Israel. Thus says Jehovah: What evil did your fathers find in me, that they went far from me, and went after vanity, and became vain? And they said not, Where is Jehovah, that brought us up out of the land of Egypt, that led us in the wilderness, in a land of deserts and pits, in a land of drouth and the shade of death, in a land which no man passed through, and where no man dwelt?

3 And I brought you to the land of Carmel, to eat its fruit, and its good, and you came and defiled my land, and made my inheritance an abomination.   And the priests said not, Where is Jehovah? and those who administer the laws knew me not, and the shepherds transgressed against me, and the prophets prophesied by Baal, and went after things which can not profit.   Therefore I will yet contend with you, says Jehovah, and with your sons' sons will I contend.   For pass over to the islands of the Cyprians, and see ; and send to Kedar, and consider well, and see if there has been such a thing.   Has a nation changed gods, and they are not gods? but my people have changed its glory for that which can not profit.   ⌄

 4 Be astonished, heavens, at this ; tremble and be greatly amazed, says Jehovah ; for my people have done two wrongs ; they have forsaken me, the fountain of living water, to hew out for themselves cisterns, broken cisterns, which can not hold water.   Is Israel a servant? Is he a child of the house? Why then were [men allowed] to plunder him ?   The lions roared against him, they uttered their voice and made his land a desolation ; his cities are burned without inhabitant.   Even the sons of Noph [Memphis] and Tahpanes [Daphne] have eaten off your head.   Have you not procured this for yourself by forsaking Jehovah your God, when he led you by the way?

 5 And now what have you to do in the way of Egypt, to drink the waters of Shihor [the Nile]?   And what have you to do in the way of Assyria, to drink the waters of the river [the Euphrates]? Your wickedness shall correct you, and your defections rebuke you ; and you shall know and see that it is an evil and a bitter thing that you forsook Jehovah your God, and that my fear is not in you, says the Lord Jehovah of hosts.   For from of old I broke your yoke, and burst your bands, and you said, I will not transgress.   But on every high hill, and under every green tree, you have bowed down to commit fornication.   But I planted you wholly a choice vine, a genuine seed.   How then are you changed to me, to be degenerate shoots of a strange vine ?   For though you wash yourself with niter, and take for yourself much vegetable alkali, your wickedness is written before me, says the Lord Jehovah.

 6 How can you say, I am not defiled, I have not gone after Baals ? See your way in the valley, know what you have done ; you are a swift young camel interweaving her ways ; a wild ass used to the wilderness, which in her desire snuffs the wind ; in her heat who can bring her back ?   Those that seek her will not weary them-

selves ; in her month they shall find her.   Withhold your foot from being unshod, and your throat from thirst.   But you said, There is no hope, for I love strangers, and I will go after them.

7 As a thief is ashamed when he is found out, so are the house of Israel ashamed ; they, their kings, their princes, and their priests, and their prophets, who say to the wood, Thou art my father ; and to the stone, Thou hast begotten me ; but they have turned to me the back, and not the face ; but in the time of their affliction they say, Arise and save us.   But where are your gods which you made for yourself?   Let them arise if they can save you in the time of your affliction ; for according to the number of your cities are your gods, Judah.

8 Why do you contend with me ?   All of you have transgressed against me, says Jehovah.   In vain I smote your sons ; they received not correction ; your sword has devoured your prophets like a destroying lion.   Generation, see the word of Jehovah : Have I been a wilderness to Israel?   Have I been a land of darkness ? Why do you say, my people, We have prevailed, we will go to thee no more ?   Can a young woman forget her ornamental attire ? a bride her belt ?   But my people have forgotten me days without number.

9 Why do you make good your way to seek love ?   Therefore also you have taught your ways wickedness, and on your skirts is found the blood of poor innocent souls : I found it not by secret search, but on all these.   Yet you say, Because I am innocent, his anger will surely turn away from me.   Behold, I have judged you, because you say, I have not sinned.   Why do you go so much to change your way ?   You shall be ashamed also of Egypt, as you were ashamed of Assyria, and shall go from it with your hands on your head ; for Jehovah rejects your confidences, and you shall not prosper in them.

10 It is said, If a man puts away his wife, and she goes from him and becomes [the wife] of another man, shall he return to her again ?   Shall not that land be greatly defiled ?   But you have committed fornication with many lovers, yet return to me, says Jehovah. Lift up your eyes to the high places, and see where you have not been defiled ; you sat on the ways for them, like the Arab in the desert, and have defiled the land with your fornication and with your wickedness.   Therefore shall the showers be withheld, and the vernal rain shall not come.   And you have the forehead of a woman that is a harlot ; you refuse to be ashamed.   Will you not

henceforth cry to me, My Father, thou art the companion of my youth? Will he keep his anger forever? Will he keep it eternally? Behold, you have said and done as evil as you could.

PROPHECY III.   [3, 6, 4, 4.

JEREMIAH REPROVES IDOLATRY, AND URGES A RETURN TO THE WORSHIP OF JEHOVAH.

1 JEHOVAH said to me in the days of Josiah the king, Have you seen what apostatizing Israel has done? She goes on every high mountain, and under every green tree, and commits fornication there. But I said after she had done all these things, Return to me; and she returned not; and her treacherous sister Judah saw her. And when I saw that for all these causes, because apostatizing Israel committed adultery, I put her away, and gave her a bill of her divorcement; then treacherous Judah, her sister, was not afraid; but she went and committed fornication also. And when by the report of her fornication the land was defiled, then she committed adultery with stones and trees. And for all this also her treacherous sister Judah turned not to me with all her heart, but with falsehood, says Jehovah.

2 And Jehovah said to me, As to the righteousness of her soul, apostatizing Israel is better than treacherous Judah. Go and proclaim these words to the north, and say, Return, apostatizing Israel, says Jehovah; I will not cause my face to frown on you; for I am kind, says Jehovah, I will not keep [anger] forever. Only acknowledge your wickedness, that you have transgressed against Jehovah your God, and gone away to strangers under every green tree, and obeyed not my voice, says Jehovah.

3 Return, backsliding sons, says Jehovah; for I am your Lord, and I will take you one of a city and two of a family, and bring you to Zion, and give you shepherds after my heart, who shall feed you with knowledge and understanding. And when you shall be multiplied and be fruitful in the earth, in those days, says Jehovah, they shall not say any more, The ark of the covenant of Jehovah; neither shall it come into mind; they shall not remember it, neither shall they visit it; nor shall this be done any more. At that time they shall call Jerusalem the throne of Jehovah, and all nations shall wait on the name of Jehovah at Jerusalem; neither shall they go any more after the hardness of their hearts for evil.

4 In those days the house of Judah shall go with the house of
Israel, and they shall come together from the north country to the
land which I caused their fathers to inherit.   But I said, How shall
I put you among sons, and give you the desirable land, the glorious
possession of the hosts of nations ?   And I said, You shall call me,
My Father, and turn not away from following me ; but as a woman
deals treacherously with her friend, so have you, house of Israel,
dealt treacherously with me, says Jehovah.

5 A voice is heard on the hills, the weeping, the supplications of
the sons of Israel, because they perverted their way, they forgot
Jehovah their God.   Return, backsliding sons ; I will heal your defections.   Behold us ; we come to thee, for thou art Jehovah our
God.   Surely, in vain from the hills is [sought] the abundance of
the mountains ; but in Jehovah our God is the salvation of Israel.
For shame has consumed the labor of our fathers from our youth ;
their sheep and their cattle, their sons and their daughters.   We
lie down in our shame, and our confusion covers us ; for we have
sinned against Jehovah our God, we and our fathers from our
youth, even to this day, and obeyed not the voice of Jehovah our God.

6 If you will return, Israel, says Jehovah, return to me.   And if
you will put away your abominations from before me, then you shall
not remove.   If you swear, As the Lord lives, in truth and justice,
and righteousness, then shall the nations bless themselves in him,
and in him shall they glory ; for thus says Jehovah to the men of
Judah and Jerusalem : Break up for yourselves fallow ground, and
sow not among thorn bushes ; circumcise yourselves to Jehovah,
and put away the foreskins of your hearts, men of Judah and inhabitants of Jerusalem, lest my indignation go forth like fire, and
burn, and there be none to extinguish it, on account of the evil of
your doings.

PROPHECY IV.   4, 5, 5, 20.

JEREMIAH PREDICTS THE BABYLONIAN INVASION AND LAMENTS
ITS MISERIES.

1 DECLARE in Judah, and publish in Jerusalem, and say, Blow a
trumpet in the land.   Cry, Fill [your notes], and say, Assemble
yourselves together, and let us go to the fortified cities.   Set up a
standard toward Zion ; flee, stop not ; for I will bring evil from
the north, and a great destruction.   A lion has gone up from his

thicket, and a destroyer of nations has broken up his camp ; he has gone out from his place to make your land a desolation ; and your cities shall be consumed without inhabitant. For this gird yourselves with sackcloth ; mourn and lament, for the fierce anger of Jehovah has not turned away from us.

2 And in that day, says Jehovah, the heart of the king shall perish, and the heart of the princes ; and the priests shall be astonished, and the prophets amazed. Then I said, Ah, Lord Jehovah, surely thou hast greatly deceived this people and Jerusalem, saying, You shall have peace ; but the sword reaches to the soul. At that time it shall be said to this people, and to Jerusalem, A dry wind from the hills in the desert, by the way of the daughter of my people, not to fan nor to clean, — a wind stronger than for these things, — shall come for me ; now also I will pronounce judgments on them.

3 Behold, one shall come up like clouds, and his chariots shall be like a whirlwind ; his horses are swifter than eagles. Woe to us, for we are destroyed. Wash your heart from wickedness, Jerusalem, that you may be saved. How long shall vain thoughts lodge in you ? For a voice declares from Dan, and publishes evil from mount Ephraim, announce to the nations, behold, publish against Jerusalem, Watchmen have come from a distant country, and have given their voice against the cities of Judah. They are around her like keepers of a field, on every side ; for she has rebelled against me, says Jehovah. Your way and your doings have done these things to you ; this is your wickedness, for it is bitter, for it reaches to your heart.

4 My bowels ! my bowels ! I am pained in the walls of my heart. My heart is disquieted within me, I can not be still ; for thou hearest, my soul, the sound of the trumpet, the war shout. Destruction on destruction is proclaimed, for all the earth is laid waste ; my tents are destroyed suddenly, and my curtains in a moment. How long shall I see the standard and hear the sound of the trumpet. For my people are foolish, they know me not ; they are sons of the bearers of burdens, and not intelligent [men] ; they are wise for evil, but to do good they know not.

5 I saw the earth, and behold, it was empty and waste ; and the heavens, and their light was gone ; I saw the mountains, and behold they shook, and all the hills were moved ; I saw, and behold, there was no man, and all the birds of heaven had fled ; I saw, and behold, Carmel was a desert, and all its cities were thrown down

before Jehovah, before his fierce anger. For thus says the Lord : All the earth shall be a desolation ; but I will not make a complete destruction. For this let the earth mourn, and the heavens put on blackness from above ; because I have spoken, I have purposed, and I will not change my mind, nor turn from it.

6 At the noise of the horseman and of the bowman every city shall flee ; they shall go to the thickets, and ascend to the hills ; every city shall be forsaken, and not a man shall dwell in them ; and when you are destroyed, what will you do ? Though you clothe yourself with crimson, though you adorn yourself with gold, though you rend your eyes with eye-paint, you shall make yourself fair in vain ; your lovers have rejected you, they shall seek your life. For there is a voice as of a woman in childbirth ; I hear distress, as of one that bears [her] first born ; it is the voice of the daughter of Zion ; she sobs, she stretches out her hands : Woe now is me, for my soul has languished for murderers !

7 Run about Jerusalem, and see now, and know, and inquire in the streets, if you can find a man, if there is one that does justice, that seeks truth, and I will forgive you. But when they say, As Jehovah lives, therefore they swear falsely. Are not thy eyes, Jehovah, on the truth ? Thou didst smite them, but they were not sick ; thou didst consume them, [but] they refused to receive correction ; they made their faces harder than a rock, they refused to turn. Then I said, Surely these are the weak, they are foolish, because they know not the way of Jehovah, the justice of their God. I will get me to the great men, and speak to them ; for they know the way of Jehovah, the justice of their God. Indeed, they have broken the yoke altogether, they have burst the bands ; therefore a lion from the forest shall smite them, and a wolf of the evenings destroy them ; a leopard shall watch over their cities ; every one that goes out of them shall be torn to pieces ; for their transgressions are many, and their backslidings great.

8 Why should I forgive you for this ? Your sons have forsaken me, and sworn by things which are not gods. And I satisfied them, but they committed adultery, and assembled themselves in crowds at the house of the harlot. They are fed horses roaming about, they each one neigh for his neighbor's wife. Shall I not visit for these things, says Jehovah ? And shall not my soul be avenged on such a nation as this ?

9 Go up on her walls and destroy, but make not a complete de-

struction. Take away her tendrils, for they belong not to Jehovah; for the house of Israel and the house of Judah have dealt very treacherously with me, says Jehovah; they have denied Jehovah, and said, He is not [God]; evil shall not come on us, neither shall we see sword nor famine; and the prophets are wind, and have not the word. Thus shall it be done to them.

10 Therefore thus says Jehovah the God of hosts : Because you say this word, behold, I will make my word in your mouth a fire, and this people wood, and it shall consume them. Behold, I will bring on you a nation from afar, house of Israel, says Jehovah. It is a strong nation; it is an ancient nation; you shall not know its language, nor understand what they say. Its quiver is an opened grave; all of them are mighty men; and it shall eat up your harvest and your bread; it shall consume your sons and your daughters; it shall consume your flocks and your herds; it shall consume your vines and your fig trees; it shall possess your fortified cities, in which you trust, with the sword. But in those days, says Jehovah, I will not make a complete destruction of you. And when they shall say, Why has Jehovah our God done all these things to us? then say to them, According as you have forsaken me, and served strange gods in your land, so shall you serve strangers in a land not yours.

PROPHECY V. [5, 21, 6.

JERUSALEM TO BE ENTIRELY DESTROYED; THE REJECTION OF THE WICKED.

1 DECLARE this to the house of Jacob, and publish it in Judah, saying, Hear now this, foolish people and of no mind, who have eyes, and see not; ears, and hear not : will you not fear me? says Jehovah; will you not tremble before me, who have set the sand a bound to the sea, a perpetual ordinance, and it can not pass over it; and though its waves rage and roar, they can not pass over it? But the heart of this people is perverse and rebellious; they have departed and gone; and they said not in their heart, Let us now fear Jehovah our God, who gives rain, both the autumnal rain and the vernal rain in their time, and keeps for us the appointed weeks of the harvest. Your wickedness has turned away these things, and your sins have withheld good from you. For wicked men are found among my people, who watch like the crouching of fowlers, who set

snares that they may take men.   As a cage is full of birds, so their
houses are full of deceit; therefore have they become great and
rich; they are fat, they shine, they also abound in evil deeds; they
judge not the cause, the cause of the fatherless, but they prosper;
and the cause of the needy they judge not.   Shall I not visit for
these things? says Jehovah.   Shall not my soul be avenged on such
a nation as this?

2 An astonishment and a horrible wickedness is committed in the
earth.   The prophets prophesy falsely, and the priests rule by their
hands; and the people love to have it so.   But what will you do in
the latter end of it?

3 Flee, sons of Benjamin, from the midst of Jerusalem, and in
Tekoah blow a trumpet, and in Beth-hakkerem set up a signal, for
evil comes hurrying from the north, and a great destruction.   I
have likened the daughter of Zion to a fair and delicate woman.
Shepherds shall come against her, and their flocks; they shall pitch
their tents against her on every side; they shall feed each one in his
place.   Declare war against her; arise, and let us go up at noon.
Woe to us, for the day is spent, for the shadows of evening incline.
Arise, and let us go up by night, and destroy her palaces.

4 For thus says Jehovah of hosts, Cut down trees, and throw up
a mound about Jerusalem.   She is a city to be punished; she is all
oppression in the midst of her.   As a fountain sends forth its
waters, so she sends forth her wickedness; violence and oppression
are heard in her; bruises and wounds are continually before my
face.   Be instructed, Jerusalem, lest my soul be alienated from you;
lest I make you a desolation, a land not inhabited.   Thus says Jehovah of hosts: They shall thoroughly glean as a vine the remnant
of Israel; return your hand like a grape gatherer to the baskets.

5 To whom shall I speak and testify, that they may hear?   Behold, their ear is uncircumcised, that they can not attend; behold,
the word of Jehovah is to them a reproach, they do not delight in
it.   But I am full of the indignation of Jehovah; I am tired of containing it; I will pour it out on the children in the streets, and on
the company of young men together; for both the man and the wife
shall be taken, and the elder with him that is full of days; and their
houses shall be transferred to others, their fields and their wives together; for I will stretch out my hand against the inhabitants of
the earth, says Jehovah; for from the least to the greatest, every
one practices fraud; and from the prophet to the priest, every one

utters falsehood.   They have healed the wound of the daughter of my people slightly, saying, Peace, peace, when there is no peace. Were they ashamed when they committed an abomination ?   Indeed, they were not at all ashamed; indeed, they know not how to be confounded.   Therefore they shall fall with the fallen ; in the time of their visitation they shall be cast down, says Jehovah.

6 Thus says Jehovah: Stand in the ways and see, and inquire for the old paths ; where is the good way ? and walk in it, and find rest to your souls.   But they said, We will not walk in it.   And I set watchmen over you [saying], Attend to the voice of the watchmen ; and they said, We will not attend.   Therefore hear, nations, and know, assembly, which is among them.   Hear, earth ; behold, I will bring evil on this people, the fruit of their thoughts, because they attend not to my words, and refuse my law.

7 Why is this, that incense comes to me from Sheba, and sweet cane from a distant land ?   Your burnt offerings are not acceptable, nor your sacrifices agreeable to me.   Therefore thus says Jehovah : Behold, I will lay stumbling blocks before this people, and they shall stumble on them, fathers and sons together ; and neighbor and friend shall perish.

8 Thus says Jehovah : Behold, a people has come from the land of the north, and a great nation is raised up from the sides of the earth.   They shall hold the bow and spear ; they are cruel, and shall not pity ; their voice shall roar like the sea, and they shall ride on horses arranged like men for battle against you, daughter of Zion.   We heard the report of them ; our hands hung down, [and] distress seized us, [and] pain as a woman in childbirth.   Go not into the country, walk not in the way, for the sword of the enemy is a terror on every side.   Daughter of my people, gird on sackcloth, roll yourself in ashes, make a mourning as for an only son, a bitter lamentation ; for a destroyer shall come on us suddenly.

9 I have made you the fortress of an assayer among my people, that you may know and try their way ; all of them are perverse revolters, going about with slander ; they are all of them brass and iron ; they are destroyers.   The bellows is dried up by their white heat ; he melts and tries in vain ; the wicked are not plucked away. Rejected silver shall men call them, for Jehovah has rejected them.

PROPHECY VI. [7, 1-28.

JEREMIAH CALLS THE NATION TO HOLINESS, AND PREDICTS THE DESTRUCTION OF THE COMMONWEALTH.

1 THE word which came to Jeremiah from Jehovah, saying, Stand in the gate of the house of Jehovah, and proclaim there this word, and say, Hear the word of Jehovah, all Judah that go in at these gates to worship Jehovah. Thus says Jehovah of hosts, the God of Israel : Make good your ways and your doings, and I will dwell among you in this place ; but trust not for yourselves in lying words, saying, The temple of Jehovah, the temple of Jehovah, the temple of Jehovah ! these [shall save us]. For if you make your ways and your doings really good ; if you do justice between a man and his neighbor ; if you oppress not the stranger, the widow, and the fatherless, nor shed innocent blood in this place, nor go after other gods to your injury, then I will dwell with you in this place, in the land which I gave to your fathers from of old and forever.

2 Behold, you trust in lying words, which can not profit. Will you steal, kill, and commit adultery, and swear falsely, and burn incense to Baal, and walk after other gods which you have not known, and come and stand before me in this house, which is called by my name, and say, We are delivered up to do all these abominations ? Is this house which is called by my name a den of robbers in your sight ? I also, behold, I have seen [your wickedness], says Jehovah.

4 For go now to my place, which is in Shiloh, where I dwelt at first, and see what I did to it on account of the wickedness of my people Israel. And now, because you have done all these works, says Jehovah, and I spoke to you, rising early and speaking, and you obeyed not; and I called, and you answered not ; therefore I will do to the house which is called by my name, and to the place which I gave to you and to your fathers, as I did to Shiloh, and will cast you out from before me, as I cast out your brothers, all the children of Ephraim.

5 And now as for you, pray not for this people, nor lift up for them cry or prayer, neither intercede with me, for I will not hear you. Do you not see what they do in the cities of Judah, and in the streets of Jerusalem ? The sons collect wood, and the fathers kindle a fire, and the women knead dough to make cakes for the

queen of heaven, and to pour out libations to other gods, that they may provoke me. Do they provoke me? says Jehovah. Do they not rather [vex] themselves, to the confusion of their faces? Therefore, thus says the Lord Jehovah: Behold, my anger and my indignation are poured out on this place, on man and on beast, and on the trees of the field, and on the fruits of the ground; and it shall burn, and not be extinguished.

6 Thus says Jehovah of hosts, the God of Israel: Add your burnt offerings to your sacrifices, and eat meat, for I spoke not to your fathers, nor commanded them in the day that I brought them out of the land of Egypt, concerning the matter of burnt offerings and sacrifices, but I commanded them this word, saying, Obey my voice, and I will be your God, and you shall be my people; and walk in all the way which I command you, that it may be well with you. But they obeyed not, nor inclined their ear, but walked in the counsels of their hard hearts to do evil, and were behind, and not before.

7 For from the day in which your fathers came up from the land of Egypt to this day, I sent to you all my servants the prophets daily, rising early and sending them. But they obeyed me not, nor inclined their ear, and they hardened their neck to do worse than their fathers. Therefore, you shall say to them all these words; but they will not hear you; and call to them, but they will not answer. Then say to them, This is a nation which obey not the voice of Jehovah their God, nor receive instruction; truth has perished, and is cut off from before them.

PROPHECY VII.　　　　[7, 29, 8, 13.

HUMAN SACRIFICES REPROVED.

1 Cut off your hair, and cast it away, and take up a lamentation, for Jehovah has rejected, he has cast off the generation of his wrath. For the sons of Judah did evil in my sight, says Jehovah; they put their abominations in the house which is called by my name, to defile it; and built altars in Tophet, which is in the valley of the son of Hinnom, to burn their sons and their daughters with fire, which I commanded not, neither did it come into my mind. Therefore behold, the days come, says Jehovah, in which it shall no more be called Tophet, or valley of the son of Hinnom, but valley of the slaughter; and they shall bury in Tophet, till there is no

13 *

place.   And the dead bodies of this people shall be for food to the birds of heaven, and to the beasts of the earth ; and none shall frighten them away.   And I will cause the voice of joy and the voice of gladness, the voice of the bridegroom and the voice of the bride, to cease from the cities of Judah and from the streets of Jerusalem, for the land shall be desolate.

2 At that time, says Jehovah, they shall bring out the bones of the kings of Judah, and the bones of his princes, and the bones of the priests, and the bones of the prophets, and the bones of the inhabitants of Jerusalem from their graves, and shall spread them out before the sun, and before the moon, and before all the host of heaven, which they loved and which they served, and after which they walked, and which they sought and worshiped.   They shall not be gathered up nor buried, [but] shall be for dung on the face of the ground.   And death shall be chosen rather than life, by all the remnant who remain of this evil family, in all places in which I drive out those who remain, says Jehovah of hosts.

3 And say to them, Thus says Jehovah : Shall they fall, and not rise ?   Shall they turn away, and not return ?   Why has this people of Jerusalem backslidden with a perpetual backsliding ?   They hold fast to lies, they refuse to turn.   I attended and heard ; they spoke not right ; none changed his mind concerning his wickedness, saying, What have I done ?   They all turned to their race, as the horse rushes to battle.   Even the stork in the heavens knows her times, and the turtle dove and swallow, and the chattering swallow, observe the time of their coming, but my people know not the justice of Jehovah.   How say you, We are wise, and the law of Jehovah is with us ?   Behold, surely he made it in vain ; the pen of the scribes [writes] falsehood.

4 The wise are ashamed, they are confounded and taken ; behold, they have rejected the word of Jehovah, and what wisdom have they ?   Therefore I will give their wives to others, and their fields to those who shall possess them ; for from the least to the greatest, every one commits fraud ; from the prophet to the priest, every one practices falsehood.   And they have healed the wound of the daughter of my people slightly, saying, Peace, peace, when there was no peace.   Were they ashamed when they committed abomination ?   Indeed, they were not at all ashamed, and know not how to blush ; therefore they shall fall with those that fall ; in the time of their visitation they shall fall, says Jehovah.   I will entirely con-

sume them, says Jehovah ; there shall be no grapes on the vine, nor figs on the fig tree ; and the leaf shall wither, and I will deliver them to those that shall cause them to pass away.

PROPHECY VIII.   [8, 14, 9.

THE BABYLONIAN INVASION AT HAND.

1 WHY do we remain here ?   Assemble yourselves, and let us go to the fortified cities, and be silent there ; for Jehovah our God has destroyed us, and made us drink the waters of the poppy ; for we have sinned against Jehovah.   We wait for peace, and there is no good ; for a time of healing, and behold terror.   The snorting of his horses is heard from Dan ; at the neighing of his mighty ones the whole earth shakes ; and they shall come and consume the land and all it contains, the city and those who dwell in it.   For behold, I will send against you serpents, vipers, which it is impossible to charm, and they shall bite you, says Jehovah.

2 My joy [is turned] into sorrow within me ; my heart within me is sick.   Behold the voice of the cry of the daughter of my people, from a distant land.   Is not Jehovah in Zion ?   Is not her king in her ?   Why then did they provoke me with their carved images, with their strange vanities ?   The grain harvest is past ; the fruit harvest has ended, and we are not saved [gathered in].   For the wound of the daughter of my people am I wounded ; I am black. Astonishment has seized me.   Is there no balsam in Gilead ?   Is there no physician there ?   Why then comes no healing to the daughter of my people ?   O that my head was water, and my eyes a fountain of tears, that I might weep day and night for the killed of the daughter of my people !   O that I had in the wilderness a traveler's lodge, that I might forsake my people, and go from them ! for they are all an assembly of robbers ; they bend their tongues as bows for lies, but are not valiant for truth in the earth ; for they go from wickedness to wickedness, and know not me, says Jehovah.

3 Beware every man of his friend, nor trust any one in his brother ; for every brother will certainly overreach, and every friend will go about with slander.   And they deceive every one his friend, and speak not the truth : they teach their tongues to speak lies, and tire themselves to act perversely.   Your dwelling is in the midst of deceit ; through deceit they refuse to know me, says Jehovah.

Therefore thus says Jehovah of hosts : Behold, I will melt and try them ; for what shall I do on account of the daughter of my people ?   Their tongue is a slaughtering arrow, they speak deceit with their mouth ; one speaks peace to his friend, but in his heart he lies in wait for him.   Shall I not punish them for these things, says Jehovah ?   Shall not my soul be avenged on such a nation as this ?

4 I will take up a weeping and lamentation for the mountains, and a lamentation for the pastures of the wilderness.   For they are burned up, with none passing through, and they hear not the voice of cattle ; from the birds of heaven to the beasts of the field, they have fled and gone.   For I will make Jerusalem heaps, a den of jackals ; and the cities of Judah will I make a desolation without inhabitant.   Who is a wise man, that he may understand this ? and one to whom the mouth of Jehovah has spoken, that he may declare it ?   Why is the land destroyed, and the wilderness burned up, without any passing through?   And Jehovah said, Because they forsook my law, which I set before them, and obeyed not my voice, nor walked according to it, but walked after the hardness of their heart, and after the Baals which their fathers taught them ; therefore.thus says Jehovah of hosts, the God of Israel : Behold, I will feed this people with wormwood, and give them the water of the poppy to drink ; and I will scatter them among nations which they have not known, they nor their fathers, and send the sword after them till I have consumed them.

5 Thus says Jehovah of hosts : Attend, and call the wailers, that they may come, and send for skillful [wailers], that they may come ; and let them make haste, and take up a lamentation for us, that our eyes may run down with tears, and our eyelids flow with water.   For a voice of wailing is heard from Zion : How are we destroyed ! we are exceedingly ashamed, for we have forsaken the land, for they have thrown down our dwellings.   But hear, women [wailers], the word of Jehovah, and let your ear receive the word of his mouth, and teach your daughters wailing, and every woman her companion lamentation ; for death has come up into our windows, it has entered our palaces, to cut off the child from without, and the young man from the streets.   Say, thus says Jehovah : For the dead bodies of men shall fall like dung on the field, and like the bundle of those that follow the reaper, and none shall gather them up.

6 Thus says Jehovah : Let not the wise man glory in his wis-

dom, nor the mighty man glory in his might, nor the rich man glory in his riches ; but let him that glories glory in this, that he understands and knows me ; for I am Jehovah, performing kindness, justice, and righteousness in the earth ; for in these things I delight, says Jehovah. Behold, the days come, says Jehovah, in which I will punish all the circumcised with the uncircumcised. Egypt, and Judah, and Edom, and the sons of Ammon, and Moab, and all with cut hair who live in the wilderness ; for all the nations are uncircumcised, and all the house of Israel are uncircumcised in heart.

PROPHECY IX. [10, 1–16.

IDOLS AND HEATHEN SUPERSTITIONS NOTHING ; JEHOVAH IS THE CREATOR.

1 HEAR this word which Jehovah speaks to you, house of Israel. Thus says Jehovah : Be not instructed in the way of the nations, nor be dismayed at the signs of heaven, for the nations are dismayed at them. For the customs of the peoples are vanity ; for a tree is cut from the forest, the work of the hands of the workman, with an axe ; he beautifies it with silver and gold, and they fasten it with nails and hammers, that it can not be moved. They are like a palm tree, a turned work ; they speak not ; they must be entirely carried, for they can not go ; fear them not, for they can not do evil, neither is it in their power to do good.

2 They are in nothing like thee, Jehovah ; thou art great, and thy name is of great power. Who will not fear thee, King of the nations? for to thee shall [men] come ; for among all the wise men of the nations, and in all their kingdoms, there is none like thee. They are altogether brutish and foolish ; the wood is a doctrine of vanities. Silver plate is brought from Tarshish, and gold from Uphaz, the work of the workman, and of the hands of the founder ; blue and purple are their clothing ; all of them the work of the skillful. But Jehovah is the true God ; he is the living God, and the eternal King ; at his wrath the earth shakes, and the nations can not withstand his indignation.

3 Say thus to them : The gods who made not the heavens and the earth shall perish from the earth, and from under these heavens ; he made the earth by his power, he established the world by his wisdom ; and by his understanding he stretched out the heavens.

When he utters his voice, there is an abundance of water in the heavens, and he causes his clouds to ascend from the ends of the earth. He makes lightnings for rain, and brings forth wind from his treasuries. Every man is brutish in respect to knowledge, every founder is ashamed of his work, for his cast image is a lie ; there is no breath in them. They are vanity, and a work of deceptions ; in the time of their visitation they shall perish. The portion of Jacob is not like these ; for he is the former of all things, and Israel is the rod of his inheritance ; Jehovah of hosts is his name.

PROPHECY X.   [10, 17-25.

THE BABYLONIAN INVASION PREDICTED.

1 TAKE away your bundle from the land, inhabitant of the fortress, for thus says Jehovah : Behold, I will sling out the inhabitants of the land at this time, and distress them till they find trouble. Woe is me on account of my wound ; my blow is grievous ; but I said, This surely is my affliction, and I must bear it. My tent is destroyed, all my pins are torn away ; my sons have gone forth from me, and are not ; there is no more any one to stretch my tent, nor to set up my curtains ; for the shepherds have become brutish, and seek not Jehovah ; therefore they shall not prosper, and all their flocks shall be scattered.

2 A voice, a report, behold, it has come, and there is a great tumult from the land of the north, to make the cities of Judah a desolation, a habitation of jackals. I know Jehovah, that his way is not in man ; that it is not of man that walks to make his steps firm. Correct me, Jehovah, but with justice, not in anger, lest thou bring me to nothing. Pour out thy indignation on the nations who know thee not, and on families that call not on thy name ; for they have devoured Jacob, they both devour him and destroy his habitation.

PROPHECY XI.   [11.

GOD INSISTS ON HIS COVENANT ; HE REVEALS A CONSPIRACY AGAINST THE PROPHET.

1 THE word which came to Jeremiah from Jehovah, saying, Hear the words of this covenant, and speak to the men of Judah, and

the inhabitants of Jerusalem, and say to them, Thus says Jehovah the God of Israel : Cursed is the man who will not obey the words of this covenant, which I commanded your fathers, in the day in which I brought them out of the land of Egypt, out of the iron furnace, saying, Hear my words and do them, according to all that I shall command you, and be my people, and I will be your God, in order to confirm the oath which I swore to your fathers, to give them a land flowing with milk and honey, as at this day.   Then I answered and said, Amen, Jehovah.

2 Then Jehovah said to me, Proclaim all these words in the cities of Judah, and in the streets of Jerusalem, saying, Hear the words of this covenant, and do them.   For I solemnly testified to your fathers, from the day in which I brought them up out of the land of Egypt to this day, rising early ; and I testified, saying, Hear my voice.   But they heard not, nor inclined their ear, but walked every man after the hardness of his evil heart.   Then I brought on them all the words of this covenant, which I commanded them to do, and they did them not.

3 Then Jehovah said to me, A conspiracy is formed among the men of Judah and the inhabitants of Jerusalem.   They have turned to the wickedness of their fathers before, who refused to obey my words, and they went after other gods to serve them.   The house of Israel and the house of Judah broke my covenant which I formed with their fathers.

4 Therefore, thus says Jehovah : Behold, I will bring on them evil, from which they shall not be able to go away ; and they shall cry to me, and I will not hear them.   And the cities of Judah, and the inhabitants of Jerusalem, shall go and cry to the gods to whom they burned incense, and they shall not save them in the time of their trouble.   For according to the number of your cities were your gods, Judah, and according to the number of the streets of Jerusalem have you set up altars to shame, altars to burn incense to Baal.   Therefore, pray not for this people, lift not up for them cry or prayer, for I will not hear when they cry to me on account of their trouble.

5 What has my beloved to do in my house, to commit the wickedness of the great ?   And they have caused the holy flesh to pass away from you ; for when you feed yourself, then you exult.   Jehovah called you a green olive tree, fair and of beautiful fruit ; with a great noise he kindled fires against it, and they consumed its

branches. For Jehovah of hosts, who planted you, has spoken evil against you, because of the evil of the house of Israel, and of the house of Judah, which they have done to provoke me by burning incense to Baal.

6 Then Jehovah informed me, and I knew ; then thou didst show me their works. For I was like a gentle young sheep which is led to slaughter, and knew not that they formed plots against me [saying], Let us destroy the tree with its fruit ; let us cut him off this day, that his name may be no more remembered. But Jehovah of hosts judges righteously ; he tries the soul and heart ; I shall see thy vengeance on them, for to thee have I laid open my cause.

7 Therefore, thus says Jehovah concerning the men of Anathoth, who seek your life, saying, Prophesy not in the name of Jehovah, that you die not by our hands ; therefore, thus says Jehovah of hosts : Behold, I will punish you ; your young men shall die by the sword, your sons and your daughters shall die by famine, and you shall have no remnant, for I will bring evil on the men of Anathoth, the year of their visitation.

PROPHECY XII.   [12.

GOD'S JUSTICE QUESTIONED IN SUFFERING THE WICKED TO PROSPER ; HIS JUDGMENTS.

1 Thou art righteous, Jehovah ; but let me contend with thee, let me even speak with thee of justice. Why does the way of the wicked prosper ? and all that deal treacherously are at rest. Thou plantest them, and they take root, they grow, and also bear fruit. Thou art near in their mouth, but far from their souls. But thou, Jehovah, hast known me ; thou hast seen me, and tried my heart with thee.

2 Wilt thou not separate them as sheep for slaughter, and set them apart for a day of slaughter ? How long shall the earth mourn ? and all the plants of the field be dried up on account of the wickedness of its inhabitants ? The beasts and birds are destroyed ; but they say, He will not see our latter end. If you have run with the footmen, and they wearied you, how will you contend with horses ? And if [they have wearied you] in a land of peace, in which you had confidence, what will you do in the pride of the

Jordan? For even your brothers and the house of your fathers, even they have dealt treacherously with you, and have called after you in full numbers, so that you can not trust them when they speak kindly to you.

3 I have forsaken my house, I have torn up my inheritance, I have given the delight of my soul to the hand of her enemies; my inheritance has become to me like a lion in the forest; she gives her voice against me; therefore I hate her. My inheritance has become to me a ravenous beast, a hyena; come, ravenous beasts, against her on every side; assemble yourselves, all the beasts of the field; let them come to devour. Many shepherds have destroyed my vineyard, they have trodden down my portion, they have made my desirable portion a desolate wilderness. Being made desolate, it mourns, desolate to me; all the land is destroyed, but no man lays it to heart. Therefore have destroyers come up on all the hills of the wilderness, for the sword of Jehovah devours from one end of the land to the other, and no flesh has peace. They have sown wheat and reap thorns; they weary themselves, but shall accomplish nothing; and they are ashamed of their produce from the fierce anger of Jehovah.

4 Thus says Jehovah concerning all my evil neighbors, who smite the inheritance which I caused my people Israel to inherit: Behold, I will pluck them off from their land, and the house of Judah I will pluck out from the midst of them. And after I have plucked them out, I will again have mercy on them, and restore them every one to his inheritance, and every one to his land; and if they will truly learn the ways of my people, to swear by my name, as Jehovah lives, according as my people learned to swear by Baal, then they shall be built up in the midst of my people. But if you will not obey, I will surely pluck up that nation, and it being plucked up, shall perish, says Jehovah.

PROPHECY XIII.   [13.

JEREMIAH'S PARABLE OF THE GIRDLE.

1 THUS said Jehovah to me: Go and buy you a linen girdle, and put it on your loins, and let it not come into water. And I bought a girdle, according to the word of Jehovah, and put it on my loins. And the word of Jehovah came to me a second time, saying, Take

the girdle which you bought, which is on your loins, and arise and go to the Euphrates, and hide it there in a cleft of the rock. And I went and hid it by the Euphrates, as Jehovah commanded me.

2 And after many days, Jehovah said to me, Arise, go to the Euphrates, and take from there the girdle which I commanded you to hide there. And I went to the Euphrates, and dug, and took the girdle from the place where I hid it, and behold the girdle was spoiled, and was good for nothing.

3 Then the word of Jehovah came to me, saying, Thus says Jehovah: Thus will I destroy the beauty of Judah, and the great beauty of Jerusalem. This evil people refuse to hear my word; they walk after the stubbornness of their hearts, and go after other gods, to serve them and to worship them; and they shall be like this girdle, which is good for nothing. For as a girdle adheres to the loins of a man, so did I cause all the house of Israel, and all the house of Judah, to adhere to me, says Jehovah, to be to me for a people, and for a name, and for a praise, and for a glory, and they obeyed not. Say to them, therefore, this word: Thus says Jehovah, the God of Israel: Let every bottle be filled with wine; and they shall say to you, Do we not know very well that every bottle is filled with wine? Then say to them, Thus says Jehovah: Behold, I will fill all the inhabitants of this land, and the kings who sit on the throne of David, and the priests, and the prophets, and all the inhabitants of Jerusalem, with drunkenness, and dash them one against another, both fathers and sons together, says Jehovah; and I will not pity, nor spare, nor have mercy on them, not to destroy them.

4 Hear and attend; be not proud, for Jehovah speaks; give glory to Jehovah your God before he cause darkness, and before your feet stumble on the dark mountains. Then you shall look for light, and he will make it the shade of death; he will make it thick darkness. But if you will not hear, my soul shall weep in secret places for [your] pride, and my eyes shall run down with tears when the flock of Jehovah is carried away captive.

5 Say to the king and to the queen, Humble yourselves and sit down, for your beautiful crowns shall come down from your heads. The cities of the south are shut up, and no one opens them. Judah has gone into captivity, all of it; she is entirely carried away captive. Lift up your eyes, and see those that come from the north; where is the flock that was given you, your beautiful flock? What

will you say when he shall punish you? for you have taught [men] to be hard masters over you. Will not pains seize you as a woman in childbirth? And when you shall say in your heart, Why have these things come on me? For the multitude of your sins are your skirts removed, and your heels made bare.

6 Can the Ethiopian change his skin, or the leopard his spots? then will you be able to do good, who are accustomed to do evil; therefore I will scatter you like straw which flies before the wind of the desert. This is your lot, your measured portion from me, says Jehovah, because you have forgotten me, and trusted in lies. And I will also strip off your skirts over your head, and your shame shall appear; I have seen your adulteries, and your neighings, and your schemes of fornications on the hills of the field, your abominations. Woe to you, Jerusalem! How long ere you will be pure?

PROPHECY XIV.   14, 15.

Word which came to Jeremiah concerning the drouth; [the prophet persecuted, but to be protected.]

1 JUDAH mourns, and her gates languish; they mourn on the ground, and a cry ascends from Jerusalem; for their nobles sent their little ones for water; they went to the cisterns, they found no water; they returned with their vessels empty; they were ashamed and confounded, and covered their heads, because the ground is dismayed, for there has been no rain on the earth. The husbandmen are ashamed, they cover their heads; for even the hind of the field has brought forth, and deserted [her young], because there is no green herb; and the wild asses stand on the hills, they snuff up the air like jackals, their eyes fail because there is no green herb.

2 Though our wickedness testifies against us, Jehovah, do for thy name; for our defections are multiplied, we have sinned against thee. Hope of Israel, his saviour in time of trouble, why art thou like a stranger in the land, like a traveler who spreads his tent to lodge [for a night]? Why art thou like a man astonished, like a mighty man who is not able to save? For thou art in the midst of us, Jehovah, and thy name is called on us; forsake us not.

3 Thus says Jehovah concerning this people: They have so loved to wander, and so little restrained their feet, that Jehovah has not accepted them; now he will remember their wickedness, and pun-

ish their sins. Then Jehovah said to me, Pray not for this people for [their] good ; though they fast, I will not hear their cry, and though they offer burnt offerings and bread offerings, I will not accept them, but will consume them with the sword, and with famine, and with pestilence. Then I said, Ah, Lord Jehovah ! behold, the prophets say to them, You shall not see the sword, nor have famine, but I will give you true peace in this place.

4 Then Jehovah said to me, The prophets prophesy lies in my name ; I sent them not, nor commanded them, neither did I speak to them ; they prophesy to you a false vision, a divination, a vanity, and a deceit of their heart. Therefore thus says Jehovah concerning the prophets, who prophesy in my name, and I sent them not ; and they say, There shall not be sword nor famine in this land : by sword and famine shall these prophets be consumed, and the people to whom they prophesy shall be cast forth in the streets of Jerusalem from before the famine and the sword, and shall have none to bury them, they, their wives, and their sons, and their daughters ; for I will pour out on them their wickedness.

5 And say to them this word : My eyes shall run down with tears night and day, and shall not rest, for the virgin daughter of my people has been wounded with a great wound, and an exceedingly grievous blow. If I go forth to the fields, then behold the killed with the sword ; and if I come to the city, then behold the consumed with famine ; for both the prophet and the priest go about in the earth, they know not whither.

6 Have you entirely rejected Judah ? does your soul abhor Zion ? Why have you smitten us, so that we have no healing ? We looked for peace, and there is no good ; for a time of healing, and behold terror. We know, Jehovah, our wickedness [and] the sin of our fathers, for we have sinned against thee. Reject us not for thy name, dishonor not the throne of thy glory, remember and break not thy covenant with us. Are there among the vanities of the nations any that can cause rain ? or can the heavens give showers ? Art not thou he, Jehovah our God ? And we will trust in thee, for thou doest all these things.

7 Then Jehovah said to me, Though Moses and Samuel stood before me, my soul should not be to this people. Send them from my sight, and let them go. And if they say to you, Whither shall we go ? then say to them, Thus says Jehovah : Those for pestilence, to pestilence ; and those for the sword, to the sword ; and those for

famine, to famine; and those for captivity, to captivity. For I have appointed over them four families, says Jehovah; the sword to kill, and the dogs to drag them about, and the birds of heaven and the beasts of the earth, to devour and destroy. And I will give them over to ill treatment in all the kingdoms of the earth, because of Manasseh the son of Hezekiah, king of Judah, for what he did in Jerusalem. Who then will pity you, Jerusalem, and who will console you, or turn aside to ask for your welfare?

8 You rejected me, says Jehovah, you went back; therefore I will stretch out my hand on you and destroy you. I am tired of pitying, and I will scatter them with a winnowing shovel at the gates of the land. I will bereave, I will destroy my people; they turn not from their ways. Their widows shall be more numerous than the sands of the sea. I will bring up against their mothers the young man that destroys at noon; I will cause anguish and terrors to fall on them suddenly. She that has borne seven shall languish, her soul shall expire, her sun shall go down while it is yet day; she shall be ashamed and confounded; and those that remain of them will I give to the sword before their enemies, says Jehovah.

9 Alas for me, my mother, that you have borne me a man of contention and a man of strife to all the land. For I have not borrowed, nor have men lent me, but they every one curse me. Jehovah said, I will surely release you for good, [and] in a time of trouble and in a time of distress will cause your enemies to come as suppliants to you. Can one break iron, iron from the north, and brass? Your wealth and your treasures I will give for plunder without price, both for all your sins, and in all your bounds. And I will cause [you] to serve your enemies in a land which you know not; for a fire is kindled in my anger which shall burn against you.

10 Thou knowest, Jehovah; remember me, and visit me, and avenge me on my persecutors; do not by thy long suffering take me away; know that for thy sake I bear reproach. Thy words were found, and I eat them, and thy words were to me the joy and gladness of my heart; for thy name was called on me, Jehovah, God of hosts. I sat not in the assembly of dancers, nor rejoiced on account of thy hand; I sat alone, for thou didst fill me with indignation. Why is my pain perpetual, and my wound mortal? It refuses to be healed. Thou hast been to me like a lie, like waters that are not durable.

11 Therefore thus says Jehovah: If you return, then I will

14 *

restore you, and you shall stand before me ; and if you cause the precious to go out from the vile, you shall be as my mouth.   They shall
turn to you, but turn not to them ; and I will make you against this
people a strong brazen wall, and they shall fight against you, but
shall not prevail ; for I am with you to save you, and to deliver
you, says Jehovah ; and I will deliver you from the hand of the
wicked, and redeem you from the hand of tyrants.

PROPHECY · XV.   [16, 17, 4.

THE DESTRUCTION AND CAPTIVITY OF THE JEWS PREDICTED,
AND THEIR RESTORATION.

1 AND the word of Jehovah came to me, saying, Take not a
wife, and have no sons nor daughters in this place ; for thus says
Jehovah concerning the sons and daughters born in this place, and
concerning the mothers that bear them, and concerning the fathers
that beget them in this land : They shall die by fatal diseases ; they
shall not be lamented, nor buried ; they shall be for dung on the
face of the earth ; they shall be consumed by the sword and by
famine, and their dead bodies shall be food for the birds of heaven
and the beasts of the earth.

2 For thus says Jehovah : Go not into a house of wailing, and go
not to lament nor condole with them, for I have taken away my
peace from this people, says Jehovah, the kindness and the mercies.
The great and the small in this land shall die ; they shall not be
buried, and men shall not lament for them, and none shall cut himself, or be the subject of baldness for them ; and men shall not
break bread for them on account of grief, to comfort them for the
dead, nor give them the cup of consolation to drink for their fathers
or for their mothers.   And go not to a house of feasting, to sit
down with them to eat and drink, for thus says the Lord Jehovah,
the God of Israel : Behold, I will cause to cease from this place, before your eyes and in your days, the voice of joy and the voice of
gladness, the voice of the bridegroom and the voice of the bride.

3 And when you declare to this people all these words, and they
say to you, Why has Jehovah spoken against us all these great
evils ? and what is our wickedness, and what is our sin, that we
have committed against Jehovah our God ? then say to them, Because your fathers forsook me, says Jehovah, and went after other

gods, and served them, and worshiped them, and forsook me, and
kept not my law ; and you have done worse than your fathers.
For behold, you walk every one after the hardness of his heart to
do evil, not to obey me.   Therefore I will take you up from this
land to a land which you have not known, neither your fathers ;
and there you shall serve other gods day and night, because I will
show you no favor.

4 Therefore, behold, the days come, says Jehovah, when it shall
not be said any more, As Jehovah lives, who brought up the sons
of Israel from the land of Egypt, but, As Jehovah lives, who brought
up the sons of Israel from the land of the north, and from all lands
to which I had driven them.   For I will bring them again to their
land which I gave to their fathers.   Behold, I will send many fishermen, says Jehovah, and they shall fish them, and afterwards I will
send many hunters, and they shall hunt them from every mountain,
and from every valley, and from the clefts of the rocks ; for my
eyes are on all your ways, they shall not be concealed from me, as
your wickedness has not been concealed from my sight.   And I
will repay their former repeated wickedness, and their sin, because
they defiled my land with the dead bodies of their detestable things,
and filled my inheritance with their abominations.

5 Jehovah, my strength, and my fortress, and my refuge in the
day of distress, to thee shall the nations come from the ends of the
earth, and say, Truly, our fathers inherited a lie, a vanity, and they
did not profit them.   Shall a man make for himself gods which are
not gods ?   Therefore, behold, I will this time cause them to know ;
I will make them know my hand and my power, and they shall
know that my name is Jehovah.

6 The sin of Judah is written with a pen of iron, it is engraved
with the point of a diamond on the tablet of their hearts, and on
the horns of your altars, as their children remember their altars, and
their asherahs, by the green trees on the high hills.   My mountain,
with the country I will give, your wealth and all your treasures, to
be plundered, your high places with your sins in all your bounds ;
you shall depart from your inheritance which I gave you, and I will
make you serve your enemies in a land which you have not known,
for you have kindled a fire of my anger which shall burn forever.

PROPHECY XVL   [17, 5-18.

PIETY CONDUCTS TO PROSPERITY, AND SIN TO MISERY; THE PROPHET SEEKS PROTECTION FROM GOD.

1 THUS says Jehovah: Cursed is the man that trusts in man, and makes flesh his arm, and whose heart departs from Jehovah. He shall be like a ruin in a desert, and shall not see when good comes, but he shall occupy the parched places in the desert, a land of salt, and one not inhabited. Blessed is the man who trusts in Jehovah, and has Jehovah for his confidence. For he shall be like a tree planted by waters, and he shall send out his roots by the stream, and shall not fear when heat comes; and his leaf shall be green, and he shall not be anxious in the year of drouth, nor cease from bearing fruit. The heart is deceitful above all things, and is desperately wicked; who can know it? I Jehovah search the heart, I try the soul, to give every man according to his way, according to the fruit of his doings.

2 He that gathers riches, and not by justice, is a partridge that sits on eggs which she has not laid. In the midst of his days he shall leave [his stores], and in his latter end shall be a fool. The place of our sanctuary has been a glorious height from the beginning. Jehovah, the hope of Israel, all that forsake thee shall be put to shame, and those that depart from thee shall be written in the earth, for they depart from the fountain of living water, from Jehovah.

3 Heal me, Jehovah, and I shall be healed; save me, and I shall be saved; for thou art my praise. Behold, they say to me, Where is the word of Jehovah? let it come, I pray you. As for me, I have not withdrawn myself from being a shepherd after thee, and have not desired the fatal day, thou knowest; the words of my lips have been right before thee. Be not a terror to me; thou art my refuge in the evil day. Let my persecutors be ashamed, but let not me be ashamed; let them be confounded, but let me not be confounded; bring on them the evil day, and destroy them with a double destruction.

PROPHECY XVII.   [17, 19-27.

GOD DEMANDS THE OBSERVANCE OF THE SABBATH.

1 THUS said Jehovah to me : Go and stand in the gate of the sons of the people, through which the kings of Judah come in and go out, and in all the gates of Jerusalem, and say to them, Hear the word of Jehovah, kings of Judah, and all Judah, and all you inhabitants of Jerusalem who go through these gates. Thus says Jehovah : Take heed to yourselves, and carry no load on the Sabbath day, when you enter into the gates of Jerusalem ; and carry not forth a load from your houses on the Sabbath day, and do no work, but hallow the Sabbath day, as I commanded your fathers. But they heard not, nor inclined their ear, and made their neck stiff, that they might not hear, nor receive correction.

2 But if you will attentively hear me, says Jehovah, not to bring in a load by the gates of this city on the Sabbath, and to hallow the Sabbath day, not to do in it any work, then there shall go through the gates of this city kings and princes sitting on the throne of David, riding in chariots and on horses, they and their princes, the men of Judah and the inhabitants of Jerusalem ; and this city shall be inhabited forever. Then shall they come from the cities of Judah, and from about Jerusalem, and from the land of Benjamin, and from the low country, and from the mountain, and from the south, bringing burnt offerings and sacrifices, and bread offerings and frankincense, and bringing thank offerings to the house of Jehovah. But if you will not hear me, to hallow the Sabbath day, and not carry loads and go into the gates of Jerusalem on the Sabbath day, then I will kindle a fire in her gates, and it shall consume the palaces of Jerusalem, and shall not be extinguished.

PROPHECY XVIII.   [18.

THE POTTER AND HIS WORK A TYPE OF GOD AND HIS WORK.

1 THE word which came to Jeremiah from Jehovah, saying, Arise and go down to the house of the potter, and there I will cause you to hear my word. Then I went down to the house of the potter, and behold, he was making a work on the wheel. And the vessel

which he made of the clay was spoiled in the hand of the potter; and he changed his purpose, and made it another vessel, as it was right in the sight of the potter to do.

2 Then the word of Jehovah came to me, saying, Can I not do to you, house of Israel, like the potter, says Jehovah? Behold, like clay in the hand of the potter, so are you in my hand, house of Israel; when I speak concerning a nation and concerning a kingdom, to pluck up, and to cast down, and to destroy, and that nation turns from its wickedness, on account of which I spoke against it, then I will change my mind in respect to the evil which I designed to do it.

3 And when I speak concerning a nation and concerning a kingdom, to build up and to plant, and it does evil in my sight, not to obey my voice, then I will change my mind in respect to the good which I said I would do to it. And now say, I pray you, to the men of Judah, and to the inhabitants of Jerusalem, Thus says Jehovah: Behold, I create evil against you, and devise against you a device. Turn, I pray you, every man from his evil way, and make your ways and your works good. But they said, It is in vain, for we will walk after our devices, and will do every man according to the hardness of his evil heart.

4 Therefore thus says Jehovah: Ask, I pray you, among the nations, Who has heard of such things? The virgin of Israel has committed a horrible deed. Will the snow of Lebanon forsake the rock of the field? Will the streams reject the cold strange waters? Yet my people have forgotten me, that they may burn incense to vanity; they cause men to stumble in their highways, the ancient ways, to walk in paths a way not thrown up; to make their land a desolation, an eternal hissing; every one that passes by it shall be astonished and shake his head. I will scatter them before the enemy as with an east wind; I will show them the back, and not the face, in the day of their calamity.

5 Then they said, Come, let us devise devices against Jeremiah, for the law shall not perish from the priest, nor counsel from the wise, nor the word from the prophet; come, let us smite him with the tongue, and not attend to any of his words. Do thou attend to me, Jehovah, and hear the voice of my adversaries. Shall evil be repaid for good? for they have dug a pit for my life. Remember how I stood before thee and spoke good for them, to turn away thy indignation from them. Therefore give their sons to famine, and

deliver them up to the power of the sword; and let their wives be childless and widows, and let their men be killed with pestilence, and their young men be smitten with the sword in battle. Let a cry be heard from their houses when thou shalt bring a troop on them suddenly; for they have dug a pit to take me, and have laid snares for my feet. But thou, Jehovah, knowest all their counsel against me for death; forgive not their wickedness, nor blot out their sin from before thee, but let them be overthrown before thee; deal with them in the time of thine anger.

PROPHECY XIX.   [19.

THE DESTRUCTION OF JERUSALEM REPRESENTED BY BREAKING AN EARTHEN BOTTLE.

1 THUS says Jehovah: Go and take a bottle, a potter's vessel, and some of the elders of the people, and some of the elders of the priests, and go to the Valley of the son of Hinnom, which is at the entrance of the pottery gate, and proclaim there the word which I shall speak to you, and say, Hear the word of Jehovah, kings of Judah and inhabitants of Jerusalem; thus says Jehovah of hosts, the God of Israel: Behold, I will bring evil on this place, at which all ears that hear shall tingle. Because they have forsaken me, and estranged this place, and burned incense in it to other gods, whom neither they, nor their fathers, nor the kings of Judah knew, and filled this place with the blood of innocents [children]; and built altars to Baal, to burn their sons with fire as burnt offerings to Baal, which I neither commanded nor required, neither did it come into my mind: therefore, behold, the days shall come, says Jehovah, in which this place shall be called no longer Tophet, and Valley of the son of Hinnom, but Valley of the Slaughter.

2 For I will bring to naught the counsel of Judah and Jerusalem in this place, and will cause them to fall by the sword of their enemies, and by the hand of those that seek their life; and I will give their bodies to be food for the birds of heaven and the beasts of the earth, and make this city a desolation and a hissing; all that pass through it shall be astonished and hiss, on account of all its plagues. And I will cause them to eat the flesh of their sons, and the flesh of their daughters; and a man shall eat the flesh of his friend, in the siege and in the distress with which their enemies and those

that seek their lives shall distress them.   Then break the bottle in
the sight of the men who went with you, and say to them, Thus
says Jehovah of hosts : In this manner will I break this people, as
one breaks a potter's vessel, so that it can no more be repaired ;
and they shall be buried in Tophet till there shall be no place for
burial.   Thus will I do to this place, says Jehovah, and to its inhabitants, and make this city like Tophet.   And the houses of Jerusalem and the houses of the kings of Judah shall be impure, like
the place of Tophet, with all the houses on the roofs of which they
have burned incense to all the host of heaven, and poured out libations to other gods.

3 Then Jeremiah came from Tophet, where Jehovah sent him to
prophesy, and stood in the court of the house of Jehovah, and said
to all the people : Thus says Jehovah of hosts, the God of Israel :
Behold, I will bring on this city, and on all its cities, all the evil which
I have spoken against it, because they have hardened their neck
not to obey my words.

PROPHECY XX.   [20.

THE JUDGMENT OF PASHUR FOR PERSECUTION ; THE PROPHET'S CONSOLATIONS, AND HIS EXTREME ANGUISH.

1 THEN Pashur the son of Immer the priest, who was chief prefect of the house of Jehovah, heard Jeremiah when he prophesied
these words ; and Pashur smote Jeremiah the prophet, and put him
in the stocks, which were at the high gate of Benjamin, which was
by the house of Jehovah.

2 And on the next day Pashur took Jeremiah out of the stocks,
and Jeremiah said to him, Jehovah has not called your name Pashur,
but Magor Misabib [terror is on every side] ; for thus says Jehovah :
Behold, I will make you a terror to yourself, and to all your friends ;
and they shall fall by the sword of their enemies, and your eyes shall
see it ; and I will give all Judah into the hands of the king of Babylon,
and he shall carry them away captive to Babylon, and smite them
with the sword.   And I will give all the wealth of this city, and all
its labor, and all its precious things, and all the treasures of the
kings of Judah, into the hand of their enemies ; and they shall
plunder them, and take them, and carry them to Babylon.   And
you, Pashur, and all the inhabitants of your house, shall go into

exile; and you shall go to Babylon, and there you shall die, and there be buried, and all your friends to whom you prophesy falsely.

3 Thou didst persuade me, Jehovah, and I was persuaded; thou art stronger than I, and dost prevail. I am an object of derision all the day; every one mocks me. For as often as I speak, I cry out on account of violence and oppression; for the word of Jehovah is to me a reproach and derision all the day. Then I said, I will not mention him, I will not speak any more in his name; but [his word] was in my heart, like a burning [fire] shut up in my bones, and I was tired of holding in, and could not [be silent]. I heard, indeed, the slander of many; fear was on every side. Tell, that we may report against him; all my familiar friends, that watch at my side, say, Perhaps he will be persuaded, that we may prevail against him, and take our revenge of him.

4 But Jehovah is with me like a mighty man of power; therefore my persecutors shall stumble, and not prevail; because they have not prospered they shall be greatly ashamed with shame that shall never be forgotten. For Jehovah of hosts proves the righteous, he sees soul and heart. I shall see thy vengeance on them, for to thee have I made known my cause. Sing to Jehovah; praise Jehovah; for he delivers the life of the needy from the hand of the wicked.

5 Cursed be the day in which I was born; let not the day in which my mother bore me be blessed. Cursed be the man who brought the good news to my father, saying, A male child is born to you, making him very glad; and let that man be like the cities which Jehovah overthrew, and pitied not; and let him hear a cry in the morning, and a battle shout at noon, because he killed me not from birth, and my mother was not my grave, and her womb with child forever. Why was I born to see trouble and sorrow, that my days should be spent in shame?

PROPHECY XXI.   [21.

THE CAPTURE OF JERUSALEM PREDICTED.

1 THE word which came to Jeremiah from Jehovah, when king Zedekiah sent Pashur the son of Malchiah, and Zephaniah the son of Maaseiah the priest, to him, saying, Inquire, I pray you, concern-

ing us of Jehovah; for Nebuchadrezzar the king of Babylon has made war on us; perhaps Jehovah will do with us according to all his wonderful works, that [Nebuchadrezzar] may go up from us.

2 Then Jeremiah said to them, Say thus to Zedekiah: Thus says Jehovah, the God of Israel: Behold, I will turn back the weapons of war which are in your hands, with which you fight against the king of Babylon and the Chaldeans, that besiege you without the wall, and will assemble them in the midst of this city, and will fight against you with an outstretched hand and a strong arm, and with anger and indignation and great wrath; and I will smite the inhabitants of this city, both man and beast, and they shall die with a great pestilence. And afterward, says Jehovah, I will give Zedekiah king of Judah, and his servants, and the people, and all that remain in this city from the pestilence, from the sword, and from the famine, into the hand of Nebuchadrezzar king of Babylon, and into the hand of their enemies, and into the hand of those that seek their life; and he shall smite them with the edge of the sword; he shall not spare them, nor have mercy on them, nor pity them.

3 And say to this people, Thus says Jehovah: Behold, I set before you the way of life and the way of death; he that remains in this city shall die by the sword, and by famine, and by pestilence; and he that goes out and goes over to the Chaldeans that besiege you, shall live; and his life shall be given him for a prey; for I have set my face against this city for evil, and not for good, says Jehovah; it shall be given into the hand of the king of Babylon, and he shall burn it with fire.

4 And [say] to the house of the king of Judah, Hear the word of Jehovah: House of David, thus says Jehovah: Administer justice in the morning, and deliver the oppressed from the hand of the oppressor, lest my indignation go forth like fire, and burn, and there be none to extinguish it, on account of the evil of your doings.

5 Behold, I am against you, inhabitant of the valley, rock of the plain, says Jehovah, who say, Who shall come down to us? and who shall enter our dwellings? For I will punish you according to the fruit of your doings, says Jehovah; for I will kindle a fire in your forest, and it shall consume all around you.

PROPHECY XXII.

THE HOUSE OF THE KING ADMONISHED ; JEHOIAKIM AND CONIAH TO BE PUNISHED.

1 THUS said Jehovah : Go down to the house of the king of Judah, and speak there this word, and say, Hear the word of Jehovah, king of Judah, who sits on the throne of David, you, and your servants, and your people who go in at these gates.   Thus says Jehovah : Do justice and righteousness, deliver the oppressed from the hand of the oppressor, and do no wrong and no violence to the stranger, and the widow, and the fatherless, and shed not the blood of the innocent in this place ; for if you really do this, then there shall go in at the gates of this house kings sitting for David on his throne, riding in chariots and on horses, they and their servants and their people. .

2 But if you hear not these words, I have sworn by myself, says Jehovah, that this house shall be a ruin. For thus says Jehovah concerning the house of the king of Judah : You are Gilead to me, and the top of Lebanon ; but I will make you a wilderness, and cities not inhabited.   For I have appointed over you destroyers, every man with his weapon, and they shall cut down your choice cedars, and cast them into the fire.   And many nations shall pass by this city, and say every man to his neighbor, Why has Jehovah done thus to this great city ?   And they shall say, Because they forsook the covenant of Jehovah their God, and worshiped other gods, and served them.

3 Weep not for the dead, nor lament for him ; weep bitterly for the living, for he shall return no more, nor see his native land. For thus says Jehovah concerning Shallum the son of Josiah king of Judah, who reigned in the place of Josiah his father, who went forth from this place : He shall return there no more ; but in the place where they have carried him away captive, there shall he die, and see this land no more.

4 Woe to him who builds his house with unrighteousness, and his chambers with injustice ; that makes his neighbor serve him for nothing, and gives him not [a compensation] for his work.   He says, I will build me a large house, and airy apartments, and he rends himself windows, and covers it with cedar, and paints it with

red. Shall you reign because you contend with the cedar ?   Did
not your father eat and drink while he did justice and righteousness ? then it was well with him. He judged faithfully the cause
of the poor and needy ; then it was well.   Is not this to know me ?
says Jehovah.   But you have no eyes nor heart except for your
unrighteous gain, and for the blood of the innocent, to pour it out,
and to practice violence and oppression.

5 Therefore thus says Jehovah concerning Jehoiakim the son of
Josiah king of Judah : They shall not lament for him.   Alas, my
brother ! Alas, my sister ! and Alas, the majesty !   He shall be
buried with the burial of an ass, dragged along and cast forth far
from the gates of Jerusalem.

6 Go up to Lebanon and cry ; lift up your voice in Bashan, and
cry from Abarim [mountains east of the Jordan], for all your friends
are destroyed.   I spoke to you in your prosperity, and you said, I
will not hear.   This has been your way from your youth, for you
heard not my voice.   The wind shall consume your shepherds, and
your friends shall go into exile ; then shall you be ashamed and
confounded for all your wickedness.   You dwelt in Lebanon, and
made your nest in the cedars ; how will you be pitied when pains
come on you like the distress of a woman in childbirth ?

7 As I live, says Jehovah, surely though Coniah the son of Jehoiakim king of Judah were a seal on my right hand, yet from that
would I pluck you, and give you into the hand of those that seek
your life, and into the hand of those whom you fear, even into the
hand of Nebuchadrezzar king of Babylon, and into the hand of the
Chaldeans.   And I will carry you forth, and your mother who bore
you, to a foreign land, where you were not born ; and there you
shall die ; but to the land to which they shall lift up their souls to
return, they shall not return.

8 Is this man Coniah an earthen vessel, despised [and] broken ?
Is he a vessel in which no pleasure is taken ?   Why are he and his
children carried away and cast down in a land which they have not
known ?   Earth, earth, earth, hear the word of Jehovah.   Thus
says Jehovah : Write this man childless ; a man that shall not
prosper in his days, for none of his children shall prosper, nor sit on
the throne of David his father, nor bear rule any longer in Judah.

PROPHECY XXIII.

THE SHEPHERDS TO BE PUNISHED, AND THE JEWS YET TO BE RESTORED TO THEIR LAND UNDER A SON OF DAVID.

1 Woe to the shepherds who destroy and scatter the flock of my feeding, says Jehovah. Therefore thus says Jehovah the God of Israel concerning the shepherds who feed my people : You have scattered my flock, and driven them away, and have not taken care of them ; behold, I will punish you for the evil of your doings, says Jehovah, and will gather the remnant of my flock from all the lands in which I have driven them, and bring them back to their pasture, and they shall be fruitful and multiply ; and I will raise up shepherds over them who shall feed them ; and they shall fear no more, nor be dismayed, nor punished, says Jehovah.

2 Behold, the days come, says Jehovah, in which I will raise up to David a righteous sprout ; and a king shall reign, and he shall be wise, and do justice and righteousness in the land. In his days Judah shall be saved and Israel dwell safely, and this shall be the name by which he shall be called : Jehovah is our righteousness. Therefore, behold, the days shall come, says Jehovah, when they shall no more say, As Jehovah lives, who brought up the sons of Israel from the land of Egypt ; but, As Jehovah lives, who brought up and led the children of the house of Israel from the land of the north, and from all lands to which I have driven them; and they shall live in their land.

PROPHECY XXIV.

CONCERNING THE PROPHETS.

1 My heart is broken within me ; all my bones are relaxed ; I am like a drunken man whom wine has overcome, because of Jehovah, and because of his holy words. For the land is full of adulterers, for the land mourns because of the curse ; the pastures of the wilderness are dried up ; for their oppression is evil, and their power is not just. For both the prophet and the priest are profane, and in my house I have found their wickedness, says Jehovah. Therefore shall their ways be like slippery places ; they shall be driven

away into darkness, and fall in it; for I will bring evil on them the year of their visitation, says Jehovah.

2 And I saw folly in the prophets of Samaria; they prophesied by Baal, and caused the people of Israel to err; and I see horrible wickedness in the prophets of Jerusalem; they commit adultery, and walk in lies, and strengthen the hands of the wicked, that they may all of them become to me like Sodom, and her inhabitants like Gomorrah. Therefore thus says Jehovah of hosts concerning the prophets: Behold, I will feed them with wormwood, and give them an infusion of the poppy to drink; for profaneness has gone forth from the prophets of Jerusalem to all the land.

3 Thus says Jehovah of hosts: Hear not the words of the prophets who prophesy to you; they corrupt you, they speak a vision of their heart, not from the mouth of Jehovah; they say continually to those that despise me, Jehovah says, You shall have peace; and to every one that walks in the hardness of his heart, they say, Evil shall not come on you; for who has stood in the council of Jehovah, and seen and heard his word? who has attended to his word and heard it? Behold, the indignation of Jehovah has gone forth like a whirlwind, and a violent whirlwind shall strike the head of the wicked; the anger of Jehovah shall not turn back till he shall perform, till he shall accomplish the purposes of his heart. In the latter days, you shall learn from it knowledge. I sent not these prophets, but they ran; I spoke not to them, but they prophesied. But if they had stood in my council, and caused my people to hear my words, then they would have turned them from their evil way, and from the evil of their doings.

4 Am I a God at hand, says Jehovah, and not a God at a distance? Can any one hide himself in secret places, that I shall not see him, says Jehovah? Do I not fill heaven and earth? says Jehovah. I have heard what the prophets say, who prophesy in my name falsely, saying, I have dreamed, I have dreamed. How long shall this be in the hearts of the prophets who prophesy falsely, and prophesy the deceit of their heart, [and] design to make the people forget my name, for their dreams which they tell every man to his neighbor, as their fathers forgot my name for Baal? Let the prophet who has a dream tell a dream; and let him who has my word speak my word truly. What is the straw to the wheat, says Jehovah? Has not my word been hitherto like a fire, says Jehovah, and like a hammer which breaks the rock?

Therefore, behold, I am against the prophets, says Jehovah, who steal away my word, each one from his neighbor; behold, I am against the prophets, says Jehovah, who take their tongues and utter oracles; behold, I am against the prophets of false dreams, says Jehovah, for they tell them, and cause my people to err with their lies, and with their boasting; and I sent them not, nor commanded them, and they can not profit this people at all, says Jehovah.

5 And when this people, or a prophet, or a priest, asks you, saying, What is the burden of Jehovah? then say to them, What burden? For I have rejected you, says Jehovah. And as to the prophet, and priest, and people, who shall say, The burden of Jehovah, I will punish that man and that house. Say thus every man to his neighbor, and every man to his brother: What has Jehovah answered? and, What has Jehovah spoken? And you shall not mention any more the burden of Jehovah, but his word shall be to every man a burden; for you have perverted the words of the living God, of our God, Jehovah of hosts. Thus shall you say to the prophet: What has Jehovah answered? and, What has Jehovah spoken? If you say, The burden of Jehovah, therefore thus says Jehovah: Because you say this word, The burden of Jehovah, when I sent to you saying, You shall not say, The burden of Jehovah, therefore, behold, I will entirely forget you, and reject you, and this city which I gave you and your fathers, from before me. And I will put on you eternal reproach and eternal shame, which shall not be forgotten.

PROPHECY XXV.   [24.

THE PARABLE OF THE FIGS.

1 JEHOVAH showed me, and behold, two baskets of figs were set before the temple of Jehovah, after Nebuchadrezzar king of Babylon, carried away captive Jechoniah the son of Jehoiachim king of Judah, and the princes of Judah, and the carpenters and the smiths from Jerusalem, and brought them to Babylon. One basket was of very good figs, like the first ripe figs, and the other basket was of very bad figs, that could not be eaten from badness.

2 And Jehovah said to me, What do you see, Jeremiah? And I said, Figs; the good figs, very good; and the bad, very bad, which can not be eaten from badness. And the word of Jehovah came to me, saying, Thus says Jehovah, the God of Israel: Like these good

figs, so will I regard the captives of Judah, whom I have sent from this place to the land of the Chaldeans, for good. And I will set my eyes on them for good, and restore them to this land, and build them up, and not pull them down ; and plant them, and not pull them up. For I will give them a heart to know me, that I am Je-hovah ; and they shall be my people, and I will be their God ; for they shall turn to me with all their heart.

3 And like the bad figs, which can not be eaten from badness, says Jehovah, so will I make Zedekiah the king of Judah, and all his princes, and the remnant of Jerusalem that remain in this land, and those that live in the land of Egypt ; and I will give them up to agitation and affliction in all the kingdoms of the earth ; and for a reproach, and a proverb, and a derision, and a curse in all places where I shall drive them. And I will send on them the sword, and famine, and pestilence, till they shall be destroyed from the land which I gave to them and to their fathers.

PROPHECY XXVI.   [25.

JEREMIAH PREDICTS THE EXILE OF 70 YEARS IN BABYLON, AND THE JUDGMENTS OF OTHER NATIONS.

1 THE word which came to Jeremiah concerning all the people of Judah in the fourth year of Jehoiakim son of Josiah king of Judah, — this was the first year of Nebuchadrezzar king of Babylon, — which Jeremiah the prophet spoke to all the people of Judah, and to all the inhabitants of Jerusalem, saying, From the 13th year of Josiah the son of Amon king of Judah even to this day, the 23d year, came the word of Jehovah to me, and I spoke to you, rising early and speaking, and you heard not. And Jehovah sent to you all his servants the prophets, rising early and sending them, and you heard not, nor inclined your ear to hear. They said, Turn, we pray you, every man from his evil way, and from the evil of your doings, and live in the land which Jehovah gave to you and to your fathers forever and ever. But go not after other gods to serve them, that you provoke me not with the work of your hands, and I will not do you harm. But you heard me not, says Jehovah, that you might provoke me to anger with the work of your hands to your injury.

2 Therefore thus says Jehovah of hosts : Because you obeyed not my word, behold, I will send and take all the families of the north,

says Jehovah, and Nebuchadrezzar king of Babylon my servant, and bring them against this land and against its inhabitants, and against these nations around, and destroy them, and make them an astonishment and a hissing, and eternal desolations. And I will cause to perish from them the voice of joy and the voice of gladness, and the voice of the bridegroom and the voice of the bride, and the sound of millstones and the light of a lamp. And all this land shall be a waste and a desolation, and these nations shall serve the king of Babylon 70 years.

3 And when the 70 years are completed, I will punish the king of Babylon, and that nation, says Jehovah, for their wickedness, and the land of the Chaldeans, and make it eternal desolations. And I will bring on that land all my words which I have spoken against it, all which are written in this book, in which Jeremiah prophesied concerning all nations. For they also shall serve many and great nations and great kings ; and I will repay them according to their doings, and according to the work of their hands.

4 For thus said Jehovah the God of Israel to me : Take this cup of the wine of indignation from my hand, and give drink from it to all the nations to which I shall send you ; and they shall drink, and be agitated and rage, because of the sword which I will send to them. And I took the cup from the hand of Jehovah, and gave drink to all the nations to whom Jehovah sent me ; to Jerusalem and the cities of Judah, and her kingdoms and her princes, to make them a waste and a desolation, a hissing and a curse, as at this day ; to Pharaoh king of Egypt, and his servants and his princes, and all his people, and all the mixed people, and all the kings of the land of Uz, and all the kings of the land of the Philistines, and to Ascalon and Gaza and Ekron and the remnant of Ashdod, to Edom and Moab and the sons of Ammon, and to all the kings of Tyre and all the kings of Zidon, and to the kings of Ai which are beyond the lake, to Dedan and Tema, and to Buz, and to all who have the hair cut, and all the kings of the Arabs and all the kings of the mixed people who live in the wilderness, and to all the kings of Zimri and all the kings of Elam, and to all the kings of Media and all the kings of the north, near and remote with respect to each other, and to all the kingdoms of the world which are on the face of the earth, and the king of Sheshach [Babylon] shall drink after them. And say to them, Thus says Jehovah of hosts, the God of Israel : Drink, and be drunk and vomit, and fall and rise not before the sword

which I will send among you.   And when they refuse to take the
cup from your hand and drink, then say to them, Thus says Jehovah of hosts : You shall surely drink : for behold, I have begun to
inflict evil on the city which is called by my name, and shall you be
entirely unpunished ?   You shall not be unpunished, for I will call
a sword on all the inhabitants of the earth, says Jehovah of hosts.

5 Therefore prophesy against them all these words, and say to
them, Jehovah will roar from on high, from his holy habitation he
will utter his voice ; he will surely roar against their habitation ; he
will shout like those who tread out the wine against all the inhabitants of the earth, [and] the sound shall reach to the ends of the
earth ; for Jehovah will contend with the nations, he will judge
all flesh, and give the wicked to the sword.

6 Thus says Jehovah of hosts : Behold, evil shall go forth from
nation to nation, and a great whirlwind shall be excited from the
sides of the earth.   In that day the killed by Jehovah shall extend
from one end of the earth to the other ; they shall not be lamented,
nor gathered together, nor buried ; they shall be for dung on the
face of the earth.   Lament, shepherds ; cry and roll in the dust,
chiefs of the flock, for your days have fully come for slaughter, and
I will dash you to pieces, and you shall fall like a desirable vessel.
Flight shall perish from the shepherds, and escape from the chiefs
of the flock.

7 There is a voice of the cry of the shepherds, and of the wailing
of the chiefs of the flock, because Jehovah has destroyed their pasture ; and the peaceful pastures shall be destroyed from before
the fierce anger of Jehovah.   He shall leave like a lion his covert,
for their land shall be a desolation from before cruel wrath, and from
before the fierceness of [God's] anger.

PROPHECY XXVII.   [26.

JEREMIAH PREDICTS THE DESTRUCTION OF THE TEMPLE, AND IS
TRIED FOR HIS LIFE AND ACQUITTED.

1 In the beginning of the reign of Jehoiakim the son of Josiah
king of Judah came this word from Jehovah, saying, Thus says Jehovah : Stand in the court of the house of Jehovah, and speak to
all the cities of Judah, which come to the house of Jehovah to worship, all the words which I command you to speak to them ; with-

hold not a word. Perhaps they will hear, and turn every man from his evil way, and I will change my mind concerning the evil which I have thought to do to them because of the evil of their doings. And say to them, Thus says Jehovah: If you will not hear me, to walk in my law which I set before you, to obey the words of my servants the prophets whom I send to you, rising early and sending them, and you hear not, then I will make this house like Shiloh, and this city a curse to all the nations of the earth.

2 Then the priests and the prophets and all the people heard Jeremiah speak these words in the house of Jehovah. And when Jeremiah finished speaking all that Jehovah commanded him to speak to all the people, then the priests and prophets and all the people took him, saying, You shall surely die. Why have you prophesied in the name of Jehovah, saying, This house shall be like Shiloh, and this city shall be burned without inhabitant? And all the people were assembled together against Jeremiah in the house of Jehovah.

3 And the princes of Judah heard of these things, and went up from the house of the king to the house of Jehovah, and sat at the entrance of the new gate of Jehovah, and the priests and prophets spoke to the princes and to all the people, saying, [Give] judgment of death against this man; for he prophesies against this city, as you have heard with your ears.

4 But Jeremiah spoke to all the princes and to all the people, saying, Jehovah sent me to prophesy, against this house and against this city, all the words which you have heard. And now make your ways and your works good, and hear the voice of Jehovah your God, that Jehovah may change his mind concerning the evil which he has spoken against you. But as for me, behold, I am in your hands; do with me as is good and right in your sight; only know surely, that if you kill me, you will bring the blood of an innocent [man] on yourselves, and on this city, and on its inhabitants; for Jehovah certainly sent me to you to speak in your ears all these words.

5 Then said the princes and all the people to the priests and prophets, [We can not give] judgment of death against this man, for Jehovah our God sent him to speak to us. Then some of the elders of the land arose, and spoke to all the assembly of the people, saying, Micah the Morashthite was a prophet in the days of Hezekiah king of Judah, and he spoke to all the people of Judah,

saying, Thus says Jehovah of hosts : Zion shall be plowed as a
field, and Jerusalem shall be a heap of ruins, and the mountain of
the house, high places of a forest.   Did Hezekiah king of Judah and
all Judah kill him ?   Did they not fear Jehovah, and beseech the
face of Jehovah, so that Jehovah changed his mind concerning the
evil which he spoke against them ?   And shall we do this great
wrong against ourselves ?

6 And [another] man also prophesied in the name of Jehovah,
Urijah the son of Shemaiah, of Kirjathjearim, and he prophesied
against this city, and against this land, according to all the words
of Jeremiah ; and king Jehoiakim and all his mighty men and all
his princes heard his words, and the king sought to kill him, and
Urijah heard of it, and was afraid, and fled, and went to Egypt.   And
king Jehoiakim sent men to Egypt, Elnathan the son of Akbor, and
certain men with him, and they brought Urijah from Egypt, and
took him to king Jehoiakim, and he smote him with the sword, and
cast his dead body into the graves of the common people.   Nevertheless, the hand of Ahikim the son of Shaphan was with Jeremiah, not
to give him into the hand of the people that they should kill him.

PROPHECY XXVIII.   [27.

JEREMIAH ADVISES SUBMISSION TO THE KING OF BABYLON.

1 IN the beginning of the reign of Jehoiakim the son of Josiah
king of Judah came this word to Jeremiah from Jehovah, saying,
Thus said Jehovah to me : Make you bands and a yoke, and put
them on your neck, and send them to the king of Edom, and the
king of Moab, and the king of the sons of Ammon, and the king of
Tyre, and the king of Zidon, by the hand of messengers that come
to Jerusalem, to Zedekiah king of Judah ; and command them for
their masters, saying, Thus says Jehovah of hosts the God of
Israel, Say thus to your masters : I made the earth, and the men
and beasts which are on the face of the earth, by my great power
and outstretched arm, and give the earth to whom I judge best.
And now I have given all these lands into the hand of Nebuchadnezzar king of Babylon, my servant, and have also given him the
beasts of the field to serve him.   And all nations shall serve him,
and his son, and his son's son, till the time of his land shall come,
even his ; and many nations shall serve him, and great kings.   And

the nation and kingdom that will not serve Nebuchadnezzar king of Babylon, and submit its neck to the yoke of the king of Babylon, I will punish that nation, says Jehovah, with the sword, and with famine, and with pestilence, till they shall be consumed by his hand.   Therefore hear not your prophets, nor your diviners, nor your dreamers, nor your magians, nor your sorcerers, who speak to you, saying, Serve not the king of Babylon, for they prophesy a lie to you to remove you far from your land, and that I should drive you out to perish.   But the nations that bring their necks under the yoke of the king of Babylon and serve him, them will I cause to remain in their land, says Jehovah, and they shall cultivate and inhabit it.

2 And I spoke according to all these words to Zedekiah king of Judah, saying, Bring your necks under the yoke of the king of Babylon, and serve him, and be his people.   Why will you die, you and your people, by the sword, and by famine, and by pestilence, as Jehovah has said concerning the nations that will not serve the king of Babylon?   Therefore hear not the words of the prophets who speak to you, saying, Serve not the king of Babylon, for they prophesy to you a lie.   For I sent them not, says Jehovah, but they prophesy falsely in my name, that I may drive you out to perish, you and the prophets who prophesy to you.

3 And I spoke also to the priests and all this people, saying, Thus says Jehovah : Hear not the words of the prophets who prophesy to you, saying, Behold, the vessels of the house of Jehovah shall be brought back from Babylon now shortly, for these prophets prophesy to you a lie.   Hear them not ; serve the king of Babylon and live.   Why should this city become a desolation?   But if they are indeed prophets, and if the word of Jehovah is with them, let them make intercession, I pray you, to Jehovah of hosts, that the vessels which are left in the house of Jehovah, and in the house of the king of Judah, and in Jerusalem, may not go to Babylon.   For thus says Jehovah of hosts concerning the pillars, and the sea, and the bases, and the rest of the vessels which are left in this city, which Nebuchadnezzar king of Babylon took not when he carried away captive Jeconiah the son of Jehoiakim king of Judah from Jerusalem to Babylon, with all the nobles of Judah and Jerusalem ; for thus says Jehovah of hosts, the God of Israel, concerning the vessels left of the house of Jehovah, and of the house of the king of Judah and of Jerusalem : They shall be carried to Babylon, and there shall they

be till the day when I shall visit them, says Jehovah. Then will I bring them up, and restore them to this place.

PROPHECY XXIX.   [28.

THE PROPHET HANANIAH ; HIS PROPHECIES AND DEATH.

1 AND in the same year, in the beginning of the reign of Zede-kiah king of Judah, in the 4th [year], in the fifth month, Hananiah the son of Azzur the prophet, who was in Gibeon, spoke to me in the house of Jehovah, in the sight of the priests and of all the peo-ple, saying, Thus says Jehovah of hosts, the God of Israel : I will break the yoke of the king of Babylon. Within two years I will restore to this place all the vessels of the house of Jehovah which Nebuchadnezzar king of Babylon took from this place and carried to Babylon ; and Jechoniah the son of Jehoiakim king of Judah, and all the captives of Judah who went to Babylon, will I bring again to this place, says Jehovah ; for I will break the yoke of the king of Babylon.

2 Then Jeremiah the prophet spoke to Hananiah the prophet, in the sight of the priests, and of all the people who stood in the house of Jehovah ; and Jeremiah the prophet said, Amen, so may Jehovah do ; may Jehovah establish your word which you have prophesied, to restore the vessels of the house of Jehovah, and all the captives from Babylon to this place. Nevertheless, hear, I pray you, this word which I speak in your ears, and in the ears of all the people. The prophets who were before me, and before you, from of old, also prophesied against many lands and great kingdoms, of war, and evil, and pestilence. The prophet who prophesies of peace, when the word of the prophet comes to pass, the prophet shall be known, that Jehovah sent him in truth.

3 Then Hananiah the prophet took the yoke from the neck of Jeremiah the prophet, and broke it ; and Hananiah spoke in the sight of all the people, saying, Thus says Jehovah : In this manner will I break the yoke of Nebuchadnezzar king of Babylon, within two years, from the neck of all nations ; and Jeremiah the prophet went his way.

4 Then the word of Jehovah came to Jeremiah after Hananiah the prophet broke the yoke from the neck of Jeremiah the prophet, saying, Go and speak to Hananiah, saying, Thus says Jehovah :

You broke a yoke of wood, but I will make in the place of it a yoke of iron ; for thus says Jehovah of hosts, the God of Israel : I have put a yoke of iron on the neck of all these nations, that they may serve Nebuchadnezzar king of Babylon ; and they shall serve him ; and I have given him also the beasts of the field.

5 Then said Jeremiah the prophet to Hananiah the prophet, Hear, I pray you, Hananiah : Jehovah did not send you, and you have made this people trust in a lie ; therefore thus says Jehovah : Behold, I will cast you on the face of the ground ; this year you shall die ; for you have taught defection from Jehovah.   And the prophet Hananiah died that year in the seventh month.

PROPHECY XXX.   [29.

JEREMIAH'S LETTER TO THE CAPTIVES AT BABYLON.

1 AND these are the words of the letter which Jeremiah the prophet sent from Jerusalem to the rest of the elders of the exiles, and the priests, and prophets, and all the people, whom Nebuchadnezzar carried away captive from Jerusalem to Babylon, after the departure of Jechoniah the king, and the queen, and the eunuchs, the princes of Judah and of Jerusalem, and the carpenters and smiths from Jerusalem, by the hand of Eleasah the son of Shaphan, and Gemariah the son of Hilkiah, whom Zedekiah king of Judah sent to Nebuchadnezzar king of Babylon, saying, Thus says Jehovah of hosts, the God of Israel, to all the exiles whom I have carried into exile from Jerusalem to Babylon : Build houses and live in them, and plant vineyards and eat their fruit ; take wives, and have sons and daughters ; and take wives for your sons, and give your daughters to husbands, that they may have sons and daughters ; and increase there, and be not few.   And seek the peace of the city where I have carried you into exile, and pray for it to Jehovah, for in its peace shall you have peace.

2 For thus says Jehovah of hosts, the God of Israel : Let not your prophets which are in the midst of you, and your magi, deceive you ; and hear not to your dreams which you cause to be dreamed ; for they prophesy falsely to you in my name ; I sent them not, says Jehovah.   For thus says Jehovah : At the completion of 70 years in Babylon I will visit you, and confirm toward you my good word, that I would bring you back to this place ; for I

know the purposes which I purpose concerning you, says Jehovah, purposes of peace, and not of evil, to give you a latter end and hope.

3 Then you shall call on me, and go and pray to me, and I will hear you ; and you shall seek me, and find me, when you seek me with all your heart. And I will be found by you, says Jehovah, and I will bring back your captives, and gather them from all nations, and from all places to which I have driven you, says Jehovah, and bring you again to the place from which I caused you to be carried into exile.

4 Since you say, Jehovah has raised us up prophets in Babylon, surely thus says Jehovah concerning the king who sits on the throne of David, and all the people that dwell in this city, your brothers who went not forth with you into captivity ; thus says Jehovah of hosts : Behold, I will send on them the sword, and famine, and pestilence, and make them like bad figs, that can not be eaten from badness. And I will pursue them with sword, and famine, and pestilence, and give them up for ill treatment to all kingdoms of the earth, for a a curse, and an astonishment, and a hissing, and for a reproach among all nations whither I drive them ; because they did not hear my word, says Jehovah, when I sent to them my servants the prophets, rising early and sending them, but you would not hear, says Jehovah. Hear, therefore, the word of Jehovah, all you exiles whom I have sent from Jerusalem to Babylon.

5 Thus says Jehovah of hosts, the God of Israel, concerning Ahab the son of Kolaiah, and Zedekiah the son of Maaseiah, who prophesy to you a lie in my name : Behold, I will give them into the hand of Nebuchadrezzar king of Babylon, and he shall smite them in your sight. And a curse shall be taken from them by all the exiles of Judah in Babylon, saying, May Jehovah make you like Zedekiah and like Ahab, whom the king of Babylon roasted with fire ; because they practiced folly in Israel, and committed adultery with the wives of their friends, and spoke words falsely in my name, which I did not command •them ; but I knew it, and was a witness, says Jehovah.

6 And to Shemaiah the Nehelamite, speak, saying, Thus says Jehovah of hosts, the God of Israel : Because you sent letters in your name, saying to all the people at Jerusalem, and to Zephaniah the son of Maaseiah the priest, and to all the priests, saying that Jehovah has made you priest, that there should be officers of the house of Jehovah for every one that is mad, and that prophesies,

and that you should put him in stocks, and in racks; now, therefore, why have you not rebuked Jeremiah of Anathoth, who prophesies to you? For he sent letters to us at Babylon, saying, This exile is long; build houses and live; and plant vineyards, and eat the fruit of them. And Zephaniah the priest read this letter in the ears of Jeremiah the prophet.

7 Then came the word of Jehovah to Jeremiah the prophet, saying, Send to all the exiles, saying, Thus says Jehovah concerning Shemaiah the Nehelamite: Because Shemaiah prophesied to you, and I sent him not, and he caused you to trust in a lie, therefore thus says Jehovah: Behold, I will punish Shemaiah the Nehelamite, and his children. There shall not be a man descending from him remaining in the midst of this people, neither shall he see the good which I will do my people, says Jehovah, because he has taught defection from Jehovah.

PROPHECY XXXI.   [30, 31.

A RETURN FROM THE BABYLONIAN EXILE PREDICTED.

1 THE word which came to Jeremiah from Jehovah, saying, Thus said Jehovah, the God of Israel: Write all the words which I have spoken to you in a book; for behold, the days come, says Jehovah, in which I will bring back the exiles of my people, Israel and Judah, says Jehovah, and cause them to return to the land which I gave their fathers, and they shall possess it; and these are the words which Jehovah spoke concerning Israel and Judah.

2 For thus says Jehovah: We heard a voice of trembling; there is fear, and not peace. Ask, I pray you, and see: does a male bear children? Why do I see every man with his hands on his loins, like a woman in childbirth? And all faces are turned to paleness. Alas! for great is that day, so that none is like it, for it is the time of Jacob's trouble, but he shall be saved from it.

3 For in that day, says Jehovah of hosts, I will break off his yoke from your neck, and burst your bands, and strangers shall no more cause them to serve; but they shall serve Jehovah their God, and David their king, whom I will raise up for them. Therefore fear not my servant, Jacob, says Jehovah, nor be dismayed, Israel, for behold, I will save you from afar, and your children from the land of their captivity, and Jacob shall return and be quiet and flourish,

16 *

and none shall make him afraid. For I will be with you, says Jehovah, to save you; for I will make a destruction of all nations among which I have dispersed you, but will not make a destruction of you, but will correct you justly, and not leave you entirely unpunished.

4 For thus says Jehovah: Your bruise is desperate, and your wound incurable. No one has given advice for a cure, no healing applications have been made to you. All your friends have forgotten you, they inquire not for you; for I smote you with the wound of an enemy, with a severe correction, on account of the magnitude of your wickedness, because your sins were great. Why do you cry because of your bruise? Your pain is without remedy, on account of the magnitude of your wickedness. Because your sins were great have I done these things to you. Therefore all that consume you shall be consumed, and all your adversaries shall go into captivity, and all that plundered you shall be for plunder, and all that preyed on you shall be for a prey; for I will restore soundness to you, and heal your wounds, says Jehovah, though they call you Zion the outcast, whom no man inquires for.

5 Thus says Jehovah: Behold, I will bring back the exiles of the tents of Jacob, and have mercy on his dwelling places; and the city shall be built on its ruins, and the palace be inhabited in its [former] manner; and thanksgiving shall go forth from them, and the voice of dancers; and I will increase them, and they shall not be few, and glorify them, and they shall not be small; and their children shall be as of old, and their congregation shall be established before me, and I will punish all their oppressors. And their chief shall proceed from themselves, and their ruler go forth from the midst of them; and I will cause them to approach, and they shall come near to me; for who is he that has pledged his heart to come near to me? says Jehovah. And you shall be my people, and I will be your God.

6 Behold, a tempest of the indignation of Jehovah has gone forth; a storm stirs itself up, and shall fall on the head of the wicked; the anger of Jehovah shall not turn back till he executes, till he accomplishes the purposes of his heart. In the latter days you shall understand it fully. At that time, says Jehovah, I will be a God to all the families of Israel, and they shall be my people.

7 Thus says Jehovah: The people, the remains of the sword, shall find favor in the wilderness when I go to cause Israel to rest. Je-

hovah appeared to me from afar, [saying], And I loved you with an eternal love ; therefore have I prolonged [my] kindness to you. I will yet build you up, and you shall be built up, virgin of Israel ; you shall yet adorn yourself with tabrets, and go forth with the dance of the dancers ; you shall yet plant vines on the mountains of Samaria ; the planters shall plant and gather for common use ; for the time shall come when the watchmen on mount Ephraim shall cry, Arise, and let us go up to Zion, to Jehovah our God.

8 For thus says Jehovah : Sing for Jacob [with] gladness ; shout for the chief of the nations ; declare, cry aloud, and say, Jehovah, let thy people, the remnant of Israel, be saved.   Behold, I will bring them from the land of the north, and gather them from the sides of the earth, [and] with them the blind and lame, her that is with child, and her that is bearing children together ; a great company shall return thither ; they shall come with weeping, and I will bring them with supplications, and conduct them to streams in a plain way, in which they shall not stumble, for I will be a father to Israel, and Ephraim shall be my first born.

9 Hear the word of Jehovah, nations, and declare it to the distant islands, and say, He that scattered Israel will gather him, and keep him as a shepherd [keeps] his flock.   For Jehovah will redeem Jacob, and ransom him from the hand of those that are stronger than he ; and they shall come and sing on the heights of Zion, and flow to the good of Jehovah, to the grain, and wine, and oil, and to the young of the flocks and herds, and they shall be plentifully supplied, and be anxious no more.   Then shall the virgin rejoice in the dance, and young men and old men together, for I will change their mourning into rejoicing, and have mercy on them, and make them glad from their sorrow.   And I will plentifully supply the priests with fatness, and my people shall be satisfied with good, says Jehovah.

10 Thus says Jehovah : A voice is heard in Ramah, lamentation and bitter weeping ; Rachel weeping for her sons, she refuses to be comforted for her sons, because they are not.   Thus says Jehovah : Restrain your voice from weeping, and your eyes from tears, for there shall be a reward of your work, says Jehovah, and they shall return from the land of the enemy.   There is hope for your latter end, says Jehovah, that your sons shall return to their bounds.

11 I have long heard Ephraim mourn : Thou hast corrected me, and I was corrected like a bullock untaught ; turn me, that I may

be turned, for thou art Jehovah my God; for after I have turned I
will change my mind, and after I am made to understand, I will
smite on [my] thigh.   I am ashamed and confounded, for I have borne
the reproach of my youth.   Is Ephraim my dear son? is he a
pleasant child? for as often as I speak of him I affectionately remember him still.   Therefore my bowels are pained for him; I will
surely have mercy on him, says Jehovah.

12 Set up pillars for yourself, set up for yourself columns, give
your attention to the way which you went; return, daughter of
Israel, return to these your cities.   How long will you wander
about, refractory daughter? for Jehovah has created a new thing on
the earth : the female shall protect the male.

13 Thus says Jehovah of hosts, the God of Israel : They shall yet
say this word in the land of Judah, and in its cities, when I return
their exiles: May Jehovah bless you, habitation of righteousness,
mountain of holiness; and Judah shall dwell in it and in all his cities
together; husbandmen also shall go forth with flocks.   For I will sati-
ate the soul of the thirsty, and fill every hungry soul.   For this I
will awake and see, and my sleep shall be sweet to me.

14 Behold, the days come, says Jehovah, in which I will sow
the house of Israel and the house of Judah with the seed both of
man and beast; and as I have watched over them to pluck up and
throw down, and destroy and injure, so will I watch over them to
build up and plant, says Jehovah.   In those days they shall no
more say, The fathers eat sour grapes, and the children's teeth are
blunted, but every man shall die for his wickedness, and every man
who eats sour grapes shall have his teeth blunted.

15 Behold, the days come, says Jehovah, in which I will make with
the house of Israel and the house of Judah a new covenant, not according to the covenant which I made with their fathers, in the day in
which I took them by the hand to bring them up out of the land of
Egypt; for they broke my covenant, and I rejected them, says Jehovah.   But this is the covenant which I will make with the house
of Israel, after those days, says Jehovah.   I will put my law within
them, and write it on their hearts, and will be their God, and they
shall be my people.   And they shall no more teach every one his
friend, and every one his brother, saying, Know Jehovah; for all of
them shall know me, from the least to the greatest, says Jehovah;
for I will forgive their wickedness, and their sins I will remember
no more.

16 Thus says Jehovah, who gives the sun for a light by day, the ordinances of the moon and stars for a light by night, who stirs up the sea that its waves roar; Jehovah of hosts is his name: If these ordinances shall depart from before me, says Jehovah, then also shall the posterity of Israel cease to be a nation before me forever. Thus says Jehovah: If the heavens can be measured above, and the foundations of the earth searched out below, then will I also reject all the posterity of Israel for all that they have done, says Jehovah.

17 Behold the days come, says Jehovah, in which the city of Jehovah shall be built up from the tower of Hanameel to the corner gate, and the measuring line shall go forth over against it, even to the hill of Gareb, and shall extend around to Goath; and all the valley of the dead bodies and of the ashes, and all the fields to the brook Kidron, to the corner of the horse gate towards the east, shall be a sanctuary of Jehovah; it shall not be plucked up, nor thrown down forever.

PROPHECY XXXII. [32.

JEREMIAH'S LAND PURCHASE.

1 THE word which came to Jeremiah in the 10th year of Zedekiah king of Judah, which was the 18th year of Nebuchadrezzar. And at that time the army of the king of Babylon was besieging Jerusalem, and Jeremiah the prophet was shut up in the court of the prison, which was in the house of the king of Judah. For Zedekiah the king of Judah shut him up, saying, Why have you prophesied, saying, Thus says Jehovah: Behold, I will give this city into the hand of the king of Babylon, and he shall take it, and Zedekiah king of Judah shall not be delivered from the hand of the Chaldeans, but shall surely be given into the hand of the king of Babylon; and he shall speak with him mouth to mouth, and his eyes shall see his eyes; and he shall lead Zedekiah to Babylon, and there shall he be till I visit him, says Jehovah; though you fight with the Chaldeans, you shall not prosper?

2 Then Jeremiah said, The word of Jehovah came to me, saying, Behold, Hanameel the son of Shallum your uncle will come to you, saying, Buy for yourself my field which is in Anathoth, for the right of redemption belongs to you to buy. And Hanameel my uncle's son came to me according to the word of Jehovah, to the court of

the prison; and he said to me, Buy, I pray you, my field which is in Anathoth in the land of Benjamin, for the right of inheritance belongs to you, and the redemption belongs to you; buy it for yourself. Then I knew that it was the word of Jehovah, and I bought the field, which is in Anathoth, of Hanameel my uncle's son, and weighed him the silver, 17 shekels of silver [$9.52], and wrote it in a book, and sealed it up, and took witnesses, and weighed the silver in scales.

3 And I took the book of purchase [the deed], that which was sealed according to the law and ordinances, and that which was open; and I gave the book of purchase to Baruch, the son of Neriah the son of Maaseiah in the presence of Hanameel my uncle, and in the presence of the witnesses who subscribed [their names] in the book of purchase, before the Jews who sat in the court of the prison. And I charged Baruch in their presence, saying, Thus says Jehovah of hosts, the God of Israel: Take these books, this book of purchase that is sealed, and this book which is open, and put them in an earthen vessel, that they may continue many days. For thus says Jehovah of hosts, the God of Israel: Houses and fields and vineyards, shall yet be bought in this land.

4 And after I gave the book of the purchase to Baruch the son of Neriah, I prayed, saying, Ah, Lord Jehovah, behold, thou hast made the heavens and the earth by thy great power, and by thy outstretched arm, and nothing is too wonderful for thee. Thou showest kindness to thousands, and repayest the wickedness of fathers into the bosom of their children after them; God the great, the mighty, Jehovah of hosts, is his name; great in counsel and mighty in action, whose eyes are open on all the ways of the sons of men, to give each man according to his ways, and according to the fruit of his doings; who hast shown signs and wonders in the land of Egypt even to this day, both in Israel and among [other] men, and hast made thee a name as at this day; and thou didst bring thy people Israel out of the land of Egypt with signs and wonders, and with a strong hand, and with an outstretched arm, and with great terror, and give them this land, which thou didst swear to their fathers that thou wouldst give them, a land flowing with milk and honey.

5 And they went in and possessed it, but obeyed not thy voice, and walked not in thy law, [and] did not all which thou commandedst them; and thou hast called [down] on them all this evil. Behold, the mounds of the enemy have already come against the city

to take it, and the city is given up to the hand of the Chaldeans, who fight against it with the sword, and famine, and pestilence; and what thou saidst has occurred, and behold, thou seest it. But thou saidst to me, Lord Jehovah, Buy you a field for money, and take witnesses, though this city is given into the hand of the Chaldeans.

6 And the word of Jehovah came to Jeremiah, saying, Behold, I Jehovah am the God of all flesh; is any thing too wonderful for me? Therefore thus says Jehovah : Behold, I will give this city into the hand of the Chaldeans, and into the hand of Nebuchadrezzar king of Babylon, and he shall take it. And the Chaldeans shall come and fight against this city, and set this city on fire, and burn it, and the houses on whose roofs they have burned incense to Baal, and poured out libations to other gods, to provoke me to anger. For the sons of Israel and the sons of Judah have done only evil in my sight from their youth; indeed, the sons of Israel have only provoked me to anger with the work of their hands, says Jehovah. For this city has been an object of my anger and my indignation from the day in which they built it to this day, that I might remove it from my sight, for all the wickedness of the sons of Israel and the sons of Judah, which they have committed to provoke me to anger, they, their kings, their princes, their priests, and their prophets, both the men of Judah and the inhabitants of Jerusalem.

7 For they have turned to me the back, and not the face; though I taught them, rising early and teaching, yet they heard not to receive correction. And they set their abominations in the house which is called by my name, to defile it, and built the high places to Baal which are in the valley of the son of Hinnom, to cause their sons and their daughters to pass through [the fire] to Moloch, which I commanded them not; and it came not into my mind that they should commit this abomination to cause Judah to sin.

8 And now, therefore, thus says Jehovah, the God of Israel, to this city, of which you say, It is given into the hand of the king of Babylon by the sword, and famine, and pestilence : Behold, I will gather them from all the lands to which I drive them in my anger, and in my indignation, and in great wrath, to this place, and will cause them to live securely; and they shall be my people, and I will be their God; and I will give them one heart, and one way to fear me forever for their good, and for the good of their sons after them.

9 And I will make with them an eternal covenant that I will not turn away from them, but will do them good, and put my fear in their heart, that they may not depart from me ; and I will rejoice over them to do them good, and plant them in this land in truth, with all my heart and with all my soul.   For thus says Jehovah : As I have brought on this people all this great evil, so will I bring on them all the good which I promise them.   And fields shall be bought in this land, of which you say, It is a desolation without man or beast ; it is given into the hand of the Chaldeans.   They shall buy fields for money, and write them in books, and seal them, and witness them, in the land of Benjamin, and in the places about Jerusalem, and in the cities of Judah, in the cities of the mountain, and in the cities of the plain, and in the cities of the south, for I will bring back their captives, says Jehovah.

PROPHECY XXXIII.   [33.

JEREMIAH PREDICTS THE RETURN FROM THE BABYLONIAN EXILE.

1 AND the word of Jehovah came to Jeremiah a second time, while he was yet shut up in the court of the prison, saying, Thus says Jehovah, who made [Zion], who formed her and established her ; Jehovah is his name.   Call on me, and I will answer you, and show you great things and difficult, which you know not.   For thus says Jehovah, the God of Israel, concerning the houses of this city, and the houses of the kings of Judah, which are thrown down for the mounds and for the sword that are about to fight with the Chaldeans, and to fill them with the dead bodies of the men whom I have smitten in my anger, and in my indignation, because I have hid my face from this city on account of all their wickedness.

2 Behold, I will apply to her a bandage and healing, and I will heal them, and show them an abundance of peace and truth.   And I will restore the captives of Judah and the captives of Israel, and will build them up as at first ; and I will purify them from all their wickedness which they commit against me, and will forgive all their wickedness which they commit against me, and in which they transgress against me ; and [the city] shall be to me a name of joy and praise and beauty to all nations of the earth, which shall hear of all the good that I do them ; and they shall fear and tremble on account of all the good and all the peace which I bestow on it.

3 Thus says Jehovah : There shall yet be heard in this place of which you say, It is waste, without man and without beast, in the cities of Judah and in the streets of Jerusalem, which are destroyed without man, and without inhabitant, and without beast, the voice of joy and the voice of gladness, the voice of the bridegroom and the voice of the bride, the voice of those who say, Praise Jehovah of hosts ; for Jehovah is good ; for his kindness is forever, of those that bring a thank offering to the house of Jehovah ; for I will restore the captives of the land as at first, says Jehovah.

4 Thus says Jehovah of hosts : There shall yet be in this place, which is waste, with no man, and not even a beast in all his cities, a pasture of shepherds causing flocks to lie down. In the cities of the mountain, in the cities of the plain, and in the cities of the south, and in the land of Benjamin, and in the environs of Jerusalem, and in the cities of Judah, shall flocks yet pass on the hands of him that counts them, says Jehovah.

5 Behold, the days come, says Jehovah, in which I will perform my good word which I spoke to the house of Israel, and concerning the house of Judah. In those days and at that time I will cause to grow to David a sprout of righteousness, and he shall do justice and righteousness in the earth. In those days Judah shall be saved, and Jerusalem shall be inhabited in security ; and this is the name by which they shall be called, Jehovah is our righteousness. For thus says Jehovah : There shall not be cut off from David a man sitting on the throne of the house of Israel ; and of the priests [and] scribes a man shall not be cut off from before me, to offer the burnt offerings, and to furnish bread offerings, and to offer sacrifices forever.

6 And the word of Jehovah came to Jeremiah, saying, Thus says Jehovah : If you can break my covenant of day and my covenant of night, that there shall not be day and night in their time, then may my covenant with David my servant be broken, that he shall not have a son reigning on his throne, and with the Levites [and] priests, my ministers. As the host of heaven, which can not be numbered, and the sand of the sea, which can not be measured, so will I multiply the children of David my servant, and the Levites my ministers.

7 And the word of Jehovah came to Jeremiah, saying, Have you not seen what this people say ? The two families which Jehovah chose, them has he also rejected ; and they despise my people as

being no longer a nation before them. Thus says Jehovah : If I have not established my covenant with day and night, the ordinances of heaven and earth, then will I reject the children of Jacob and of David my servant, not to take of his children for rulers over the children of Abraham, Isaac, and Jacob ; for I will restore their captives, and have mercy on them.

PROPHECY XXXIV.   [34, 1-7.

THE CAPTURE AND DESTRUCTION OF JERUSALEM PREDICTED, AND THE HONORABLE BURIAL OF ZEDEKIAH.

1 THE word which came to Jeremiah from Jehovah, when Nebuchadnezzar king of Babylon, and all his host, and the kingdoms of the earth, the dominion of his hand, and all the peoples fought against Jerusalem, and against all her cities, saying, Thus says Jehovah, the God of Israel : Go and say to Zedekiah king of Judah, Thus says Jehovah : Behold, I will give this city into the hand of the king of Babylon, and he shall burn it with fire, and you shall not be delivered from his hand ; for you shall surely be taken, and given into his hand, and your eyes shall see the eyes of the king of Babylon, and his mouth shall speak to your mouth, and you shall go to Babylon.

2 But hear the word of Jehovah, Zedekiah king of Judah. Thus says Jehovah concerning you : You shall not die by the sword ; you shall die in peace, and they shall burn you with the burnings of the first kings your fathers, who were before you ; and they shall lament for you, Alas, lord! for I have spoken [this] word, says Jehovah.

3 And Jeremiah the prophet spoke all these words to Zedekiah king of Judah in Jerusalem; and the army of the king of Babylon fought against Jerusalem and against all the cities of Judah that were left, against Lachish, and against Azeka ; for they were left of the cities of Judah, fortified cities.

PROPHECY XXXV.　　　　[34, 8-22.

THE LIBERATION OF SERVANTS, AND THEIR REDUCTION TO SERVI-
TUDE A SECOND TIME ; GOD'S WORD ON THE OCCASION.

1 THE word which came to Jeremiah from Jehovah, after king
Zedekiah made a covenant with all the people which were in Jerusalem, to proclaim liberty to them, that each man should let go his
man servant, and each man his female servant, a Hebrew and a He-
brewess, free, that they should not cause them to serve any man his
brother that was a Jew.　And all the princes obeyed, and all the
people who came into covenant that each one should let his man
servant and each one his female servant go free, not to serve them
any more ; and they obeyed, and let them go.　Then they turned
afterward, and took back their man servants and female servants
whom they had let go free, and subjugated them for man servants
and female servants.

2 Then came the word of Jehovah to Jeremiah from Jehovah,
saying, Thus says Jehovah the God of Israel : I made a covenant
with your fathers in the day in which I brought them out of the land
of Egypt, out of the house of servants, saying, At the end of seven
years you shall let go every man his brother, a Hebrew, who has
been sold to you.　When he has served you six years, then you shall
let him go free from being with you ; and your fathers obeyed me
not, nor inclined their ear.　But you turned this day, and did that
which is right in my sight, to proclaim liberty every one to his
friend ; and you made a covenant before me in the house which is
called by my name.　Then you turned and profaned my name, and
took back every man his man servant, and every man his female
servant, whom you had let go free for their lives, and you subjugated them to be your man servants and your female servants.

3 Therefore thus says Jehovah : You have not obeyed me to proclaim liberty every man to his brother, and every man to his friend.
Behold, I proclaim to you liberty, says Jehovah, for the sword, for
pestilence, and for famine ; and I will give you up for injurious
treatment to all kingdoms of the earth ; and I will give the men
who transgress my covenant, who perform not the words of the
covenant which they made before me, when they cut the bullock in

two, and passed between its pieces ; the princes of Judah and the princes of Jerusalem, the eunuchs and priests, and all the people of the land who passed between the pieces of the bullock, I will even give them into the hand of their enemies, and into the hand of those that seek their life ; and their dead bodies shall be for food to the birds of heaven and beasts of the earth. And I will give Zedekiah king of Judah and his princes into the hand of their enemies, and into the hand of those that seek their life, and into the hand of the army of the king of Babylon, which has gone up from against you. Behold, I will command, says Jehovah, and bring them back to this city, and they shall fight against it, and take it, and burn it with fire ; and the cities of Judah will I make a desolation without inhabitant.

PROPHECY XXXVI.   [35.

THE FILIAL PIETY OF THE RECHABITES ; THE JEWS REPROVED BY IT ; THE RECHABITES BLESSED FOR IT.

1 THE word which came to Jeremiah from Jehovah, in the days of Jehoiakim the son of Josiah king of Judah, saying, Go to the house of the Rechabites, and speak to them, and bring them to the house of Jehovah, to one of the chambers, and give them wine to drink. Then I took Jaazaniah the son of Jeremiah son of Habaziniah, and his brothers, and all his sons, and all the house of the Rechabites, and brought them to the house of Jehovah, to the chamber of the sons of Hanan the son of Igdaliah, a man of God, which was by the side of the chamber of the princes, that was over the chamber of Maaseiah the son of Shallum the doorkeeper.

2 And I set before the sons of the house of the Rechabites goblets and cups full of wine, and said to them, Drink wine. But they said, We do not drink wine, for Jonadab the son of Rechab our father commanded us, saying, You shall not drink wine, you nor your sons forever, nor build houses, nor sow seed, nor plant vineyards, nor have them ; but you shall live in tents always, that your days may be many on the face of the earth in which you live as strangers. And we have obeyed the voice of Jonadab the son of Rechab our father, in respect to all which he commanded us, not to drink wine, we, our wives, our sons, and our daughters ; nor to build houses to live in ; and we have no vineyards, fields, nor seed ;

but live in tents, and do according to all that Jonadab our father commanded us.   But when Nebuchadrezzar king of Babylon came up against the land, we said, Come, let us go to Jerusalem from before the army of the Chaldeans, and from before the army of Syria ; so we live in Jerusalem.

3 Then came the word of Jehovah to Jeremiah, saying, Thus says Jehovah of hosts, the God of Israel : Go and say to the men of Judah and the inhabitants of Jerusalem, Will you not receive correction to hear my words, says Jehovah ?   The words of Jonadab the son of Rechab, who commanded his sons not to drink wine, are performed, and they drink not wine to this day, for they obey the command of their father ; but I spoke to you, rising early and speaking, and you obey me not.   And I sent you all my servants, the prophets, rising early and sending, saying, Turn, I pray you, every man from his evil ways, and make your works good, and go not after other gods to serve them, and live in the land which I gave to you and to your fathers ; and you incline not your ear, and obey me not.   For the sons of Jonadab the son of Rechab perform the command of their father which he commanded them ; but this people do not obey me.   Therefore thus says Jehovah, the God of hosts, the God of Israel : Behold, I will bring on Judah, and on all the inhabitants of Jerusalem, all the evil which I have spoken against them ; because I spoke to them, and they did not hear ; I called them, and they did not answer.

4 But to the house of the Rechabites Jeremiah said, Thus says Jehovah of hosts, the God of Israel : Because you obey the command of Jonadab your father, and keep all his commands, and do according to all that he commanded you, therefore thus says Jehovah of hosts, the God of Israel : There shall not fail a man from Jonadab the son of Rechab to stand before me forever.

PROPHECY XXXVII.   [36.

JEREMIAH'S PROPHECIES WRITTEN, AND READ TO THE PEOPLE, AND BURNED.

1 AND in the 4th year of Jehoiakim son of Josiah king of Judah came this word to Jeremiah from Jehovah, saying, Take a book roll, and write on it the words which I have spoken to you concerning Israel and Judah, and all nations, from the day that I spoke to you,

17 *

from the days of Josiah to this day. Perhaps the house of Judah
will hear all the evil which I purpose to do to them, that they may
turn every man from his evil way, and I will forgive their wickedness and their sins.

2 Then Jeremiah called Baruch the son of Neriah; and Baruch
wrote from the mouth of Jeremiah all the words of Jehovah which
he had spoken to him on the book roll. And Jeremiah commanded
Baruch, saying, I am shut up, I can not go to the house of Jehovah;
but do you go and read from the roll, which you have written from
my mouth, the words of Jehovah in the ears of the people, in the
house of Jehovah, on the day of the fast; and read them also in the
ears of all Judah that go in at their gates. Perhaps they will fall
down in their supplications before Jehovah, and turn every man
from his evil way; for great is the anger and indignation which
Jehovah has spoken against this people. And Baruch the son of
Neriah did according to all which Jeremiah the prophet commanded,
and read from the book the words of Jehovah, in the house of
Jehovah.

3 And in the 5th year of Jehoiakim the son of Josiah king of Judah, in the ninth month, they proclaimed a fast before Jehovah for all
the people in Jerusalem, and all the people that came to Jerusalem
from the cities of Judah. And Baruch read in the book the words
of Jeremiah in the house of Jehovah, in the chamber of Gemariah
the son of Shaphan the scribe, in the high court, at the entrance of
the new gate of the house of Jehovah, in the ears of all the people. And Micah the son of Gemariah the son of Shaphan heard
all the words of Jehovah from the book; and he went down to the
king, to the chamber of the scribe, and behold, all the princes were
sitting there — Elishama the scribe, Dalaiah the son of Shemaiah,
and Elnathan the son of Akbor, and Gemariah the son of Shaphan,
and Zedekiah the son of Hananiah, and all the princes.

4 And Micah told them all the words which he heard when
Baruch read in the book in the ears of the people. Then all the
princes sent Jehudi the son of Nethaniah son of Shelemiah son of
Cushi, saying, Take in hand the roll which you read in the ears of
the people, and come. And Baruch the son of Neriah took the
roll in his hand, and went to them. And they said to him, Sit
down, we pray you, and read it in our ears; and Baruch read in
their ears.

5 And when they heard all the words, they were afraid every

man of his friend, and said to Baruch, We must surely tell the king all these words. And they asked Baruch, saying, Tell us, we pray you, how did you write all these words from his mouth? And Baruch said to them, He pronounced to me all these words, and I wrote them in the book with ink. Then said the princes to Baruch, Go and hide yourself, you and Jeremiah, and let no man know where you are.

6 And they went to the king to the court, but the roll they laid up in the chamber of Elishama the scribe. And they told all things in the ears of the king, and the king sent Jehudi to take the roll, and he took it from the chamber of Elishama the scribe, and Jehudi read it in the ears of the king, and in the ears of all the princes that stood before the king. And the king sat in his winter house, in the ninth month, and the stove was burning before him; and when he had read three or four columns, he cut it with a writer's knife, and cast it into the fire which was in the stove, till all the roll was consumed in the fire which was in the stove.

7 And neither the king nor any of his servants who heard all these words were afraid, nor rent their garments; and though Elnathan, and Delaiah, and Gemariah interceded with the king not to burn the roll, yet he heard not to them. And the king commanded Jerameel the king's son, and Seraiah the son of Azriel, and Shelemiah the son of Abdiel, to take Baruch the scribe, and Jeremiah the prophet; but Jehovah concealed them.

8 Then came the word of Jehovah to Jeremiah, after the king burned the roll, and the words which Baruch had written from the mouth of Jeremiah, saying, Again take another roll, and write on it all the former words which were on the first roll that Jehoiakim king of Judah burned; and say concerning Jehoiakim the king, Thus says Jehovah: You burned that roll, saying, Why did you write on it, saying, The king of Babylon shall come and destroy this land, and make man and beast to cease out of it? Therefore thus says Jehovah, concerning Jehoiakim king of Judah, He shall not have one to sit on the throne of David, and his dead body shall be cast out to the heat by day and the frost by night. And I will punish him and his children and his servants for their wickedness, and bring on them, and on the inhabitants of Jerusalem, and on the men of Judah, all the evil which I have spoken against them, and they heard not.

9 Then Jeremiah took another roll, and gave it to Baruch the son

of Neriah the scribe, and he wrote on it from the mouth of Jeremiah
all the words of the roll which Jehoiakim king of Judah burned
with fire ; and besides, many similar words were added to them.

PROPHECY XXXVIII.   [37, 38.

JEREMIAH IMPRISONED, SAVED FROM PERISHING BY EBED MELECK, AND ADVISING THE KING.

1 AND king Zedekiah the son of Josiah reigned instead of Coniah the son of Jehoiakim, whom Nebuchadrezzar king of Babylon
made king in the land of Judah.   But neither he, nor his servants,
nor the people of the land obeyed the words of Jehovah which he
spoke by the hand of Jeremiah the prophet.   And king Zedekiah
sent Jehucal son of Shelemiah, and Zephaniah son of Maaseiah the
priest to Jeremiah the prophet, saying, Pray, I beseech you, for us
to Jehovah our God.

2 And Jeremiah came in and went out in the midst of the people,
for they had not [yet] cast him into prison.   And Pharaoh's army
came forth from Egypt, and the Chaldeans, who were besieging Jerusalem, heard the report of them, and went up from Jerusalem.

3 And the word of Jehovah came to Jeremiah the prophet, saying, Thus says Jehovah, the God of Israel : Say thus to the king of
Judah, who sends you to me to inquire of me : Behold, the army of
Pharaoh, which is coming out to you for help, will return to its land,
to Egypt, and the Chaldeans will return and fight against this city,
and burn it with fire.   Thus says Jehovah : Deceive not yourselves,
saying, The Chaldeans will surely go up from us ; for they shall not
go.   But if you had smitten all the army of the Chaldeans that fight
against you, and there remained only wounded men among them
each in his tent, they should rise up and burn this city with fire.

4 And when the army of the Chaldeans went up from Jerusalem,
from before the army of Pharaoh, then Jeremiah went down from
Jerusalem to go to the land of Benjamin, to receive his portion there
among the people.   And when he was in the gate of Benjamin, a
master of the guards was there, whose name was Irijah, son of
Shelemiah, son of Hananiah, and he took Jeremiah the prophet,
saying, You are deserting to the Chaldeans.   And Jeremiah said, It
is false ; I am not deserting to the Chaldeans.   But he did not
hear to him ; and Irijah took Jeremiah and brought him to the

princes; and the princes were angry at Jeremiah, and smote him, and cast him into prison in the house of Jonathan the scribe, for they made that a prison.

5 But when Jeremiah had gone into the dungeon, and into the stocks, and had remained there many days, then king Zedekiah sent and took him out; and the king asked him in his house privately, and said, Is there any word from Jehovah? And Jeremiah said, There is; and he said, You shall be given into the hand of the king of Babylon.

6 And Jeremiah said to king Zedekiah, What sin have I committed against you, or your servants, or this people, that you put me in prison? And where are your prophets that prophesied to you, saying, The king of Babylon shall not come against you, nor against this land? But now hear, I pray you, my lord the king; let my supplication, I pray you, be acceptable before you, and send me not back to the house of Jonathan the scribe, that I may not die there.

7 Then Zedekiah the king commanded that they should keep Jeremiah in the court of the prison, and he gave him a loaf of bread daily from the bakers' street, till all the bread was consumed from the city, and Jeremiah remained in the court of the prison.

8 And Shephatiah, son of Mattan, and Gedaliah, son of Pashur, and Jucal, son of Shelemiah, and Pashur, son of Malchiah, heard the words which Jeremiah spoke to all the people, saying, Thus says Jehovah: He that remains in this city shall die by the sword, and famine, and pestilence, but he that goes out to the Chaldeans shall live, and he shall have his life for a prey, and shall live; thus says Jehovah: This city shall surely be given into the hand of the army of the king of Babylon, and he shall take it. Then said the princes to the king, Let this man, we pray you, be put to death; because he weakens the hands of the men of war who remain in this city, and the hands of all the people, by speaking to them according to these words; for this man seeks not the peace of this people, but their injury. Then king Zedekiah said, Behold, he is in your hands, for the king can do nothing against you.

9 Then they took Jeremiah and cast him into the dungeon of Malkiah, the son of Hammelech, which was in the court of the prison, and let Jeremiah down with cords, and there was no water in the dungeon, but mud, and Jeremiah sunk in the mud. And Ebed Melech the Ethiopian, a eunuch, heard, for he was in the house of the king, that they had put Jeremiah into the dungeon, and

the king sat in the gate of Benjamin.   Then went Ebed Melech
from the house of the king, and spoke to the king, saying, My lord
the king, those men have done evil in all that they have done to
Jeremiah the prophet, whom they have cast into the dungeon ; for
he was dead in his place from famine, for there is no more bread in
the city.   And the king commanded Ebed Melech the Ethiopian,
saying, Take with you from here 30 men, and bring up Jeremiah the
prophet from the dungeon before he dies.

10 And Ebed Melech took with him 30 men, and went to the
house of the king, to the room under the treasury, and took from it
torn rags and worn-out rags, and let them down to Jeremiah, into
the dungeon, with cords.   And Ebed Melech the Ethiopian said to
Jeremiah, Put, I pray you, the torn and worn-out rags under the
sides of your hands, under the cords ; and Jeremiah did so.   And
they drew up Jeremiah with the cords, and took him up out of the
dungeon, and Jeremiah remained in the court of the prison.

11 Then king Zedekiah sent and took Jeremiah the prophet to him
in the third entrance of the house of Jehovah.   And the king said to
Jeremiah, I will ask you a thing ; hide not a word from me.   And
Jeremiah said to Zedekiah, When I tell you, will you certainly not
kill me ? and if I give you advice, will you hear me ?   And king
Zedekiah swore to Jeremiah secretly, saying, As Jehovah lives, who
has made for us this life, I will not kill you, nor give you into the
hands of those men who seek your life.

12 And Jeremiah said to Zedekiah, Thus says Jehovah, the God
of hosts, the God of Israel : If you will go forth to the princes of
the king of Babylon, then you shall preserve your life, and this city
shall not be burned with fire, and you shall live, you and your house ;
but if you will not go out to the princes of the king of Babylon,
then this city shall be given into the hand of the Chaldeans, and
they shall burn it with fire, and you shall not be delivered from their
hand.   And king Zedekiah said to Jeremiah, I am afraid of the
Jews who have deserted to the Chaldeans, lest they should give me
into their hands, and they will mock me.

13 And Jeremiah said, They shall not give you up.   Hear, I pray
you, the voice of Jehovah, according to what I speak to you, that it
may be well with you, and that you may preserve your life.   But if
you refuse to go out, this is the word which Jehovah has shown me :
Behold, all the women which are left in the house of the king of
Judah shall be brought out to the princes of the king of Babylon ;

and behold, they shall say, Your friends have incited you, and prevailed against you ; your feet have sunk down in the mire, they are turned back. And all your wives and your sons shall they bring out to the Chaldeans, and you shall not be delivered from their hand, but shall be taken by the hand of the king of Babylon, and this city shall be burned with fire.

14 Then said Zedekiah to Jeremiah, Let no man know of these words, and you shall not die. And if the princes hear that I have spoken with you, and come and say to you, Tell us, we pray you, what you said to the king, and what the king said to you, and hide it not from us, and we will not kill you ; then say to them, I presented my supplication before the king, that he would not send me back to the house of Jonathan to die there.

15 Then came all the princes to Jeremiah, and asked him, and he told them according to these words which the king commanded, and they withdrew quietly from him, for the matter was not heard. And Jeremiah remained in the court of the prison till the day on which Jerusalem was taken.

PROPHECY XXXIX.   [39.

JERUSALEM TAKEN AND DESTROYED ; MISERIES INFLICTED ON THE JEWS ; FAVOR SHOWN TO JEREMIAH, ETC.

1 AND when Jerusalem was taken, in the 9th year of Zedekiah king of Judah, in the tenth month, came Nebuchadrezzar king of Babylon and all his army to Jerusalem, and besieged it. In the 11th year of Zedekiah, in the fourth month, on the 9th day of the month, was the city taken ; and all the princes of the king of Babylon came and sat in the middle gate. Nergal Sharezer, Samgarnebo, Sarsechim, prefects of the eunuchs, Nergal Sharezer prefect of the Magi, and all the rest of the princes of the king of Babylon. And when Zedekiah king of Judah saw them and all the men of war, then they fled, and went out by night from the city, by the way of the king's garden, by the gate between the two walls, and they went toward the wilderness.

2 But the army of the Chaldeans pursued them, and overtook Zedekiah in the wilderness of Jericho, and they took him, and carried him up to Nebuchadrezzar king of Babylon, to Riblah, in the land of Hamath, and he pronounced judgment on him. And the

king of Babylon killed the sons of Zedekiah in Riblah before his
eyes, and the king of Babylon killed all the nobles of Judah, and
he put out the eyes of Zedekiah, and bound him with fetters of
brass, to bring him to Babylon.

3 And the Chaldeans burned the house of the king and the
houses of the people with fire, and threw down the walls of Jerusalem. And the rest of the people that remained in the city, and the
deserters who had deserted to him, and the rest of the people that
remained, did Nebuzaradan, chief of the executioners, carry captive
to Babylon. But Nebuzaradan, chief of the executioners, caused
the poor of the people, who had nothing, to remain in the land of
Judah, and gave them vineyards and fields at that time.

4 And Nebuchadrezzar king of Babylon commanded concerning
Jeremiah, by the hand of Nebuzaradan, chief of the executioners,
saying, Take him and set your eyes on him, and do him no injury;
but do to him as he shall say to you. Then sent Nebuzaradan,
chief of the executioners, and Nebushazban, chief of the eunuchs,
and Nergal Sharezer, chief of the Magi, and all the chiefs of the
king of Babylon; then they sent and took Jeremiah from the court
of the prison, and gave him to Gedaliah, the son of Ahikam, the
son of Shaphan, that they should carry him home; and he lived in
the midst of the people.

5 And the word of Jehovah came to Jeremiah when he was shut
up in the court of the prison, saying, Go and speak to Ebed Melech
the Ethiopian, saying, Thus says Jehovah of hosts, the God of Israel: Behold, I will bring my words on this city for evil, and not
for good, and they shall be before you in that day; but in that day
I will deliver you, says Jehovah, and you shall not be given into the
hand of men whom you fear, for I will deliver you, and you shall
not fall by the sword; you shall have your life for a prey, because
you have trusted in me, says Jehovah.

PROPHECY XL. [40, 41.

JEREMIAH'S RETURN TO GEDALIAH; GEDALIAH'S DEATH, AND EVENTS THAT FOLLOWED IT.

1 THE word which came to Jeremiah from Jehovah, after Nebuzaradan, chief of the executioners, sent him from Ramah, where
he had taken him, and he was bound with chains in the midst of

all the captives of Jerusalem and Judah who were carried away captive to Babylon.

2 The chief of the executioners took Jeremiah, and said to him, Jehovah your God spoke this evil against this place, and Jehovah brought it to pass, and did as he said, for you sinned against Jehovah, and obeyed not his voice; therefore has this thing come on you. And now, behold, I release you this day from the manacles which are on your hands. If it seems good to you to go with me to Babylon, then I will set my eyes on you; but if it is evil in your eyes to go with me to Babylon, forbear; see, all the land is before you; where it is good and right in your eyes to go, there go.

3 And when he did not yet return, [he said], Return to Gedaliah, the son of Ahikam, the son of Shaphan, whom the king of Babylon has placed over the cities of Judah, and live with him in the midst of the people; or, wherever it is right in your eyes to go, go. And the chief of the guards gave him an allowance for the way, and a present, and dismissed him. And Jeremiah came to Gedaliah, the son of Ahikam, at Mizpah, and lived with him in the midst of the people who remained in the land.

4 And all the captains of the forces which were in the country, and their men, heard that the king of Babylon had made Gedaliah, the son of Ahikam, governor in the land, and that he had committed to him men and women and children and some of the poor of the land, of those that they had not carried away captive to Babylon; and they came to Gedaliah to Mizpah, both Ishmael, son of Nethaniah, and Johanan and Jonathan, sons of Kareah, and Seriah, son of Tanhumeth, and the sons of Ephai the Netophathite, and Jazaniah, son of the Maachathite, and their men. And Gedaliah, son of Ahikam, son of Shaphan, swore to them and to their men, saying, Fear not to serve the Chaldeans; live in the land and serve the king of Babylon, and it shall be well with you. And as for me, behold, I will live at Mizpah, to stand before the Chaldeans who will come to us; but do you collect wine and fruits and oil, and put them in your vessels, and live in your cities which you have taken. And all the Jews also who were in Moab, and among the sons of Ammon, and in Edom, and who were in all lands, heard that the king of Babylon had given a remnant to Judah, and placed Gedaliah, the son of Ahikam, the son of Shaphan, over them; and all the Jews returned from all places to which they had been driven, and came to the land

of Judah to Gedaliah, to Mizpah, and collected wine and fruit a great abundance.

5 And Johanan, the son of Kareah, and all the captains of the forces which were in the country, came to Gedaliah, to Mizpah, and said to him, Do you know certainly that Baalis, king of the sons of Ammon, has sent Ishmael, the son of Nethaniah, to kill you? And Gedaliah, son of Ahikam, did not believe them. And Johanan, son of Kareah, spoke to Gedaliah secretly in Mizpah, saying, Let me go, I pray you, and I will smite Ishmael, son of Nethaniah, and not a man shall know it. Why should he kill you, and all the Jews that are gathered together to you be scattered, and the remnant of Judah perish? And Gedaliah, son of Ahikam, said to Johanan, son of Kareah, You shall not do this thing, for you speak falsely against Ishmael.

6 And in the seventh month, Ishmael, the son of Nethaniah, Elishama, of the royal family, and one of the chiefs of the king, and 10 men with him, came to Gedaliah, son of Ahikam, at Mizpah, and they eat bread there together in Mizpah. And Ishmael, the son of Nethaniah, and the 10 men who were with him, arose and smote Gedaliah, son of Ahikam, son of Shaphan, with the sword, and killed him, whom the king of Babylon had placed over the land. And Ishmael smote all the Jews who were with Gedaliah in Mizpah, and the Chaldeans who were found there, and the men of war.

7 And the second day after he had killed Gedaliah, no man knew it; and 80 men came from Shechem, from Shiloh, and from Samaria, with their beards shaved and their clothes rent, and having cut themselves, and with a bread offering and frankincense in their hands, to bring to the house of Jehovah. And Ishmael, son of Nethaniah, went out to meet them from Mizpah, weeping as he went; and when he approached them, he said to them, Come to Gedaliah, the son of Ahikam. And when they came into the midst of the city, then Ishmael, the son of Nethaniah, and the men that were with him, killed them, and cast them into the pit.

8 But 10 men were found among them, who said to Ishmael, Kill us not, for we have wheat, and barley, and oil, and honey, hid in the field. And he forbore, and did not kill them, with their brothers. And the pit into which Ishmael cast the bodies of the men whom he killed, with Gedaliah, was that which king Asa made, on account of Baasha, king of Israel. Ishmael, son of Nethaniah, filled it with the killed. And Ishmael took captive all the rest of

the people who were in Mizpah, the daughters of the king, and all the people who were left in Mizpah, over whom Nebuzaradan, the chief executioner, had set Gedaliah, the son of Ahikam; Ishmael, the son of Nethaniah, took them captive, and went to pass over to the sons of Ammon.

9 And Johanan, the son of Kareah, and all the captains of the forces which were with him, heard of all the evil which Ishmael, the son of Nethaniah, had done, and they took all the men and went to fight with Ishmael, the son of Nethaniah. And they found him at the great waters which were in Gibeon. And when all the people who were with Ishmael saw Johanan, the son of Kareah, and all the captains of the forces who were with him, they were glad; and all the people whom Ishmael had carried away captive from Mizpah turned about, and returned and went to Johanan, the son of Kareah. And Ishmael, the son of Nethaniah, escaped with eight men from before Johanan, and went to the sons of Ammon.

10 And Johanan, son of Kareah, and all the captains of the forces who were with him, took all the rest of the people whom he had recovered from Ishmael, son of Nethaniah, from Mizpah, after he had smitten Gedaliah, the son of Ahikam, mighty men, men of war, and women and children and eunuchs, whom he brought back from Gibeon; and they went and stopped at the encampment of Chimham, which is by the side of Bethlehem, for journeying to go to Egypt from before the Chaldeans, for they were afraid of them, because Ishmael, son of Nethaniah, had smitten Gedaliah, son of Ahikam, whom the king of Babylon placed over the land.

PROPHECY XLI.   42, 43, 7.

THEY ASK THE PRAYERS AND ADVICE OF JEREMIAH, BUT DO NOT FOLLOW HIS ADVICE; THEIR CONDUCT DENOUNCED.

1 AND all the captains of the forces, and Johanan, son of Kareah, and Jazaniah, son of Hoshaiah, and all the people, from the least to the greatest, came near and said to Jeremiah the prophet, Let our supplication, we pray you, be accepted before you, and pray for us to Jehovah your God, for all this remnant; for we are left a few from many, as your eyes see us; that Jehovah your God may show us the way in which we should go, and the thing which we should do.

2 And Jeremiah the prophet said to them, I hear; behold, I will

pray to Jehovah your God, according to your words, and all that Jehovah shall answer you, I will tell you ; I will keep back nothing from you.   And they said to Jeremiah, Let Jehovah be to us a true and faithful witness, that according to all the words which Jehovah your God shall send us, so will we do ; whether it is good, or whether it is evil, we will obey the voice of Jehovah our God, to whom we send you, that it may be well with us when we obey the voice of Jehovah our God.

3 And at the end of 10 days the word of Jehovah came to Jeremiah, and he called Johanan, son of Kareah, and all the captains of the forces who were with him, and the people, from the smallest to the greatest, and said to them, Thus says Jehovah, the God of Israel, to whom you sent me to present your supplications before him : If you will settle permanently in this land I will build you up, and not pull you down ; and plant you, and not pull you up.   For I have changed my mind in respect to the evil which I have done you.   Fear not the king of Babylon, of whom you are afraid, says Jehovah, for I will be with you to save you, and to deliver you from his hand ; and will show you mercies, and he shall have mercy on and restore you to your land.

4 But if you say, We will not live in this land, and obey not the voice of Jehovah your God, saying, No, but we will go to the land of Egypt, where war is not seen, and the sound of the trumpet not heard, and there is no want of bread, and there will we live ; then hear now the word of Jehovah, remnant of Judah.   Thus says Jehovah of hosts, the God of Israel : If you really set your faces to go to Egypt, and go to live there, then the sword of which you are afraid shall overtake you there in the land of Egypt ; and the famine about which you are anxious shall follow you there to Egypt, and there you shall die ; and all the men who set their faces to go to Egypt to live there shall die by sword, by famine, and by pestilence ; and there shall not be to them a remnant, or any that escape from the evil which I will bring on them.   For thus says Jehovah of hosts, the God of Israel : As I have poured out my anger and my indignation on the inhabitants of Jerusalem, so shall my indignation be poured out on you when you come to Egypt, and you shall be a curse, and an astonishment, and a contempt and reproach, and shall see this place no more.

5 Jehovah says to you, remnant of Judah, Go not to Egypt. Know, surely, that I have warned you this day.   For you err against

your lives ; for you sent me to Jehovah your God, saying, Pray for us to Jehovah our God, and according to all that Jehovah our God shall say to us, so tell us, and we will do it. And I tell you this day, and you will not obey the voice of Jehovah your God in any thing for which he has sent me to you. And now, know surely, that by the sword, by famine, and by pestilence, you shall die in the place where you are pleased to go to live there.

6 And when Jeremiah had finished speaking to the people all these words of Jehovah their God, with which Jehovah their God had sent him to them, [even] all these words, then spoke Azariah, the son of Hoshaiah, and Johanan, the son of Kareah, and all the proud men, to Jeremiah, saying, You say what is false ; Jehovah our God has not sent you, saying, You shall not go to Egypt to live there ; but Baruch, the son of Neriah, has incited you against us, to give us into the hand of the Chaldeans to kill us, and to carry us away captives to Babylon.

7 And neither Johanan, the son of Kareah, nor any of the captains of the forces, nor any of the people, obeyed the voice of Jehovah, to live in the land of Judah. And Johanan, the son of Kareah, and all the captains of the forces, took all the remnant of Judah who had returned from all nations to which they were driven, to live in the land of Judah, the men, and women, and children, and the daughters of the king, and every soul which Nebuzaradan, chief of the executioners, had left with Gedaliah, son of Ahikam, son of Shaphan, and Jeremiah the prophet, and Baruch, the son of Neriah, and they went to the land of Egypt ; for they obeyed not the voice of Jehovah ; and they went to Tahpanhes [Daphne].

PROPHECY XLII. [43, 8–13, 44.

JEREMIAH PREDICTS THE CONQUEST OF EGYPT BY NEBUCHAD-
REZZAR, AND THE DESTRUCTION OF THE JEWS IN EGYPT.

1 THEN came the word of Jehovah to Jeremiah in Tahpanhes, saying, Take in your hand great stones, and hide them in the mortar in the brick kiln, which is at the entrance of the house of Pharaoh, in Tahpanhes, in the sight of the Jews, and say to them, Thus says Jehovah of hosts, the God of Israel : Behold, I will send and take Nebuchadrezzar, king of Babylon, my servant, and set his throne on these stones which I have hid, and he shall stretch his

18 *

splendor over them, and shall come and smite the land of Egypt.
Those who are for death [shall be given up] to death, and those
who are for captivity to captivity, and those who are for the sword
to the sword. And I will kindle a fire in the houses of the gods
of Egypt, and he shall burn them, and carry them away captive,
and put on the land of Egypt, as a shepherd puts on his garment,
and go from it in peace. And he shall break in pieces the images
of Bethshemesh, which are in the land of Egypt, and burn them
with fire.

2 The word which came to Jeremiah concerning all the Jews living in the land of Egypt, in Migdol, and at Tahpanhes, and at Noph,
and in the land of Pathros, saying, Thus says Jehovah of hosts, the
God of Israel: You have seen all the evil which I brought on
Jerusalem, and on all the cities of Judah, and behold, they are a desolation this day, and none lives in them, because of their wickedness
which they committed to provoke me to anger, in going to burn incense to serve other gods, which neither you nor your fathers knew.
And I sent to you all my servants the prophets, rising early and sending, saying, Do not, I pray you, this abominable thing which I hate.
And they obeyed not, nor inclined their ear, to turn from their wickedness, not to burn incense to other gods. Therefore my indignation and my anger have been poured out, and have consumed the
cities of Judah and the streets of Jerusalem, and they have become
a waste and a desolation as at this day.

3 And now, thus says Jehovah, the God of hosts, the God of
Israel: Why do you commit this great evil against your lives, to
cut off from yourselves man and woman, child and nursing infant,
from the midst of Judah, so as to leave you no remnant, to provoke
me to anger with the work of your hands, to burn incense to other
gods in the land of Egypt, where you have gone to live, to cut yourselves off, and that you may be a curse and reproach among all
nations of the earth? Have you forgotten the wickedness of your
fathers, and the wickedness of the kings of Judah, and the wickedness
of their wives, and your wickedness, and the wickedness of your
wives, which they committed in the land of Judah and in the streets
of Jerusalem? They have not been humbled to this day, neither
have they feared nor walked in my law and in my ordinances,
which I set before you and before your fathers.

4 Therefore thus says Jehovah of hosts, the God of Israel:
Behold, I have set my face against you for evil, even to cut off all

Judah. And I will take the remnant of Judah which set their faces to go to the land of Egypt to live there, and they shall all be consumed in the land of Egypt; they shall fall by the sword and by famine; they shall be consumed, from the least to the greatest, by the sword, and they shall die by famine; and they shall be a curse, an astonishment, and a contempt and reproach. And I will punish those who live in the land of Egypt, as I punished Jerusalem, with the sword, with famine, and with pestilence; and there shall not be any to escape or remain of the remnant of Judah that have gone to live in the land of Egypt, and to return to the land of Judah, to which they lift up their souls to return to live; for there shall none return, except a [few] that escape.

5 Then all the men who knew that their wives burned incense to other gods, and all the women who stood by, a great company, and all the people who lived in the land of Egypt and in Pathros, answered Jeremiah, saying, As for this word which you have spoken to us in the name of Jehovah, we will not obey you. But we will surely perform all the words which have gone out of our mouth, to burn [incense] to the queen of heaven, and to pour out to her libations as we have done, we and our fathers, our kings and our princes, in the cities of Judah and in the streets of Jerusalem; and we were satisfied with bread, and were prosperous, and saw no evil. But from the time that we ceased to burn incense to the queen of heaven, and to pour out libations to her, we have wanted all things, and been consumed by sword and famine. And [the women said], But when we burned incense to the queen of heaven, and poured out libations to her, did we, without our husbands, make cakes to worship her, and pour out libations to her?

6 Then said Jeremiah to all the people, to the men and women, and to all the people who gave him that answer, As to the burning of incense which you performed in the cities of Judah and in the streets of Jerusalem, you and your fathers, your kings and your princes, and the people of the land, did not Jehovah remember them? And did they not come into his mind? And Jehovah could no longer bear the evil of your doings, and the abominations which you committed; therefore has your land become a desolation, and an astonishment, and a curse, without inhabitant, as at this day. Because you burned incense, and because you sinned against Jehovah, and obeyed not the voice of Jehovah, nor walked in his

law, nor in his ordinances, nor in his precepts; therefore has this evil come on you as at this day.

7 Then Jeremiah said to all the people, and to all the women, Hear the word of Jehovah, all Judah which is in the land of Egypt. Thus says Jehovah of hosts, the God of Israel: You and your wives speak with your mouths and perform with your hands, saying, We will perform our vows which we have vowed, to burn incense to the queen of heaven, and to pour out libations to her. You will certainly perform your vows, and will certainly accomplish your vows. Therefore hear the word of Jehovah, all you Jews who live in the land of Egypt: Behold, I have sworn by my great name, says Jehovah, that my name shall no more be pronounced by the mouth of any man of Judah, saying, As the Lord Jehovah lives, in all the land of Egypt. Behold, I will watch over them for evil, and not for good, and all the men of Judah who are in the land of Egypt shall be destroyed by the sword and by famine, till they are consumed. And those that escape from the sword shall return from the land of Egypt to the land of Judah, few in number; and all the remnant of Judah which have gone to the land of Egypt to live there, shall know whose word shall stand, mine or theirs. And this shall be a sign to you, says Jehovah; for I will punish you in this place, that you may know that my words shall surely stand against you for evil.

8 Thus says Jehovah: Behold, I will give Pharaoh Hophra king of Egypt into the hand of his enemies, and into the hand of those that seek his life, as I gave Zedekiah king of Judah into the hand of Nebuchadrezzar king of Babylon, that sought his life.

PROPHECY XLIII.   [45.

JEREMIAH COMFORTS BARUCH.

1 THE word which Jeremiah the prophet spoke concerning Baruch, the son of Neriah, after he had written these words in the book from the mouth of Jeremiah, in the fourth year of Jehoiakim, the son of Josiah, king of Judah, saying, Thus says Jehovah, the God of Israel, concerning you, Baruch: You have said, Woe is me now, for Jehovah will add grief to my sorrow; I shall be weary with my sighing, and find no rest. Thus say to him: Thus says Jehovah:

Behold, that which I built I will break down, and that which I planted I will pull up, even all this land; and you seek great things for yourself; seek them not, for behold, I will bring evil on all flesh, says Jehovah; but I will give you your life for a prey, in all places to which you shall go.

PROPHECY XLIV. [46, 1–12.

The word of Jehovah which came to Jeremiah the prophet concerning the nations. To the Egyptians, concerning the army of Pharaoh Necho king of Egypt, which was by the river Euphrates at Carchemish, which Nebuchadrezzar king of Babylon smote, in the 4th year of Jehoiakim, son of Josiah king of Judah.

1 PREPARE the shield and buckler [heavy shield] and come near to battle. Harness the horses, let the horsemen mount, set yourselves with helmets, polish the lances, put on the cuirasses. Why do I see them dismayed, turned back; and their mighty men are smitten, they fly, they turn not back; fear is on every side, says Jehovah. The swift shall not escape, the mighty shall not be delivered; at the north, by the bank of the river Euphrates, they have stumbled and fallen.

2 Who is this that comes up like the Nile, and his waters rage like floods? Egypt comes up like the Nile, and [his] waters rage like floods. For he said, I will go up, I will cover the earth, and destroy cities and those that live in them. Go up, horses, run about, chariots, and let the mighty men of Ethiopia and Lybia, that hold the shield, and the Lydians, that hold [and] bend the bow, go forth, for it is the day of the Lord Jehovah of hosts, the day of vengeance, that he may be avenged of his adversaries, and the sword shall devour and be satisfied, and be soaked with blood, for the Lord Jehovah of hosts has a sacrifice in the land of the north, by the river Euphrates.

3 Go up to Gilead, and take balsam, virgin daughter of Egypt; you multiply medicines in vain; there is no healing for you. The nations hear your shame, and your cry fills the earth; for the mighty have stumbled on the mighty, and both have fallen together.

PROPHECY XLV.

The word which Jehovah spoke to Jeremiah the prophet of the coming of Nebuchadrezzar king of Babylon, to smite the land of Egypt.

1 TELL in Egypt, and proclaim in Migdol, and publish in Noph and Tahpanes, say, Set yourselves and stand firm, for the sword is devouring around you. Why are your mighty men swept away. He stood not, because Jehovah smote him. He stumbled greatly ; he also fell on his friend. Then they said, Arise, let us return to our people, and to the land of our birth, from the edge of the cruel sword. They cry there, Pharaoh king of Egypt, destruction [has overtaken you] ; he has passed beyond his appointed time. As I live, says the king, Jehovah of hosts is his name ; surely he shall come like Tabor, on the mountains, like Carmel on the sea. Make for yourself implements for exile, inhabitant daughter of Egypt, for Noph shall be a desolation, it shall be burned without inhabitant.

2 Egypt is a tolerably fair heifer : destruction has come from the north, it has come ; and her mercenaries in the midst of her are like cattle of the stall ; for they also turn back, they flee together, they stand not, for the day of their calamity has come on them, the time of their visitation. Its voice shall come like a serpent ; but they shall come with a host, and fall on her with axes, like woodcutters. They shall cut down her forest, says Jehovah, though it has not been explored [from its extent], for they exceed the migratory locusts, and are innumerable. The daughter of Egypt is brought to shame ; she is given into the hand of the people of the north.

3 Jehovah of hosts, the God of Israel, says, Behold, I will punish Amon of No [the supreme god of the Egyptians], and Pharaoh, and Egypt, and all her gods, and her kings, both Pharaoh and all that trust in him. And I will give them into the hand of those that seek their life, and into the hand of Nebuchadrezzar king of Babylon, and into the hand of his servants ; but afterward it shall be inhabited as in days of old, says Jehovah.

4 And as for you, fear not, my servant Jacob, and be not dismayed, Israel, for behold, I will save you from afar, and your children from the land of their captivity. And Jacob shall return and be quiet,

and at ease, and none shall make him afraid. As for you, fear not, my servant Jacob, says Jehovah, for I am with you; for I will make a complete destruction of all the nations whither I have driven you, but I will not make a complete destruction of you, but will correct you moderately, and not leave you entirely unpunished.

PROPHECY XLVI. [47.

The word of Jehovah which came to Jeremiah the prophet, concerning the Philistines, before Pharaoh smote Gaza.

THUS says Jehovah: Behold, waters come up from the north, and they are an overflowing river, and overflow the earth and all it contains, the city and those who live in it; and men shall cry, and all the inhabitants of the earth lament. From the noise of the rushing of the hoofs of his steeds, from the rumbling of his chariots, the noise of his wheels, fathers turn not back for sons, from weakness of hands, because the day has come to destroy all the Philistines, to cut off from Tyre and Zidon every remnant of a helper, for Jehovah will destroy the Philistines that remain from the island of Caphtor [Crete]. Baldness has come on Gaza; Ascalon is destroyed, the remnant of their valley; how long will you cut yourself? Alas! sword of Jehovah, how long ere you will be quiet? Be returned to your scabbard, rest, and be still. How can you be quiet, when Jehovah has commanded you against Ascalon, and against the sea coast? There has he appointed you.

PROPHECY XLVII. [48.

Concerning Moab.

1 THUS says Jehovah of hosts, the God of Israel: Alas for Nebo; for it is put to shame. Kirjathaim is taken; Misgab is taken and confounded; there is no more any praise of Moab; in Heshbon they have devised evil against her. Come, let us cut her off from being a nation; you also, Madmen, shall be silent; the sword shall go after you. There is the voice of a cry from Horonaim, wasting and a great destruction. Moab is broken down; her little ones raise a cry; for at the ascent of Luhith, weeping shall go up on weeping; for at the descent of Horonaim they have heard the assailants'

cry of destruction; flee, save your lives, and be like ruins in a desert.

2 For because you trusted in your works, and in your treasures, you shall also be taken, and Chemosh shall go into exile, his priests and his princes together. A destroyer shall come on every city, and not a city shall be delivered; and the valley shall perish, and the plain be destroyed, because Jehovah has said it. Give wings to Moab, that she may go quickly, for her cities shall be a desolation, without inhabitant. Cursed be he that does the work of Jehovah deceitfully; and cursed be he that holds back his sword from blood.

3 Moab has been at ease from his youth; he has been quiet on his lees; he has not been emptied from vessel to vessel, nor gone into exile; therefore his taste remains in him, and his odor is not changed. Therefore behold, the days come, says Jehovah, in which I will send him turners, who shall turn him, and empty his vessels, and break his bottles. And Moab shall be ashamed of Chemosh, as the house of Israel was ashamed of Bethel their confidence. How will you say, We are mighty men, and men of valor for war? Moab is destroyed; her cities have gone up [to heaven in smoke], and her choice young men have gone down to slaughter, says the King; Jehovah of hosts is his name. The calamity of Moab is near to come, and his affliction hastens on exceedingly. All that are about him run about for him, and all that know his name say, How is the strong rod broken, the beautiful staff.

4 Come down from glory, sit in thirst, inhabitant daughter of Dibon, for the destroyer of Moab has come up against you to destroy your fortresses. Stand in the way and watch, inhabitant of Aroer; ask him that flees and has escaped, say, What has happened? Moab is put to shame, for it is crushed; lament and cry; tell in Arnon that Moab is destroyed, and judgment has come on the country of the plain, on Holon, and Jazah, and Mephaath, and Dibon, and Nebo, and Bethdiblathaim, and Kirjathaim, and Bethgamul, and Bethmeon, and Kerioth, and Bozrah, and all the cities of the land of Moab, far and near. The house of Moab is cut off and his arm broken, says Jehovah. Make him drunk, for he has magnified himself against Jehovah, and Moab shall wallow in his vomit, and be a laughing stock, even he. For was not Israel a laughing stock to you, when he was found among thieves? for as often as you spoke of him you shook yourself [in scorn]. Forsake

the cities and live in the rock, inhabitants of Moab; and be like the dove that makes her nest deep in the mouth of a pit.

5 We have heard of the pride of Moab; he is very proud; and of his dignity, and his grandeur, and his majesty, and the exaltation of his heart [mind]. I know, says Jehovah, his wrath, and he shall not be so; and his lies, and he shall not do so. Therefore I will lament for Moab, for all Moab will I cry; for the men of Kirheres I will mourn. I will weep for you with the weeping of Jazar, vine of Sibmah; your shoots went to the lake, they reached to the lake of Jazar. A destroyer has fallen on your fruit harvest, and on your vintage, and joy and gladness are taken away from the fruitful field, and from the land of Moab; and I have caused the wine to cease from the presses. The joyful shouting shall not be trod, the shouting shall not be shouting. From the cry of Heshbon to Elealeh [and] to Jahaz, they utter their voice; from Zoar to Horonaim, she is a three year old heifer, for the waters of Nimrim also shall be desolate; and I will cause to cease from Moab, says Jehovah, him that offers on high places, and him that burns incense to his god.

6 Therefore my heart shall sound for Moab like pipes, and my heart shall sound for the men of Kirheres like pipes; because the abundance which they gained has perished. For baldness is on all heads, and all beards are cut off; on all hands are cuttings, and on all loins is sackcloth. On all the roofs of Moab, and in all her streets, is lamentation; for I have broken Moab like a vessel in which no pleasure is taken, says Jehovah. Lament; how are you broken! how has Moab turned the back ashamed! Moab is a laughing stock, and an object of merriment to all around him. For thus says Jehovah: Behold, one shall fly like an eagle, and spread his wings over Moab. Kerioth is taken, the fortresses are seized, and the hearts of the mighty men of Moab shall be in that day like the heart of a woman in distress. Moab is destroyed from being a people, for he magnified himself against Jehovah. Fear, and a pit, and a snare, are on you, inhabitant of Moab, says Jehovah. He that flees from the fear shall fall into the pit; and he that comes up from the pit shall be taken in the snare; for I will bring on Moab the year of their visitation, says Jehovah.

7 In the shade of Heshbon the fugitives shall stop for want of strength; for a fire shall go out of Heshbon, and a flame from the midst of Sihon, and shall consume the extremities of Moab and the crown of the head of the sons of destruction. Alas for you, Moab,

the people of Chemosh have perished, for your sons and your daughters are taken into captivity. But I will restore the captives of Moab in after times, says Jehovah. Hitherto the judgment of Moab.

PROPHECY XLVIII. [49, 1-6.

Concerning the sons of Ammon.

1 THUS says Jehovah: Has Israel no sons? has he no heir? Why [then] does Malcom [Moloch] inherit Gad, and his people live in its cities? Therefore behold, the days come, says Jehovah, in which I will cause the war shout to be heard at Rabbah of the sons of Ammon, and it shall be a desolate heap, and her daughters shall be burned with fire, and Israel shall possess his possessions, says Jehovah.

2 Lament, Heshbon, for Ai is destroyed; cry, daughters of Rabbah, gird on sackcloth, lament, and run about in the inclosures, for Malcom shall go into exile, his priests and his princes together. Why do you boast of valleys? Your valley flows with blood, rebellious daughter, that trust in your treasures. Who will come against me? Behold, I will bring on you fear, says the Lord Jehovah of hosts, from all that are around you, and you shall be driven out each one directly forward, and none shall gather the fugitives. But afterwards I will restore the captives of the sons of Ammon, says Jehovah.

PROPHECY XLIX. [49, 7-22.

Concerning Edom.

1 THUS says Jehovah of hosts: Is wisdom no more in Teman? Has counsel perished from the intelligent? Is their wisdom poured out? Flee, turn, make your dwelling in deep places, inhabitants of Dedan, for I have brought the calamity of Esau on him, the time of my visiting him. If vintagers come to you, will they not leave gleanings? If thieves by night, they will plunder till they have enough; but I have stripped Esau bare, and have carried away his concealed treasures, and he shall not be able to be hid. His children are destroyed, and his brothers and his neighbors, and nothing is left of him. Leave your fatherless ones with me; I will preserve [them]; and let your widows trust in me. For thus says

Jehovah : They have drunk deeply of the cup, to whom it was not adjudged, and shall you be altogether unpunished? You shall not be unpunished, but shall drink deeply. For I have sworn by myself, says Jehovah, that Bozrah shall be a desolation, a reproach, a waste, and a curse, and all her cities eternal desolations.

2 I have heard a report from Jehovah, and a messenger is sent among the nations [saying], Assemble yourselves and come against her, arise to battle. For behold, I have made you small among the nations, [and] despised among men. Your terribleness has deceived you, the pride of your heart, inhabitant of the tops of the rock, possessor of high hills. Though you set your nest on high, like the eagle, thence will I bring you down, says Jehovah.

3 Edom is a desolation; all that pass by it are astonished and hiss for all her plagues. Like the overthrow of Sodom and Gomorrah and their neighbors, says Jehovah, not a man of high degree shall live there, not a son of man of low degree shall inhabit it. Behold, one shall come up like a lion from the pride of the Jordan, against the perennial pasture; I will bring him up, I will cause him to run up her ascents; and what chosen one shall I place over her? For who is like me? and who will teach me? and who is the shepherd that can stand before me? Therefore hear the counsel of Jehovah which he has taken against Edom, and his purposes which he has formed against the inhabitants of Teman. Surely they shall drag them forth [like] the smallest of the sheep; surely he shall make them forget their pasture; at the noise of their fall the earth shall quake, and the sound of her cry shall be heard to the Red sea.

4 Behold, one shall come up like an eagle, and fly and spread his wings over Bozrah, and the heart of the mighty men of Edom shall be in that day like the heart of a woman in distress.

PROPHECY L. [49, 23-27.

Concerning Damascus.

HAMATH and Arpad are ashamed, for they have heard an evil report ; they have fainted ; there is anxiety on the sea, it can not be quiet. Damascus desists, she turns to flee, she has taken to trembling ; distress and anguish have seized her, like a woman in childbirth. Why was not the city of praise forsaken, the city of my joy? Therefore her young men shall fall in her streets, and all

the men of war be silent in that day, says Jehovah of hosts ; and I
will kindle a fire on the wall of Damascus, and it shall consume
the palaces of Benhadad.

PROPHECY LI. |49, 28–33.

*Concerning Kedar and the kingdoms of Hazor, which Nebuchad-
rezzar, king of Babylon, smote.*

1 THUS says Jehovah : Arise, go up to Kedar, and plunder the
sons of the east ; their tents and their flocks shall be taken, their
curtains and all their goods, and their camels shall bear [them away]
for them, and they shall cry to them, Fear is on every side. Fly,
flee for your lives, go deep down to live, inhabitants of Hazor, says
Jehovah, for Nebuchadrezzar, king of Babylon, has taken counsel
against you, and formed a purpose against you.

2 Arise, go up to a nation at rest, living in security, says Jehovah ; it has no doors nor bars ; they live alone ; and his camels
shall be a prey, and the multitude of his possessions a spoil, and I
will scatter them to all winds, with their cut-off locks, and from all
quarters, says Jehovah, will I bring their calamity on them.   And
Hazor shall be a habitation of jackals, a desolation forever ; not a
man of high degree shall dwell there, nor a son of man of low degree live in it.

PROPHECY LII. |49, 34–39.

*Word of Jehovah which came to Jeremiah the prophet concerning
Elam, in the beginning of the reign of Zedekiah.*

THUS says Jehovah of hosts : Behold, I will break the bow of
Elam, the beginning of their strength, and bring on Elam the four
winds from the four quarters of heaven, and scatter them to all these
winds, and there shall not be a nation to which the outcasts of
Elam shall not come.   And I will confound Elam before their enemies, and before those that seek their life, and bring evil on them,
my fierce anger, says Jehovah, and send a sword after them till I
have consumed them ; and I will set my throne in Elam, and destroy
thence king and princes, says Jehovah.   But in after times I will
restore the captives of Elam, says Jehovah.

PROPHECY LIII.   [50, 51, 58.

The word which Jehovah spoke concerning Babylon [and] the land of the Chaldeans, by Jeremiah the prophet.

1 TELL the nations, and publish, lift up a standard, publish and conceal it not; say, Babylon is fallen, Bel is ashamed, Merodach is confounded, her idols are ashamed, her blocks are confounded. For a nation has come up against her from the north, which shall make her land a desolation, and there shall not be an inhabitant in it; from man to beast, all have fled [and] gone.

2 In those days and at that time, says Jehovah, the sons of Israel shall come, and the sons of Judah together, and shall go with weeping as they go, and seek Jehovah their God; they shall inquire the way to Zion, with their faces towards it; they shall go and be joined to Jehovah, [and their] eternal covenant shall not be forgotten.

3 My people were a flock of lost sheep; their shepherds caused them to stray; the mountains turned them aside; they went from mountain to hill; they forgot their resting place. All that found them devoured them, and their adversaries said, We shall not be held guilty, because they sinned against Jehovah, the habitation of righteousness, and Jehovah was the hope of their fathers.

4 Flee from the midst of Babylon, and go 'out from 'the land of the Chaldeans, and be like the he goats before the flock. For behold, I raise up and bring up against Babylon an assembly of great nations from the land of the north, and they shall prepare against her means by which she shall be taken; his arrows are like a skillful warrior's, he shall not return empty; and the Chaldeans shall be a spoil, and all that plunder them shall be satisfied, says Jehovah, because you rejoiced and exulted, spoilers of my inheritance; because you sported like a bullock [in] tender grass, and neighed like horses. Your mother is greatly ashamed; she that bore you is confounded. Behold, the latter end of nations is a parched wilderness and a desert. From the wrath of Jehovah, she shall not be inhabited, and all her land shall be desolate; every one that passes by Babylon shall be astonished, and hiss at all her plagues.

5 Prepare against Babylon on every side; all you who bend the
19 *

bow, shoot at her ; spare not the arrows ; for she has sinned against Jehovah.　Shout against her on every side ; she gives her hand ; her pillars fall, her walls are overthrown ; for it is the vengeance of Jehovah ; be revenged on her ; do to her as she has done.　Cut off the sower of seed from Babylon, and him that handles the sickle in the time of harvest ; from before the cruel sword let them turn every one to his people, and flee every one to his land.

6 Israel was a lost sheep which the lions drove away.　The king of Assyria devoured him first, and Nebuchadrezzar, king of Babylon, afterwards picked his bones.　Therefore thus says Jehovah of hosts, the God of Israel : Behold, I will punish the king of Babylon and his land, as I punished the king of Assyria.　And I will restore Israel to his pasture, and he shall feed on Carmel and Bashan, and his soul be satisfied on mount Ephraim and Gilead.　In those days and at that time, says the Lord Jehovah, the wickedness of Israel shall be sought for, and there shall be none ; and the sins of Judah, and they shall not be found ; for I will forgive those whom I cause to remain.

7 *Against the land of Merathaim* [*double rebellion*].　Go up against her, against the inhabitants of Pekod [punishment] ; lay waste and utterly destroy their hereafter, says Jehovah, and do according to all that I command you.　There is a noise of war in the earth, and great destruction.　How is the hammer [desolator] of all the earth cut down and broken !　How has Babylon become a desolation among the nations !　I set a snare for you, and you are taken, Babylon, and knew it not ; you are found and also taken, because you contended with Jehovah.　Jehovah opened his armory, and brought out the implements of his indignation ; for this is the work of the Lord Jehovah of hosts in the land of the Chaldeans.　Come against her from the end [of the world], open her storehouses, cast her up like heaps, and destroy her entirely ; let her have no remnant ; destroy all her heifers, let them go down to slaughter.　Alas for them, for their day has come, [and] the time of their visitation.　There is a noise of the fleeing and those escaping from the land of Babylon, to tell Zion of the vengeance of Jehovah our God, the vengeance of his temple.

8 Publish against Babylon ; chiefs all bending the bow, encamp against her on every side, let none escape ; repay her according to her work, do to her according to all that she has done ; for she has acted proudly against Jehovah, against the Holy One of Israel ;

therefore her young men shall fall in her streets, and all her men of war be silent in that day, says Jehovah. Behold, I am against you, Pride, says the Lord Jehovah of hosts, for your day has come, the time of your visitation ; and Pride has stumbled and fallen ; he shall not rise ; and I will burn his cities with fire, and it shall consume all around him.

9 Thus says Jehovah of hosts : The sons of Israel and the sons of Judah were oppressed together, and all that took them captives held them fast, they refused to let them go. But their Redeemer is mighty ; Jehovah of hosts is his name ; he will surely vindicate their cause, that he may give rest to the earth, but he will disquiet the inhabitants of Babylon. There is a sword on the Chaldeans, says Jehovah, and on the inhabitants of Babylon, and on her princes, and on her wise men ; there is a sword on the liars, and they have become fools ; a sword on her mighty men, and they are confounded ; a sword on their horses and on their chariots, and on all the mixed multitude in the midst of her, and they have become women ; and a sword on her treasures, and they are plundered ; a drouth on her waters, and they shall be dried up ; for it is a land of carved images, and they are mad with terrors [idols]. Therefore the wild beasts of the desert shall dwell [in it], and the daughters of the ostrich return to it, and it shall no more be inhabited forever, nor dwelt in from generation to generation. As Jehovah overthrew Sodom and Gomorrah, and their neighbors, a man of high degree shall not live there, nor the son of man of low degree dwell there.

10 Behold, a people have come from the north, and a great nation and mighty kings are raised up from the sides of the earth ; they shall hold bow and javelin ; they are cruel, and shall not pity ; their voice shall roar like the sea, and they shall ride on horses set in order like men for battle, against you, daughter of Babylon. The king of Babylon heard the report of them, and his hands hung down, and distress seized him, and pain [as] a woman in childbirth. Behold, he shall come up like a lion from the pride of the Jordan to the perennial pasture, for I will wink, I will cause them to run off from it ; and who is the chosen one that I shall appoint against her ? for who is like me ? and who can cause me to know ? and who is the shepherd that can stand against me ? Therefore hear the counsel of Jehovah, which he has taken against Babylon, and his purposes, which he has purposed against the land of the Chaldeans. They shall surely drag them forth [like] the smallest of the flock, and he will

appoint them a habitation. At the noise of the taking of Babylon, the earth quaked, and a cry was heard among the nations.

11 Thus says Jehovah: Behold, I will raise up against Babylon, and against the inhabitants of the heart of my adversaries, a destroying wind; and I will send against Babylon winnowers, and they shall winnow it, and make its land empty, for they shall be against her from every side in that evil day. God shall bend the bow, [as] he that bends his bow, and God shall lift himself up in his cuirass; then spare not her chosen men, destroy utterly all her host. For the wounded have fallen in the land of the Chaldeans, and the killed in her streets. For Israel and Judah are not forsaken by their God, by Jehovah of hosts, though their land was full of blame from the Holy One of Israel.

12 Flee from the midst of Babylon, and save every man his life, that you be not cut off in her wickedness; for this is the time of Jehovah's vengeance, the recompense which he renders her. Babylon was a gold cup in the hand of Jehovah, making all the earth drunk with her wine; the nations drank, therefore the nations were mad; suddenly has Babylon fallen, and she shall be broken to pieces. Lament for her; take balsam for her pain; perhaps she may be healed. We have healed Babylon, but she is not healed; leave her, and let us go every man to his land, for her judgment reaches to heaven, and rises up to the skies. Jehovah brings out our righteousness; come and let us declare in Zion the work of Jehovah our God.

13 Sharpen the arrows; fill the shields: Jehovah has excited the spirit of the kings of Media, for his purpose is against Babylon to destroy it; for this is the vengeance of Jehovah, the vengeance of his temple. Set up a standard against the walls of Babylon, strengthen the watch, establish guards, provide liers in wait, for Jehovah has both purposed and done that which he spoke against the inhabitants of Babylon. You dwelt on great waters, with great treasures; your end has come, and the measure of your extortion. Jehovah of hosts has sworn by himself, Surely will I fill you with men, as with winged locusts, and they shall raise the war-shout against you.

14 He made the earth by his strength, he established the world by his wisdom, and by his understanding he stretched out the heavens. At the uttering of [his] voice there is an abundance of water in the heavens, and he causes the clouds to ascend from the ends

of the earth; he makes lightnings for the rain, and brings the wind out of his armories. Every man without knowledge [image] is a brute; every founder is ashamed of a carved image; but his casting is a lie, and there is no breath in them; they are vanity, [and] a work of delusions; in the time of their visitation they shall perish. Not like these is the portion of Jacob, for he is the maker of all things, and is the staff [support] of his inheritance; Jehovah of hosts is his name.

15 You have been my beetle, my implement of war; and I broke in pieces the nations with you, and with you destroyed kingdoms; and I smote with you the horse and his rider; and I smote with you man and woman; and I smote with you elder and child; and I smote with you young man and young woman; and I smote with you the shepherd and his flock; and I smote with you the husbandman and his team; and I smote with you governors and prefects; but I will return to Babylon, and to all the inhabitants of Chaldea, all their evil which they did to Zion, before your eyes, says Jehovah.

16 Behold, I am against you, destroying mountain, says Jehovah, the destroyer of all the earth; and I will stretch out my hand against you, and roll you down from the rocks, and make you a mountain of fire; and they shall not take from you a stone for a corner, nor a stone for foundations, for you shall be eternal desolations, says Jehovah.

17 Set up a standard in the earth; blow a trumpet among the nations; call out the nations against her; call against her the kingdoms of Ararat, Minni, and Ashchenaz; appoint against her military governors; bring up the horse like bristling, hairy locusts; call out against her the nations of the kings of Media, her governors and all her prefects, and all the land of their dominion; and let the earth quake and be in pain, for Jehovah has established [his] purposes against Babylon to make the land of Babylon a desolation without inhabitant.

18 The mighty men of Babylon have ceased to fight, they sit down in the strongholds, their might is dried up, they are women; her dwellings are burned, her bars are broken down; courier runs to meet courier, and messenger to meet messenger, to tell the king of Babylon that his city is taken from end [to end], that the passages are seized, and the reeds [fortifications] are burned with fire, and the men of war are in consternation. For thus says Jehovah

of hosts, the God of Israel : The daughter of Babylon shall be like a threshing floor at the time of its threshing ; yet a little while, and the harvest time will come to it.

19 Nebuchadrezzar, king of Babylon, devoured us, he entirely destroyed us, he made us an empty vessel, he swallowed us up like a dragon [a serpent], he filled his belly with our delicacies, he thrust us away. Let my violence and my flesh [which he has devoured] be on Babylon, shall the inhabitant of Zion say, and my blood on the inhabitants of Chaldea, shall Jerusalem say. Therefore thus says Jehovah : Look to me to maintain your cause, and I will execute your vengeance ; and I will dry up her sea, and make dry her fountain, and Babylon shall become heaps, a habitation of jackals, a desolation, a hissing, without inhabitant. They shall roar together like lions, they shall be roused up like young lions ; in their heat I will give them their drink, and make them drunk, that they may exult ; then they shall sleep an eternal sleep, and not awake, says Jehovah. I will bring them down like lambs for slaughter, like rams with he goats.

20 How is Sheshach taken, and the praise of all the earth caught! How is Babylon a desolation among the nations ! The sea went up against Babylon, [and] she was covered with the abundance of its waves. Her cities are a desolation, the land is dry, and the land is a desert in which no man of high degree shall live, and through which no son of man of low degree shall pass ; and I have punished Bel, with Babylon, and brought out what he has swallowed from his mouth, and the nations shall flow to him no more.

21 The wall, also, of Babylon has fallen down. Go out of the midst of her, my people ; save every man his life from the fierce anger of Jehovah, lest your heart also faint, and you be afraid of the report which is reported in the earth, when one report comes in one year, and the year after another, that violence is in the earth, and ruler against ruler.

22 Therefore behold, the days come in which I will punish the carved images of Babylon, and all her land shall be ashamed, and her wounded shall fall in the midst of her. Then sing against Babylon, heaven, and earth, and all that is in them, for from the north destroyers shall come on her, says Jehovah. As Babylon was for the fall of the wounded of Israel, so on Babylon the wounded of all the earth shall fall. You that have escaped from the sword, go, stop not, remember Jehovah from afar, and let Jerusalem come into your mind.

23 We were ashamed, because we heard reproach; confusion covered our faces, for strangers came against the holy things of the house of Jehovah. Therefore behold, the days come, says Jehovah, in which I will punish her carved images, and the wounded shall groan in all her land. Though Babylon should go up to heaven, and cut off her strength [make herself inaccessible] on high, destroyers from me shall come on her, says Jehovah.

24 There is the sound of a cry from Babylon, and of a great destruction from the land of the Chaldeans. For Jehovah destroys Babylon, and he has destroyed out of it the great noise; though their waves roared like many waters, he gave their noise to destruction. For a destroyer has come on Babylon, and her mighty men are taken, their bows are broken; for the God of retributions, Jehovah, will certainly repay. Then [says God] I will make her princes, and her wise men, and her governors, and her prefects, and her mighty men, drunk; and they shall sleep an eternal sleep, and not awake, says the king; Jehovah of hosts is his name.

25 Thus says Jehovah of hosts: The broad walls of Babylon shall be razed to the ground, and her high gates burned with fire, and the labor of peoples shall be for nothing, and the toil of nations for the fire.

PROPHECY LIV. [51, 59-64.

THE SINKING OF THE BOOK OF THESE PROPHECIES IN THE EUPHRATES.

1 THE word which Jeremiah the prophet commanded Seraiah, son of Neriah, son of Mahseiah, when he went with Zedekiah, king of Judah, to Babylon, in the 4th year of his reign. And Seraiah was the chamberlain. Then Jeremiah wrote all the evil which should come on Babylon in one book, all those words which are written against Babylon; and Jeremiah said to Seraiah, When you come to Babylon, then see and read all these words; then say, Thou, Jehovah, hast spoken against this place, to cut it off, that there shall not be an inhabitant in it, man nor beast, but that it shall be eternal desolations.

2 And when you have finished reading this book, bind on it a stone, and cast it into the midst of the Euphrates, and say, Thus sh..ll Babylon sink and not rise, before the evil which I will bring on her, and they shall fly away. Thus far the words of Jeremiah.

ARTICLE LV.   [52.

THE REIGN OF ZEDEKIAH, THE DESTRUCTION OF JERUSALEM, AND
THE FORTUNES OF JEHOIAKIM.

1 ZEDEKIAH was 21 years old when he began to reign, and he
reigned 11 years in Jerusalem, and his mother's name was Hamutal,
daughter of Jeremiah of Libnah.   And he did evil in the sight of
Jehovah, according to all that Jehoiakim did.   For through the
anger of Jehovah it happened to Jerusalem and Judah, that he cast
them out from his presence when Zedekiah rebelled against the king
of Babylon.

2 And in the 9th year of his reign, in the tenth month, on the
10th [day] of the month, came Nebuchadrezzar, king of Babylon,
and all his host, against Jerusalem; and he encamped against it,
and built against it watch towers on every side.   And the city was
besieged till the 11th year of king Zedekiah.

3 In the fourth month, on the 9th [day] of the month, the famine in the city was severe, and there was no bread for the people
of the country.   Then the city was taken, and all the men of war
fled and went out of the city by night, by way of the gate between
the two walls which was by the king's garden, and the Chaldeans
were against the city on every side, and they went by the way to
the desert.

4 But the army of the Chaldeans pursued after the king, and took
Zedekiah in the deserts of Jericho, and all his army were scattered from him; and they took the king and brought him to the
king of Babylon at Riblah, in the land of Hamath, and he pronounced judgment on him; and the king of Babylon killed the sons
of Zedekiah before his eyes, and also all the princes of Judah did he
kill at Riblah.   Then he put out the eyes of Zedekiah, and bound
him in fetters of brass; and the king of Babylon carried him to
Babylon, and put him in prison till the day of his death.

5 And in the fifth month, on the 10th [day] of the month, which
was the 19th year of king Nebuchadrezzar, king of Babylon, Nebuzaradan, chief of the executioners, who stood before the king of
Babylon, came to Jerusalem, and burned the house of Jehovah, and
the king's house, and all the houses of Jerusalem, and all the large
houses he burned with fire.   And all the army of the Chaldeans

which was with the chief of the executioners broke down the wall of Jerusalem on every side. And some of the poor of the people, and the rest of the people that remained in the city, and the deserters that deserted to the king of Babylon, and the rest, a great multitude, and the poor from the country, did Nebuzaradan, chief of the executioners, cause to remain for vine dressers and husbandmen.

6 And the pillars of brass which belonged to the house of Jehovah, and the bases, and the brass sea which was in the house of Jehovah, the Chaldeans broke up, and carried all the brass to Babylon. And they took the pots, and shovels, and snuffers, and basins, and bowls, and all the brass utensils with which they ministered; and the chief of the executioners took the dishes, and fire pans, and basins, and pots, and lamps, and bowls, and cups for libations, — what was gold as gold, and what was silver as silver, — two pillars, one sea, 12 oxen of brass which were under the bases, that king Solomon made for the house of Jehovah; their brass was not weighed, all these vessels. And as to the pillars, the height of each pillar was 18 cubits, and a line of 12 cubits went round it, and its thickness was 4 fingers; [it was] hollow. And there was a capital on it of brass, and the height of each capital was 5 cubits, and a lattice work and pomegranates on the capital entirely round it, all of brass; and the same of the second pillar, and the pomegranates. And there were 96 pomegranates in the air; all the pomegranates were 100 around the lattice work.

7 And the chief of the executioners took Seraiah, the chief priest, and Zephaniah, the second priest, and the three door keepers, and from the city he took one eunuch, who was prefect of the men of war, and seven men who saw the face of the king, who were found in the city, and the scribe, the prince of the army, who mustered the people of the country for war, and 60 men of the people of the country who were found in the city. Then Nebuzaradan, chief of the executioners, took them and brought them to the king of Babylon at Riblah, and the king of Babylon smote them and killed them at Riblah, in the land of Hamath, and he carried Judah away captive from his land.

8 These are the people whom Nebuchadrezzar carried away captive in the 7th year : Jews, 3,023 ; in the 18th year of Nebuchadrezzar, from Jerusalem, 832 souls ; in the 23d year of Nebuchadrezzar, Nebuzaradan, chief of the executioners, carried away captive, Jews, 745 souls ; all the souls were 4,600.

9 And in the 37th year of the captivity of Jehoiachin, king of Judah [B. C. 561], in the twelfth month, on the 25th day of the month, Evil Merodach, king of Babylon, in the first year of his reign, lifted up the head of Jehoiachin, king of Judah, and brought him out of prison, and spoke kindly to him, and gave him a seat above the seats of the kings who were with him in Babylon. And he changed his prison clothes, and he eat bread before him continually all the days of his life ; and his allowance was given him continually, an allowance from the king of Babylon, the portion of the day for its day, till the day of his death, all the days of his life.

11. EZEKIEL.

PROPHECY I.   [1, 2, 3, 21.

EZEKIEL'S VISION OF GOD AND THE CHERUBS AT THE RIVER CHEBAR, AND HIS CALL TO THE PROPHETIC OFFICE.

1 AND in the 30th year, in the fourth month, on the 5th day of the month, as I was among the captives by the river Chebar, the heavens were opened, and I saw visions of God. On the 5th day of the month, in that 5th year of king Jehoiachin's captivity, came the word of Jehovah to Ezekiel, the son of Buzi the priest, in the land of the Chaldeans, by the river Chebar, and the hand of Jehovah was on him there.

2 And I saw, and behold, a storm-wind came from the north, a great cloud, and a fire taking hold of itself, and a brightness around it ; and within it there was, as it were, the brilliancy of polished brass in the fire. And in it was the likeness of four living ones ; and this was their appearance : they had the form of a man, and each of them had four faces and four wings, and their feet were straight, and the sole of their feet was like the sole of a calf's foot, and they sparkled like the brilliancy of polished brass.

3 And a man's hands were under their wings on their four sides, and they four had their faces and their wings ; their wings were joined one to another ; they turned not when they went ; they went each one straight forward.

4 And as to the form of their faces, the four had the face of a man and the face of a lion on the right side, and the four had the face of an ox on the left side, and the four had the face of an eagle; and their faces and their wings were extended upwards; two wings were joined one to another, and two covered their bodies. And they went each one straight forward; to where the spirit was to go, they went; they turned not when they went. And as to the likeness of the living ones, their appearance was like burning coals of fire, like the appearance of lamps. This [appearance] went about between the living ones, and it had the brightness of fire, and from the fire went forth lightning; and the living ones ran and returned, like the appearance of lightning.

5 And I saw the living ones, and behold, there was one wheel on the earth by the side of [each of] the living ones, with its four faces. The appearance of the wheels and their work was like the brilliancy of Topaz, and the four had one form; and their appearance and their work was, as it were, of a wheel in a wheel. When they went, they went on their four sides; they turned not when they went. And as to their rims, they were high and fearful, and the rims of the four were full of eyes on every side.

6 And when the living ones went, the wheels went beside them; and when the living ones were lifted up from the earth, the wheels were lifted up. Where the Spirit was to go, there they went; and the wheels were lifted up against them, for the Spirit of the living one was in the wheels. When these went, they went; and when these stood still, they stood still; and when these were lifted up from the earth, the wheels were lifted up against them; for the spirit of the living one was in the wheels.

7 And over the heads of the living one was a floor, like the appearance of a stupendous crystal, extended over their heads above. And their wings under the floor were extended one to another, and each had two, that covered their bodies.

8 And I heard the sound of their wings, like the sound of many waters, like the voice of the Almighty. When they went, the sound of the noise was like the sound of a host. When they stood, they let down their wings, and there was a voice from above the floor which was over their heads. And above the floor which was over their heads, there was, as it were, the appearance of a sapphire stone, of the likeness of a throne; and on the likeness of the throne was a likeness like the appearance of a man above.

9 And I saw, as it were, the appearance of polished brass, like the appearance of fire, within itself on every side; from the appearance of his loins and upwards, and the appearance of his loins and downwards, I saw, as it were, the appearance of a man, and he had a brightness around him like the appearance of the bow which is on a cloud in a day of rain. Such was the appearance of the brightness around. This was the appearance of the likeness of the glory of Jehovah; and I saw and fell on my face, and heard a voice speak and say to me, Son of man, stand on your feet, and I will speak with you. And the Spirit came on me as he spoke to me, and set me on my feet, and I heard him that spoke to me.

10 And he said to me, Son of man, I send you to the sons of Israel, to a rebellious nation which has rebelled against me. They and their fathers have transgressed against me to this very day. And I send you to sons of a hard face and a strong will, and do you say to them, Thus says the Lord Jehovah; and whether they will hear, or whether they will forbear — for they are a rebellious house — that they may know that there is a prophet among them.

11 And as for you, son of man, be not afraid of them, and fear not their words, though they are rebels and thorns to you, and you live among scorpions. Be not afraid of their words, nor be confounded at their faces, for they are a rebellious house. And do you speak my words to them, whether they hear or whether they forbear, for they are rebellious.

12 And as for you, son of man, hear what I tell you; be not rebellious like [this] rebellious house; open your mouth and eat what I give you. And I saw, and behold, a hand was sent to me, and behold, in it was a roll of a book, and he spread it before me, and it was written within and on the back side; and there was written on it, Lamentations, Sighing, and Woe.

13 And he said to me, Son of man, what you find, eat; eat this roll, and go speak to the house of Israel. Then I opened my mouth, and he caused me to eat the roll, and said to me, Son of man, let your belly eat, and your bowels be filled with this roll which I give you; and as you eat, it shall be in [your] mouth like honey for sweetness.

14 Then he said to me, Son of man, go, go to the house of Israel, and speak my words to them, for you are not sent to a people of dark speech and hard tongue, [but] to the house of Israel; not to many peoples of a dark speech and a hard tongue, whose

words you can not understand ; did I send you to them, they would hear you. But the house of Israel will not hear you, for they will not hear me ; but all the house of Israel are of a hard face and of a hard heart. Behold, I will make your face strong against their faces, and your brow strong against their brows ; I will make your brow harder than a crystal, harder than a rock ; fear them not, nor be dismayed before them, for they are a rebellious house.

15 And he said to me, Son of man, all the words which I tell you receive in your mind, and hear with your ears, and go to the exiles of the sons of my people, and speak to them, and say to them, Thus says the Lord Jehovah ; whether they will hear, or whether they will forbear.

16 Then the Spirit took me up, and I heard behind me the sound of a great tumult [saying], Blessed is the glory of Jehovah in his place ; and there was a noise of the wings of the living ones that touched each other, and a noise of the wheels against them, and a noise of a great tumult ; and the Spirit lifted me up and took me, and I went sorrowful, with great excitement of my spirit, for the hand of Jehovah was strong on me. And I went to the exiles at Telabib, who live by the river Chebar, and to those who live there ; and I staid there seven days astonished among them.

17 And at the end of seven days the word of Jehovah came to me, saying, Son of man, I have made you a watchman of the house of Israel ; hear, therefore, the word from my mouth, and warn them from me. When I say to the wicked man, You shall surely die, and you do not warn him, nor speak to warn the wicked man from his evil way to save his life, that wicked man shall die for his wickedness, but his blood will I require from your hand. But if you warn the wicked man, and he turns not from his wickedness, nor from his wicked way, he shall die for his wickedness, but you have saved your life.

18 And when a righteous man turns from his righteousness, and does evil, and I put destruction before him, that he may die, if you do not warn him, he shall die for his sin, and his righteousness which he performed shall not be remembered, but his blood will I require from your hand. But if you warn the righteous man not to sin, and he sins not, be shall surely live, because he was warned, and you shall save your life.

20 *

PROPHECY II.   [3, 22, 4.

EZEKIEL ADMONISHED ; HE REPRESENTS THE SIEGE AND DISTRESS OF JERUSALEM BY SYMBOLICAL ACTIONS.

1 AND the hand of Jehovah was on me there, and he said to me, Arise and go to the valley, and there I will speak with you.   Then I arose and went to the valley, and behold, there was the glory of Jehovah standing, like the glory which I saw by the river Chebar ; and I fell on my face.   And the Spirit came on me, and caused me to stand up on my feet ; and he spoke with me, and said to me, Go and be shut up in your house.

2 And, son of man, behold, cords shall be put on you, and they shall bind you with them, and you shall not go out among them. And I will cause your tongue to cleave to your throat, and you shall be dumb, and shall not be to them for a reprover, for they are a rebellious house.   But when I speak to you I will open your mouth, and you shall say to them, Thus says Jehovah : Let him that hears hear, and let him that forbears forbear ; for they are a rebellious house.

3 And, son of man, take for yourself a brick, and put it before you, and portray on it the city Jerusalem.   And put a siege against it, and build against it a watch-tower, and cast up against it an embankment, and set against it camps, and place against it battering-rams on every side ; and take for yourself an iron frying-pan, and set it for an iron wall between you and the city, and set your face against it, and let it be in a state of siege, and distress it : this shall be a sign to the house of Israel.

4 And do you lie on your left side, and put the wickedness of the house of Israel on it ; the number of days during which you shall lie on it you shall bear their wickedness.   And I will assign for you the years of their wickedness according to the number of days, 390 days ; and you shall bear the wickedness of the house of Israel. When you complete these, then lie on your right side a second time, and bear the wickedness of the house of Judah 40 days ; I assign you a day for every year.

5 And set your face against the siege of Jerusalem, and let your arm be uncovered, and prophesy against it.   And behold, I will put cords on you, and you shall not change from side to side till you

have finished the days of your siege. And take wheat, and barley, and beans, and lentiles, and millet, and spelt, and put them in one vessel, and prepare them for yourself for food the number of days during which you lie on your side ; 390 days shall you eat it. And your food which you eat shall be by weight, 20 shekels [11 oz.] a day ; from time to time shall you eat it. And you shall drink water by measure, a sixth of a hin [1.6 pints] ; from time to time shall you drink it. And you shall eat barley cakes ; and with balls of men's dung shall [the bread] be baked in their sight. And Jehovah said, Thus shall the sons of Israel eat their bread impure among the nations to which I will drive them.

6 Then I said, Alas, Lord Jehovah, behold, I have not been defiled, and from my youth to this day I have not eaten of a creature that died [of itself], or that was torn [by beasts] ; and impure food has not come into my mouth. Then he said to me, See, I have appointed you cattle's dung instead of man's, and do you make your bread over it. And he said to me, Son of man, behold, I will break the staff of bread in Jerusalem, and they shall eat bread by weight and with anxiety, and drink water by measure and with consternation, that they may want bread and water, and be astonished, one and another, and perish for their wickedness.

PROPHECY III.　　　　　[5.

THE SLAUGHTER AND DISTRESS OF THE JEWS REPRESENTED BY OPERATING ON HAIRS.

1 AND do you, son of man, take a sharp sword, a razor of the barbers [in sharpness], and pass it over your head and over your chin, and take scales for weighing, and divide the hairs. A third part burn with fire in the city, when the days of the siege are completed ; and take a third part, and smite with the sword about it, and scatter a third part to the wind, and I will draw out a sword after them ; and take thence a small number, and bind them on your skirts. And of them again take some, and cast them into the fire, and burn them with fire. A fire shall go forth from it to all the house of Israel.

2 Thus says the Lord Jehovah : This is Jerusalem ; I put her in the midst of the nations, and around her were the lands ; but she changed my judgments to wickedness more than the nations and

my ordinances more than the lands which were around her, for they refused my judgments, and walked not in my ordinances.   Therefore thus says the Lord Jehovah : Because your tumult has been greater than that of the nations which were around you, and you have not walked in my ordinances, nor performed my judgments, nor done according to the judgments of the nations which were around you [but worse], therefore thus says the Lord Jehovah : Behold, I am against you, even I ; and I will execute judgments among you, in the sight of the nations, and do to you that which I have not done, and the like of which I will not do again, because of all your abominations.   Therefore fathers shall eat their sons among you, and sons shall eat their fathers ; and I will execute judgments on you, and scatter all that shall remain of you to all winds.   Therefore, as I live, says the Lord Jehovah, surely, because you have defiled my sanctuary with all your detestable things, and with all your abominations, therefore I also will take [you] away, my eye shall not spare, neither will I pity.   A third part of you shall die with pestilence, and be consumed with famine in the midst of you ; and a third part shall fall by the sword in the places around you ; and a third part will I scatter to all winds, and draw out a sword after them ; and my anger shall be accomplished, and my indignation appeased on them, and I will be avenged ; and they shall know that I Jehovah have spoken in my jealousy when I accomplish my indignation on them.

3 And I will make you a waste and a reproach among the nations which are around you, in the sight of all that pass by.   And you shall be a reproach, and a reviling, a correction, and an astonishment to the nations which are around you, when I execute judgments on you with anger, and indignation, and indignant rebukes : I Jehovah have spoken it ; when I send on you the malignant arrows of famine, which are for destruction, which I will send on you to destroy you ; and I will add famine on you, and break your staff of bread ; and I will send famine on you, and evil beasts, and they shall bereave you, and pestilence and blood shall pass on you, and I will bring on you the sword ; I, Jehovah, have said it.

PROPHECY IV.　　　　　　　[6.

AGAINST THE MOUNTAINS OF ISRAEL.

1 AND the word of Jehovah came to me, saying, Son of man, set your face against the mountains of Israel, and prophesy against them, and say, Mountains of Israel, hear the word of the Lord Jehovah: Thus says the Lord Jehovah to the mountains and to the hills, to the streams and to the valleys: Behold, I will bring a sword on you, and destroy your high places. And your altars shall be laid waste, and your Hammons [objects of idolatrous worship] shall be broken down; and I will cast down your wounded before your blocks, and I will put the dead bodies of the sons of Israel before their blocks, and scatter their bones around their altars. In all your habitations your cities shall be laid waste, and your high places be made desolate, that your altars may be destroyed and punished. And your blocks shall be broken to pieces, and your Hammons be cut down, and your works destroyed; and the wounded shall fall in the midst of you, and you shall know that I am Jehovah.

2 But I will cause some of you to remain, who shall escape from the sword among the nations when I scatter you in the lands; and those of you that escape shall remember me among the nations by whom they are carried away captive, when I break their adulterous heart which departs from me, and their eyes which go adulterously after their blocks; and they shall loathe themselves in their own sight, on account of the wickedness which they have committed, for all their abominations; and they shall know that I am Jehovah, and that I said not in vain that I would do them this evil.

3 Thus says the Lord Jehovah: Smite with your hand, and stamp with your feet, and say, Alas, for all the evil abominations of the house of Israel, who shall fall by the sword, and by famine, and by pestilence. He that is far off shall die by pestilence; and he that is near shall fall by the sword; and he that remains, and is shut up, shall die with famine; and I will consume them with my indignation, and you shall know that I am Jehovah, when your killed shall be in the midst of your blocks, around your altars, on every high hill, on all the tops of the mountains, and under every green tree, and under every terebinth of thick foliage, places where they offered sweet odors to all their blocks. And I will stretch out my hand

against them, and make the land a greater desolation and astonishment than the wilderness of Riblah, in all your habitations; and they shall know that I am Jehovah.

PROPHECY V.   [7.

EZEKIEL PROCLAIMS THE SPEEDY AND COMPLETE DESTRUCTION OF THE LAND.

1 AND the word of Jehovah came to me, saying, And now, son of man, thus says the Lord Jehovah to the land of Israel: An end has come, an end on the four quarters of the land. Now the end is on you, and I will send my anger on you, and judge you according to your ways, and put on you all your abominations. My eye shall not spare you, neither will I pity, for I will put your ways on you, and your abominations shall be within you, and you shall know that I am Jehovah.

2 Thus says the Lord Jehovah: An evil, an only evil; behold, it comes. An end comes, the end against you; behold, it comes. The cycle comes on you, inhabitant of the land; the time comes, the day of tumult is at hand, but not the rejoicing of mountains. Now I will shortly pour out my indignation on you, and accomplish my anger on you, and judge you according to your ways, and put on you all your abominations; and my eye shall not spare, neither will I pity. I will deal with you according to your ways, and your abominations shall be within you, and you shall know that I am Jehovah who smite.

3 Behold the day; behold, it comes. The cycle comes; the rod glitters [with flowers], pride blossoms, violence rises up for a rod of wickedness, and there is nothing of them, and nothing of their multitude, and nothing of their riches, and nothing brilliant among them. The time has come, the day has arrived; let not the buyer rejoice, nor the seller mourn; for fierce anger is on all her multitude; for the seller shall not return to that which is sold, while yet their life is among the living. For the vision is against all her multitude. They shall not return, neither shall they preserve any man his life by his wickedness. Blow the trumpet to cause all to prepare, but none goes to battle; for my fierce anger is on all her multitude.

4 The sword is without, and pestilence and famine within; he

that is in the field shall die with the sword; and him that is in the city famine and pestilence shall consume; but some of them shall escape, and be on the mountains, all of them mourning, like doves of the valleys, each one for his wickedness. All hands shall be feeble, and all knees flow with water; and they shall put on sackcloth, and trembling cover them, and shame be on all faces, and on all heads baldness; their silver they shall cast away in the streets, and their gold shall be an object of detestation; and their silver and their gold shall not be able to deliver them in the day of the wrath of Jehovah. Their desire they shall not satisfy, nor shall they fill their bowels [with it]; for it is the stumbling block of their wickedness. They rejoiced with pride in the beauty of its ornaments, they made of it their abominations, and their detestable things; therefore will I make it an object of detestation to them, and give it into the hand of strangers for plunder, and of the wicked of the earth for spoil, and they shall profane it.

5 Make a chain, for the land is full of bloody judgment, and the city full of violence; and I will bring the shepherds of the nations, and they shall possess their houses; and I will cause the splendor of the strong ones to cease, and their holy things shall be profaned. Terror shall come, and they shall seek for peace, and there be none. Calamity shall come on calamity, rumor shall be on rumor, and they shall seek a vision of the prophet, but law shall perish from the priest, and counsel from the elders. The king shall mourn, the prince shall be clothed with astonishment, and the hands of the people of the land shall be troubled. I will deal with them and judge them according to their judgments, and they shall know that I am Jehovah.

PROPHECY VI. [8, 9, 10, 11.

VISIONS OF GOD WITH THE CHERUBS REPEATED AT JERUSALEM.

1 AND in the 6th year, in the sixth month, on the 5th day of the month, I sat in my house, and elders of Judah sat before me; and the hand of the Lord Jehovah fell on me there; and I saw, and behold, a form like the appearance of fire; from the appearance of his loins and downwards, even of fire; and from his loins and upwards, like the appearance of brightness, like the brilliancy of polished brass. And he put forth the form of a hand, and took me by the hair of my head, and the spirit bore me between the earth and

heaven, and brought me to Jerusalem, in visions of God, to the entrance of the interior gate which opens to the north, where there was a seat of the image of jealousy which sells Israel.

2 And behold, there was the glory of the God of Israel, according to the appearance which I saw in the valley. And he said to me, Son of man, lift up now your eyes towards the north. Then I lifted up my eyes towards the north, and behold, north of the gate was an altar of this image of jealousy at the entrance. And he said to me, Son of man, do you see what they do, the great abominations which the house of Israel commit here, which should be far from before my sanctuary? But return again; you shall see greater abominations.

3 Then he brought me to the entrance of the court, and I saw, and behold, there was a hole in the wall. And he said to me, Son of man, dig now in the wall. And I dug in the wall, and behold, an entrance. And he said to me, Go in, and see the evil abominations which they commit here. And I went in and saw, and behold, every form of reptile and abominable beast, and all the blocks of the house of Israel, were portrayed on the wall on every side; and 70 men of the elders of the house of Israel — and Jazaniah, the son of Shaphan, standing among them — stood before them, and each one with his censer in his hand, and a thick cloud of incense went up. Then he said to me, Have you seen, son of man, what the elders of the house of Israel do in darkness, each in the chambers of his imagery? For they say, Jehovah does not see us, Jehovah has forsaken the earth.

4 Then he said to me, Return again, and you shall see greater abominations which they do. Then he brought me to the entrance of the gate of the house of Jehovah which is towards the north, and behold, there were women sitting weeping for Tammuz [Adonis]. Then he said to me, Have you seen, son of man? Return again; you shall see greater abominations than these.

5 Then he brought me to the interior court of the house of Jehovah, and behold, at the entrance of the temple of Jehovah, between the porch and altar, there were about 25 men with their backs to the temple of Jehovah, and their faces to the east, and they worshiped the sun towards the east. Then he said to me, Do you see, son of man? Is it too little for the house of Judah to commit the abominations which they commit here, but they fill the land with violence, and return to provoke me? but they put the branch to their nose [an idolatrous service] in vain. For I also will execute

indignation ; my eye shall not spare, neither will I pity ; and they shall cry in my ears with a loud voice, but I will not hear them.

6 Then he cried in my hearing with a loud voice, saying, Approach, [angel] overseers of the city, and each with his destroying weapon in his hand. Then, behold, 6 men came from the way of the High Gate, which opens towards the north, and each with his slaughter weapon in his hand, and one man among them was clothed with linen, and a writer's inkstand was at his loins. And they came and stood beside the altar of brass. And the glory of the God of Israel was taken up from the cherub on which it was, to the threshold of the house ; and he called to the man clothed with linen, at whose loins was the writer's inkstand, and Jehovah said to him, Pass through the city, through Jerusalem, and set a mark on the foreheads of the men that sigh and cry for all the abominations which are done in it. Then he said to the others in my hearing, Go through the city after him, and smite ; let not your eye spare, neither pity ; kill and destroy elder and young man, young woman and little one, and women ; but come not near any man who has on him the mark, and begin at my sanctuary ; and they began with the elders who were before the house. And he said to them, Defile the house, and fill the courts with the killed ; go. Then they went, and smote in the city.

7 And when they had smitten them, and I was left, then I fell on my face and cried, and said, Ah, Lord Jehovah, will you destroy all the remnant of Israel in pouring out your indignation on Jerusalem ? And he said to me, The wickedness of the house of Israel and Judah is very great, and the land is filled with blood, and the city with wrong ; for they say, Jehovah has forsaken the earth, and Jehovah sees not. But as for me, my eye shall not spare, neither will I pity ; I will put their way on their head. And behold, the man clothed with linen, at whose loins was the inkstand, brought back word, saying, I have done as you commanded.

8 Then I looked, and behold, on the floor which was over the head of the cherubs was, as it were, a sapphire stone, the likeness of a throne ; [and one] was seen on it. And he said to the man clothed with linen, Go in between the wheels, under the cherubs, and fill your hand with coals of fire from between the cherubs, and scatter them through the city. And he came before me, and the cherubs stood on the right side of the house, where the man went in, and the cloud filled the interior court. Then the glory of Je-

hovah ascended from the cherub to the threshold of the house, and the house was filled with the cloud, and the court was full of the brightness of the glory of Jehovah. And the sound of the wings of the cherubs was heard to the exterior court, like the voice of God Almighty when he speaks. And when he commanded the man clothed with linen, saying, Take fire from between the wheels from between the cherubs, then he went and stood beside a wheel. And the cherub reached his hand from between the cherubs to the fire which was between the cherubs, and took [some], and put it in the hands of the man clothed with linen, and he took it and went away. And the form of the hand of a man was seen to belong to the cherubs under their wings.

9 And I saw, and behold, four wheels by the cherubs, one wheel by one cherub, and another wheel by another cherub ; and the appearance of the wheels was like the luster of a topaz. And as to their appearances, the four had one form, as if a wheel was in a wheel. When they went, they went on their four sides ; they turned not when they went, but to the place to which the head was directed they went ; they turned not when they went.

10 And all their flesh, and backs, and hands, and wings, and wheels, were full of eyes on every side. The four had their wheels ; and as to the wheels, one called them in my hearing, Whirlwinds. Each one had four faces ; the first face was the face of a cherub, the second face the face of a man, and the third the face of a lion, and the fourth the face of an eagle.

11 And the cherubs were lifted up. This was the living one which I saw by the river Chebar. And when the cherubs went, the wheels went beside them, and when the cherubs raised their wings to ascend from the earth, the wheels did not turn from being beside them. When these stood, they stood, and when these were lifted up, they were lifted up ; for the spirit of the living one was in them.

12 And the glory of Jehovah went from the threshold of the house, and stood on the cherubs. And the cherubs lifted up their wings and ascended from the earth in my sight ; and when they went, the wheels were also against them. And they stood at the entrance of the gate of the house of Jehovah on the east, and the glory of the God of Israel was on them above [the floor].

13 This was the living one which I saw under the God of Israel, by the river Chebar, and I knew that they were cherubs. Each had four faces, and each had four wings, and the likeness of the hands

of a man was under their wings ; and as to the form of their faces, they were the faces which I saw by the river Chebar, their appearances and themselves ; they went each one directly forward.

14 Then the spirit took me up, and brought me to the east gate of the house of Jehovah, that opens to the east, and behold, at the entrance of the gate were 25 men, and I saw among them Jazaniah, the son of Azzur, and Pelatiah, the son of Benaiah, princes of the people. And he said to me, Son of man, these are the men that devise wickedness, and give evil counsel in this city, who say, The time has not come for building houses. This city is the pot, and we are the meat ; therefore prophesy against them ; prophesy, son of man. Then the Spirit of Jehovah fell on me, and he said to me, Say, Thus says Jehovah : Thus do you say, house of Israel ; and as for the thoughts of your mind, I know them ; you multiply your killed in this city, and fill its streets with the killed. Therefore thus says the Lord Jehovah : Your killed whom you put in it, they are the meat, and it is the pot ; but I will bring you out of it, and will give you into the hand of strangers, and execute judgments on you. You shall fall by the sword on the border of Israel ; I will judge you, and you shall know that I am Jehovah. This shall not be to you a pot, nor you be meat in it ; on the border of Israel [at Riblah] will I judge you, and you shall know that I am Jehovah, in whose ordinances you have not walked, and whose judgments you have not performed, but have done according to the judgments of the nations around you.

15 And when I prophesied, Pelatiah, the son of Benaiah, died ; then I fell on my face, and cried with a loud voice, and said, Ah, Lord Jehovah, wilt thou make an entire destruction of the rest of Israel ? Then the word of Jehovah came to me, saying, Son of man, the inhabitants of Jerusalem say to your brothers, your brothers, the men of your connection, and all the house of Israel, all of them, Put Jehovah far away from us, for this land is given to us for a possession. Therefore say, Thus says the Lord Jehovah : I will surely put them far off among the nations, and I will surely scatter them in the lands ; but I will be to them for a sanctuary in a little while, in lands to which they go.

16 Therefore say, Thus says the Lord Jehovah : Then I will gather you from the peoples, and assemble you from the lands whither I scatter you, and give you the land of Israel. And they shall come there, and put away all its detestable things and all its abominations

from it. And I will give them one heart, and a new spirit will I put within them ; and I will take away the heart of stone from their flesh, and give them a heart of flesh, that they may walk in my ordinances, and keep my judgments, and do them ; and they shall be my people, and I will be their God. But as for those whose heart goes after the heart of their detestable things, and of their abominations, I will put their way on their heads, says the Lord Jehovah.

17 Then the cherubs raised their wings, and the wheels were against them, and the glory of the God of Israel was on them above. And the glory of Jehovah went up from the city, and stood on a mountain east of the city. Then the spirit took me up, and brought me to Chaldea, to the exiles, in vision by the Spirit of God ; and the vision which I saw went up from me. Then I spoke to the exiles all the words of Jehovah which he showed me.

PROPHECY VII. [12.

EZEKIEL PREDICTS THE CAPTIVITY OF ZEDEKIAH.

1 THEN the word of Jehovah came to me, saying, Son of man, you live in the midst of a rebellious house, which have eyes to see, but see not ; which have ears to hear, but hear not; for they are a rebellious house.

2 And as for you, son of man, make instruments of exile, and remove by day before their eyes; and remove from your place to another place before their eyes ; perhaps they will see ; for they are a rebellious house. And bring out your goods, like goods for exile, by day before their eyes, and go out in the evening before their eyes, as those carrying things away ; break through the wall before their eyes, and go out by the [breach] ; bear loads on [your] shoulders ; go in the evening ; cover your face ; see not the ground ; for I have made you a sign to the house of Israel.

3 Then I did as I was commanded. I carried out my goods, as goods for exile by day, and in the evening I dug through the wall with [my] hand, and went out in the evening, [and] bore [things] on my shoulder, before their eyes.

4 Then the word of Jehovah came to me in the morning, saying, Son of man, does not the house of Israel, the rebellious house, say to you, What are you doing ? Say to them, Thus says the Lord Jehovah : The prince [shall bear] this burden in Jerusalem, and all

the house of Israel, in the midst of whom he is. Say, I am your sign ; as I have done so shall it be done by them; they shall go into exile, into captivity. The prince who is in the midst of them shall bear [loads] in the evening on [his] shoulder, and go forth ; he shall dig through the wall, to go out by it ; he shall cover his face, that the earth may not be seen by his eyes ; but I will spread my net on him, and he shall be taken in my snare ; and I will bring him to Babylon, the land of the Chaldeans, but he shall not see it, and he shall die there. And all that are about him, his help and all his armies, will I scatter to all winds, and draw out a sword after them. And they shall know that I am Jehovah, when I scatter them among the nations, and disperse them in the lands. But I will leave a few of them from the sword, from famine, and from pestilence, that they may declare all their abominations to the nations to which they go ; and they shall know that I am Jehovah.

5 And the word of Jehovah came to me, saying, Son of man, eat your bread with agitation, and drink your water with trembling and anxiety, and say to the people of the land, Thus says the Lord Jehovah of the inhabitants of Jerusalem in the land of Israel : They shall eat their bread with anxiety, and drink their water with astonishment, that their land may be desolated in respect to all it contains, on account of the violence of all who live in it. And the inhabited cities shall be laid waste, and the land be a desolation ; and you shall know that I am Jehovah.

6 And the word of Jehovah came to me, saying, What is this proverb which you have in the land of Israel, saying, The days are prolonged, and every vision fails ? Therefore say to them,.Thus says the Lord Jehovah : I will cause this proverb to cease, and they shall not say it any more in Israel; but say to them, The days are at hand, and the accomplishment of every vision. For no vision [from me] shall any longer be in vain, nor any divination false among the house of Israel. For I am Jehovah ; I will speak the word which I please, and it shall be done, it shall no longer be deferred ; for in your days, rebellious house, I will speak a word, and do it, says the Lord Jehovah.

7 And the word of Jehovah came to me, saying, Son of man, behold, the house of Israel say the vision which he sees is for many days, and he prophesies for distant times ; therefore say to them, Thus says the Lord Jehovah : None of my words shall any longer be deferred, for I will speak a word and it shall be done, says the Lord Jehovah.

21 *

PROPHECY VIII.   [13.

AGAINST THE FALSE PROPHETS.

1 AND the word of Jehovah came to me, saying, Son of man,
prophesy against the prophets of Israel that prophesy; and say
to those that prophesy from their heart, Hear the word of Jehovah.
Thus says the Lord Jehovah : Woe to the foolish prophets that
walk after their spirit, and see nothing.   Your prophets, Israel, are
like jackals of the deserts; you go not up into the breaches,
neither do you build a wall around the house of Israel, that they
may stand in battle in the day of Jehovah.   They see vanity and a
lying divination, saying, Jehovah says, when Jehovah did not send
them; and they wait for [their] word to come to pass.   Do you not
see a false vision, and tell a lying divination, when you say, Jehovah says, and I spoke not ?

2 Therefore thus says the Lord Jehovah : Because you speak
vanity and see a lie, therefore behold, I am against you, says the
Lord Jehovah; and my hand shall be on the prophets who see
vanity and divine a lie; they shall not be in the assembly of my
people, nor be written on the roll of the house of Israel, nor come
to the land of Israel; and you shall know that I am Jehovah.   Because they lead my people astray, saying, Peace, when there is no
peace; and one builds a wall [of a house], and behold, they plaster
it with mortar.   Say to them that plaster it with mortar, that it shall
fall; there shall be an overflowing rain, and I will cause hailstones
to fall on it, and a storm wind shall rend it, and behold, the wall
shall fall; and shall it not be said to you, Where is the plastering
with which you plastered it ?

3 Therefore thus says the Lord Jehovah : I will cause a storm-
wind to break forth in my indignation, and there shall be an overflowing rain in my anger, and hailstones to destroy in [my] indignation; and I will break down the wall which you have plastered
with mortar, and raze it to the ground, and its foundation shall be
laid bare, and it shall fall, and you shall be destroyed with it; and
you shall know that I am Jehovah.   And I will accomplish my indignation on the wall, and on those that plaster it with mortar, and
say to you, There is no wall, and they that plastered it are no more ;
the prophets of Israel who prophesy to Jerusalem, and see for it a

vision of peace when there is no peace [shall perish], says the Lord Jehovah.

4 And as for you, son of man, set your face against the daughters of my people, who prophesy from their heart, and prophesy concerning them, and say, Thus says the Lord Jehovah : Woe to those that sew cushions for all the joints of the hand [the knuckles], and make quilts for the head of every statue, to hunt souls. You hunt my people, even [their] lives, that you may go and live ; and you profane me among my people, for bundles of barley and for pieces of bread, to kill those that should not die, and to preserve alive those that should not live, by your lying to my people who obey lying.

5 Therefore thus says the Lord Jehovah : Behold, I am against your cushions with which you hunt souls for the birds, and I will tear them off from your arms, and will let the souls go, the souls which you hunt for the birds ; and your quilts also will I tear away, and deliver my people from your hands ; and they shall no more be in your hand for a prey, and you shall know that I am Jehovah.

PROPHECY IX.   [14, 1-11.

EZEKIEL REPROVES MEN FOR WORSHIPING IDOLS IN THEIR HEARTS.

1 THEN came to me men from the elders of the Jews ; and the word of Jehovah came to me, saying, Son of man, these men set up their blocks in their hearts, and put the stumbling block of their wickedness before their face. Shall I be inquired of at all by them ? Therefore speak to them, and say to them, Thus says the Lord Jehovah : Every man of the house of Israel who sets up his blocks in his heart, and puts the stumbling block of his wickedness before his face, and goes to a prophet, I Jehovah will answer him that comes with the multitude of his blocks, to take the house of Israel by their hearts, who are all estranged from me by their blocks.

2 Therefore say to the house of Israel, Thus says the Lord Jehovah : Turn, and turn [yourselves] from all your blocks, and turn your faces from all your abominations. For every man of the house of Israel, and of the strangers who live in Israel, who departs from me, and sets up his blocks in his heart, and puts the stumbling block of his wickedness before his face, and comes to a prophet to inquire of him from me, I Jehovah will answer him from myself, and set

my face against that man, and make him a sign and a proverb, and cut him off from among my people; and you shall know that I am Jehovah.

3 And as for a prophet, when he is deceived and speaks a word, I Jehovah will deceive that prophet, and stretch out my hand on him, and destroy him from among my people Israel; and they shall bear their wickedness. The wickedness of him that inquires and the wickedness of the prophet shall be the same, that the house of Israel may not wander from me any more, nor sin any more, with all their transgressions; and they shall be my people, and I will be their God, says the Lord Jehovah.

PROPHECY X.   14, 12, 15.

GOD'S JUDGMENTS NOT TO BE AVERTED FROM THE GUILTY.

1 AND the word of Jehovah came to me, saying, Son of man, when a land sins against me, and deals treacherously, and I stretch out my hand against it, and break its staff of bread, and send famine on it, and cut off from it man and beast, and these three men are in it, Noah, Daniel, and Job, they shall save their lives by their righteousness, says the Lord Jehovah. If I cause evil beasts to pass through a land, and they cut off its children, and it becomes a desolation, with none passing through, on account of the beasts, these three men in it, as I live, says the Lord Jehovah, shall not save sons nor daughters; they only shall be saved, and the land shall be a desolation.

2 Or if I bring a sword on that land, and say, Sword, pass through the land, and cut off from it man and beast, then these three men in it, as I live, says the Lord Jehovah, shall not save sons nor daughters, but they only shall be saved. Or if I send pestilence on that land, and pour out my indignation on it with blood, to cut off from it man and beast, and Noah, Daniel, and Job are in it, as I live, says the Lord Jehovah, they shall not save son nor daughter; they shall save themselves [only] by their righteousness.

3 For thus says the Lord Jehovah: How much more when I send my four evil judgments, sword, and famine, and evil beasts, and pestilence, on Jerusalem, to cut off from it man and beast! Yet behold, there shall be left of it a remnant, that shall be brought forth,

sons and daughters ; behold, they shall come forth to you, and you shall see their way and their doings, and be comforted for the evil which I bring on Jerusalem, for all which I bring on it ; and they shall comfort you, for you shall see their way and their doings, and know that I did not in vain all. that I did to her, says the Lord Jehovah.

4 And the word of Jehovah came to me, saying, What is the vine tree more than any other tree ? Is it a branch which is on the trees of the forest ? Can timber be taken from it to make any work ? Can a pin be taken from it to hang any thing on ? Behold, it is given to the fire for fuel, and the fire consumes the two ends, and its middle is burned. Is it fit for a work [then] ? Behold, when it was perfect, it could not be made into any work ; how much less when the fire has consumed it, and it is burned, can it be made into a work then ! Therefore thus says the Lord Jehovah : As the vine tree among the trees of the forest, which I have given to the fire to consume, so will I give the inhabitants of Jerusalem ; and I will set my face against them, and they shall go from one fire, and another fire shall consume them ; and you shall know that I am Jehovah, when I set my face against them ; and I will make the land a desolation, because they have dealt treacherously, says the Lord Jehovah.

PROPHECY XI.   [16.

JERUSALEM, A BRIDE AND A HARLOT, TO BE PUNISHED AND RECLAIMED, WITH SODOM AND SAMARIA.

1 AND the word of Jehovah came to me, saying, Son of man, make Jerusalem know her abominations, and say, Thus says the Lord Jehovah to Jerusalem : Your birth and nativity were in the land of the Canaanite, your father was an Amorite, and your mother a Hittite ; and as to your nativity, in the day in which you were born, none cut your navel cord, nor were you washed with water to be seen, nor sprinkled with salt, nor wound with bandages. No eye pitied you, to do for you one of these things, that pity should be shown you, and you were cast out on the face of the field, with a loathing of your life, in the day in which you were born.

2 Then I passed by you, and saw you wallowing in your blood, and said to you in your blood, Live. Yes, I said to you in your blood, Live, and caused you to grow like a sprout of the field ; and

you grew and became great, and came to be a beauty of beauties. Your breasts stood out, your hair was long, but you were naked and bare. Then I passed by you and saw, and behold, your time was the time of love, and I spread my skirt over you, and covered your nakedness, and swore to you, and entered into covenant with you, says the Lord Jehovah, and you became mine.

3 Then I washed you with water, and swept away with a flood your blood from you, and anointed you with oil, and clothed you with embroidered work, and shod you with sealskins, and bound you with fine linen [about your head], and covered you with [a mantle of] silk, and adorned you with ornaments, and put bracelets on your hands, and a chain on your neck ; and I put a jewel in your nose, and rings in your ears, and a beautiful crown on your head, and you were adorned with gold and silver, and clothes of fine linen, and silk and embroidered work, and I caused you to eat fine flour, honey, and oil, and you became exceedingly fair, and were a prosperous kingdom.

4 And your name went out among the nations for your beauty, for it was perfect, through the excellency which I put on you, says the Lord Jehovah. But you trusted in your beauty, and committed fornication against my name, and poured out your fornications on every one that passed by, to be with him ; and took your clothes and made yourself variegated tabernacles, and committed fornication in them ; things which had not come, and shall not be [again] ; and you took my beautiful ornaments of gold and of silver, which I gave you, and made images of men, and committed fornication with them, and took your embroidered garments and covered them, and set my oil and my incense before them ; and my bread which I gave you, the fine flour, and oil, and honey which I caused you to eat, and set it before them for a sweet odor ; and it was so, says the Lord Jehovah.

5 And you took your sons and your daughters, whom you bore to me, and sacrificed them for the [idols] to eat. Was this a small part of your fornication, that you killed my sons, and gave them up, to cause them to pass through fire ? And in all your abominations and fornications you remembered not the days of your infancy, when you were naked and bare, and wallowing in your blood.

6 And after all your wickedness, woe, woe to you, says the Lord Jehovah, then you built you a brothel, and made you a high place in every street ; at the head of every way you built your high place,

and caused your beauty to be abhorred, and opened your feet to every one who passed by, and multiplied your fornications. And you committed fornication with the sons of Egypt, your neighbors of great flesh, and multiplied your fornications to provoke me. Then, behold, I stretched out my hand against you, and gave you to the desire of those that hated you, the daughters of the Philistines, who were ashamed of your lewd ways; and you committed fornication with the sons of Assyria, but they did not satisfy you; yes, you committed fornication with them, and were not satisfied; and you increased your fornications in the land of Canaan to Chaldea, and were not satisfied with this. How did your heart languish, says the Lord Jehovah, when you did all these things, the work of a harlot princess! When you built your brothel at the head of every way, and made your high place in every street, then you were not like the harlot to scorn the price; [you were] the adulterous wife, who takes strangers instead of her husband. To all harlots they give a liberal gift; but you give your liberal gifts to all your lovers, and bribe them to come to you for your fornications from every side. Your habit is the reverse of that of harlots in your fornications; and there is no harlot after your method, even in your giving the reward, and the reward is not given to you, so that you are the reverse [of harlots].

7 Therefore hear, harlot, the word of Jehovah: Thus says the Lord Jehovah: Because your brass [money] is poured out, and your nakedness uncovered in your fornications with your lovers, and with all the blocks of your abominations, even according to the blood of your sons which you have given them, therefore, behold, I will gather all your lovers with whom you have had intercourse, and all whom you have loved, with all whom you have hated, I will even gather them to you from every side, and uncover your nakedness to them, and they shall see all your nakedness. And I will judge you with the judgments of adulteresses, and of those that shed blood, and give you blood, indignation, and hatred, and give you into their hand; and they shall tear down your brothel, and break down your high places, and strip you of your clothes, and take away your jewels, and leave you naked and bare. And they shall bring up against you an assembly, and stone you with stones, and cut you in pieces with their swords, and burn your house with fire, and execute judgments on you, in the sight of many women; and I will cause you to cease from being a harlot, and you shall not

give harlot hire any more.   Then I will rest from my indignation against you, and my jealousy shall depart from you, and I will be quiet, and not be angry any more.   Because you forget the days of your youth, and displease me with all these things, therefore I also will put your way on your head, says the Lord Jehovah, that you may not commit wickedness with all your abominations.

8 Behold, all that make proverbs shall make a proverb against you, saying, Like mother and like daughter.   You are the daughter of a mother who cast off her husband and her sons, and you are the sister of your sisters who cast off their husbands and their sons ; your mother was a Hittite, and your father an Amorite.   Your elder sister is Samaria, who sat on your left hand ; and your younger sister, who sits on your right hand, is Sodom and her daughters.   But you have not walked in their ways, nor done according to their abominations ; that was despised as little.   You have been more corrupt than they in all your ways.   As I live, says the Lord Jehovah, surely Sodom, your sister, and her daughters, did not do as you and your daughters have done.   Behold, this was the sin of your sister Sodom, pride, fullness of bread, and she and her daughters had careless ease ; and she did not strengthen the hand of the poor and needy ; and they were haughty, and committed abominations before me ; and when I saw it I took them away.   And Samaria did not commit half your sins ; but you have multiplied your abominations more than they, and justify your sisters by all your abominations which you commit.   Do you also bear your shame according as you judged your sisters, for your sins, by which you have made yourself more abominable than they, — they are more righteous than you, — and be ashamed, and bear your confusion, for your justification of your sisters.

9 But I will restore the captives of Sodom and her daughters, and the captives of Samaria and her daughters, and with them I will restore your captives, that you may bear your confusion, and be confounded for all that you have done, when you change your minds in regard to it.   And your sister Sodom and her daughters shall return to their former state ; and Samaria and her daughters shall return to their former state ; and you and your daughters shall return to your former state.   But Sodom, your sister, was not heard of from your mouth in the day of your pride, before your wickedness was discovered, as in the time of your reproach by the daughters of Syria, and all that were around her, the daughters of the

Philistines, who despised you on all sides, [and] you bore your wickedness and your abominations, says Jehovah.

10 For thus says the Lord Jehovah : I will do to you as you did, who despised the oath and broke the covenant. But I remember my covenant with you in the days of your youth, and will confirm [it] to you for an eternal covenant ; and you shall remember your ways, and be confounded when you receive your sisters, your elder sisters, and those younger than you ; and I will give them to you for daughters, but not from your covenant. And I will confirm my covenant with you, and you shall know that I am Jehovah, that you may remember and be ashamed, and not open your mouth any more on account of shame, when I forgive you all that you have done, says the Lord Jehovah.

PROPHECY XII.   [17.

THE PARABLE OF THE EAGLES.

1 AND the word of Jehovah came to me, saying, Son of man, tell a riddle and put forth a parable to the house of Israel, and say, Thus says the Lord Jehovah : A great eagle with large wings, of long feathers full of feathers, which were of various colors, came to Lebanon, and took a lock of the cedar. He broke off the top of its twigs, and brought it to the land of Canaan, [and] set it in a city of merchants. And he took of the seed of the land, and put it in a field for seed ; and he took it to great waters, and set it for a willow tree. But it grew and became a spreading vine of low stature, whose branches turned towards him, and its roots were under him, and it became a vine, and produced branches, and sent forth shoots.

2 And there was another great eagle, with great wings and many feathers ; and behold, this vine turned its roots to him, and sent forth its shoots for him, that he should water it in the beds where it was planted. It was planted in a good soil, by much water, to pro- duce branches and bear fruit, and to be a noble vine. Say, Thus says the Lord Jehovah : Shall it prosper ? Will he not pull up its roots ? And will he not pluck off its fruit, and all the fresh foliage of its branches become dry ? And will he not [come] with a great arm and a mighty people to take it up by its roots ? And behold, shall the plant prosper ? When the east wind touches it, will it

not wither? It will be entirely dried up on the beds where it grew.

3 And the word of Jehovah came to me, saying, Say, I pray you, to the rebellious house, Do you not know what these things mean? Say, Behold, the king of Babylon came to Jerusalem, and took her king and her princes, and brought them to him at Babylon. And he took one of the royal family, and made a covenant with him, and brought him into an oath, and took away the mighty men of the land, that the kingdom might be humble, and not exalt itself, and keep his covenant, and confirm it. Then he rebelled against him, and sent his messengers to Egypt, that it should furnish him horses and many people. Shall he prosper? Shall he be delivered that does these things? And shall one break a covenant and be delivered?

4 As I live, says the Lord Jehovah, surely in the place of the king who made him king, whose oath he has despised, and whose covenant he has broken, in the midst of Babylon he shall die; and not with [his] great army and vast assembly will Pharaoh do any thing for him in battle when [the enemy] casts up mounds and builds watch-towers to cut off many souls. And he despised the oath, to break the covenant, when behold, he gave his hand. All these things also has he done; he shall not be delivered.

5 Therefore thus says the Lord Jehovah : As I live, surely it is my oath which he despised, and my covenant which he broke, and I will put it on his head, and spread my net over him, and he shall be taken in my fortress ; and I will bring him to Babylon, and judge him there for his crime which he has committed against me. And all his fugitives and all his armies shall fall by the sword, and those that remain shall be scattered to all winds; and you shall know that I Jehovah have spoken.

6 Thus says the Lord Jehovah : I also will take one from the locks of a cedar, and put him on high, and crop off the top of his tender branches, and plant him on a mountain high and exalted. On the mountain of the height of Israel will I plant him, and he shall put forth branches, and bear fruit, and be a noble cedar. And under him shall dwell all birds of every wing ; they shall live in the shade of his branches ; and all the trees of the field shall know that I Jehovah abase the high tree and exalt the low tree, dry up the green tree and make the dry tree fruitful. I Jehovah have spoken, and will do it.

PROPHECY XIII.   [18.

GOD'S JUSTICE ASSERTED ; HE DEALS WITH MEN ACCORDING TO THEIR DOINGS.

1 THEN the word of Jehovah came to me, saying, Why do you use this proverb concerning the land of Israel, saying, The fathers eat sour grapes, and the children's teeth are blunted. As I live, says the Lord Jehovah, surely you shall no longer have this proverb in Israel. Behold, all souls are mine ; behold, the soul of the father and the soul of the son are alike mine. The soul that sins shall die.

2 But if a man is righteous, and does justice and righteousness ; eats not on the mountains, and lifts not up his eyes to the blocks of the house of Israel ; nor defiles his friend's wife, nor approaches a woman [in her] impurity ; nor oppresses any man ; [but] restores his pledge for debt ; commits no robbery ; gives his bread to the hungry, and covers the naked with clothing ; gives not for usury, and takes not increase ; keeps back his hand from evil ; renders a true judgment between man and man ; walks in my ordinances, and keeps my judgments to perform truth, — he is a righteous man ; he shall live, says the Lord Jehovah.

3 If he begets a son of violence, that sheds blood, and does not according to any of these things, but eats on the mountains, and defiles his friend's wife, oppresses the poor and needy, commits robbery, restores not the pledge, and lifts up his eyes to blocks, commits abomination, lends for usury, takes increase, shall he live ? He shall not live. If he has done all these abominations, he shall surely die ; his blood [the blood which he has shed] shall be on him.

4 Behold, if he has a son, and he sees all the sins of his father which he commits, and fears, and does not do like them ; eats not on the mountains, and lifts not up his eyes to the blocks of the house of Israel ; defiles not his friend's wife ; and oppresses no man, takes not a pledge, and commits not robbery ; gives his bread to the hungry, and covers the naked with clothing ; [with] his hand turns back oppression from the poor, and takes not increase ; performs my judgment, walks in my ordinances, — he shall not die for the wickedness of his father ; he shall surely live. Because his father committed oppression, robbed his brother, and did that which is not good among his people, therefore, behold, he shall die for his wickedness.

5 But you say, Why? Does not the son suffer for the wickedness of the father? If the son does justice and righteousness, [and] keeps all my ordinances, and does them, he shall surely live. The soul that sins shall die; the son shall not suffer for the wickedness of the father, nor the father suffer for the wickedness of the son; the righteousness of the righteous shall be on him, and the wickedness of the wicked shall be on him.

6 And when a wicked man turns from all his sins which he has committed, and keeps all my ordinances, and does justice and righteousness, he shall surely live; he shall not die. None of his transgressions which he committed shall be remembered against him; for his righteousness which he has done, he shall live. Do I delight at all in the death of the wicked, says the Lord Jehovah, [and] not in his turning from his way, that he may live?

7 And when a righteous man turns from his righteousness, and does evil, doing according to all the abominations which the wicked man does, shall he live? None of his righteousness which he has done shall be remembered; for his crime which he commits, and for his sin which he sins, he shall die. But you say, The way of the Lord is not equal. Hear, I pray you, house of Israel: Is not my way equal? Are not your ways unequal? When a righteous man turns from his righteousness, and does evil, then he shall die for it; for his evil which he does he shall die. But when a wicked man turns from his wickedness which he has done, and does justice and righteousness, he shall preserve his life. Because he feared and turned from all his transgressions which he committed, he shall surely live; he shall not die.

8 But the house of Israel say, The way of the Lord is not equal. Are not my ways equal, house of Israel? Are not your ways unequal? Therefore will I judge every man according to his way, house of Israel, says the Lord Jehovah. Turn and turn [yourselves] from all your transgressions, that wickedness may not be your ruin. And cast away from you all your transgressions which you have committed, and make you a new heart, and a new spirit; for why will you die, house of Israel? For I have no pleasure in the death of mortal, says the Lord Jehovah. Therefore turn and live.

PROPHECY XIV.   [19.

A LAMENTATION FOR THE KINGS OF JUDAH.

1 AND take up a lamentation for the princes of Israel, and say,
How did your mother lie a lioness among lions? Among young
lions she brought up her young. And she brought up one of her
young; he became a lion, and learned to catch prey; he devoured
men. And the nations heard of him; he was taken in their pit,
and they brought him with hooks to the land of Egypt. And when
she saw that she waited [in vain], her expectation [from him] perished, and she took another of her young, and made him a young
lion. And he went about among lions; he was a young lion, and
learned to take prey; he devoured men. And he knew their
widows, and desolated their cities, and made the land desolate, and
filled it with the noise of his roaring.

2 Then the nations on every side, from the provinces, assailed
him, and spread their net for him, and he was taken in their pit;
and they put him in a cage with hooks, and brought him to the king
of Babylon, and brought him to fortresses, that his voice might no
more be heard on the mountains of Israel.

3 Your mother was like a vine on your high places, planted by
waters; she was fruitful and full of branches from many waters, and
had strong rods for the scepters of rulers; and its height was great
even to the clouds, and it was seen by reason of its height, and by
reason of the multitude of its branches. Then it was plucked up
with indignation; it was cast down on the ground, and an east wind
dried up its fruit. Its strong scepters are broken and dried up, and
the fire has consumed it. And now it is planted in a desert, in a
dry and thirsty land; and a fire has gone out from a rod of its
limbs, and consumed its fruit, and it has no strong rod for a ruler's
scepter. This is a lamentation, and shall be a lamentation.

22 *

PROPHECY XV.

GOD'S DEALINGS WITH THE ISRAELITES RECOUNTED ; THEIR EXILE
AND RESTORATION PREDICTED.

1 AND in the 7th year, in the fifth month, on the 10th day of the
month, came men from the elders of Israel to inquire of Jehovah,
and sat before him. Then the word of Jehovah came to me, saying, Son of man, speak to the elders of Israel, and say to them,
Thus says the Lord Jehovah : Do you come to inquire of me ? As
I live, I will not be inquired of by you, says the Lord Jehovah.
Will you judge them ? will you judge them, son of man ? Make
them know the abominations of their fathers ; and say to them,
Thus says the Lord Jehovah : In the day in which I chose Israel, I
lifted up my hand to the posterity of the house of Jacob, and was
made known to them in the land of Egypt ; and I lifted up my
hand to them, saying, I am Jehovah your God. In that day I lifted
up my hand to them, to bring them out from the land of Egypt to a
land which I looked out for them, flowing with milk and honey,
which is the glory of all lands.

2 And I said to them, Cast away every one of you the abominations of his eyes, and defile not yourselves with the blocks of Egypt ;
I am Jehovah your God. But they rebelled against me, and would
not hear me ; they cast not away every man the abominations of his
eyes, nor forsook the blocks of Egypt. Then I said that I would
pour out my indignation on them, to accomplish my anger on them,
in the land of Egypt. But I had regard for my name, that it might
not be profaned in the sight of the nations among whom they were,
before whose eyes I was made known to them, to bring them out from
the land of Egypt ; and I brought them out from the land of Egypt,
and brought them into the wilderness.

3 Then I gave them my ordinances, and taught them my judgments, which if man does, he shall live by them ; and I gave them
my Sabbaths also, to be a sign between me and them, that they
might know that I am Jehovah, who sanctifies them. But the house
of Israel rebelled against me in the wilderness ; they walked not in
my ordinances, and refused my judgments, which if a man does, he
shall live by them ; and my Sabbaths they profaned exceedingly.
Then I said that I would pour out my indignation on them in the

wilderness, to consume them. But I had regard for my name, that it might not be profaned in the sight of the nations before whose eyes I brought them forth.

4 And I also lifted up my hand to them in the wilderness, not to bring them into the land which I gave [them], flowing with milk and honey, which is the glory of all lands, because they rejected my judgments, and walked not in my ordinances, and profaned my Sabbaths, because their heart went after their blocks. But my eye spared them, not to destroy them, nor did-I make an end of them in the wilderness.

5 Then I said to their sons in the wilderness, Walk not in the ordinances of your fathers, nor keep their judgments, nor defile yourselves with their blocks; I am Jehovah your God; walk in my ordinances, and keep my judgments and do them, and hallow my Sabbaths, that they may be a sign between me and you, that you may know that I am Jehovah your God. But the sons rebelled against me; they walked not in my ordinances, nor kept my judgments to do them, which if a man does, he shall live by them; and they profaned my Sabbaths. Then I said that I would pour out my indignation on them, to accomplish my anger on them in the wilderness. But I took back my hand, and had regard for my name, that it might not be profaned in the sight of the nations before whose eyes I brought them out.

6 I also lifted up my hand to them in the wilderness, to scatter them among the nations, and to disperse them in the lands, because they performed not my judgments, and rejected my ordinances, and profaned my Sabbaths, and their eyes were after the blocks of their fathers. Then I also gave them ordinances that were not good, and judgments by which they could not live, and defiled them with their offerings, in causing every first born of a mother to pass through the fire, that I might destroy them, that they might know that I am Jehovah.

7 Therefore speak to the house of Israel, son of man, and say to them, Thus says the Lord Jehovah: Your fathers reproached me in this way, by dealing treacherously with me; for I brought them into the land which I lifted up my hand to give them, and they saw the high hills, and all the shady trees, and sacrificed there their sacrifices, and set [objects] of displeasure among them, and there placed their sweet odors, and there poured out their libations. Then I said to them, What is the high place to which you come? But they call its name High Place to this day.

8 Therefore say to the house of Israel, Thus says the Lord Jehovah : Are you defiled after the manner of your fathers, and after their blocks P Do you commit fornication P And by presenting your gifts, and causing your sons to pass through fire, are you defiled, with all your blocks, to this day P And shall I be inquired of by you, house of Israel P As I live, says the Lord Jehovah, I will not be inquired of by you. And that which you intend, shall not be, when you say, We will be like the nations, like the families of the lands to serve wood and stone.

9 As I live, says the Lord Jehovah, surely, with a strong hand, and with an outstretched arm, and with indignation poured out, I will rule as king over you, and bring you out from the peoples, and gather you from the lands in which you are scattered, with a strong hand, and with an outstretched arm, and with indignation poured out. And I will bring you to the wilderness of the peoples, and judge you there face to face ; as I judged your fathers in the wilderness of the land of Egypt, thus will I judge you, says the Lord Jehovah.

10 And I will pass you under the rod, and bring you into the bond of the covenant, and purge out from you the rebels ; and those that transgress against me will I bring forth from the land where they live, and none shall come into the land of Israel ; and you shall know that I am Jehovah.

11 And as for you, house of Israel, thus says the Lord Jehovah : Go and serve every man his blocks, if you will not hereafter obey me ; but profane not my holy name any more with your gifts and your blocks. But on my holy mountain, on the mountain of the height of Israel, says the Lord Jehovah, there shall all the house of Israel, all in their land, serve me ; and there I will require your offerings, and the first fruits of your gifts, with all your holy things.

12 I will accept you for a sweet odor when I bring you from the peoples, and gather you from the lands in which I have scattered you, and I will be hallowed among you in the sight of the nations ; and you shall know that I am Jehovah when I bring you to the land of Israel, which I lifted up my hand to give to your fathers. And you shall remember then your ways and all your doings with which you defiled yourselves, and shall loathe yourselves for all your wickedness which you committed, and shall know that I am Jehovah when I deal with you for my name, not according to your evil ways, nor according to your corrupt doings, house of Israel, says the Lord Jehovah.

PROPHECY XVI.   [21, 22.

1 AND the word of Jehovah came to me, saying, Son of man, set your face towards the south, and drop [a word] against the south, and prophesy against the forest in the fields of the south, and say to the forest of the south, Hear the word of Jehovah : Thus says the Lord Jehovah : Behold, I will kindle in you a fire, and it shall consume in you every green tree and every dry tree ; the burning flame shall not be extinguished, and all faces from south to north shall be scarred with it ; and all flesh shall see that I Jehovah kindled it : it shall not be extinguished. Then I said, Ah Lord Jehovah ! they will say to me, Does he not speak parables ?

2 Then the word of Jehovah came to me, saying, Son of man, set your face against Jerusalem, and drop [a word] against the sanctuaries, and prophesy against the land of Israel, and say to the land of Israel, Thus says Jehovah : Behold, I am against you, and will draw forth my sword out of its sheath, and cut off from you the righteous and wicked. Because I cut off the righteous and wicked, therefore my sword shall go forth from its sheath against all flesh from south to north, and all flesh shall know that I Jehovah draw my sword from its sheath, [and] it shall not return again.

3 And sigh, son of man, with a breaking of loins, and sigh bitterly before their eyes ; and when they say to you, Why do you sigh ? then say, For a report, for it has come, and all hearts melt, and all hands are weak, and all spirits faint, and all knees flow with water. Behold, it shall come, and be accomplished, says the Lord Jehovah.

4 And the word of Jehovah came to me, saying, Son of man, prophesy and say, Thus says Jehovah ; say, A sword, a sword — it is sharpened, and also made bright ; it is sharpened for great slaughter ; it is made bright, that it may shine like lightning against the prince, the tribe of my son, which rejects every tree. And he gave it to be sharpened, that he might take it in hand ; this sword is made sharp, it is made bright, that he may give it into the hand of the slaughterer. Cry and lament, son of man, for it is for my people, it is for all the princes of Israel ; they are cast down before the sword with my people. Therefore smite on your thigh, for there

is a trial [at hand], and what if the scornful tribe shall be no more?
says the Lord Jehovah.

5 But as for you, son of man, prophesy, and smite hand to hand,
for the sword shall be repeated thrice; it shall be the sword of the
killed, a sword of great slaughter, which besieges them, so that
their hearts melt, and many fall. I will put heaps slaughtered by
the sword in all their gates. Alas! it has done shining, covered
with slaughter. Collect yourself, turn to the right; set yourself,
turn to the left, wherever your face turns; and I also will smite my
hands together, and rest from my indignation. I Jehovah have
spoken.

6 And the word of Jehovah came to me, saying, And as for you,
son of man, appoint two ways for the sword of the king of Babylon to come, and let them both come from one land, and make a
place, make it at the head of the way to the city; and make a way
for the sword to come to Rabbah, of the sons of Ammon, and to
Judah, with Jerusalem, the fortified city. For the king of Babylon
shall stop at the commencement of the way, at the head of the two
ways, to use a divination; he shall shake his arrows; he shall ask
the teraphim [household gods]; he shall inspect the liver. In his
right hand shall be the divination of Jerusalem, to set battering-
rams; to open the mouth with clamor; to lift up the voice with the
shout; to set the battering-rams at the gates; to throw up a mound;
to build towers. And this shall appear to them like a false divination in their sight, the swearing of oaths to them. But he shall
bring to remembrance [wickedness], that it may be taken.

7 Therefore thus says the Lord Jehovah: Because you make
your wickedness to be remembered by the discovery of your transgressions, to cause your sins to be seen in all your doings, because
you make yourselves to be remembered, you shall be taken in hand.
And you, profane and wicked prince of Israel, whose day has come,
there is an end of the time of wickedness. Thus says the Lord
Jehovah: Remove the tiara [of the priest], and take off the crown
[of the king]; this shall not be this; exalt the low, and abase the
high. I will make her an entire destruction; and this [kingdom]
shall exist no more till he comes to whom justice belongs, and I
give it to him.

8 And as for you, son of man, prophesy and say, Thus says the
Lord Jehovah concerning the sons of Ammon and their reproach;
say, A sword, a sword — it is drawn for slaughter; it is sharpened

to devour, that it may shine like lightning, while you see vanity,
while you divine a lie, to give you to the necks of the killed, of the
wicked whose day has come, an end to the time of wickedness.
Return the sword to its sheath; in the place in which you were created, in the land of your nativity I will judge you,—and pour out on
you my indignation, and blow on you with the fire of my wrath,
and give you to the hands of savage men, skillful to destroy.   You
shall be fuel for the fire ; you shall be dung on the earth ; you shall
not be remembered, for I Jehovah have spoken.

9 And the word of Jehovah came to me, saying, Will you judge,
will you judge, son of man, the bloody city, and make it know all
its abominations.   And say, Thus says the Lord Jehovah : City
which sheds blood in the midst of her, to cause her time to come,
and makes blocks against herself for sin, for the blood which you
shed you are condemned, and by your blocks which you make you
are defiled ; and you shall cause your days to draw near, and
your years to come.   Therefore I will make you the reproach of
the nations, the scorn of all lands ; the near and the distant
shall deride you ; your name shall be infamous ; you shall be full of
confusion.

10 Behold, the princes of Israel have been each one of them
according to his arm among you to shed blood.   They despise father
and mother in you ; they deal unjustly and oppressively with the
stranger ; they oppress in you the fatherless and widow ; my holy
things you despise, and my Sabbaths you profane.   In you are slan-
derers to shed blood ; and they eat on the mountains in you ; they
commit lewdness in you ; in you one uncovers the nakedness of his
father [his father's wife], and they humble the defiled from impurity.
And one commits an abomination with his friend's wife, and another
defiles his daughter-in-law with wickedness, and another humbles
his sister, the daughter of his father, in you.   They take bribes in
you to shed blood ; you take usury and increase, and you plunder
your friend with fraud, and forget me, says the Lord Jehovah.
And behold, I have smitten my hands together at your oppression, which you commit, and at your blood, which is in the midst
of you.

11 Can your heart endure and your hands be strong in the
days in which I shall deal with you ?   I Jehovah have spoken,
and I will do.   I will scatter you among the nations, and disperse
you in the lands, and consume your impurity out of you ; and you

shall be defiled in the sight of the nations, and know that I am
Jehovah.

12 And the word of Jehovah came to me, saying, Son of man,
the house of Israel have become dross to me ; all of them are brass,
and tin, and iron, and lead, in the furnace ; they are the scoriæ of
silver.   Therefore thus says the Lord Jehovah : Because you are
all of you dross, therefore, behold, I will gather you into Jerusalem,
a collection of silver, and brass, and iron, and lead, and tin, in the
furnace, to kindle a fire on it to melt it ; so will I collect you in my
anger and in my indignation, and place you and melt you.   And I
will collect you, and blow on you with the fire of my wrath, and you
shall be melted in [Jerusalem].   As silver is melted in a furnace,
so shall you be melted in her ; and you shall know that I Jehovah
have poured out my indignation on you.

13 And the word of Jehovah came to me, saying, Son of man,
say to her, You are a land which is not purified ; it has not been
rained on in the day of indignation.   There is a conspiracy of her
prophets in her ; they devour the lives of men like a roaring lion
seizing the prey ; they take treasures and precious things ; they
multiply her widows in her ; her priests violate my law and profane
my holy things ; they distinguish not between the holy and profane,
nor teach the difference between the impure and the pure ; and my
Sabbaths they hide from their eyes, and I am profaned among them.
Her princes in her are like wolves tearing the prey, to shed blood,
to destroy lives, that they may take plunder.   Her prophets plaster
them with mortar, they see vanity, they divine for them a lie ; they
say, Thus says the Lord Jehovah, but Jehovah spoke not ; the people of the land practice oppression, they commit robbery, they oppress the poor and needy, and wrongfully use violence against the
stranger.

14 And I sought for a man of them to build a wall, and stand in
the breach before me, that I should not destroy the land, and found
none.   Therefore I will pour out on them my indignation ; I will
consume them with the fire of my wrath ; I will put their way on
their heads, says the Lord Jehovah.

PROPHECY XVII.

THE PARABLE OF THE LEWD SISTERS.

1 AND the word of Jehovah came to me, saying, Son of man, there were two women, daughters of one mother, and they committed fornication in Egypt; in their youth they committed fornication; there their breasts were pressed, and their virgin breasts handled. And their names were Aholah the elder, and Aholibah her sister; and they became mine, and bore sons and daughters. And as to their names, Aholah is Samaria, and Aholibah Jerusalem.

2 And Aholah committed fornication under me, and doted on her lovers, on the Assyrians that were near, who were clothed in blue, governors and prefects, all of them desirable young men, horsemen riding on horses. And she lavished her fornications on them, all of them choice young men of Assyria, and with all on whom she doted, and was defiled with all their blocks. And she did not forsake her fornications from Egypt, for they had been with her in her youth, and handled her virgin breasts, and poured out their fornications on her. Therefore I gave her into the hand of her lovers, into the hand of the sons of Assyria, on whom she doted. These uncovered her nakedness; they took her sons and her daughters, and killed her with the sword; and she became a name for women, and they executed judgments on her.

3 And her sister Aholibah saw, but was more corrupt in her inordinate desires than she, and her fornications were greater than those of her sister. She doted on the sons of Assyria, governors and prefects, that were near, clothed with perfection, horsemen riding on horses, all of them desirable young men. And I saw that she was defiled; they both had one way. But she added to her fornications; for she saw men on the wall, images of the Chaldeans, portrayed in red, girded with girdles on their loins, hanging with turbans from their heads; in their appearance, all of them princes, after the likeness of the sons of Babylon, of Chaldea, the land of their nativity; and she loved them at the sight of her eyes, and sent messengers to them to Chaldea. And the sons of Babylon came into her bed of love, and defiled her with their fornications, and she was defiled with them, and her soul was alienated from them.

4 And she discovered her fornications, and discovered her naked-

ness, and I was alienated from her as I had been alienated from her
sister.   And she multiplied her fornications by remembering the
days of her youth, in which she had committed fornication in the
land of Egypt, and doted on her paramours, whose flesh was the
flesh of asses, and whose emission was the emission of horses ; and
you returned to the lewdness of your youth when your breasts were
handled by the Egyptians, for the breasts of your youth.

5 Therefore, Aholibah, thus says the Lord Jehovah : Behold, I
will raise up against you your lovers, from whom you are alienated,
and bring them against you from every side ; the sons of Babylon
and all the Chaldeans, prefects, nobles, princes, all the sons of Assyria with them, desirable young men, governors, prefects, all of
them distinguished men and renowned, all of them riding on horses.
And they shall come against you with weapons, chariots, and wheels,
with an assembly of peoples, with shield, and buckler, and helmet ;
they shall set themselves against you on every side, and I will set
judgment before them, and they shall judge you according to their
judgments, and I will set my jealousy against you, and they shall
deal with you in indignation ; they shall take away your nose and
your ears, and the rest of you shall fall by the sword ; they shall take
away your sons and your daughters, and your children shall be consumed with fire.

6 And they shall strip you of your clothes, and take away
your jewels ; and I will cause your lewdness to cease from you, and
your wickedness from the land of Egypt, and you shall not lift up
your eyes to them, nor remember Egypt any more.   For thus says
the Lord Jehovah : Behold, I will give you into the hand of those
whom you hate, and into the hand of those from whom you are
alienated, and they shall deal with you in hatred, and take away all
your labors, and leave you naked and bare, and the nakedness of
your lewdness, and of your wickedness, and your prostitution shall
be uncovered.   These things will I do to you, for your fornication
with the nations, because you have defiled yourself with their blocks ;
you walk in the way of your sister, and I will give her cup into
your hand.

7 Thus says the Lord Jehovah : You shall drink of your sister's
cup, which is deep and large, and shall become a laughing stock and
derision from the much which it contains.   You shall be filled with
drunkenness and sorrow.   The cup of your sister is a cup of astonishment and consternation ; but you shall drink it, and suck it out,

and chew up the pieces of the cup, and you shall tear your breasts, for I have spoken, says the Lord Jehovah. Therefore thus says the Lord Jehovah: Because you have forgotten me, and cast me behind your back, you also shall bear your wickedness and your fornications.

8 And Jehovah said to me, Son of man, will you judge Aholah and Aholibah? Yes, declare to them their abominations, for they commit adultery, and blood is on their hands, for they commit adultery with their blocks, and even their sons whom they bear to me do they cause to pass through the fire to them for food. And more, they do this to me: they defile my sanctuary on the same day, and profane my Sabbaths. And when they kill their sons for their blocks, they go also to my sanctuary on the same day to profane it; and behold, you do thus in my house. Yes, furthermore, you sent for men to come from afar, to whom messengers were sent; and behold, they came, for whom you washed yourself, and painted your eyes, and put on your ornaments, and you sat on a magnificent couch, and a table was spread before you, and you put my incense and my oil on it; and the voice of a multitude at ease was with you, and together with men from the common multitude were brought in Sabeans from the wilderness, and they put bracelets on their hands, and a crown of beauty on their heads.

9 Then I said concerning her that was already worn out with adulteries, Will they commit fornication with her? even with her? And they went in to her as one goes in to a harlot; so they went in to Aholah and to Aholibah, women of lewdness. But righteous men shall judge them with the judgment of adulteresses, and with the judgment of those who shed blood, for they are adulteresses, and blood is on their hands. For thus says the Lord Jehovah: I will bring up against them an assembly, and give them up to be injuriously treated and plundered, and the assembly shall stone them with stones, and cut them to pieces with swords, and they shall kill their sons and their daughters, and burn their houses with fire; and I will make lewdness to cease from the land, and all women shall be admonished not to copy after their lewdness; and they shall put your lewdness on you, and you shall bear the sins of your blocks, and shall know that I am the Lord Jehovah.

PROPHECY XVIII. [24.

THE PARABLE OF THE POT OF MEAT.

1 AND the word of Jehovah came to me in the 9th year, in the tenth month, on the 10th day of the month, saying, Son of man, write the name of the day, this very day; the king of Babylon has approached Jerusalem this very day. Speak a parable to the rebellious house, and say to them, Thus says the Lord Jehovah: Set on the pot, set it on, and pour water in it, put together its pieces into it, all the best pieces, the ham, the shoulder, and fill it with choice bones; take the choice of the flock. And as to the pot of bones, put stuff under it, make it boil violently, and boil its bones which are in it.

2 Therefore thus says the Lord Jehovah: Woe to the bloody city, to the pot which has a disease in it, and its disease will not depart from it; bring it out piece by piece, and let no lot fall for it. For her blood is within her; she has put it on the bare rock, she has poured it not on the ground, that she might cover it with earth; to execute indignation and take vengeance, I will put her blood on the bare rock, that I may not cover it.

3 Therefore thus says the Lord Jehovah: Woe to the bloody city, for I will make the pile great, increase the wood, kindle the fire, finish the meat, put in the spices, and let the bones be burned. Then set it on the coals empty, that its brass may be hot and burn, and its impurity within it be removed, and its disease consumed. It has wearied me with labors, but its multitudinous disease has not gone from it, its disease stands the fire. Wickedness is your defilement, for I purified you and you were not purified. You shall no more be purified from your defilement till I rest from my indignation against you; I Jehovah have spoken it; it shall come; and I will do, I will not let you go unpunished, I will not spare, nor pity; they shall judge you according to your ways and according to your works, says the Lord Jehovah.

4 And the word of Jehovah came to me, saying, Son of man, behold, I will take away from you the desire of your eyes at one blow; but lament not, nor weep, nor let your tears come forth; sob in silence, make no mourning for the dead, bind on your turban, and put your shoes on your feet, cover not your lips, and eat not the bread of men.

5 Then I spoke to the people in the morning, and my wife died in the evening; and I did in the morning [following] as I was commanded. And the people said to me, Will you not tell us what these things are to us, that you do them? And I said to them, The word of Jehovah came to me, saying, Say to the house of Israel, Thus says the Lord Jehovah: Behold, I will profane my sanctuary, the pride of your strength, the desire of your eyes, the delight of your souls, and your sons and your daughters whom you have left shall fall by the sword; and you shall do as I have done; you shall not cover your lip, nor eat the bread of men; your turbans shall be on your heads, and your shoes on your feet; you shall not lament nor weep, but shall pine away for your wickedness, and sigh one to another; and Ezekiel shall be to you a sign; according to all that he has done, you shall do: when it comes, you shall know that I am the Lord Jehovah.

6 And as for you, son of man, have I not taken from them in a day their strength, their glorious rejoicing, the desire of their eyes, and the burden of their souls, their sons and their daughters? In that day shall one that has escaped come to bring you the news in their hearing; in that day your mouth shall be opened, and you shall speak, and not be silent any more; and you shall be to them for a sign, and they shall know that I am Jehovah.

PROPHECY XIX.　　　[25.

AGAINST THE AMMONITES, MOABITES, EDOMITES, AND PHILISTINES.

1 AND the word of Jehovah came to me, saying, Son of man, set your face against the sons of Ammon, and prophesy against them, and say to the sons of Ammon, Hear the word of the Lord Jehovah: Thus says the Lord Jehovah: Because you said Aha! against my sanctuary when it was profaned, and against the land of Israel when it was made desolate, and against the house of Judah when they went into exile, therefore behold, I will give you to the sons of the east for a possession; and they shall set their encampments in you, and make their dwellings in you, and they shall eat your fruit and drink your milk.

2 And I will make Rabbah a pasture for camels, and the country of the sons of Ammon a resting place for flocks; and you shall know that I am Jehovah. For thus says the Lord Jehovah: Be-

cause you clapped your hands, and stamped with your foot, and rejoiced in all your contempt with the soul, against the land of Israel, therefore behold, I will stretch out my hand against you, and give you to be plundered by the nations, and cut you off from the nations, and destroy you from the lands : I will destroy you, and you shall know that I am Jehovah.

3 Thus says the Lord Jehovah : Because Moab and Seir said, Behold, the house of Judah is like all the nations, therefore behold, I will open the side of Moab from cities, from his cities on his border, the glory of the country, Beth-jeshimoth, Baal-meon, and Kirjathaim, and give it for a possession to the sons of the east over the sons of Ammon, that the sons of Ammon may not be remembered among the nations. And I will execute judgments on Moab, and they shall know that I am Jehovah.

4 Thus says the Lord Jehovah : Because Edom acted against the house of Israel by taking vengeance, and they greatly transgressed and took vengeance on them, therefore thus says the Lord Jehovah : I will stretch out my hand on Edom, and smite of it man and beast, and make it a desolation from Teman ; they shall fall by the sword to Dedan. And I will take my vengeance on Edom by the hand of the people of Israel, and they shall deal with Edom according to my anger and my indignation ; and they shall know my vengeance, says the Lord Jehovah.

5 Thus says the Lord Jehovah : Because the Philistines dealt with vengeance, and took vengeance with contempt and soul, to destroy with eternal hostility, therefore thus says the Lord Jehovah : Behold, I will stretch out my hand against the Philistines, and cut off the Cherethites, and destroy the remnant on the sea coast, and execute great vengeance on them with indignant rebukes ; and they shall know that I am Jehovah, when I put my vengeance on them.

PROPHECY XX.   [26, 27, 28, 1–19.

AGAINST TYRE.

1 AND in the 11th year, on the first day of the month, the word of Jehovah came to me, saying, Son of man, because Tyre said against Jerusalem, Aha! the gate of the nations is broken, they are turned to me ; I shall be full, she shall be desolate ; therefore thus says the Lord Jehovah : Behold, I am against you, Tyre, and

will bring up against you many nations, like the coming up of the sea with its waves; and they shall destroy the walls of Tyre, and throw down her towers; and I will sweep off her earth from her, and make her a naked rock; she shall be a spreading of nets in the midst of the sea, for I have spoken, says the Lord Jehovah; and she shall be plundered by the nations, and her daughters who are in the country they shall kill with the sword; and they shall know that I am Jehovah.

2 For thus says the Lord Jehovah : Behold, I will bring against Tyre Nebuchadrezzar, king of Babylon, from the north, the king of kings, with horses, and chariots, and horsemen, and an assembly, and a great people; and your daughters in the country shall he kill with the sword; and he shall set watch-towers against you, and raise a mound against you, and raise up the shield against you, and set the head of his powerful battering-rams against your walls, and break down your towers with his axes. From the multitude of his horses, their dust shall cover you : at the noise of his horsemen, and wheels, and chariots, your walls shall shake, when he enters your gates as men enter a city that is broken into. With the hoofs of his horses he shall tread down all your streets; your people he shall kill with the sword; and the pillars of your strength he shall bring down to the ground.

3 And they shall plunder your wealth, and make a prey of your merchandise, and throw down your walls, and break down your desirable houses; and they shall put your stones, and your timbers, and your dust, into the waters. And I will cause the tumult of your songs to cease, and the sound of your harps shall be heard no more; and I will make you a naked rock; you shall be a spreading of nets; you shall not be built any more, for I Jehovah have spoken, says the Lord Jehovah.

4 Thus says the Lord Jehovah to Tyre : Behold, the islands shall shake at the noise of your fall, with the groaning of your wounded, and with the great slaughter within you. All the princes of the sea shall come down from their thrones, and put off their robes, and be stripped of their embroidered garments; they shall be clothed with trembling; they shall sit on the ground, and tremble incessantly, and be astonished at you. And they shall take up a lamentation over you, and say to you, How are you destroyed, you that dwelt on the seas, the glorious city which was strong by the sea, she and her inhabitants, who gave their dread to all the inhabitants [of the

sea]! Now the sea coasts shall tremble at your fall, and the islands which are in the sea be astonished at your destruction.

5 For thus says the Lord Jehovah: When I make you a desolate city, like the cities which are not inhabited; when I bring against you the deep, and cover you with many waters, then I will bring you down to those who go down to the pit, to the people of old, and cause you to live in the under world, amid ruins which have been from of old, with those that go down to the pit, that you may be inhabited no more; but I will put glory in the land of the living. I will make you an object of terror, and you shall not be sought for any more, nor be found any more forever, says the Lord Jehovah.

6 And the word of Jehovah came to me, saying, As for you, son of man, take up a lamentation over Tyre, and say to Tyre, You that dwell at the entrance of the sea, the merchant of the nations to many islands, thus says the Lord Jehovah: Tyre, you have said, I am the perfection of beauty; your boundary is in the heart of the seas, your builders completed your beauty. They built you with cypresses from Senir, for all your bounds; they took cedars from Lebanon to make masts for you; they made oaks of Bashan your oars, and your benches they made of ivory, the daughter of sherbin cedars from the coasts of Cyprus. Embroidered linen from Egypt was spread out for your sails; blue and purple from the coasts of Elis were your covering. The inhabitants of Zidon and of Arvad were your rowers; your skillful men, Tyre, who were in you, were your sailors. The old men of Gebal and its skillful men were in you for repairers; all the ships of the sea and their mariners were in you, to take part in your commerce. Persia, and Lud, and Libya, were in your army, your men of war; they hung up the shield and helmet in you, they gave you glory. The sons of Arvad and your army were on your walls on every side, and bold warriors were in your towers; they hung up their shields on your walls on every side; they perfected your beauty.

7 Tarshish was your merchant from the abundance of all riches; they furnished your markets with silver, iron, tin, and lead. Ionia, Tubal, and Meshech were your merchants; they furnished your market with souls of men and vessels of brass. From the house of Togarmah [Armenia], they gave your market horses, horsemen, and mules. The sons of Dedan were your merchants; many islands were merchants of your hand; they returned you gifts with horns of ivory and ebony. Syria was your merchant, from the abundance

of your fabrics; they furnished your market with gems, purple and embroidered work, and fine linen, and high priced things, and rubies. Judah and the land of Israel were your merchants; they furnished your market with wheat from Minnith, and pastry, and honey, and oil, and balsam. Damascus was your merchant, from the abundance of your fabrics, from an abundance of all riches, with the wine of Helbon and white wool. And Dan and Ionia furnished your markets from Uzal [Yemen in Arabia], wrought iron, cassia, and sweet cane; they were in your market. Dedan was your merchant, with carpets for riding and driving.

8 Arabia and all the princes of Kedar were merchants of your hand, furnishing you with lambs, and rams, and goats. The traveling merchants of Sheba and Raamah were your traveling merchants, and furnished your markets with the chief of all spices, and all precious stones, and gold. Haran, and Canneh, and Eden, the traveling merchants of Sheba, Assyria, [and] Chilmad, were your traveling merchants; they were your traveling merchants in splendid garments, in mantles of blue, and embroidered work, in chests of variegated stuffs, bound with cords and made of cedar, in your fairs. The ships of Tarshish were your caravans for your traffic, and you were filled and glorified exceedingly in the heart of the seas.

9 The rowers brought you into many waters; the east wind broke you in the heart of the seas. Your riches and your markets, your merchandise, your mariners, and your sailors, your repairers, and your commission merchants, and all your men of war who are in you, in all the assembly which is in you, shall fall in the heart of the seas, in the day of your fall. At the voice of the cry of your sailors, the places around shall shake; and all that handle the oar, mariners, and all sailors on the sea, shall come down from their ships; they shall stand on the land, and publish against you with their voice, and cry bitterly; and they shall cast dust on their heads; they shall roll in ashes. And they shall make themselves entirely bald for you, and gird on sackcloth, and weep for you with bitterness of soul, with bitter lamentation.

10 And their sons shall take up a lamentation for you, and lament for you. What city is like Tyre, like the destroyed in the sea? By the going forth of your goods from the seas you satisfied many nations; by the multitude of your riches and of your merchandise you enriched the kings of the earth. Now you are destroyed from the seas in the depths of the waters; your merchandise and all your

assembly within you have fallen; all the inhabitants of the islands are astonished at you, and their kings are greatly afraid; their countenances are agitated. The merchants of the peoples hiss at you; you are suddenly destroyed, and shall exist no more forever.

11 And the word of Jehovah came to me, saying, Son of man, say to the prince of Tyre, Thus says the Lord Jehovah: Because your heart is proud, and you say, I am a god, I sit in the seat of God in the heart of the seas, and you are a man and not God, though you set your heart like the heart of God, behold, you are wiser than Daniel; they can hide no secret from you. By your wisdom and by your understanding you have obtained wealth, and put gold and silver in your treasuries. By your great wisdom [and] by your traffic you have made your wealth great, and your heart is lifted up by your wealth. Therefore thus says the Lord Jehovah: Because you make your heart like the heart of a god, therefore, behold, I will bring strangers against you, the powerful of the nations, and they shall draw their swords against the beauty of your wisdom, and defile your beauty. They shall bring you down to the pit, and you shall die the death of the killed in the heart of the seas. Will you say, I am God, before him that kills you? You shall be a man, and not God, in the hand of him that kills you. You shall die the death of the uncircumcised by the hand of strangers; for I have spoken it, says the Lord Jehovah.

12 And the word of Jehovah came to me, saying, Son of man, take up a lamentation against the king of Tyre, and say to him, Thus says the Lord Jehovah: You are a seat of perfection, full of skill and perfect in beauty; you are in Eden, the garden of God; all precious stones are your covering, the ruby, the topaz, the onyx, the chrysolite, the sardonyx, and the jasper, the sapphire, the carbuncle, the emerald, and gold ⟶ the work of your drums and your [jewel] holes are in you; they were made on the day in which you were born. Your are an expanded protecting cherub, and I set you in the holy mountain; you are a god, you walk about in the stones of fire; you were perfect in your ways from the day in which you were created till wickedness was found in you. Through the abundance of your merchandise your soul is filled with violence, and you have sinned; therefore I will cast you out as profane from the mountain of God, and destroy you, protecting cherub, from the stones of fire. Your heart is lifted up by your beauty; you have corrupted your wisdom on account of your splendor. I will cast

you on the earth before the kings ; I will make you a gazing stock. By the multitude of your wicked acts, by the evil of your traffic, you have defiled your sanctuaries ; therefore I will bring out a fire from you, which shall consume you, and make you ashes on the earth, in the sight of all that see you. All that know you among the nations shall be astonished at you ; you shall be suddenly destroyed, and exist no more forever.

PROPHECY XXI.   [28, 20-26.

AGAINST ZIDON.

1 AND the word of Jehovah came to me, saying, Son of man, set your face against Zidon, and prophesy against it, and say, Thus says the Lord Jehovah : Behold, I am against you, Zidon, and will be glorified in you ; and you shall know that I am Jehovah when I execute judgments in you, and am sanctified in you. And I will send on her pestilence and blood in her streets, and the killed shall fall in her by the sword on every side, and they shall know that I am Jehovah.

2 And the house of Israel shall not have any more a painful thorn, or an afflictive thorn bush, of all that are around them, that hate them ; and they shall know that I am Jehovah.

3 Thus says the Lord Jehovah : When I gather the house of Israel from the nations in which they are dispersed, then I will be sanctified by them in the sight of the nations, and they shall dwell in their land which I gave to my servant, to Jacob ; and they shall dwell in it securely, and build houses and plant vineyards, and dwell securely, when I execute my judgments on all that hate them of those around them ; and they shall know that I am Jehovah.

PROPHECY XXII.   [29, 1-16.

EZEKIEL'S FIRST PROPHECY AGAINST EGYPT.

1 IN the 10th year, in the tenth month, on the 12th day of the month, the word of Jehovah came to me, saying, Son of man, set your face against Pharaoh, king of Egypt, and prophesy against him, and against all Egypt. Speak and say, Thus says the Lord Jehovah : Behold, I am against you, Pharaoh, king of Egypt, the

great crocodile that lies in its river, which says, My river belongs to me, for I made it; and I will put hooks into your jaws, and cause all the fish of your river to adhere to your scales, and bring you up from your rivers, and all the fish of your rivers which shall adhere to your scales, and will cast you down in the wilderness, you and all ths fish of your rivers, and you shall fall on the face of the field; you shall not be gathered, you shall not be collected together, and I will give you for food to the beasts of the earth, and to the birds of heaven; and all the inhabitants of Egypt shall know that I am Jehovah; because they have been a staff of reed to the house of Israel; when they took hold of you with the hand, you broke and pierced them through the whole shoulder; and when they leaned on you, you broke, and made all their loins shake.

2 Therefore thus says the Lord Jehovah: Behold, I will bring the sword against you, and cut off from you man and beast, and the land of Egypt shall be a desolation and a waste; and they shall know that I am Jehovah; because he said, The river is mine; I made it. Therefore behold, I am against you, and against your rivers, and will make the land of Egypt desolate wastes, a desolation from Migdol to Syene, and to the boundaries of Ethiopia. The foot of man shall not pass through it, nor the foot of beast pass through it, neither shall it be inhabited, 40 years. And I will make the land of Egypt a desolation among lands that are desolate, and her cities shall be waste, a desolation among cities that are wastes, 40 years; and I will scatter the Egyptians among the nations, and disperse them in the lands.

3 Yet thus says the Lord Jehovah: At the end of 40 years I will gather Egypt from the nations in which they were scattered, and bring back the captives of Egypt, and cause them to return to the land of Pathros, to the land of their nativity, and they shall there be a depressed kingdom. It shall be the most depressed of kingdoms, and shall no more exalt itself over the nations; and I will make them small, that they may no more rule over the nations; and it shall no more be the confidence of the house of Israel, to cause them to remember wickedness, in turning after them; and they shall know that I am the Lord Jehovah.

PROPHECY XXIII. [29, 17, 30, 19.

EZEKIEL'S SECOND PROPHECY AGAINST EGYPT.

1 AND in the 27th year [B. C. 571], in the first month, on the first day of the month, the word of Jehovah came to me, saying, Son of man, Nebuchadrezzar, king of Babylon, caused his army to perform a great service against Tyre. Every head became bald, and every shoulder was skinned, and he obtained no reward from Tyre for the service which he performed against it. Therefore thus says the Lord Jehovah: Behold, I will give Nebuchadrezzar, king of Babylon, the land of Egypt, and he shall take away its multitude, and take its spoil, and plunder it, and it shall be the reward of his army. For his work which he performed against it I will give him the land of Egypt, because they did it for me, says the Lord Jehovah. In that day will I cause the horn of Israel to grow, and give free speech among you ; and they shall know that I am Jehovah.

2 And the word of Jehovah came to me, saying, Son of man, prophesy and say, Thus says the Lord Jehovah: Lament, alas for the day ! for the day is at hand, for the day of Jehovah is at hand. The day of the nations shall be a day of clouds, and the sword shall come on Egypt and pain on Ethiopia, when the wounded fall in Egypt, and they shall take away her multitude, and her foundations shall be destroyed. Ethiopia, and Libya, and Lud, and all the mixed multitude, and Nubia, and the sons of the land of the covenant shall fall with them by the sword. Thus says Jehovah : They that uphold Egypt for the pride of her power shall come down ; from Migdol to Syene they shall fall in her by the sword, says the Lord Jehovah. And they shall be made desolate among the lands that are desolated, and her cities shall be among cities that are laid waste ; and they shall know that I am Jehovah, when I put a fire in Egypt, and all her helpers are broken down. In that day shall messengers go from me in ships to terrify Ethiopia in her security, and pain shall fall on them like the day of Egypt, for behold, it shall come.

3 Thus says the Lord Jehovah : I will remove the multitude of Egypt by the hand of Nebuchadrezzar, king of Babylon. He and his people with him, the strong ones of the nations, shall be brought to destroy the land, and they shall draw their swords against Egypt,

and fill the land with the killed. And I will make the rivers dry, and sell the land into the hand of evil men, and make the land waste, and all that is in it, by the hand of strangers. I Jehovah have spoken it.

4 Thus says the Lord Jehovah: I will destroy the blocks and remove the vanities from Noph, and there shall no more be a prince of the land of Egypt; and I will put fear on the land of Egypt, and make Pathros desolate, and set fire to Zoan, and execute judgments on No, and pour out my indignation on Sin, the fortress of Egypt, and cut off the multitude of No, and set fire to Egypt; Sin shall be in pain, No shall be taken, and Noph [be a prey to] the enemies of their day. The young men of On and Pibeseth shall fall by the sword, and these [cities] shall go into captivity. And at Tahpenhes the day shall be darkened when I break there the yoke of Egypt, and the pride of her strength shall cease within her, a cloud shall cover her, and her daughters shall go into captivity; and I will execute judgments on Egypt, and they shall know that I am Jehovah.

PROPHECY XXIV. [30, 20, 31.

EZEKIEL'S THIRD PROPHECY AGAINST EGYPT.

1 AND in the 11th year [B. C. 588], in the first month, on the 7th day of the month, the word of Jehovah came to me, saying, Son of man, I will break the arm of Pharaoh, king of Egypt, and behold, it shall not be bound up, for the application of healing medicines, to apply a bandage to bind it up to strengthen it, to hold the sword. Therefore thus says the Lord Jehovah: Behold, I am against Pharaoh, king of Egypt, and will break his strong arm, and it shall be broken, and I will make his sword fall from his hand, and scatter the Egyptians among the nations, and disperse them among the lands, and strengthen the arm of the king of Babylon, and put a sword in his hand; and the arms of Pharaoh shall fall down; and they shall know that I am Jehovah when I put my sword into the hand of the king of Babylon, and he shall stretch it out against the land of Egypt. And I will scatter the Egyptians among the nations, and disperse them in the lands; and they shall know that I am Jehovah.

2 And in the 11th year, in the third month, on the first day of the month, the word of Jehovah came to me, saying, Son of man, say

to Pharaoh, king of Egypt, and to his multitude, To whom are you like in your greatness? Behold, the Assyrian was a cedar of Lebanon with fair branches ; he was a thick, shady forest, and his height was great, and his foliage was interwoven among his branches. Waters made him great, the deep exalted him, going round his plantation with its streams, and sending for him its water-courses to all the trees of the field.

3 Therefore his height was exalted above all the trees of the field, his boughs were multiplied, and his green branches elongated when he shot forth from many waters. All the birds of heaven made their nests on his boughs, and under his green branches all the beasts of the field brought forth, and all great nations sat in his shade. And he was beautiful in his greatness, with his long branches, for his root was by many waters. The cedars in the garden of God did not excel him, the cypresses did not equal his branches, and the plane trees were not like his branches, nor was any tree in the garden of God like him in his beauty. I made him beautiful, with his many limbs, and all the trees of Eden which were in the garden of God envied him.

4 Therefore thus says the Lord Jehovah ; Because you exalt yourself in height, and he puts his branches amid the foliage, and his heart is lifted up with its height, therefore I will give him to the hand of mighty nations, and they shall deal with him, and drive him out for his wickedness, and strangers of savage nations shall cut him down, and cast him on the mountains, and his limbs shall fill in all the valleys, and his green branches be broken in all the ravines of the earth, and all the nations of the earth shall withdraw from his shade and leave him, and all the birds of heaven occupy his ruin, and his green branches be for all the beasts of the field, that none of all the trees by the waters may exalt themselves in their places, nor set their branches in the thick foliage, and that none of the [trees] that drink water may stand by them, for all are delivered to death to the under world, among sons of men that have gone down to the pit.

5 Thus says the Lord Jehovah : In the day in which he goes down to Hades I will cause the deep to mourn and cover it for him, and restrain its streams, and the great waters shall be kept back, and I will clothe Lebanon in black for him, and all the trees of the field shall languish for him. By the noise of his fall I will shake the nations, when I bring him down to Hades, to those that have

gone down to the pit, and all the sons of Eden in the under world shall be comforted, the choice and good trees of Lebanon, all that drink water, for they also shall go down to Hades with him, to the killed with the sword, and [the men] of his arm shall sit in his shade among the nations.

6 Which do you resemble, in glory and greatness, of the trees of Eden? For you are brought down to the trees of Eden of the under world; you shall lie with the uncircumcised, the killed with the sword. This is Pharaoh and all [his] multitude, says the Lord Jehovah.

PROPHECY XXV.   [32, 1–16.

EZEKIEL'S FOURTH PROPHECY AGAINST EGYPT.

1 AND in the 12th year [B. C. 587], in the twelfth month, on the 1st day of the month, came the word of Jehovah to me, saying, Son of man, take up a lamentation for Pharaoh, king of Egypt, and say to him, You are like a young lion of the nations, and like a sea monster in the seas, and you broke forth into the rivers, and made turbid the water with your feet, and disturbed the rivers.

2 Thus says the Lord Jehovah: I will spread my net over you with an assembly of many peoples, and they shall draw you up with my net, and I will cast you down on the earth, I will lay you on the open field, and cause all the birds of heaven to dwell on you, and satisfy with you the beasts of all the earth, and put your flesh on the mountains, and fill the valleys with your heaps, and water the land with an inundation of your blood on the mountains, and the valleys shall be filled from you. And I will cover heaven when I extinguish your light, and make the stars dark, and cover the sun with a cloud, and the moon shall not give her light. All the bright luminaries of heaven I will make dark over you, and put darkness on your land, says the Lord Jehovah.

3 And I will cause the hearts of many peoples to grieve, when I bring your destruction to the nations in lands which you have not known. Yes, I will make many peoples amazed at you, and kings shall be greatly afraid on your account; when I brandish my sword before them, then they shall tremble incessantly, every one for his life, in the day of your fall.

4 For thus says the Lord Jehovah: The sword of the king of Babylon shall come on you; by the swords of the mighty I will cause

your multitude to fall, all of them, the strong ones of the nations, and they shall lay waste the pride of Egypt, and all its multitude shall be destroyed. And I will destroy all her beasts from the side of her great waters, and the foot of man shall not disturb them any more, nor the hoofs of beasts. Then I will make their waters quiet, and cause their rivers to flow like oil, says the Lord Jehovah, when I make the land of Egypt a desolation ; and the land shall be bereft of all it contains when I smite all its inhabitants ; and they shall know that I am Jehovah.

5 This is the lamentation with which they shall lament ; the daughters of the nations shall lament with it concerning Egypt ; and concerning all her multitude shall they lament with it, says the Lord Jehovah.

PROPHECY XXVI.   [32, 17–32.

EZEKIEL'S FIFTH PROPHECY AGAINST EGYPT.

1 AND in the 12th year, on the 15th day of the month, came the word of Jehovah to me, saying, Son of man, Lament for the multitude of Egypt, and bring it down, with her and her daughters of the illustrious nations, to the under world, to those that have gone down to the pit.

2 Whom do you exceed in beauty ? Go down and lie with the uncircumcised. They shall fall with the killed by the sword. The sword is given ; draw her out and all her multitudes [for slaughter]. The gods of the mighty from the midst of Hades shall tell him of his helpers, who went down, and lie [with] the uncircumcised, the killed with the sword.

3 There is Assyria and all her assembly ; around it are its graves ; all of them are killed, fallen by the sword. Their graves are placed in the sides of the pit, and her assembly is around her grave, all of them killed, fallen by the sword, who inspired fear in the land of the living.

4 There is Elam and all her multitude around her grave, all of them killed, fallen by the sword, who went down uncircumcised to the under world, who set their fear in the land of the living ; but they bear their shame with those that go down to the pit. They put a bed for her among the killed, with all her multitude. Around it are her graves ; all of them are uncircumcised, killed by the sword. Though they were feared in the land of the living, yet they bear

24 *

their shame with those that go down to the pit. She is placed among the killed.

5 There is the land of the Moschi and Tiburani, and all her multitude ; its graves are around her, all of them uncircumcised, killed with the sword, though they set their fear in the land of the living. But they lie not with the mighty who have fallen, of the uncircumcised who go down to Hades with their weapons of war ; and they put their swords under their heads, and their wickedness is on their bones, though [they were] the fear of the mighty in the land of the living ; but you shall be destroyed with the uncircumcised, and lie with the killed by the sword.

6 There are Edom and her kings, and all her princes, who, with their power, are laid with the killed by the sword ; they lie with the uncircumcised, with those that go down to the pit. There are the anointed of the north, all of them, and all the Zidonians, who have gone down to the killed with their fear, ashamed of their power ; and they lie uncircumcised, with the killed by the sword, and bear their shame with those that have gone down to the pit.

7 Pharaoh shall see them, and be comforted concerning all his multitude, the killed by the sword, Pharaoh and all his host, says the Lord Jehovah. Though I put his fear in the earth, yet he shall be laid with the uncircumcised, with the killed by the sword, Pharaoh and all his multitude, says the Lord Jehovah.

PROPHECY XXVII.   [33, 1-20.

THE DUTIES OF A PROPHET.

1 AND the word of Jehovah came to me, saying, Son of man, speak to the sons of your people, and say to them, When I bring a sword on the land, and the people of the land take one man from their bounds, and make him their watchman, and he sees the sword come on the land, and blows the trumpet, and warns the people, then he that hears distinctly the sound of the trumpet, and receives not warning, if the sword comes and takes him away, his blood shall be on his head ; he heard the sound of the trumpet, and received not warning : his blood shall be on him ; but he that received warning saved his life.

2 But if a watchman sees the sword come, and sounds not the trumpet, and the people are not warned, if the sword comes and

takes any of them away, that soul is taken away in his wickedness, but his blood will I require at the watchman's hand.

3 And as for you, son of man, I have made you a watchman of the house of Israel, that you may hear the word from my mouth, and warn them from me. When I say to the wicked man, Wicked man, you shall surely die, and you do not speak to warn the wicked man from his way, that wicked man shall die for his wickedness, but his blood will I require at your hand. But if you warn the wicked man from his way, to turn from it, and he turns not from his way, he shall die for his wickedness, but you have saved your life.

4 Say, therefore, son of man, to the house of Israel, You speak rightly, saying, If our transgressions and our sins are on us, and we are consumed by them, then how shall we live ? Say to them, As I live, says the Lord Jehovah, I have no pleasure in the death of a wicked man, but in the turning of a wicked man from his way, that he may live. Turn, turn from your evil ways, for why will you die, house of Israel ?

5 And as for you, son of man, say to the sons of my people, The righteousness of the righteous shall not save him in the day of his wickedness, nor the wickedness of the wicked cause him to fall by it in the day of his turning from his wickedness ; neither shall the righteous be able to live by his righteousness in the day of his sin. When I say to a righteous man, You shall surely live, if he trusts in his righteousness and does evil, none of his righteousness shall be remembered ; for the evil which he does, he shall die. And when I say to a wicked man, You shall surely die, if he turns from his sin, and does justice and righteousness, [if] the wicked man gives back the pledge, repays the robbery, walks in the ordinances of life to do no evil, he shall surely live, he shall not die. None of his sins which he committed shall be remembered against him ; he does justice and righteousness ; he shall surely live.

6 But the sons of your people say, The way of the Lord is not equal ; but as for them, their ways are not equal. When a righteous man turns from his righteousness, and does evil, he shall die for it ; and when a wicked man turns from his wickedness, and does justice and righteousness, on their account he shall live. But you say, The way of the Lord is not equal. I will judge you every man according to his way, house of Israel.

PROPHECY XXVIII.   [33, 21-33.

AGAINST THOSE LEFT IN JUDEA AFTER THE DESTRUCTION OF JERUSALEM.

1 AND in the 12th year of our captivity, in the tenth month, on the 5th day of the month, one that escaped came to me from Jerusalem, saying, The city is destroyed. And the hand of Jehovah was on me on the morning before the man that escaped came, and he opened my mouth till he came to me in the morning; then he opened my mouth, and I was no longer dumb.

2 And the word of Jehovah came to me, saying, Son of man, the inhabitants of these desolations in the land of Israel speak, saying, Abraham was one, and he possessed the land; but we are many, and the land is given to us for a possession. Therefore say to them, Thus says the Lord Jehovah: You eat with the blood and lift up your eyes to your blocks, and shed blood; and shall you possess the land? You stand on your swords, you commit abominations, and defile every one his friend's wife; and shall you possess the land? Say thus to them: Thus says the Lord Jehovah: As I live, those who are in the desolations shall fall by the sword, and him that is in the field will I give to the beasts, that they may devour him; and they that are in fortresses and caves shall die by pestilence. And I will make the land a desolation and a waste, and the pride of its strength shall cease, and the mountains of Israel shall be desolate, with none to pass through them; and they shall know that I am Jehovah, when I make the land a waste and a desolation, on account of all the abominations which they have committed.

3 And as for you, son of man, the sons of your people talk of you by the walls and at the doors of the houses, and one says to another, Come, I pray you, and hear what word proceeds from Jehovah. And they come to you like the coming of the people, and sit before you [like] my people, and hear your words, but do them not. For they practice love with their mouth, [but] their heart goes after unjust gain; and behold, you are to them as a song of love, of one that has a pleasant voice and plays well on an instrument, and they hear your words, but do them not. But when this comes, — behold, it shall come, — then they shall know that a prophet is among them.

PROPHECY XXIX.   [34.

AGAINST THE SHEPHERDS OF ISRAEL, THEIR RULERS.

1 AND the word of Jehovah came to me, saying, Son of man, prophesy against the shepherds [rulers] of Israel; prophesy and say, Shepherds, thus says the Lord Jehovah: Woe to the shepherds of Israel, who feed themselves. Should not the shepherds feed the flocks? You · eat the milk, you clothe yourselves with the wool, you kill the fat ones, you feed not the flock. You strengthen not the wearied, you heal not the sick; you bind not up the bruised, and the driven away you bring not back, and the lost you seek not; but you rule them with violence and oppression, and they are scattered abroad because there is no shepherd, and are food for all the beasts of the field, and are scattered abroad. My sheep wander through all the mountains, and on all the high hills, and my flock is scattered on all the face of the earth, and none inquires for them nor seeks them.

2 Therefore, shepherds, hear the word of Jehovah: As I live, says the Lord Jehovah, because my flock is a prey, and my flock is food for all the beasts of the field, with no shepherd, and the shepherds inquire not for my flock, and the shepherds feed themselves, but feed not my flock, therefore, shepherds, hear the word of Jehovah. Thus says the Lord Jehovah: Behold, I am against the shepherds, and will demand my flock from their hand, and will cause them to cease from feeding my flock, and the shepherds shall no more feed themselves; and I will deliver my flock from their mouth, and they shall not have them for food.

3 For thus says the Lord Jehovah: Behold me, for I will inquire after my flock, and search for them as a shepherd searches for his flock in the day in which he is among his scattered sheep; so will I seek for my flock, and deliver them from all places in which I have scattered them in the day of clouds and darkness. And I will bring them from the peoples, and gather them from the lands, and will bring them to their land, and feed them on the mountains of Israel, in the valleys, and in all the dwellings of the land. I will feed them in a good pasture; their pasture shall be on the high mountains of Israel; there shall they lie down in a good pasture, and eat rich food on the mountains of Israel. I will feed

my flock and cause them to lie down, says the Lord Jehovah, and will seek the lost, and bring back the driven away, and bind up the bruised, and strengthen the weak, and keep the fat and strong, and feed them with justice.

4 And as for you, my flock, thus says the Lord Jehovah : Behold, I will judge between sheep and sheep, and between the rams and the he goats. Is it too little in your sight to eat up the good feed, but the rest of your feed will you trample down with your feet ? And you drink water that has settled, but the rest you make foul with your feet ; and my sheep eat what is trodden down by your feet, and drink what your feet have made foul.

5 Therefore thus says the Lord Jehovah against them : Behold, I will judge between fat sheep and lean sheep. Because you thrust with side and with shoulder, and push with your horns all the weak till you scatter them abroad, therefore I will save my flock, and it shall no more be a prey ; and I will judge between sheep and sheep, and set over them one shepherd, and he shall feed them, my servant David ; he shall feed them and be their shepherd. And I Jehovah will be their God, and my servant David shall be a prince among them ; I Jehovah have spoken. And I will make a peaceful covenant with them, and cause evil beasts to cease from the land ; and they shall live securely in the wilderness, and sleep in the forests. And I will make them and the places around my hill a blessing, and cause the rain to descend in its time, [and] there shall be rains of blessings.

6 And the tree of the field shall yield its fruit, and the earth its increase ; and they shall be secure in their land, and know that I am Jehovah, when I break the bands of their yoke and deliver them from those that destroyed them. And they shall no more be a prey to the nations, neither shall the beasts of the earth devour them ; but they shall live securely, and none shall make them afraid. And I will establish for them a plantation for my name, and they shall no more be consumed with famine in the land, nor bear any more the reproach of the nations ; and they shall know that I Jehovah their God am with them, and that they are my people of the house of Israel, says the Lord Jehovah ; for you, my flock, the flock of my feeding, are mine ; I am your God. savs the Lord Jehovah.

PROPHECY XXX.   [35.

AGAINST THE EDOMITES.

1 AND the word of Jehovah came to me, saying, Son of man, set your face against mount Seir, and prophesy against it, and say to it, Thus says the Lord Jehovah: Behold, I am against you, mount Seir, and will stretch out my hand against you, make you a waste and a desolation; I will lay your cities waste, and you shall be a desolation, and shall know that I am Jehovah.

2 Because you had a perpetual grudge, and delivered the sons of Israel to the sword, in the time of their calamity, in the time of the end of their wickedness, therefore, as I live, says the Lord Jehovah, I will surely make you blood, and blood shall pursue you; since you do not hate blood, therefore blood shall pursue you; and I will make mount Seir a waste and a desolation, and will cut off from it him that passes by and returns, and fill his mountains with the killed; and on your hills, and in your valleys, and in all your ravines, shall fall the killed with the sword. And I will make you eternal desolations, and your cities shall not be inhabited; and you shall know that I am Jehovah.

3 Because you said, These two nations and these two lands shall be mine, we will possess them, but Jehovah was there; therefore, as I live, says the Lord Jehovah, I will do according to your anger, and according to your hatred which you exercised in your hatred of them, and I will be known by them when I judge you. And you shall know that I Jehovah heard all the contemptuous words which you spoke against the mountains of Israel, saying, They are destroyed, they are given to us to be consumed; and you magnified yourselves against me with your mouth, and made your words strong against me; I heard it.

4 Thus says the Lord Jehovah: When all the earth rejoices, I will make you a desolation. As you rejoiced over the inheritance of the house of Israel, because it was a desolation, so will I do to you. Mount Seir shall be a desolation, and all Edom, all of it; and they shall know that I am Jehovah.

PROPHECY XXXI.   [36.

1 AND as for you, son of man, prophesy to the mountains of Israel, and say, Mountains of Israel, hear the word of Jehovah. Thus says the Lord Jehovah: Because the enemy said against you, Aha, the high places of old have become a possession for us, therefore prophesy and say, Thus says the Lord Jehovah: Because, even because of desolations, and a panting after you from every side, that you should be a possession of the remnant of the nations, and you come on the lip of the tongue [of slander], and are the slander of the people, therefore, mountains of Israel, hear the word of the Lord Jehovah.   Thus says the Lord Jehovah to the mountains and hills, to streams and valleys, and to deserts and wastes, and to the forsaken cities which are for plunder and derision to the remnant of the nations which are on every side; therefore thus says the Lord Jehovah: Surely with the fire of my jealousy I speak against the remnant of the nations, and against Edom, all of it; because they gave my land to them for a possession with the rejoicing of the whole heart, with contempt of soul, to plunder it for a prey; therefore prophesy concerning the land of Israel, and say to the mountains and hills, Thus says the Lord Jehovah: Behold, in my jealousy and indignation I said that you should bear the shame of the nations; therefore thus says the Lord Jehovah: I lift up my hand, that surely the nations which are around you shall bear their shame.

2 But you, mountains of Israel, shall put forth your branches, and bear your fruit for my people Israel, for they are near to come.   For behold, I am for you, and will turn to you, and you shall be tilled and sown, and I will multiply men on you, all the house of Israel, all of it, and the cities shall be inhabited, and the wastes built up. I will multiply on you men and beasts, and they shall increase and be fruitful, and I will cause you to be inhabited as you formerly were, and do better by you than of old; and you shall know that I am Jehovah.   And I will cause men to walk on you, my people of Israel, and they shall possess you, and you shall be their inheritance, and no more bereave them.

3 Thus says the Lord Jehovah: Because they say to you, You

are a consumer of men, you bereave your nation, therefore you shall not consume men any more, and your nation you shall no more bereave, says the Lord Jehovah, neither will I any more cause to be heard against you the revilings of the nations ; and the reproaches of the peoples you shall no more endure, and your nation you shall bereave no more, says the Lord Jehovah.

4 And the word of Jehovah came to me, saying, Son of man, the house of Israel lived in their land and defiled it with their way and with their works ; their way before me was like the most detestable impurity. Then I poured out my indignation on them for the blood which they shed in my land, and defiled it with their idols ; and scattered them among the nations ; and they are dispersed in the lands. I judged them according to their way and their doings. Then they went to the nations to which they went, and profaned my holy name by its being said of them, These are the people of Jehovah, and they have gone out from their land. But I will spare my holy name which the house of Israel profane among the nations to which they have gone.

5 Therefore say to the house of Israel, Thus says the Lord Jehovah : Not for your sakes will I do it, house of Israel, but for the sake of my holy name which you profane among the nations to which you have gone. And I will hallow my name greatly which is profaned among the nations among whom you profane it ; and the nations shall know that I am Jehovah, says the Lord Jehovah, when I am hallowed by you in their sight. Then I will take you from the nations, and gather you from all lands, and bring you to your land, and sprinkle pure water on you, and you shall be pure from all your defilements, and from all your blocks. I will purify you, and I will give you a new heart, and a new spirit will I put within you ; and I will put away the heart of stone from your flesh, and give you a heart of flesh ; and my Spirit will I put within you, and cause you to walk in my ordinances, and keep my judgments and do them ; and you shall dwell in the land which I gave your fathers, and shall be my people, and I will be your God.

6 Then I will save you from all your defilements, and call for grain and increase it, and not put famine on you. And I will increase the fruit of the tree and the produce of the field, that you may no more have the reproach of famine among the nations.

7 Then you shall remember your evil ways, and your doings which were not good, and loathe yourselves on account of your sins

and on account of your abominations. Not for your sakes will I
do this, says the Lord Jehovah, be it known to you : be ashamed
and confounded on account of your ways, house of Israel.

8 Thus says the Lord Jehovah : In the day in which I purify you
from all your sins, then I will cause your cities to be inhabited, and
your desolations shall be built up ; and the destroyed land shall be
cultivated, instead of its being a desolation in the sight of every one
that passes by.   Then shall they say, This land which was laid waste
is like the garden of Eden ; and the cities which were desolated,
and laid waste, and thrown down, shall be inhabited as fortified cities.   Then shall the nations which remain around you know that I
Jehovah build up the thrown down, and plant the desolate ; I Jehovah have spoken, and I will do it.

9 Thus says the Lord Jehovah : Yet this will I be ˙asked by the
house of Israel to do for them : I will increase them like hosts
of men, like hosts of angels, like the hosts of Jerusalem at her
stated feasts ; so shall the destroyed cities be full of hosts [multi-
tudes] of men ; and they shall know that I am Jehovah.

PROPHECY XXXII.   [37.

RESURRECTION AND RESTORATION OF ALL THE JEWISH NATION, AND THE POST-RESURRECTIONARY KINGDOM OF DAVID.

1 THE hand of Jehovah was on me, and he brought me by the
Spirit of Jehovah, and set me down in a valley, and it was full of
bones.   Then he caused me to pass over them on every side, and
behold, they were many exceedingly on the face of the valley ; and
behold, they were extremely dry.   Then he said to me, Son of man,
shall these bones live again ?   And I said, Lord Jehovah, thou
knowest.   Then he said to me, Prophesy concerning these bones,
and say to them, Dry bones, hear the word of Jehovah : Thus says
Jehovah to these bones : Behold, I will bring into you spirit, and
you shall live.   And I will put on you tendons, and lay on you flesh,
and cover you with skin, and put spirit in you ; and you shall live,
and know that I am Jehovah.

2 Then I prophesied as I was commanded ; and there was a voice
as I prophesied ; and behold, there was a shaking, and the bones
approached, bone to its bone.   Then I saw, and behold, there were
tendons on them, and flesh came up, and a skin covered them over ;

but there was no spirit in them.   Then he said to me, Prophesy to
the spirit, prophesy, son of man, and say to the spirit, Thus says
the Lord Jehovah : Come, spirit, from the four winds, and breathe
on these killed, that they may live.

3 Then I prophesied as I was commanded, and the spirit came
into them, and they lived, and stood on their feet, a host exceedingly great.

4 Then he said to me, Son of man, these bones are all the house
of Israel ; and behold, they say, Our bones are dried up, our expectation has perished, we are cut off.   Therefore prophesy and say
to them, Thus says the Lord Jehovah : Behold, I will open your
graves, and bring you up out of your graves, my people, and cause
you to come to the land of Israel ; and you shall know that I am
Jehovah when I open your graves, and bring you up out of your
graves, my people.   And I will put my spirit in you, and cause you
to live, and give you rest in your land ; and you shall know that I
Jehovah have spoken and done it, says the Lord Jehovah.

5 Then the word of Jehovah came to me, saying, And, son of
man, take one stick, and write on it, For Judah, and for the sons
of Israel his companions ; and take another stick, and write on it,
For Joseph, the stick of Ephraim, and of all the house of Israel his
companions.   Then bring them together one to the other, for one
stick, and let them be one in your hand.   And when the sons of
your people say to you, Will you not tell us what these things
mean ? say to them, Thus says the Lord Jehovah : Behold, I will
take the stick of Joseph, which is in the hand of Ephraim, and the
tribes of Israel his companions, and put them on the stick of Judah,
and make them one stick, and they shall be one in my hand.   Then
let the sticks on which you have written be in your hand before
their eyes, and say to them, Thus says the Lord Jehovah : Behold,
I will take the sons of Israel from among the nations to which they
have gone, and collect them from every side, and cause them to
come to their land, and make them one nation in the land on the
mountains of Israel ; and one king shall be over them for a king,
and they shall no more be two nations, neither shall they be divided any more into two kingdoms ; and they shall no more be
defiled with their blocks, and with their abominations, and with all
their transgressions ; and I will save them from all their habitations
in which they sinned, and purify them ; and they shall be my people, and I will be their God.

6 Then my servant David shall be king over them, and they shall all have one shepherd, and walk in my judgments, and keep my ordinances and do them ; and they shall live in the land which I gave to my servant Jacob, in which your fathers lived ; then they shall live in it, and their sons, and their sons' sons, forever.   And I will make with them a peaceful covenant ; it shall be an eternal covenant with them ; and I will plant them, and multiply them, and put my sanctuary among them, forever ; and my tabernacle shall be over them, and I will be their God, and they shall be my people ; and the nations shall know that I am Jehovah that sanctify Israel, when my sanctuary is among them forever.

PROPHECY XXXIII.   [38, 39.

GOG AND MAGOG, OR THE POST-RESURRECTIONARY DESTRUCTION OF THE ENEMIES OF ISRAEL, THE WICKED.

1 THEN came a word of Jehovah to me, saying, Son of man, set your face against Gog, of the land of Magog [the extreme north], the head chief of the Moschi and Tibareni [barbarous tribes near the Black Sea], and prophesy against him, and say, Thus says Jehovah : Behold, I am against you, Gog, head chief of the Moschi and Tibareni, and will cause you to return, and put hooks in your jaws, and bring you out, and all your host, horses and horsemen, all of them clothed with splendor, a great assembly, [with] shield and buckler, all of them carrying swords ; Persia, Ethiopia, and Libya with them, all of them with shield and helmet ; Gomer [the Crimea, a country north of the Black Sea], and all her armies ; the house of Togarmah [Armenia, or a still more northern country], on the sides of the north, and all his armies, many peoples with him.

2 Stand and be firm, you and all your assembly who are assembled to you ; and do you be the object of their attention.   After many days you shall be appointed over them : in after years you shall come to the land brought back from the sword, collected from many peoples, on the mountains of Israel, which were a perpetual desolation ; and the nation shall be brought from many peoples, and they shall live all of them securely.   Then you shall go up like a storm, and come like a cloud ; you shall cover the earth, you and all your armies, and many peoples shall be with you.

3 Thus says the Lord Jehovah : Then, in that day, thoughts shall

come into your mind, and you shall form an evil purpose, and say, I will go up to an open country ; I will come to those at rest, living securely, all of them living without walls or bars ; and they have no doors, to take a spoil, and seize a prey, and to take back your hand over wastes and desolations ; and to a people gathered from the nations, to get cattle and goods ; to those living on the height of the earth. Sheba, and Dedan, and the merchants of Tarshish, and all her young lions [princes], shall say to you, Have you come to take a spoil ? Have you assembled your assembly to get plunder, to carry off silver and gold, and to take cattle and goods, and to get much spoil ?

4 Therefore prophesy, son of man, and say to Gog, Thus says the Lord Jehovah : In the day in which you know that my people Israel live securely, then you shall come from your place, from the sides of the north, you and many peoples with you, all of them riding on horses, a great assembly and a great army ; and you shall come up against my people of Israel like a cloud, to cover the land ; it shall be in the latter days that I will bring you against my land, that the nations may know me when I am hallowed by you, Gog, before their eyes.

5 Thus says the Lord Jehovah : Are not you he of whom I spoke in ancient days by the hand of my servants, the prophets of Israel, who prophesied in those days [and] years that I would bring you against them ? And in that day, in the day when Gog shall come against the land of Israel, says the Lord Jehovah, my indignation shall come up in my face. For in my jealousy I say, in the fire of my wrath, Surely in that day there shall be a great earthquake over all the land of Israel ; and the fishes of the sea, and the birds of heaven, and the beasts of the field, and all the reptiles which creep on the earth, which are on the face of the ground, shall shake before me, and the mountains be broken down, and the precipices fall, and every wall of the earth shall fall.

6 And I will call against him the sword on all my mountains, says the Lord Jehovah, and the sword of every man shall be against his brother ; and I will judge him with pestilence and with blood ; and I will rain an overflowing shower, and hailstones, fire, and sulphur on him and on all his armies, and on the many peoples which are with him. And I will be magnified and hallowed, and known in the sight of many nations ; and they shall know that I am Jehovah.

25 *

7 And prophesy, son of man, against Gog, and say, Thus says the Lord Jehovah : Behold, I am against you, Gog, head chief of the Moschi and Tibareni ; and I will turn you again, and lead you, and bring you up from the sides of the north, and bring you on the mountains of Israel, and smite your bow from your left hand, and cause your arrows to fall from your right hand ; and you shall fall on the mountains of Israel, you and all your armies, and the peoples which are with you ; I will give you to ravenous birds of every wing, and to the beasts of the field ; and you shall fall on all the face of the field ; for I have spoken it, says the Lord Jehovah.

8 And I will send a fire on Magog, and on the inhabitants of the [Black] sea coasts, that live securely ; and they shall know that I am Jehovah. And I will make known my holy name among my people Israel, and not profane my holy name any more ; and the nations shall know that I am Jehovah, the Holy One of Israel. Behold, it shall come, it shall be, says the Lord Jehovah ; that is the day of which I have spoken.

9 Then shall the inhabitants of the cities of Israel go and burn and consume with fire the weapons, and bucklers, and shields, and bows and arrows, and canes, and lances, seven years. And they shall not take wood from the field, nor cut it from the forest, but shall burn the weapons with fire ; and they shall plunder their plunderers, and take the prey of those who preyed on them, says the Lord Jehovah.

10 And in that day I will give Gog a place of burial in Israel, the valley of passengers, east of the lake ; and it shall stop the nostrils of those that pass by ; and they shall bury Gog there, and all the multitude, and call the valley The Multitude of Gog. And the house of Israel shall bury them, to purify the land, seven months. And all the people of the land shall bury them ; and it shall be to them for a name in the day of my glorifying them, says the Lord Jehovah. And they shall separate men to pass through the land, that they who pass through the land may bury those that remain on the face of the land, to purify it. They shall search at the end of seven months ; and passengers shall pass through ; and if one sees a bone of a man, he shall set up a signal by it till the buriers bury it in the valley of The Multitude of Gog. And the name of the city [the place] shall be The Multitude, and they shall purify the land.

11 And, son of man, say, Thus says the Lord Jehovah : Speak
to birds of every wing, and to all the beasts of the field [saying],
Assemble yourselves, and come, congregate from every side to the
sacrifice which I make for you, a great sacrifice on the mountains
of Israel, and eat flesh and drink blood ; eat the flesh of mighty
men, and drink the blood of the princes of the earth, rams, lambs,
and he goats, bullocks, all of them fat from Bashan ; and eat fat till
you are satisfied, and drink blood to drunkenness, of my sacrifice
which I make for you.

12 And you shall be filled at my table with horses and chariots,
mighty men, and all men of war, says the Lord Jehovah.   And I
will set my glory in the nations, and all nations shall see my judgment which I execute, and my hand which I put on them.   And
the house of Israel shall know that I am Jehovah their God from
that day and forward ; and the nations shall know that the house
of Israel were carried away captive for their wickedness, which they
committed against me, and that I hid my face from them, and gave
them into the hand of their enemies, and they all fell by the sword.
According to their impurity and according to their transgressions I
dealt with them, and hid my face from them.

13 Therefore thus says the Lord Jehovah : Now I will bring back
the captives of Jacob, and have mercy on all the house of Israel,
and be jealous for my holy name.   Though they bore their shame
and all their treachery which they committed against me when they
lived securely in their land, and none made them afraid, when I
restore them from the nations and assemble them from the lands of
their enemies, then I will be hallowed by them in the sight of many
nations, and they shall know that I am Jehovah their God, when I
carry them away captive to the nations, and assemble them in their
land, and leave none of them behind.   And I will no more hide my
face from them, when I pour out my Spirit on the house of Israel,
says the Lord Jehovah.

PROPHECY XXXIV.   [40–48.

THE POST-RESURRECTIONARY TEMPLE, HOLY CITY, HOLY LAND, AND JEWISH COMMONWEALTH.

SECTION I.   [40.

THE POST-RESURRECTIONARY GATES, COURTS, CHAMBERS, ARCHITECTURAL ORNAMENTS, AND WALLS AROUND THE TEMPLE.

1 In the 25th year of our exile, in the first month, on the 10th day of the month, in the 14th year after the city was smitten, on that very day the hand of Jehovah was on me, and he brought me there [to Jerusalem]. In visions of God he brought me to the land of Israel, and set me on an exceedingly high mountain; and on it was as it were the building of a city, at the south. And he brought me there, and behold, there was a man whose appearance was like the appearance of brass, and a linen line was in his hand, and a measuring reed, and he stood at the gate.

2 Then the man said to me, Son of man, see with your eyes, and hear with your ears, and apply your mind to all that I cause you to see; for you are brought hither in order that I may cause you to see, that you may tell all you see to the house of Israel.

3 And behold, there was a wall on the outside of the house, extending round it, and in the hand of the man a measuring reed of 6 cubits of a cubit and a hand [of 7 hands 21 inches]. And he measured the breadth of the wall, 1 reed [10½ feet], and the height 1 reed. Then he came to the gate which opened towards the east, and went up its steps and measured [one] threshold of the gate, 1 reed broad, and the [other] threshold 1 reed broad, and the chamber 1 reed long and 1 reed broad; and between the chambers [the distance] was 5 cubits, and the threshold of the gate by the side of the interior porch of the gate was 1 reed; and he measured the interior porch of the gate 1 reed.

4 Then He measured the porch of the gate 8 cubits, and its pilaster 2 cubits, and the porch of the gate was within. And the chambers of the gate towards the east were 3 on one side and 3 on the other; the 3 had one measure, and their pilasters had one measure, on one side and on the other.

5 And he measured the breadth of the entrance of the gate 10

cubits, [and] the length of the gate 13 cubits; and there was a space before the chambers of 1 cubit [on one side] and 1 cubit on the other, and the chamber was 6 cubits on one side and 6 cubits on the other. Then he measured the gate from the roof of one chamber to the roof of another, 25 cubits broad, door against door. And he made the pilasters 60 cubits, and the gate [extended] to the pilaster of the court on every side. And from the front of the gate of entrance to the front of the interior porch of the gate was 50 cubits. And there were closed windows to the chambers and to their pilasters, on the inside of the gate on every side, and also to the verandas, and there were windows on all sides within, and on the pilasters palm trees.

6 Then he brought me to the exterior court, and behold, there were rooms and a pavement made for the court on all sides, 30 rooms on the pavement. And the pavement by the sides of the gates, opposite to the length [line] of the gates was the lower pavement. And he measured the breadth from the front of the lower gate to the front of the interior court without, 100 cubits east and north.

7 And as for the gate which opened towards the north in the exterior court, he measured its length and breadth, and its chambers, 3 on one side and 3 on the other, and its pilasters, and its verandas, and the measure was according to the measure of the first gate; its length was 50 cubits, and its breadth 25 cubits; and its windows, and its verandas, and its palm trees were according to the measure of the gate which opens towards the east; and they went up to it by 7 steps, and its verandas were before them. And the gate of the interior court was opposite to the [exterior] gate, towards the north and east; and he measured from gate to gate 100 cubits.

8 Then he led me towards the south, and behold, there was a gate towards the south, and he measured its pilasters and its verandas according to the other measures; and there were windows in it, and in the verandas around on all sides, like the other windows; the length was 50 cubits, and the breadth 25 cubits. And its ascent had 7 steps, and before them were its palm trees, 1 on this side and 1 on that side, on the pilasters; and there was a gate of the court within, towards the south, and he measured from gate to gate towards the south 100 cubits.

9 And he brought me to the interior court by the south gate, and measured the south gate according to the measures of the others,

and its chambers, and its pilasters, and its verandas were according
to the other measures; and it had windows.   And its verandas on
all sides were 50 cubits long and 25 cubits broad.   And its verandas were towards the interior court, and there were palm trees on
its pilasters, and its ascent had 8 steps.

10 And he brought me to the interior court towards the east, and
measured the gate like the other measures; and its chambers, and
its pilisters, and its verandas were like the other measures; and
it had windows.   And its verandas on every side were 50 cubits
long and 25 cubits broad.   And its verandas were towards the
outer court; and there were palm trees on its pilasters on one side
and on the other, and its ascent had 8 steps.

11 And he brought me to the north gate, and measured, like the
other measures, its chambers, and its pilasters, and its verandas;
and it had windows on all sides.   The length was 50 cubits, and the
breadth 25 cubits.   And its pilasters were towards the interior court;
and there were palm trees on its pilasters on this side and on that,
and its ascent was by 8 steps.

12 And there was a room and its door by the pilasters of the
gates, where they washed the burnt offerings.   And in the porch
of the gate were 2 tables on this side and 2 on that, on which
to kill the burnt offerings, and sin offerings, and trespass offerings.
And at the outside, as one goes up to the entrance of the north
gate, were 2 tables, and on the other side, which was at the porch
of the gate, were 2 tables; 4 tables on this side and 4 tables on that
side; 8 tables on which they slaughtered [victims].   And the four
tables for burnt offerings were of cut stone, $1\frac{1}{2}$ cubits long, $1\frac{1}{2}$ cubits
broad, and 1 cubit high.   On them they laid the instruments with
which they killed the burnt offerings and sacrifices.   And there were
forked pins of a hand [in length], set in the house around; and on
the tables was the flesh of the offering.

13 And outside of the interior gate were rooms for the singers
in the interior court, which were at the side of the north gate, and
opened to the south; one at the side of the east gate opened to
the north.   And he said to me, This room which opens towards the
south is for the priests who keep the charge of the house; and the
chamber which opens towards the north is for the priests who keep
the charge of the altar.   These are the sons of Zadok, who, of the
sons of Levi, come near Jehovah to minister to him.   Then he
measured the court, 100 cubits long and 100 cubits broad, square;
and the altar was before the house.

14 Then he brought me to the porch of the house and measured the porch, 5 cubits on one side and 5 cubits on the other side, and the breadth of the gate, 3 cubits on one side and 3 cubits on the other side. The length of the porch was 20 cubits, and the breadth 11 cubits, and they went up to it with steps, and there were columns by the pilasters, one on one side and another on the other side.

SECTION II.　　　　　　　[41.

THE POST-RESURRECTIONARY TEMPLE.

1 THEN he brought me to the temple, and measured the pilasters, 6 cubits broad on one side and 6 cubits broad on the other side; the breadth of the tabernacle and the width of the door was 10 cubits, and the sides by the door were 5 cubits on this side and 5 cubits on that side; and he measured its length, 40 cubits, and breadth, 20 cubits; and he went in and measured the pilaster of the door, 2 cubits, and the door, 6 cubits, and the breadth of the door, 7 cubits.

2 Then he measured its length, 20 cubits, and the breadth, 20 cubits, to before the temple, and said to me, This is the most holy place. Then he measured the wall of the house, 6 cubits, and the breadth of the side chambers, 4 cubits on every side around all the house; and the side chambers were chamber to chamber 33 times, and they extended to the wall of the house for side chambers to be joined [to it] on every side, but they were not joined to the wall of the house, and it was enlarged and carried round above to the side chambers; for the circuit of the house was above around [the house]. Therefore the breadth of the house was for the ascent, so that the lower part ascended to the higher through the middle part. And I saw the height of the house on every side, and the bases of the side chambers were a full reed, 6 cubits, to the knuckles [10½ feet]; and the breadth of the wall of the side chambers to the outside was 5 cubits, and the remaining part of the house was the side chambers which belonged to the house; and between the rooms was a breadth of 20 cubits around the house on every side. And the doors of the side chambers were towards the space that was left, one door towards the north, and another door towards the south; and the breadth of the space left was 5 cubits on every side.

3 And the structure which was before the inclosure on the side towards the court was 70 cubits broad, and the wall of the structure

5 cubits broad on every side, and its length was 90 cubits. And he measured the length of the house, 100 cubits, and the inclosure, and the structure and its walls, 100 long ; and the breadth before the front of the house, and of the inclosure towards the east, was 100 cubits.

4 And he measured the length of the structure which was before the inclosure, [and] that which was behind it, and the galleries on one side and the other were 100 cubits, and the interior temple and the porches of the courts, the thresholds, and the windows which were closed, and the galleries around the three sides. Opposite to the threshold was a board of wood around, and the ground extended to the windows, and the windows were covered to the space above the door, and on the interior house, and without, and on every wall around, within and without, were clothes.

5 And cherubs were made, and palm trees from cherub to cherub ; and each cherub had two faces, and the face of a man was towards the palm tree on one side, and the face of a lion towards the palm tree on the other side ; and so it was made on all the house on every side. Palm trees were made from the ground to over the door, and on the wall of the temple. The door posts of the temple were square, and the appearance of the front of the sanctuary was like the appearance [of the rest].

6 The altar was of wood, 3 cubits high, and 2 cubits long, and its corners, and its length, and its walls were of wood. And he said to me, This is the table that stands before Jehovah. And the temple and the sanctuary had two doors, and the two doors had each two leaves, that turned, two leaves for one door, and two leaves for the other door. And there were made on them, even on the doors of the temple, cherubs and palm trees, such as were made on the walls ; and a threshold of wood was before the porch without, and there were closed windows and palm trees on one side and on the other, on the sides of the porch, and the side chambers of the house, and the thresholds.

SECTION III.   [42.

BUILDINGS CONNECTED WITH THE POST-RESURRECTIONARY TEMPLE.

1 AND he brought me to the exterior court towards the north, and brought me to the rooms which were before the inclosure, and which were before the structure on the north. The length was 100 cubits before the gate towards the north, and the breadth 50 cubits. Opposite to the 20 cubits in the interior court, and opposite to the

pavement of the interior court, was gallery before gallery in three rows] ; and before the chambers was a walk of 10 cubits broad, inward, [with] a way of one cubit, and their doors towards the north. And the upper chambers were narrower — because the galleries took room away from them — than the lower and middle parts of the structure, for it was of 3 stories ; but they had no columns like the columns of the courts ; therefore they were narrower than the lowest and than the middle ones from the ground.

2 And as to the wall which was without against the chambers towards the exterior court before the chambers, its length was 50 cubits ; for the length of the rooms which were in the exterior court was 50 cubits, but before the temple 100 cubits. And under these rooms was an entry from the east as one comes to them from the exterior court. In the breadth of the wall of the court towards the east, before the inclosure and before the building, were rooms ; and there was a way before them like the appearance of the rooms which were towards the north ; their length was the same as their breadth, and their goings out and entrances were according to their fashions and their doors ; and in like manner the doors of the rooms towards the south. There was a door at the head of the way before a commodious wall, in the way towards the east as one enters.

3 And he said to me, The north rooms and the south rooms, which are before the inclosure, are holy rooms, where the priests shall eat the most holy things when they come near to Jehovah. There they shall lay the most holy things, and the bread offerings, and the sin offerings, and the trespass offerings, for the place is holy. When the priests enter in, they shall not go out from the holy place to the exterior court, but shall leave there the clothes in which they minister, for they are holy, and shall put on other clothes when they approach to the place which belongs to the people.

4 And he finished the measures of the interior house, and brought me to the gate which opens towards the east, and measured it on every side. And he measured the east side with the measuring reed, 500 reeds of the measuring reed on every side ; he measured the north side 500 reeds of the measuring reed on every side ; he measured the south side 500 reeds of the measuring reed ; he went round to the west side, [and] measured 500 reeds of the measuring reed ; he measured on the four sides its wall on every side, 500 in length and 500 in breadth, to separate between the holy and the common.

Section IV.

THE ENTRANCE OF JEHOVAH INTO THE POST-RESURRECTIONARY TEMPLE.

1 Then he brought me to the gate, the gate which opens to the east, and behold, the glory of the God of Israel came from the east, and his voice was like the voice of many waters, and the earth shone with his glory ; and the appearance was like the appearance which I saw when I came to destroy the city ; and the appearances were like the appearance which I saw by the river Chebar ; and I fell on my face.

2 Then the glory of Jehovah came to the house by the way of the gate which opens towards the east. And the Spirit took me up and brought me into the interior court, and behold, the glory of Jehovah filled the house. And I heard one speaking to me out of the house, and a man stood by me, and he said to me, Son of man, this is the place of my throne, and the place of the soles of my feet, where I will dwell in the midst of the sons of Israel forever ; and the house of Israel shall no more defile my holy name, they nor their kings, with their fornications, nor with the dead bodies of their kings when they die, by setting their threshold by my threshold, and their door posts by my door posts, so that there was only a wall between me and them ; and they defiled my holy name with their abominations, which they committed, and I consumed them in my anger. Now they shall remove far away from me their fornication, and the dead bodies of their kings, and I will dwell among them forever.

3 And, son of man, tell the house of Israel of this house, that they may be ashamed of their wickedness, and let them measure the pattern. And if they are ashamed of all that they have done, tell them the form of the house, the fashion of it, the passages for going out and coming in, and all its forms, and all its ordinances, and all its forms, and all its laws, and write it in their sight, that they may keep all its forms and all its ordinances, and do them.

4 This is the law of the house : On the top of the mountain, all within its limits on every side shall be most holy ; behold, this is the law of the house.

SECTION V.   [43, 13–27.

1 AND these are the measures of the altar by cubits, each cubit being a cubit and a hand [7 hands]. The cavity shall be a cubit high and a cubit broad, and its border, at the edge around it, shall be a span; and this shall be the upper part of the altar; and from the cavity on the ground to the lower ledge shall be 2 cubits, and the breadth 1 cubit; and from the smaller ledge to the greater ledge 4 cubits, and the breadth one cubit; and the altar shall be 4 cubits, and from the altar and upwards there shall be four horns; and the hearth shall be 12 cubits long by 12 broad, square with its four sides; and the ledge shall be 14 cubits long by 14 cubits broad on its four sides, and the border about it shall be ½ cubit, and its cavity shall be 1 cubit round, and its steps shall be towards the east.

2 And he said to me, Son of man, thus says the Lord Jehovah: These shall be the ordinances of the altar in the day when it shall be made, to offer burnt offerings on it, and sprinkle blood on it. And you shall give the priests the Levites who are of the posterity of Zadok, who come near to me, says the Lord Jehovah, to serve me, a young bullock for a sin offering; and you shall take of its blood and put it on its four horns, and on the four corners of the ledge, and on the border around, and you shall purify it, and cleanse it. And you shall take the bullock of the sin offering, and burn it in a house appointed for that purpose without the sanctuary; and on the second day you shall offer a he goat without blemish for a sin offering, and they shall purify the altar as they purified it with the bullock. And when you have finished purifying it, you shall offer a young bullock without blemish, and a ram from the flock without blemish; and you shall offer them before Jehovah, and the priests shall put salt on them, and offer them up for a burnt offering to Jehovah.

3 Seven days shall you offer daily a goat for a sin offering, and they shall sacrifice a young bullock and a ram from the flock without blemish. Seven days shall they cleanse the altar and purify it, and consecrate themselves, and they shall finish these days, and on the 8th day and forward the priests shall offer on the altar your burnt offerings and your peace offerings, and I will accept you, says the Lord Jehovah.

Section VI.   [44.

1 THEN he brought me back to the exterior gate of the sanctuary,
which opens towards the east, and it was shut.   And Jehovah said
to me, This gate shall be shut; it shall not be opened, and no man
shall enter in by it, for Jehovah the God of Israel enters in by it;
therefore it shall be shut.   As to the prince, the prince shall sit in
it to eat bread before Jehovah.   He shall go in by way of the porch
of the gate, and by that way he shall go out.

2 Then he brought me to the north gate before the house, and I
saw, and behold, the house of Jehovah was filled with the glory of
Jehovah, and I fell on my face.   And Jehovah said to me, Son of
man, attend and see with your eyes and hear with your ears all the
words which I speak with you concerning all the ordinances of the
house of Jehovah, and all its laws, and attend to the entrances of
the house, and all the ways of egress from the sanctuary; and say
to the rebellion the house of Israel, Thus says the Lord Jehovah:
Be satisfied with all your abominations, house of Israel, in your
having brought strangers, uncircumcised in heart and uncircumcised in flesh, to be in the sanctuary, to profane my house, when
you offered my food, the fat and the blood, and broke my covenant
with all your abominations, and kept not my holy charge, but took
the keepers of my charge in the sanctuary to yourselves.

3 Thus says the Lord Jehovah: No stranger, uncircumcised in
heart and uncircumcised in flesh, shall come into my sanctuary, of
all the strangers that are among the sons of Israel.   And the Levites who went far from me when Israel went astray, who went
astray from me after their blocks, shall bear their wickedness; and
they shall be servants in my sanctuary, having charges at the gates
of the house, and serving at the house; they shall kill the burnt
offerings and sacrifices of the people, and shall stand before them to
serve them.

4 Because they served them before their blocks, and were a stumbling block of wickedness to the house of Israel, therefore have I
lifted up my hand against them, says the Lord Jehovah, and they
shall bear their wickedness; and they shall not come before me to
execute the priests' office for me, nor come near to any of my holy
things in the most holy place, but they shall bear their shame and

their abominations which they committed ; and I will make them keepers of the charge of the house for all its service, and all the work which shall be done in it.

5 But the priests the Levites, the sons of Zadok, who kept the charge of the sanctuary when the sons of Israel went astray from me, shall approach me to perform my service, and to stand before me, and to present me the fat and the blood, says the Lord Jehovah. They shall come into my sanctuary, and shall come near to my table, to serve me ; they shall clothe themselves in linen garments, and no wool shall come on them, when they serve in the gates of the interior court, and in the house.

6 Linen turbans shall be on their heads, and linen breeches on their loins ; and they shall not be girded with sweat. And when they go forth into the exterior courts, to the people, they shall put off the garments with which they serve, and lay them in the holy apartment, and shall put on other garments, and shall not sanctify the people in their garments.

7 They shall not shave their heads, nor suffer their hair to grow long ; they shall shear their heads. None of the priests shall drink wine when they enter into the interior court ; neither shall they take to them for wives a widow, or a woman that has been divorced, but they shall take virgins of the race of the house of Israel, or a widow who is the widow of a priest. And they shall teach my people the difference between the holy and the profane, and cause them to distinguish between the impure and the pure. And in controversy they shall stand up to judge ; they shall judge according to my judgments, and shall keep my laws and my ordinances in all my festivals, and shall hallow my Sabbaths.

8 And they shall come to no dead person to defile themselves ; but for a father or mother, or for a son or daughter, for a brother, or sister who has no husband, they may defile themselves. And after one's cleansing, they shall reckon to him 7 days ; and on the day that he goes into the sanctuary, into the interior court, to serve in the sanctuary, he shall offer his sin offering, says the Lord Jehovah.

9 And it shall be to them for an inheritance : I am their inheritance ; and you shall give them no possession in Israel : I am their possession. They shall eat the bread offering, and sin offering, and trespass offering ; and every devoted thing in Israel shall belong to them. And the first of all the first fruits, and every offering of all

26 *

the offerings, shall belong to the priests; and you shall also give the priest the first of your coarse meal, that he may cause a blessing to rest on your house. The priests shall not eat any thing that dies of itself, or is torn, either bird or beast.

Section VII.   45, 46.

THE APPROPRIATION OF LAND FOR RELIGIOUS PURPOSES, WEIGHTS AND MEASURES, AND SACRIFICES.

1 AND when you divide the land for an inheritance, you shall offer an offering to Jehovah, a holy portion of the land; the length shall be 25,000 reeds, and the breadth 10,000; it shall be holy in all its bounds. And of this shall be for the sanctuary 500 by 500 square, and 50 cubits around it on every side for an open place. And of this place you shall measure 25,000 in length, and 10,000 in breadth; and in it shall be the sanctuary, the most holy place.

2 A holy portion of that district shall belong to the priests, who serve the temple of Jehovah, [and] who approach to serve Jehovah; and they shall have it as a place for houses, and a holy place belonging to the sanctuary. And 25,000 in length and 10,000 in breadth shall the Levites have, the ministers of the house, for their possession, [and] 20 rooms. And you shall appoint the possession of the city 5000 in breadth, and 25,000 in length, against the offering of the holy portion, that it may be a possession of all the house of Israel. And the prince shall have portions on one side and on the other side of the offering of the holy portion, and before the possession of the city, from the west side westward, and from the east side eastward; and the length shall extend along each of the portions, from the western boundary to the eastern boundary. As to the land, he shall have it for a possession in Israel; and the princes shall no more oppress my people, but give the rest of the land to the house of Israel, to their tribes.

3 Thus says the Lord Jehovah: Be satisfied, princes of Israel; put away violence and plunder; execute judgment, and do righteousness, and take off your exactions from my people, says the Lord Jehovah.

4 You shall have correct scales, a correct ephah [1⅛ bushel measure], and a correct bath [8½ gallon measure]. The ephah and the bath shall be one measure, that the bath may contain a 10th part of a homer [11¼ bushel measure], and the ephah a 10th part of a

homer ; their measure shall be according to the homer. And the shekel shall be 20 gerahs [a gerah is about 13 grains], and 60 shekels shall be to you one maneh [mina; the common mina was 100 shekels].

5 This is the wave offering which you shall offer : the 6th part of an ephah out of a homer of wheat, and the 6th part of an ephah out of a homer of barley ; and as for the ordinance concerning oil, — the bath of oil, — you shall take a 10th of a bath from a cor, which is 10 baths a homer ; for a homer is 10 baths. And you shall offer one lamb from the flock out of 200 from the pastures of Israel, for bread offerings, and for burnt offerings, and for peace offerings, to make expiation for them, says the Lord Jehovah. All the people of the land shall give their wave offering for the prince of Israel ; and it shall be the duty of the prince to give burnt offerings, and bread offerings, and libations, at the feasts and new moons, and on the Sabbaths ; and at all the religious assemblies of the house of Israel he shall present the sin offerings, and bread offerings, and burnt offerings, and peace offerings, to make expiation for the house of Israel.

6 Thus says the Lord Jehovah : In the first month, on the 1st day of the month, you shall take a young bullock without blemish, and purify the sanctuary ; and the priest shall take of the blood of the sin offering, and put it on the door posts of the house, and on the four corners of the ledge of the altar, and on the posts of the gate of the inner court. And you shall do in like manner, on the 7th day in the new moon, for him that has transgressed through error or ignorance ; and you shall expiate the house.

7 In the first month, on the 14th day of the month, you shall have the feast of the passover 7 days, [and] unleavened bread shall be eaten. And on that day the prince shall sacrifice for himself, and for all the people of the land, a bullock for a sin offering. And the 7 days of the feast he shall sacrifice to Jehovah 7 bullocks and 7 rams without blemish, daily 7 days, and a he goat daily, for a sin offering. And he shall present a bread offering, an ephah [1¼ bushels] for a bullock, and an ephah for a ram, and a hin [5 quarts] of oil to an ephah. On the seventh month, on the 15th day of the month, at the feast, he shall do in like manner 7 days, as to the sin offering, and burnt offering, and bread offering, and oil.

8 Thus says the Lord Jehovah : The gate of the interior court which opens towards the east shall be shut the six days of work ;

but on the Sabbath day it shall be opened, and on the new moon it shall be opened. And the prince shall enter by the way of the porch of the gate from without, and stand by the post of the gate; and the priests shall present his burnt offerings, and his peace offerings; and he shall worship at the threshold of the gate, and go out, but the gate shall not be shut till evening. And the people of the country shall worship at the door of this gate, on the Sabbaths and on the new moons, before Jehovah.

9 And the burnt offerings which the prince shall offer to Jehovah on the Sabbath day shall be 6 young sheep without blemish, and a ram without blemish; and the bread offering shall be an ephah to a ram, and the bread offering for the young sheep, the gift of his hand, and a hin of oil to an ephah. And on the day of the new moon there shall be a young bullock without blemish, and 6 young sheep, and a ram; they shall be without blemish. And he shall present for a bread offering an ephah for a bullock, and an ephah for a ram, and for the sheep according as his hand finds, and a hin of oil to an ephah.

10 And when the people of the land come before Jehovah in the appointed feasts, he that enters by way of the north gate, to worship, shall go out by way of the south gate; and he that enters by way of the south gate shall go out by way of the north gate. One shall not return by way of the gate by which he entered, but they shall go out opposite to it; and the prince shall be among the people when they come in and when they go out.

11 And at the feasts, and at the religious assemblies, the bread offering shall be an ephah to a bullock, and an ephah to a ram, and to a young sheep a gift of what comes to hand, and a hin of oil to an ephah. And when the prince shall present a voluntary burnt offering, or voluntary peace offerings, to Jehovah, the gate which opens to the east shall be opened to him; and he shall present his burnt offering, and his peace offerings, as he does on the Sabbath; and he shall go out, and shut the gate after his going out.

12 And you shall present a burnt offering daily to Jehovah, a young sheep a year old every morning shall you present it. And you shall present with it every morning, for a bread offering, a 6th of an ephah and a 3d of a hin of oil, to wet the fine flour, a bread offering to Jehovah, according to perpetual statutes continually. And they shall offer a young sheep, and the bread offering, and the oil every morning for continual burnt offerings.

13 Thus says the Lord Jehovah: When the prince gives a gift to any of his sons, the inheritance of it shall belong to his sons ; it shall be their possession by inheritance. But when he gives a gift from his inheritance to one of his servants, it shall be his till the year of liberty, when it shall revert to the prince ; but his inheritance [given to] his sons shall be theirs. And the prince shall not take of the inheritance of the people to drive them out from their possessions, but he shall give an inheritance to his sons from his possessions, that no one of my people may be driven from his possessions.

14 Then he brought me through the entry which was by the side of the gate, to the holy rooms for the priests, which opened towards the north, and behold, there was a place in their sides towards the west. And he said to me, This is the place in which the priests shall boil the trespass offering and sin offering, and bake the bread offering, that they may not bring [them] into the exterior court to sanctify the people.

15 Then he brought me into the exterior court, and caused me to pass round the four corners of the court, and behold, there was a court in every corner of the court. In the four corners of the court there were closed courts, 40 cubits long and 30 broad; the four corners had one measure ; and they had a wall around them, around the four, and boilers were made under the walls on every side. And he said to me, These are the boiling houses, in which the servants of the house shall boil the sacrifices of the people.

SECTION VIII.   [47, 1-12.

THE POST-RESURRECTIONARY RIVER OF LIFE.

1 THEN he brought me to the door of the house, and behold, water came out from under the threshold of the house eastward, for the house fronted the east, and the water went down from under the inside of the house south of the altar.

2 Then he brought me by way of the north gate, and took me around on the outside to the gate on the outside, which opened to the east ; and behold, water came out in drops from the right side [of the gate].

3 Then the man went east, and the line was in his hand, and he measured 1000 cubits. Then he caused me to pass through the water, the water [wet] the soles [of my feet]. Then he measured 1000 cubits, and caused me to pass through the water ; the water

[was to my] knees. Then he measured 1000 cubits, and caused me
to pass through water [to my] loins. Then he measured 1000 cubits, a river which I could not pass over, for the water was deep,
water to swim in, a river which could not be passed over.

4 Then he said to me, Do you see, son of man? Then he caused
me to go [about], and brought me back to the bank of the river.
And when I returned, then behold, on the bank of the river was a
vast number of trees here and there. Then he said to me, This
water goes east to Galilee, and goes down to the desert, and goes to
the [Dead] Sea, and is emptied into the [Dead] Sea, and [its] waters
made good. And every living soul that is produced abundantly, in
all places where the river comes, shall live; and the fish shall be
very abundant [in the Dead Sea], for when this water comes there,
then that water shall be made good, and every thing shall live where
the river comes.

5 And fishermen shall stand on it; from Engedi to Eneglaim
shall be a place for spreading nets. And as to kinds, these fish
shall be like the fish of the great sea, exceedingly abundant. In its
springs and in its pools the water shall not be made good; they
shall be left for salt. And on the river shall come up on its banks, here
and there, every [kind of] fruit trees, and their leaves shall not
wither, nor their fruit be destroyed; and they shall produce early
fruit monthly, because their water comes from the sanctuary, and
their fruit shall be for food, and their leaves for medicine.

SECTION IX.   [47, 13, 48.

**THE POST-RESURRECTIONARY DIVISION OF THE HOLY LAND TO ISRAELITES
AND STRANGERS, WITH A RESERVATION FOR JEHOVAH.**

1 THUS says the Lord Jehovah: This is the boundary according
to which you shall distribute the land to the 12 tribes of Israel; to
Joseph two portions; and you shall inherit it one like another; for
I lifted up my hand to give it to your fathers, and this land shall
fall to you for an inheritance.

2 And this shall be the boundary of the land on the north side from
the great sea, by way of Hethlon, as one goes to Zedad: Hamath,
Berothah, Sibraim, which is between the boundary of Damascus
and Hamath; Hazarhatticon, which is by the boundary of Hauran;
and the boundary from the sea shall be Hazarenan, the boundary
of Damascus, and Zaphon northward, and the boundary of Hamath;
and this shall be the north side.

3 And the east side you shall measure between Hauran and Damascus, and between Gilead and the land of Israel, the Jordan from the boundary on the Dead Sea; and this shall be the east side. And the south side shall be from Tamar to the water of strife, Kadesh [and] the stream to the great sea; and this shall be the south side. And the west side shall be the great sea, from the boundary till one comes to the part against Hamath. This shall be the west side.

4 And you shall divide this land among you according to the tribes of Israel, and shall divide it by lot for an inheritance to you and to the strangers who live with you, who have sons among you, and they shall be to you as one born in the country among the sons of Israel, and shall share the inheritance with you among the tribes of Israel. And in the tribe in which the stranger lives, there shall you give him his inheritance, says the Lord Jehovah.

5 And these are the names of the tribes from the north extremity, by the way of Hethlon, as one goes to Hamath, Hazarenan, the boundary of Damascus, northward towards Hamath; and each one shall have from the east side to the west side, Dan one; and by the boundary of Dan from the east side to the west, Ashur one; and by the boundary of Ashur from the east side to the west, Naphtali one; and by the boundary of Naphtali from the east side to the west, Manasseh one; and by the boundary of Manasseh from the east side to the west, Ephraim one; and by the boundary of Ephraim from the east side to the west, Reuben one; and by the boundary of Reuben from the east side to the west, Judah one; and by the boundary of Judah from the east side to the west shall be the offering [sacred portion of the land] which you shall set apart; 25,000 reeds in breadth, and in length like one of the [tribe] portions from the east side to the west, and in the middle of it shall be the sanctuary.

6 And the portion which you shall give to Jehovah shall be 25,000 reeds long and 10,000 broad. And of this a holy portion shall be for the priests, 25,000 reeds long towards the north, and towards the west 10,000 broad, and towards the east 10,000 broad, and towards the south 25,000 long; and the sanctuary of Jehovah shall be in it. It shall be for the priests who are sanctified of the sons of Zadok, who kept my charge, who went not astray, when the sons of Israel went astray as the Levites did; and it shall be an offering to them of the offerings of the land most holy, to the boundary of the Levites.

7 And the Levites shall have 25,000 reeds long and 10,000 broad, by the boundary of the priests ; the whole length 25,000, and the breadth 10,000.   And they shall not sell any of it, neither shall they exchange it, nor alienate the land, for it is holy to Jehovah.   And 5,000 left in breadth over against the 25,000 shall belong in common to the city, for dwellings and for open lands, and the city shall be within it.   And these are its measures : The north side 4,500, and the south side 4,500, and the east side 4,500, and the west side 4,500.   And the open area of the city shall be towards the north 250, and towards the south 250, and towards the east 250, and towards the west 250.

8 And as to the rest in length over against the sacred territory, 10,000 eastward and 10,000 westward, against the sacred territory ; its produce shall be for food for the servants of the city.   And servants of the city shall serve it from all the tribes of Israel.   All the sacred territory shall be 25,000 reeds by 25,000 ; you shall make the sacred territory square, together with the possession of the city.

9 And the rest on both sides of the sacred territory, and of the possession of the city, against the territory of the 25,000 [reeds] at the east boundary, and westward against the 25,000 on the west boundary, be the portions [for the tribes] shall belong to the prince ; and be the sacred territory of the sanctuary, and the sanctuary, the house, shall be within it.   What is left from the possession of the Levites and from the possession of the city between what belongs to the prince and the boundary of Judah, and the boundary of Benjamin, shall belong to the prince.

10 And as for the rest of the tribes from the east side to the west side, Benjamin one ; and by the boundary of Benjamin from the east side to the west side, Simeon one ; and by the boundary of Simeon from the east side to the west side, Issachar one ; and by the boundary of Issachar from the east side to the west side, Zebulun one ; and by the boundary of Zebulun from the east side to the west side, Gad one ; and by the boundary of Gad to the south side southward, the boundary shall be from Tamar to the waters of strife to Kadesh, [and] the stream to the great sea.   This is the land which you shall distribute by lot, a possession to the tribes of Israel, and these shall be their portions, says the Lord Jehovah.

11 And these shall be the extremities of the city : On the north side its measure shall be 4,500 reeds, and the gates of the city shall be after the names of the tribes of Israel ; three gates on the north, one gate of Reuben, one gate of Judah, and one gate of Levi.

12 And on the east side it shall be 4,500 reeds, and there shall be three gates; one gate of Joseph, one gate of Benjamin, [and] one gate of Dan. And on the south side the measure shall be 4,500 reeds, and there shall be three gates; one gate of Simeon, one gate of Issachar, [and] one gate of Zebulun. And on the west it shall be 4,500 [reeds], and there shall be three gates; one gate of Gad, one gate of Ashur, [and] one gate of Naphtali. Its circumference shall be 18,000 reeds, and the name of the city from that day shall be, Jehovah is there.

12. OBADIAH.

Vision of Obadiah, [the judgments of Edom.]

1 THUS says the Lord Jehovah concerning Edom: We have heard a report from Jehovah, and a messenger is sent to the nations, [saying,] Rise up, and we will rise up to battle against her. Behold, I have made you small among the nations, and you are greatly despised. The pride of your heart has deceived you, dweller in the asylum of the rocks, whose dwelling is on high; you say in your heart, Who shall bring me down to the earth? Though you exalt yourself like the eagle, and set your nest among the stars, thence will I bring you down, says Jehovah.

2 If thieves came to you, if robbers by night, how would you be destroyed! Would they not steal till they had enough? If grape gatherers came to you, would they not leave the gleanings? How is Esau searched! his concealed treasures explored! All your allies left you at [your] boundary; they that were at peace with you have deceived you; they have prevailed against you; those that eat your bread have set treachery under you; there is no understanding it. Is not that the day, says Jehovah, in which I destroyed the wise men from Edom, and understanding from mount Esau? And your mighty men, Teman, are destroyed, that each one may be cut off from mount Esau with slaughter. For violence towards your brother Jacob, shame shall cover you, and you shall be cut off forever.

3 In the day when you stood before [him], in the day in which strangers carried away captive his wealth, and foreigners went into his gate and cast lots against Jerusalem, you also were as one of them. But you should not have looked on your brother in the day of his calamity, and you should not have rejoiced over the sons of Judah in the day of their destruction, and you should not have enlarged your mouth in the day of distress; you should not have entered the gate of my people in the day of their misfortune, you should not have looked — certainly not you — on their affliction in the day of their calamity, nor have stood at the parting [of the ways] to cut off those of them that escaped, nor have delivered up those of them that escaped in the day of their distress. For the day of Jehovah is at hand against all nations. According as you have done, it shall be done to you; your deserved recompense shall return on your head. For you drank on my holy mountain; all nations shall drink continually, and drink and rave, and be as if they had not been.

4 But in mount Zion shall be the saved, and they shall be holy, and the house of Jacob shall possess their possessors. And the house of Jacob shall be a fire, and the house of Joseph a flame, and the house of Esau stubble; and they shall kindle it and consume it, and there shall not be a remnant left of the house of Esau, for Jehovah has said it.

5 And [those] of the south shall possess mount Esau, and [those] of the plain the Philistines; and they shall possess the fields of Ephraim and the fields of Samaria; and Benjamin shall possess Gilead. And the captives of this host of the sons of Israel [shall possess] what belongs to the Canaanites, to Zarephath; and the captives of Jerusalem which are at Sepharad shall possess the cities of the south, and saviours shall go up to mount Zion to judge mount Esau, and the kingdom shall be Jehovah's.

13. HAGGAI.

PROPHECY I.　　　　　　　　　　[1.

THE REBUILDING OF THE TEMPLE REQUIRED TO BE PROSECUTED, AND THE REQUIREMENT OBEYED.

1 IN the 2d year of Darius, the king, in the sixth month, on the 1st day of the month, came the word of Jehovah by the hand of Haggai, the prophet, to Zerubbabel, son of Shealtiel, governor of Judah, and to Joshua, son of Jozadak, chief priest, saying, Thus says Jehovah of hosts : This people say, The time has not come, the time for the house of Jehovah to be built.

2 Then came the word of Jehovah by the hand of Haggai, the prophet, saying, Is it time for you to live in ceiled houses, when this house is desolate ?　And now thus says Jehovah of hosts : Consider your ways.　You sow much and bring in little ; you eat and are not satisfied, you drink and are not filled ; one puts on clothes and does not become warm ; and he that earns wages earns wages for a purse with holes.

3 Thus says Jehovah of hosts : Consider your ways ; go up to the mountain and bring timber and build the house, and I will be pleased with it, and honor it, says Jehovah.　One looks for much, and behold a little ; and you bring [a thing] home, and I blow it away. Why ? says Jehovah of hosts.　Because of my house which is desolate, and you run, every man to his house.　Therefore heaven over you has withheld dew, and the earth withheld its increase ; and I have called for drouth on the earth, and on the mountains, and on grain, and on new wine, and on oil, and on [all] that the earth produces, and on man, and on beast, and on all the labor of [your] hands.

4 Then Zerubbabel, son of Shealtiel, and Joshua, son of Jozadak, chief priest, and all the rest of the people obeyed the voice of Jehovah their God, and the words of Haggai, the prophet, according to what Jehovah sent to them ; and the people feared Jehovah. Then spoke Haggai, the messenger of Jehovah, by a message from Jehovah to the people, saying, I am with you, says Jehovah.

5 Then Jehovah excited the spirit of Zerubbabel, son of Shealtiel, governor of Judah, and the spirit of Joshua, son of Jozadak,
chief priest, and the spirits of all the rest of the people, and they
came and worked on the house of Jehovah of hosts their God, on
the 24th day of the sixth month, in the 2d year of Darius, the king.

PROPHECY II.   [2, 1-9.

THE GLORY OF THE SECOND TEMPLE TO BE GREATER THAN THAT OF THE FIRST, AND GOD TO GIVE PEACE IN IT.

1 In the seventh month, on the 21st day of the month, came the
word of Jehovah by the hand of Haggai, the prophet, saying,
Speak, I pray you, to Zerubbabel, son of Shealtiel, governor of Judah, and to Joshua, son of Jozadak, chief priest, and to all the
remnant of the people, saying, Who is left among you that saw this
house in its first glory ? And what do you see it now ? Is it not in
comparison as nothing in your sight ?   But now be strong, Zerubbabel, says Jehovah, and be strong, Joshua, son of Jozadak, chief
priest, and let all the people of the country be strong, says Jehovah,
and work ; for I am with you, says Jehovah of hosts, according to
the covenant which I made with you when you came out of Egypt ;
and my spirit shall continue among you ; fear not.
2 For thus says Jehovah of hosts : Yet once, very soon, and I
will shake heaven, and earth, and sea, and all dry lands ; and I will
shake all nations, and the desire of all nations shall come ; and I
will fill this house with glory, says Jehovah of hosts.   The silver is
mine, and the gold is mine, says Jehovah of hosts ; the glory of
this latter house shall be greater than that of the former, says Jehovah of hosts. In this place will I give peace, says Jehovah of hosts.

PROPHECY III.   [2, 10-23.

IMPURITY OF THE JEWS ; BLESSINGS PROMISED, CONVULSIONS AT HAND, AND ZERUBBABEL TO BE HONORED.

1 On the 24th day of the ninth month, in the 2d year of Darius,
came the word of Jehovah by the hand of Haggai, the prophet,
saying, Thus says Jehovah of hosts : Ask, I pray you, the priests
the law, saying, If a man carries holy flesh in the skirt of his gar-

ment, and touches with his skirt bread, or boiled victuals, or wine, or oil, or any food, will it be holy ?   And the priests answered and said, No.   Then Haggai said, If an impure body touches any of these things, will they be impure ?   And the priests answered and said, They will be impure.   Then answered Haggai and said, So is this people, and so is this nation before me, says Jehovah, and so is all the work of their hands ; and that which they offer there is impure.

2 But now consider.   From this day and forward, from before a stone is laid, a stone in the temple of Jehovah, from the time when one comes to a heap of 20 [measures], and behold, there are 10 ; and he comes to a vat to draw out 50 vessels from the wine press, and there are 20.   I smote you with blasting, and paleness, and with hail in all the works of your hands ; but [you looked] not to me, says Jehovah.   Consider, I pray you, from this day and forward, from the 24th day of the ninth month, consider, from the day that the temple of Jehovah was founded.   Is [not] the seed yet in the storehouse ? and to [this day] the vine, and the fig tree, and the pomegranate, and the olive tree have not borne ; from this day will I bless you.

3 And the word of Jehovah came to Haggai a second time, on the 24th day of the month, saying, Speak to Zerubbabel, governor of Judah, saying, I will shake heaven and earth, and overturn the thrones of kingdoms, and destroy the strength of the kingdoms of the nations ; and I will destroy the chariot and those that ride in it, and horses and their riders shall come down, every one by the sword of his brother.   In that day, says Jehovah of hosts, I will take you, Zerubbabel, son of Shealtiel, my servant, says Jehovah, and make you like a signet ring, for I have chosen you, says Jehovah of hosts.

27*

14. ZECHARIAH.

PROPHECY I. [1, 1–6.

ZECHARIAH CALLS ON MEN TO TURN TO JEHOVAH.

1 In the eighth month, in the 2d year of Darius, came the word of Jehovah to Zechariah, son of Berechiah, son of Iddo the prophet, saying, Jehovah was displeased with your fathers ; but say to them, Thus says Jehovah of hosts : Turn to me, says Jehovah of hosts, and I will turn to you, says Jehovah of hosts.　Be not like your fathers, to whom the former prophets called, saying, Thus' says Jehovah of hosts : Turn, I pray you, from your evil ways, and from your evil doings ; and they heard not, nor attended to me, says Jehovah.

2 Your fathers — where are they ?　And have the prophets lived forever ?　But my words and my ordinances which I commanded my servants the prophets — did they not overtake your fathers ? But they turned not, nor said, As Jehovah of hosts purposed to do to us according to our ways, and according to our works, so has he done to us.

PROPHECY II. [1, 7–6.

HORSEMEN, HORSES, SATAN, ANGELS AND OTHER OBJECTS OF THE SPIRITUAL WORLD ; JOSHUA ENCOURAGED.

1 On the 24th day of the eleventh month, which is the month Sebat, in the 2d year of Darius [B. C. 520], came the word of Jehovah to Zechariah, son of Berechiah, son of Iddo the prophet, saying, I saw in the night, and behold, a man was riding on a red horse ; and he stood among myrtle trees, which were in a ravine ; and behind him were horses, red, fox-colored, and white.　Then I said, What are these, my lord ?　Then the angel who spoke with me said, I will show you what these are.　And the man who stood among the myrtle trees answered and said, These are [angels] whom Jehovah sends to go about in the earth.

2 Then they answered the angel of Jehovah that stood among

the myrtle trees, and said, We have gone about in the earth, and behold, all the earth is sitting still, and is at rest. And the angel of Jehovah answered and said, Jehovah of hosts, how long will you not have mercy on Jerusalem, and the cities of Judah, against which you have been indignant these 70 years? And Jehovah answered the angel that spoke with me good words and words of consolation.

3 Then the angel that spoke with me said, Proclaim, saying, Thus says the Lord Jehovah of hosts : I was jealous of Jerusalem and Zion with great jealousy; but I am indignant with great indignation against the nations that are at ease, who, when I was a little angry, helped on the evil. Therefore thus says Jehovah : I will return to Jerusalem with mercies, and my house shall be built in it, says Jehovah of hosts, and the line shall be stretched on Jerusalem. Proclaim again, saying, Thus says Jehovah of hosts : The cities shall yet be scattered abroad from prosperity ; for Jehovah will yet comfort Zion, and yet choose Jerusalem.

4 Then I lifted up my eyes and looked, and behold, four horns [animals with horns] ; and I said to the angel that spoke with me, What are these ? And he said to me, These are the horns that scattered Judah, Israel, and Jerusalem. And he showed me four workmen. Then I said, What have these come to do ? Then he spoke, saying, Those are the horns which scattered Judah till no man lifted up his head ; and these have come to frighten them off, to cast down the horns of the nations which lifted up the horn against the land of Judah to scatter it.

5 Then I lifted up my eyes again, and looked, and behold, a man with a measuring line in his hand. Then I said, Whither are you going ? And he said to me, To measure Jerusalem, to see what is its breadth, and what is its length. And behold, the angel which spoke with me went away, and another angel went to meet him, and said to him, Rise, and speak to this young man, saying, Jerusalem shall be inhabited as an open country, from the multitude of men and beasts in it ; and I will be to it, says Jehovah, a wall of fire round it, and a glory within it.

6 Ho, ho! and flee from the land of the north, says Jehovah, for I will disperse you, says Jehovah, like the four winds of heaven. Ho, Zion ! save yourself, dweller with the daughter of Babylon ! for thus says Jehovah of hosts. Glory is to come : he has sent me to the nations that plundered you, for he that touches you touches

the daughter of his eye ; for behold, I will shake my hand over them, and they shall be a prey to those that served them ; and you shall know that Jehovah of hosts has sent me.

7 Sing and rejoice, daughter of Zion ! for behold, [the time] has come, and I will dwell among you, says Jehovah. And many nations shall join themselves to Jehovah in that day, and they shall be my people, and I will dwell among you ; and you shall know that Jehovah of hosts has sent me to you. And Jehovah will possess Judah as his portion in the holy land, and again choose Jerusalem. Be silent, all flesh, before Jehovah ; for he is roused up from the habitation of his holiness.

8 Then he showed me Joshua, the chief priest, standing before the angel of Jehovah, and Satan standing at his right hand to oppose him. And Jehovah said to Satan, Jehovah rebuke you,-Satan ; even Jehovah rebuke you, who has chosen Jerusalem. Is not this [man] a brand plucked from the fire ?

9 But Joshua was clothed with filthy garments, and stood before the angel. Then he answered and spoke to those that stood before him, saying, Take off the filthy garments from him. Then he said to him, See, I will cause your wickedness to pass away from you, and clothe you with festive [costly] garments. Then I said, Let them put a pure turban on his head. Then they put a pure turban on his head, and clothed him with [costly] garments ; and the angel of Jehovah stood by.

10 Then the angel of Jehovah commanded Joshua, saying, Thus says Jehovah of hosts : If you will walk in my ways, and keep my charge, then you shall also judge my house and keep my courts, and I will give you guides among those that stand by [the angels]. Hear, I pray you, Joshua, chief priest, and your friends that sit before you, for you are representative men ; for behold, I will bring my servant, the Sprout ; for behold, the stone which I lay before Joshua ; on one stone are seven eyes ; behold, I will cut its engraving, says Jehovah of hosts, and remove the wickedness of this land in one day.˙ In that day, says Jehovah of hosts, you shall call every man to his friend to [sit] under the vine, and to [sit] under the fig tree.

11 And the angel that spoke with me came again, and awoke me as a man who is waked from sleep, and said to me, What do you see ? Then I said, I see, and behold, a candlestick, all of it of gold, and its bowl on the top of it, and its seven lamps on it, and the seven tubes of the seven lamps which are on the top of it, and

two olive trees by it, one on the right hand of the bowl and the other on its left. Then I answered and said to the angel that spoke with me, What are these, my lord? Then the angel that spoke with me answered and said to me, Do you not know what these are? Then I said, No, my lord. Then he answered and spoke to me, saying, This is the word of Jehovah to Zerubbabel, saying, Not by might nor by power, but by my Spirit, says Jehovah of hosts. Who are you, great mountain? Before Zerubbabel you shall be a plain, and one shall bring out the first stone [of the temple], with shoutings of, Beauty, beauty, to it.

12 Then the word of Jehovah came to me, saying, The hands of Zerubbabel shall found this house, and his hands shall finish it, and you shall know that Jehovah of hosts sent me to you. For who despises the day of small things? And these seven [angels] shall rejoice when they see the plummet in the hand of Zerubbabel. These are the eyes [observers] of Jehovah, going about in all the earth.

13 Then I answered and said to him, What are these two olive trees on the right side of the candlestick and on its left? Then I answered a second time, and said to him, What are these two olive branches which are by the two gold tubes, which empty the gold from them? Then he spoke to me, saying, Do you not know what these are? And I said, No, my lord. Then he said, These are the two anointed ones [superior angels], who stand before the Lord of all the earth.

14 Then I lifted up my eyes again, and looked, and behold, a flying roll. Then he said to me, What do you see? Then I said, I see a flying roll; the length of it is 20 cubits, and the breadth of it 10 cubits. Then he said to me, This is the curse which goes forth on all the face of the earth. For every one that steals shall be destroyed there, according to it, and every one that swears shall be destroyed there, according to it. I will bring it, says Jehovah of hosts, and it shall come into the house of the thief, and into the house of him that swears by my name falsely, and it shall pass the night in his house, and consume it, even all the wood and all the stones.

15 Then the angel that spoke with me went out and said to me, Lift up your eyes now, and see what is this which goes forth. And I said, What is it? And he said, This is an ephah [1¼ bushel measure]. And he said, This is their wickedness in all the land. And behold, a talent [113 lbs. 10 oz. 1 pwt. 2⅔ grs.] of lead was lifted

up, and a woman sat in the ephah. And he said, This is wickedness ; and he cast her into the ephah, and he cast the weight of lead on its mouth.

16 Then I lifted up my eyes, and looked, and behold, two women came, and a spirit was in their wings, for they had wings like the wings of a stork, and they lifted up the ephah between the earth and heaven. Then I said to the angel that spoke with me, Whither do they bear the ephah? And he said to me, To build a house for it in the land of Shinar, that it may be established there and set on its base.

17 Then I lifted up my eyes again, and looked, and behold, four chariots going from between two mountains, and the mountains were mountains of brass. In the first chariot were red horses, and in the second chariot black horses, and in the third chariot white horses, and in the fourth chariot spotted and swift horses. Then I answered and said to the angel who spoke with me, What are these, my lord? Then the angel answered and said to me, These are the four winds of heaven, which go forth and stand before the Lord of the whole earth. As to what is meant, the black horses shall go to the land of the north, and the white shall go after them ; and the spotted shall go to the land of the south, and the swift shall go and seek to go and go about in the earth. Then he said, Go and go about in the earth. Then they went about in the earth. Then he cried to me and spoke to me, saying, See, they have gone to the land of the north, and they shall give rest to my spirit in the land of the north. .

18 Then the word of Jehovah came to me, saying, Take some from the exiles, from Heldai, from Tobijah, and from Jedaiah, and go on the same day, and go to the house of Josiah, the son of Zephaniah, who came from Babylon, and take silver and gold, and make a crown, and put it on the head of Joshua, son of Jozadak, chief priest, and speak to him, saying, Thus says Jehovah of hosts : Behold, the man whose name [title] is The Sprout shall grow up in his place, and build the temple of Jehovah, and he shall put on majesty, and sit and rule on his throne ; and a priest shall be on his throne, and peaceful counsel shall be between the two. Then let Helem, and Tobiah, and Jediah, and Hen, the son of Zephaniah, have it for a memorial in the temple of Jehovah. And they that are far off shall come and build the temple of Jehovah, and you shall know that Jehovah of hosts has sent me to you ; and it shall come to pass if you will diligently obey the voice of Jehovah your God.

PROPHECY III.   [7, 8.

FASTS MAY BE EXCHANGED FOR FEASTS, BUT RIGHTEOUSNESS
MUST BE PRACTICED ; THE NATIONS TO BE CONVERTED.

1 AND in the 4th year of Darius the king [B. C. 518] came the
word of Jehovah to Zechariah, on the 4th day of the ninth month,
Chisleu ; and they sent to the house of God Sherezer, and Regem-
melek and his men, to wait before Jehovah, to speak to the priests
who belonged to the house of Jehovah of hosts, and to the prophets,
saying, Shall I weep [fast] in the fifth month, separating myself as
I have done these so many years ?

2 Then came the word of Jehovah of hosts to me, saying, Speak
to all the people of the land, and to the priests, saying, When you
fasted and lamented in the fifth month, and in the seventh, and this
for 70 years, did you fast at all to me ? And when you eat and
drank, did you not eat and drink ? Are not these the words which
Jehovah proclaimed by the former prophets when Jerusalem was
inhabited and in peace, and her cities round her, and the south and
the plain were inhabited ?

3 Then the word of Jehovah came to Zechariah, saying, Thus
says Jehovah of hosts : Judge true judgment, and exercise kindness
and mercies one to another, nor oppress the widow, the fatherless,
the stranger, nor the poor, nor devise evil in your hearts [minds]
one against another. But they refused to attend, and gave a refractory shoulder, and made their ears heavy that they might not hear,
and made their hearts adamant that they might not hear the law,
nor the words which Jehovah of hosts sent them by his Spirit, by
the former prophets ; and there was great wrath from Jehovah of
hosts. And as he called, and they did not hear, so they called, and
I would not hear, says Jehovah of hosts. And I scattered them
with a whirlwind among all nations which they had not known,
and the land was made a desolation after them, with none passing through it, nor returning, and they made a desirable land a
desolation.

4 Then the word of Jehovah of hosts came to me, saying, Thus
says Jehovah of hosts : I was jealous of Zion with great jealousy,
and jealous of her with great indignation. Thus says Jehovah : I
will return to Zion, and dwell in Jerusalem, and Jerusalem shall be

called the city of truth, the mountain of Jehovah of hosts, the holy mountain.

5 Thus says Jehovah of hosts : There shall yet live old men and old women in the streets of Jerusalem, and every one with his staff in his hand from great age. And the streets of the city shall be filled with boys and girls playing in the streets. Thus says Jehovah of hosts : If this appears difficult in the sight of the remnant of this people in these days, is it also difficult in my sight ? says Jehovah of hosts. Thus says Jehovah of hosts : Behold, I will save my people from the land of the east, and from the land of the west, and bring them, and they shall live in Jerusalem, and be my people, and I will be their God with truth and with righteousness.

6 Thus says Jehovah of hosts : Let your hands be strong, you that hear in these days these words from the mouth of the prophets, who [lived] in the day when the house of Jehovah of hosts was founded, that the temple might be built. For before their days there were no wages for men, nor any wages for beasts ; nor had he that went out or he that came in, any peace from the enemy, for I set all men every one against his friend. But now I will not be as in the former days towards the rest of this people, says Jehovah of hosts ; for the seed shall be in peace, the vine shall yield its fruit, and the earth its increase, and heaven shall give its dew, and I will cause the remnant of my people to possess all these things.

7 And as you were a curse to the nations, house of Judah and house of Israel, so will I save you, and you shall be a blessing. Fear not ; let your hands be strong, for thus says Jehovah of hosts : As I purposed to do you evil when your fathers provoked me to anger, says Jehovah of hosts, and did not pity, so have I again purposed in these days to do good to Jerusalem and the house of Judah ; fear not. These are the things which you shall do : Speak truth every one to his friend, judge according to truth, and judge the judgment of peace in your gates, devise not evil any man against his friend in your hearts [minds], and love not a false oath, for all these are things which I hate, says Jehovah.

8 Then the word of Jehovah of hosts came to me, saying, Thus says Jehovah of hosts : The fast of the fourth month, and the fast of the fifth month, and the fast of the seventh month, and the fast of the tenth month, the house of Israel may have for joy and gladness, and cheerful festivals ; but love truth and peace.

9 Thus says Jehovah of hosts : Many nations shall yet come, and

the inhabitants of many cities, and the inhabitants of one city shall go to another, saying, Let us go to wait before Jehovah, and to seek Jehovah of hosts; I will go also. And many peoples shall come, and mighty nations, to seek Jehovah of hosts in Jerusalem, and to wait before the face of Jehovah. Thus says Jehovah of hosts : In those days which shall come, ten men, of all the tongues of the nations, shall take hold of the skirt of one man that is a Jew, saying, Let us go with you, for we hear that God is with you.

PROPHECY IV. [9, 10.

SURROUNDING NATIONS TO BE SUBJUGATED TO THE ISRAELITES ; GOD TO REIGN IN ZION.

1 A BURDEN of the word of Jehovah is on the land of Hadrach, and Damascus is its resting place ; for the eyes of man and of all the tribes of Israel [shall be] to Jehovah. And as to Hamath, it shall border also on her [and on] Tyre and Zidon, though extremely wise. Though Tyre builds and heaps up silver like dust, and gold like mire of the streets, behold, the Lord will cast her out, and smite her power in the sea, and she shall be consumed with fire. Ascalon shall see it and fear ; Gaza shall be greatly distressed, and Ekron ; because her expectation shall be put to shame ; and a king shall perish from Gaza, and Ascalon not be inhabited; and a foreigner shall live in Ashdod ; and I will cut off the pride of the Philistines, and take away their blood from their mouth, and their abominations from between their teeth ; and they also shall be left for our God, and be as bullocks in Judah, and Ekron as a Jebusite. 2 And I will defend my house, as a military post, from him that passes by and him that returns, and the oppressor shall not pass through you any more, for now I will see with my eyes. Rejoice greatly, daughter of Zion ; shout, daughter of Jerusalem ; behold, your king shall come to you, righteous, and bringing salvation, meek, and riding on an ass, and on a colt the foal of an ass. And I will cut off the chariot from Ephraim and the horse from Jerusalem ; and the bow of war shall be cut off, and [God] shall speak peace to the nations, and his dominion shall be from sea to sea, and from the Euphrates to the ends of the earth. 3 And as for you also, on account of the blood of your covenant, I will liberate your prisoners from the pit which is without water, [and

say], Return to the fortress, prisoners of hope ; even to-day do I declare that I will restore you double. For I will bend Judah as a bow, and fill it with Ephraim, and raise up your sons Zion against the sons of Ionia, and make you like the sword of a mighty man. And Jehovah shall appear over them, and his arrows go like lightning ; and the Lord Jehovah shall blow with a trumpet, and go forth with whirlwinds of the south.

4 Jehovah of hosts shall protect them, and they shall consume and tread down the sling-stones, and drink and shout as from wine, and be filled like a bowl, like the corners of the altar. And Jehovah their God shall save them in that day ; he [shall save] his people like a flock, for they shall be stones of a crown lifting themselves up in his land. How great shall be their prosperity, and how great their beauty ! The young men shall produce grain, and the young women wine.

5 Ask of Jehovah rain in the time of the vernal rain. Jehovah makes the lightnings and gives them the showers of rain, and for men the plants of the field. For the teraphim spoke vanity, and the diviners saw a lie, and told false dreams ; they gave vain consolations, therefore they are removed like a flock, they are in distress, because there is no shepherd.

6 My anger is kindled against the shepherds, and I will punish the he goats ; for Jehovah of hosts will visit his flock, the house of Judah, and make them like a majestic horse in battle. From him shall come forth the corner [stone], from him the pin, from him the bow of war, from him shall come forth every ruler together, and they shall be like mighty men who tread down [their enemies in] war like the mire of the streets ; and they shall fight, because Jehovah is with them, and the riders on horses shall be ashamed.

7 Then I will strengthen the house of Judah, and save the house of Joseph, and cause them to be restored, because I have mercy on them ; and they shall be as if I had not cast them off, for I am Jehovah their God, and will answer them. And Ephraim shall be like a mighty man, and their heart shall rejoice as from wine ; and their sons shall see and rejoice, and their hearts exult in Jehovah.

8 I will call them and gather them, for I have redeemed them, and they shall be as numerous as they have been. Though I scattered them among the peoples, even in distant lands they shall remember me, and shall live ; they shall return with their sons. And I will bring them back from the land of Egypt, and gather them from

Assyria, and bring them to the land of Gilead and to Lebanon, and [places] shall not be found for them. And they shall pass through the sea [from] distress, and he shall smite the waves of the sea; and all the depths of the river [of Egypt] shall be dried up, and the pride of Assyria be brought down, and the scepter shall depart from Egypt; but I will strengthen them with Jehovah, and in his name shall they walk, says Jehovah.

PROPHECY V. [11.

JUDAH AND HER SHEPHERDS THREATENED.

1 OPEN your doors, Lebanon, and let the fire consume your cedars. Lament, cypress, for the cedar has fallen, their noble ones are destroyed. Lament, oaks of Bashan, for the lofty forest has come down. There is a voice of the lamenting of shepherds because their glory is destroyed; a voice of the roaring of young lions, because the pride of the Jordan is destroyed.

2 Thus says Jehovah my God: Feed a flock for slaughter; let their possessors kill and not be guilty; and let those who sell them say, Blessed be Jehovah, for I am rich; and let not their shepherds spare them. For I will no longer spare the inhabitants of the earth, says Jehovah; but behold, I will bring the men every one into the hand of his friend, and into the hand of his king, and they shall smite the earth, and I will not deliver from their hand.

3 Then I fed a flock for slaughter, nevertheless a poor flock. And I took me two sticks; one I called Beauty, and the other Bands, and I fed the flock. And I cut off three shepherds in one month, and was vexed with them, and they abhorred me. Then I said, I will not feed you; that which dies may die, and that which is cut off may be cut off, and those which remain may eat every one the flesh of another. Then I took my stick Beauty, and cut it in two, to break my covenant which I made with all nations. And it was broken in that day, and the poor of the flock that were with me, that observed me, knew that it was the word of Jehovah.

4 Then I said to them, If it seems good to you, give me my price; and if not, forbear. And they weighed my price, 30 shekels of silver [$16.80], and Jehovah said to me, Cast it into the treasury, the good price at which I was prized by them. Then I took the 30 shekels of silver and cast them into the house of Jehovah, to the

treasury. Then I broke my other stick, Bands, to break the brotherhood between Judah and Israel. Then Jehovah said to me again, Take the implements of a foolish shepherd; for behold, I will set up a shepherd in the land who shall not visit the destroyed, nor seek the driven away, nor heal the wounded, nor support that which stands firm, but shall eat the flesh of the fat, and break off their hoofs. Woe to the foolish shepherd that leaves the flock; a sword shall be on his arm, and in his right eye; his arm shall surely wither, and his right eye be surely made dim.

PROPHECY VI. [12, 13, 14.

Burden of the word of Jehovah concerning Israel; [its reformation, perils, deliverances, and future glories.]

1 SAYS Jehovah, who stretched out the heavens, and founded the earth, and formed the spirit of man in him, Behold, I will make Jerusalem a cup of trembling to all the peoples round, as [they] also were against Judah, in the siege of Jerusalem. And in that day I will make Jerusalem a lifting stone to all peoples. All that lift her shall surely be gashed, and all the nations of the earth shall be assembled against her.

2 In that day, says Jehovah, I will smite the horse with terror and his rider with madness; and I will open my eyes on the house of Judah, and every horse of the peoples will I smite with blindness, and the chiefs of Judah shall say in their heart, My strength is the inhabitants of Jerusalem, with Jehovah of hosts their God.

3 In that day I will make the chiefs of Judah like a basin of fire in wood, and like a lamp of fire in a sheaf [of grain], and they shall consume, on the right hand and on the left all peoples round, and Jerusalem shall again be inhabited in its place, in Jerusalem.

4 Then Jehovah shall save the tents of Judah, that the glory of the house of David and the glory of the inhabitants of Jerusalem may not exalt itself against Judah.

5 In that day Jehovah shall protect the inhabitants of Jerusalem, and the weak among them in that day shall be as David, and the house of David as God, as an angel of Jehovah before them; and in that day I will seek and destroy all nations that come against Jerusalem.

6 Then I will pour out on the house of David and on the inhab-

itants of Jerusalem a spirit of kindness and supplications, and they shall look on him whom they pierced [killed], and mourn for him like a mourning for an only son, and be in bitterness for him as one is in bitterness for a first born.

7 In that day there shall be a great mourning in Jerusalem, like the mourning of Hadadrimmon in the plain of Megiddo. And the land shall mourn families [by] families, separately; the family of the house of David separately, and their wives separately; the family of the house of Nathan separately, and their wives separately; the family of the house of Levi separately, and their wives separately; the family of Shimei separately, and their wives separately; all the families that remain, families by families separately, and their wives separately.

8 In that day a fountain shall be opened for the house of David, and for the inhabitants of Jerusalem, for sin and impurity. And in that day, says Jehovah of hosts, will I cut off the names of the idols from the earth, and they shall be remembered no more; and the prophets also, and the impure spirits will I cause to pass away from the earth.

9 And when a man shall yet prophesy, then his father and his mother who bore him shall say to him, You shall not live, for you speak falsehood in the name of Jehovah; and his father and his mother shall pierce [kill] him while he prophesies.

10 And in that day the prophets shall be ashamed each one of his vision when he prophesies, and they shall no more wear a hair mantle to deceive; and one shall say, I am not a prophet; I am a man that cultivates the field; for a man sold me from my childhood. Then one shall say to him, What are these wounds on your hands? Then he shall say, They are what I was smitten with in the house of·my friends.

11 [But first] awake, sword, against my shepherd [king], against the man of my companionship, says Jehovah of hosts. Smite the shepherd [king], and the sheep shall be scattered, and I will bring my hand back against the small ones [the common people]. And in all the earth, says Jehovah, two parts of it shall be cut off, shall die, and the third part of it shall remain. Then I will bring the third part through fire, and melt them, like the melting of silver, and try them, like the trying of gold. They shall call on my name, and I will answer them; I will say, They are my people, and they shall say, Jehovah is my God.

12 Behold, the day of Jehovah shall come, and your spoil be divided within you. For I will assemble all nations to Jerusalem to battle, and the city shall be taken, and the houses plundered, and the women ravished; and half the city shall go into exile, but the rest of the people shall not be cut off from the city. Then Jehovah shall go forth and fight with those nations, as in the day of his fighting, in the day of war. And his feet shall stand in that day on the mount of Olives, which is before Jerusalem on the east, and the mount of Olives shall open itself from its center to the east and west, an exceedingly great valley, and half the mountain shall remove north, and half of it south; and you shall flee to the valley of the mountains, for the valley of the mountains shall reach to Azel; and you shall flee as you fled before the earthquake, in the days of Uzziah, king of Judah; and Jehovah, my God, shall come, and all his angels with him.

13 And in that day there shall be no light, the brilliants [of heaven] shall be withdrawn, and it shall be one day, it shall be known to Jehovah as not day nor night; but at the time for evening there shall be light.

14 And in that day living water shall go out from Jerusalem; half of it shall go towards the Eastern [Dead] sea, and half of it towards the Western; it shall flow in summer and winter.

15 Then Jehovah shall be king over all the earth. In that day Jehovah shall be one, and his name one. And all the land shall be changed, like the desert from Geba to Rimmon before Jerusalem. Then it shall be raised up, and inhabited in its place, from the gate of Benjamin to the place of the first gate, to the gate of the corners and the tower of Hananeel, to the king's wine presses. And they shall live in it, and there shall be no more entire destruction, and Jerusalem shall dwell in security.

16 And this is the plague with which Jehovah will smite all the peoples who fight against Jerusalem: Their flesh shall waste away while they stand on their feet, and their eyes shall waste away in their holes, and their tongues shall waste away in their mouths. And in that day there shall be a great tumult from Jehovah among them, and they shall seize every man the hand of his friend, and his hand shall rise up against the hand of his friend. And Judah also shall fight at Jerusalem, and an army of all nations shall be around, gold and silver and clothes, a great abundance. And the plague of the horse, the mule, the camel, and all beasts which shall be in those camps, shall be like this plague.

17 And every one that is left of all nations that went against Jerusalem, shall go up from year to year, to worship the King, Jehovah of hosts, and to keep the feast of tabernacles. And as to those of the families of the earth who shall not go up to Jerusalem to worship the King, Jehovah of hosts, then on them shall be no rain. And if the family of Egypt go not up, and come not, and there is no [rain] on them, there shall be the plague with which Jehovah will smite the nations who go not up to keep the feast of tabernacles. This shall be the punishment of Egypt, and the punishment of all the nations which go not up to keep the feast of tabernacles.

18 In that day there shall be on the bells of the horses, Holiness to Jehovah, and the pots in the house of Jehovah shall be like the vases before the altar. Every pot in Jerusalem shall be holy to Jehovah of hosts, and all who sacrifice shall come and take of them, and boil in them, and in that day there shall no more be a Canaanite in the house of Jehovah of hosts.

---

15. MALACHI.

Burden of the word of Jehovah to Israel by the hand of Malachi.

PROPHECY I.   [1, 2.

JACOB PREFERRED TO ESAU; THE PRIESTS REPROVED; INJUSTICE TO WIVES, AND CALLING THE EVIL GOOD, DENOUNCED.

1 I HAVE loved you, says Jehovah; but you say, In what have you loved us? Was not Esau Jacob's brother? says Jehovah. But I loved Jacob, and hated Esau, and will make his mountains a desolation, and his inheritance of jackals a wilderness. For Edom says, We have been destroyed; but we will return, and build up the ruins. Thus says Jehovah of hosts: They shall build, but I will pull down; and they shall call them the border of wickedness, and the people against whom Jehovah is indignant forever; and your eyes shall see it, and say, Let Jehovah be magnified from above to the border of Israel.

2 A son should honor his father, and a servant his master; but

if I am a father, where is my honor? And if I am a master, where is my fear, says Jehovah of hosts to you priests, who despise my name, and say, In what do we despise your name? You bring to my altar bread that is defiled, and say, In what have we defiled you? In your saying of the table of Jehovah, It is contemptible. And, when you bring the blind to sacrifice, is it not evil? And when you bring the lame and sick, is it not evil? Offer them, I pray you, to your governor; will he be pleased with you, or accept your persons? says Jehovah of hosts. And now wait, I pray you, on the face of God, that he may be gracious to us. [With] this from your hands will he accept your persons? says Jehovah of hosts.

3 Who is there also among you? Then let him shut the doors, and kindle no fire on my altar in vain. I have no pleasure in you, says Jehovah of hosts, neither will I receive a bread offering from your hands. For from the rising of the sun to its going down, my name shall be great among the nations; and in all places, incense and a pure bread offering shall be brought to my name; for my name shall be great among the nations, says Jehovah of hosts. But you profane me by your saying, The table of Jehovah is defiled; and as to its produce, its food is contemptible.

4 And you say, Behold the weariness, and blow at it, says Jehovah of hosts, and bring the plundered, and lame, and sick, and bring a bread offering. Shall I accept it from your hands? says Jehovah. But cursed is the man who is able, and there is in his flock a male, and he vows, and sacrifices a destroyed [creature] to Jehovah; for I am a great king, says Jehovah of hosts, and my name to be feared among the nations.

5 And now the command is for you, priests. If you will not hear, nor lay to heart, to give glory to my name, says Jehovah of hosts, then I will send a curse on you, and curse your blessings; and I have also cursed them, because you lay not to heart [my admonitions]. Behold, I will rebuke the grain on your account, and scatter dung on your faces, the dung of your feasts; and one shall bear you to it. Then you shall know that I sent you this command, to be my covenant with Levi, says Jehovah of hosts. My covenant was, with him, life and peace; and I gave him [my] fear, and they feared me, and he had great fear of my name. The true law was in his mouth, and wickedness was not found in his lips; he walked in peace and uprightness with me, and turned many from wickedness. For the lips of the priest should keep knowledge, and they

should seek the law from his mouth, for he is a messenger of Jehovah of hosts.

6 But you have departed from the way; you have caused many to stumble at the law ; you have corrupted the covenant of Levi, says Jehovah of hosts. And I also will make you despised and base before all the people, according as you have not kept my ways, and are partial in the law.

7 Have we not all of us one Father ? Did not one God create us ? Why do we deal treacherously every man with his brother, to profane the law of our fathers ? Judah deals treacherously, and abominations are committed in Israel and in Jerusalem ; for Judah profanes the sanctuary of Jehovah which he loves, and marries the daughter of a strange god. Jehovah will cut off the man that does this, the enemy, and him that answers from the tents of Jacob, and brings a bread offering to Jehovah of hosts.

8 And this have you done again, to cover the altar of Jehovah with tears, with weeping and groaning ; so that I can no longer look at the bread offering, nor receive pleasure from your hands. But you say, Why ? Because Jehovah witnesses between you and the wife of your youth, with whom you deal treacherously ; but she is your companion, and the wife of your covenant. And did not [God] make one [wife], though he had the rest of the spirit ? and why one ? He sought children of God. Therefore take heed to yourselves, and let none deal treacherously with the wife of his youth. For I hate putting away, says Jehovah, the God of Israel ; and he heaps violence on his wife, says Jehovah of hosts ; therefore take heed to yourselves, and deal not treacherously.

9 You have wearied Jehovah with your words ; yet you say, With what have we wearied you ? By your saying, All that do evil are good in the sight of Jehovah, and he delights in them, and where is the God of justice ?

PROPHECY II.   [3.

GOD TO COME TO HIS TEMPLE.

1 BEHOLD, I will send my angel, and he shall prepare a way before you ; and the Lord, whom you seek, shall suddenly come to his temple, and the angel of the covenant, whom you delight in ; behold, he shall come, says Jehovah of hosts. But who shall abide the day of his coming ? And who shall stand when he appears ? For he

is like a refiner's fire, and like fullers' alkali ; and he shall sit as a
refiner and a purifier of silver, and shall purify the sons of Levi,
and refine them like gold and silver ; and they shall belong to Jehovah to present the bread offering in righteousness.

2 Then shall the bread offering of Judah and Jerusalem be sweet
to Jehovah, as in days of old, and the years of early times.   And
I will come near you for judgment, and be a speedy witness against
the magi, and against adulterers, and against false swearers, and
against those that deprive the hired man of his wages, the widow
and the fatherless, and turn aside the stranger, and fear not me,
says Jehovah of hosts.   For I am Jehovah : I change not; therefore you, sons of Jacob, are not consumed.   From the days of your
fathers you have gone away from my ordinances, and kept them
not: turn to me, and I will turn to you, says Jehovah of hosts.
But you say, In what shall we turn ?   Will a man rob God ?   But
you have robbed me.   Yet you say, Of what have we robbed you ?
Of tithes and offerings.   You are cursed with a curse, for you have
robbed me, even the whole nation.   Bring all the tithes into the
storehouse, and let there be meat in my house, and prove me now
by this, says Jehovah of hosts, [and see] if I will not open you the
windows of heaven, and pour you a blessing till there shall not be
enough.   And I will rebuke the devourer for you, and he shall not
destroy for you the fruit of the earth, and the vine in the field shall
not bereave you of its fruit, says Jehovah of hosts.

3 You have spoken strongly against me, says Jehovah ; but you
say, What have we spoken against you ?   You have said, It is in
vain to serve God ; and what is the profit that we have kept his
charge, and walked mournfully before Jehovah of hosts ?   And
now we will bless the proud ; those that do wickedness also shall
be built up, and those that try God shall be delivered.

4 Then those that fear God shall speak one to another, and Jehovah shall listen and hear, and a book of remembrance be written
before him, for those that fear Jehovah, and think of his name.
And they shall be mine, says Jehovah of hosts, in the day in which
I make [select my] treasures ; and I will spare them as a man
spares his son that serves him.   Then shall you return, and discern
between the righteous and wicked, between him that serves God
and him that serves him not.   For behold, the day shall come that
burns like a furnace ; and all the proud, and all that do wickedness,

shall be stubble, and the day that comes shall burn them up, says Jehovah of hosts; it shall leave them neither root nor branch.

5 But for you that fear my name the Sun of righteousness shall arise with healing in his wings, and you shall go forth and leap like bullocks of the stall, and tread down the wicked; for they shall be ashes under the soles of your feet, in the day which I appoint, says Jehovah òf hosts.

6 Remember the law of Moses my servant which I commanded him in Horeb for all Israel, the ordinances and judgments. Behold, I will send you Elijah the prophet before the coming of the great and terrible day of Jehovah; and he shall turn the hearts of the fathers to the sons, and the hearts of the sons to the fathers, lest I come and smite the earth with entire destruction.

CHRONOLOGICAL TABLE

OF JEWISH HISTORY, SHOWING THE POSITION OF THE LATER PROPHETS.

1. *Kingdom of Judah*, 390 years.

		YEARS.	B. C.
1.	Rehoboam,	17	975
2.	Abiam,	3	957
3.	Asa,	41	955
4.	Jehoshaphat,	25	914
5.	Joram,	8	889
6.	Ahaziah,	1	885
7	Athaliah,	6	884
8.	Joash,	40	878
9.	Amaziah,	29	838
	Later Prophets,	370	810
10.	Uzziah,	52	809
11.	Jotham,	16	758
12.	Ahaz,	16	741
13.	Hezekiah,	29	725
14.	Manasseh,	55	696
15.	Amon,	2	641
16.	Josiah,	31	639
17.	Jehoahaz,	0 3m.	609
18.	Jehoiakim,	11	608
19.	Jehoiachin,	0 3m.	598
20.	Zedekiah,	11	598
	Destruction of Jerusalem,		588
	Liberation of Jehoiachin,		561
	Return from Babylon,		536
	Ezra, ch. 1–6,	21	536
	Ezra, ch. 7–20,	1	458
	Nehemiah,	40	444
	End of Later Prophets,		440

2. *Kingdom of Israel.*

	YEARS.	B. C.
Jeroboam,	22	975
Nadab,	2	954
Baasha,	24	952
Elah,	2	930
Zimri,	0 7d.	928
Omri,	12	928
Ahab,	22	917
Ahaziah,	2	897
Joram,	12	896
Jehu,	28	884
Jehoahaz,	17	856
Joash,	16	840
Jeroboam, II.	41	825
Later Prophets,		810
Zachariah,	0 6m.	772
Shallum,	0 1m.	771
Menahem,	10	771
Pekaiah,	2	760
Pekah,	20	758
Hosea,	9	729
Destruction of the Kingdom,		719

It will be seen by an inspection of the above table, that the Later Prophets do not constitute an era in the Hebrew annals. They belong to the latter part of the era of the kings, and the Babylonian exile, terminating in the time of Nehemiah, in the era of the later historical books of the Old Testament.

(336)

NOTES.

NOTE I.

SUBSTITUTION OF CHANGE OF MIND FOR REPENTANCE.

1. In the Old Testament these translations represent a Hebrew verb (נָחַם), which signifies, according to Robinson, 1. To pity; 2. To grieve; 3. To repent; 4. To be comforted; 5. To avenge one's self. It also signifies, 6. To change one's mind, and was so understood and translated by the Septuagint, the Greek version of the Old Testament in common use among the Jews in our Lord's time. An example of this usage is found in Jonah, 3 : 9, 10 ; 4 : 1, where it is said in the common version, Who can tell if God will turn and repent, and turn away from his fierce anger, that we perish not ? And God saw their works, that they turned from their evil way, and God repented of the evil that he had said that he would do unto them, and he did it not. But it displeased Jonah exceedingly, and he was very angry. And he prayed unto the Lord, and said, I pray thee, O Lord, was not this my saying when I was in my country ? Therefore I fled before unto Tarshish ; for I knew that thou art a gracious God and merciful, slow to anger and of great kindness, and repentest thee of the evil. More exactly rendered this passage reads thus : Who knows but that God will turn and change [his mind] from his fierce anger, and we perish not ? Then God saw their works, that they turned from their evil way, and God changed his mind concerning the evil which he said he would do them, and did it not. Then Jonah was greatly displeased and angry at him. And he prayed to Jehovah, and said, I pray thee, Jehovah, is not this my word when I was in my land ? Therefore I undertook to flee to Tarshish, because I knew that thou art gracious and merciful, and of great kindness, and [one] that changes his mind concerning evil. With this the Septuagint agrees.

VOL. II.   29   (337)

2. Here, according to the common version, the people turn from their wickedness, and God repents. But what had God done to repent of? Did he regret his previous purpose to destroy the Ninevites for their wickedness? This will not be supposed. That purpose was right and good, and can never be regretted. Did he regret his announcement of that purpose by Jonah? This also can not be. That announcement proved a great blessing, and so far from regretting it, God had reason to be well pleased with it. Was any regret intended to be expressed in the case? Had God occasion for any? None. The original word, therefore, can not signify repentance. What then does it signify? There is but one thing which it can signify in conformity with the facts of the case, and that is change of mind. The words describe in the first instance a contingent fact, a possibility in respect to the future action of God; and in the second instance they describe that contingency as having actually occurred. This contingent fact was a change of the divine mind or purpose in regard to destroying Nineveh. It is a legitimate and necessary law of interpretation to understand words according to the facts of the case as known or viewed by the writer. This change of mind is the great fact of this case, not merely as known and viewed by us, but as known and viewed by the writer. The words, therefore, must be interpreted in conformity with this view, and the common rendering of them is erroneous. Robinson's Lexicon, therefore, is defective in not recognizing, to change one's mind, as one of the significations of the Hebrew verb נָחַם.

3. Other examples of this usage are found in 1 Sam. 15: 28, 29; Jer. 4: 28; 8: 6; 18: 7–10; Joel 2: 13, 14; and Amos 7: 2–4. In all these cases the true sense of the original is clearly shown by the context to be change, and specifically change of mind, and not repentance; and in all these passages the Septuagint is correct, and the common version erroneous, in agreement with the Vulgate, which initiates this error.

4. The Greek word which represents the Hebrew in the above instances is μετανοέω. This verb and the noun derived from it are often used in the New Testament, and in every case are translated in the common English version to repent, and repentance, and in the Vulgate, the standard Latin Bible of the Roman Catholics, to exercise penitence, and penitence. Repentance and penitence are nearly synonymous. They are different words for

the same thing. Penitence is repentance, and repentance is penitence. They both signify regret for sin, and denote a species of regrets ; and one or the other of these words is used indifferently to denote the same states of mind, — not changes, — according to the taste of the writer. Μετανοέω is a compound denominative verb, from νόος, mind. The simple denominative is νοέω. Νόος is an original stock or stem, from which many other Greek words are derived.

Scheme of Νόος and its Derivatives.

Primitive Noun.

Νόος, mind, intellect, understanding, etc.

Simple Denominative Verb.

Νοέω, to know, to think, to perceive, to understand, to exercise one's mind.

Compound Denominatives.

(1.) Ἀγνοέω, to not know, to not perceive.
(2.) Ἐννοέω, to know of, to think of, to contrive.
(3.) Ἐπινοέω, to know upon, to think over.
(4.) Μετανοέω, to know afterwards, to change one's mind, to think and purpose differently.
(5.) Προνοέω, to foreknow, to take forethought.
(6.) Ὑπερνοέω, to superknow, to reflect.

Cognate Noun derived from the Verb.

Μετάνοια, change of mind, after knowledge.

5. This verb passes into the Latin language, where it appears in the forms of nos-co, novi, notum, and their Latin compounds, which are scarcely less numerous than the Greek ; and from the Latin and Greek it comes into the English language, where it appears in the English verbs, to know, to recognize, to acknowledge, and their numerous derivatives and compounds, constituting a large and important family of English words. These words, in all the three languages, have similar meanings. True to the stem which appears in them all, the original νόος, mind, their meanings all revolve and cluster about mind. None of them, in either language, signifies repentance, unless as comprehended under the more general designation of mental exercises ; and it is then rather implied than expressed.

6. To recur to the scheme of νόος and its derivatives, it will be observed that the simple derivative takes its signification with its form directly from its primitive.   The stem is the same in both ; in the noun it has a noun termination, and in the verb a verb termination.   It was impossible for these words to become widely separated in sense, and at the same time be used together.   One would inevitably give its meaning to the other, and the derivative be held to the primitive by their common stems, and they were always in constant use together.   They were among the most used and best understood of all Greek words, like their corresponding English derivatives in our times, and like the English word *mind* and its derivatives.

7. Recurring again to that scheme, it will be seen that the compound denominatives all derive their significations from the simple denominative, with which they agree both in their stems and terminations, and from which they differ only in prefixes that modify the meaning of the primitive, but can not essentially depart from it.

8. The noun μετάνοια, change of mind, is formed from the verb for the purpose of representing its action and corresponds to it in signification.   If the verb had signified to repent, the noun would signify repentance ; but as the verb has the different signification, to change one's mind, the noun in conformity with it must signify change of mind.   Though remote from the original stock it retains it in its stem, together with the prefix which belongs to the verb ; and consists of this compound stem with a noun termination annexed.

9. The use of these words in the classic Greek authors is in conformity with the above.   Plato says in respect to change of opinion (Euthyd. 279, c.), "Having again changed my mind, I said," etc. Thucydides says (3, 36) of men who had adopted sanguinary and cruel measures against their enemies, "They had an immediate change of mind and reconsideration ;" and Polybius (4, 66, 7) tells us that Philip, learning the change of mind of the Dardanians, dismissed the Macedonians, etc.   These are specimens of classic usage in regard to these words ; and where another sense has sometimes been given to them, this is generally their true sense.   The meaning of these words was so clear and unequivocal, and they were so well defined by their derivation, that no classic writer mistook them, or deviated from the common standard.

10. With these views the Septuagint agrees.   The Septuagint is the Greek Sacred Scriptures of the Jews in the time of Christ, con-

sisting of translations of the Hebrew Scriptures made some time before, with several additional books, written originally in Greek, and known as the Apocrypha. Its usage in respect to these words appears in the following passages: 1 Sam. 15: 28, 29. And Samuel said to him, The Lord has rent away the kingdom from your hand to-day, and will give it to your neighbor, who is better than you, and Israel shall be divided in two, and shall not return nor change his mind; for he is not like a man, to change his mind. The grammatical subject of these verbs in the Septuagint is Israel; in the Hebrew it is the glory of Jehovah, put for God. In both cases, the verbs signify to change one's mind, and not to repent, and ought to be so translated. The sense of change of mind is not only permitted by the context, but demanded by it. The common version of this passage is therefore erroneous, neither representing the original Hebrew, nor the Septuagint, which conforms to the Hebrew; nor expressing a sense that is suitable to the occasion.

11. Jer. 4: 28. For these things let the land mourn, and heaven above be darkened, for I have spoken, and I will not change my mind; I have purposed, and will not turn back from it. Here the verb relates to God, and signifies evidently change of mind, and not repentance; and changing what he had spoken is parallel with turning back from what he had purposed. Repenting — the rendering of the common version — does not meet the demands of the context, and can not be right. God's supposed regret for what he had done is not at all to the purpose. The action contemplated is *pro*spective, and not *retro*spective.

12. Jer. 8: 6. Attend, therefore, and hear: They shall not speak so; he is not a man that changes his mind from his wickedness, saying, What have I done? In this case the verb is followed by a preposition signifying *from*. We repent *of* past misdeeds; we change and turn *from* sin. Repentance always has reference to the past, and is purely a retrospective affection; but conversion or turning from sin always has respect to the present and future. Repenting, therefore, does not meet the exigencies of this passage, and changing the mind does. Therefore the philological sense of the verb must be adhered to, and repenting, as it is rendered in the common version, rejected.

13. Jer. 18: 7, 8. When I speak concerning a nation and concerning a kingdom, to pluck them up and to destroy them, and that nation turns from all its wickedness, I also will change my

mind concerning the evil which I said I would inflict on them. So in verses 9, 10. In both these cases the verb is applied to God, to express what he will do in a certain contingency, and that is not to repent of any of his previous doings, nor indulge any class of regrets whatever, but to change his future action.

14. Joel 2 : 13, 14. And rend your hearts, and not your clothes, and turn to the Lord your God, for he is merciful and compassionate, of long suffering and great mercy, and changes his mind concerning evil. Who knows that he will not return and change his mind, and leave behind him a blessing, and a sacrifice, and a libation to the Lord our God? In this passage the people are called on to reform and turn to the Lord. The supposed repentance is on God's part, and is not introduced even as the most subordinate element of man's conversion. But the case calls for no repentance on the part of God. It does not represent him as having made any mistake, or regretting any of his doings; only as changing his counsels for the future, and reversing his purposes. In the common version, God is described as capable, in a certain contingency, of repenting, and that contingency is the conversion of the people. God is a being of great mercy, and repents of evil. If men become holy, perhaps he will return and repent. Neither the Hebrew nor the Septuagint teaches any such absurdity.

15. Amos 7: 2–4. And when they finished devouring the grass, then I said, Lord, Lord, be propitious; who will raise up Jacob, for he is extremely small? Change your mind, Lord, concerning this. Then the Lord said, This shall not be. The other instances in this connection are similar. The case did not demand that God should repent of what he *had* done, but desist from future action of the kind. The word is entirely prospective, not retrospective.

16. So in Jonah 3 : 8–10 ; 4 : 1, which has already been considered with respect to the Hebrew. The same considerations apply to the Greek.

17. In all these cases, μετανοέω, the Greek verb to change one's mind, is used in its philological and classic sense, and not in the erroneous sense ascribed to it in the common English version of the New Testament.

18. The Hebrew נִחָם, for which μετανοέω is used in the passages above cited, sometimes signifies to repent, and is correctly translated in that sense. In all such cases it is translated by μεταμέ-

λομαι, which signifies to repent, and not by μετανοέω, to change one's mind. The careful discrimination of the Septuagint in these cases adds strong confirmation to the above argument. The Greek verb μεταμέλομαι, which signifies to repent, may signify to change one's mind, but μετανοέω, which appropriately signifies to change one's mind, may not be used to signify repentance.

19. Matthew uses the verb three times, and the noun twice, making in all 5 instances. (1.) Matt. 3 : 1, 2. In those days came John the Baptist, preaching in the wilderness of Judea, saying, Change your minds, for the kingdom of heaven is at hand. (2.) v. 8. Bear fruit therefore worthy of a change of mind. (3.) v. 11. I indeed baptize you with water to a change of mind. (4.) 4 : 17. From that time Jesus began to preach and say, Change your minds, for the kingdom of heaven is at hand. (5.) 11 : 20. Then he began to rebuke the cities in which most of his mighty works were performed, because they changed not their minds.

20. The evangelist introduces these words without limitation or restriction. Can it be possible that he uses them to signify repent and repentance ? It can not. There is not the shadow of an indication of any such usage. Neither the subjects to which he applies them, nor the context, admit of their being understood in any such sense. The verb describes John's preaching in respect to its object, and the noun the effect of his baptism, which pertained to the same thing. What was the known object of John's preaching ? To convert men to holiness ; and the effect of his baptism, when properly received, was their actual conversion. This is appropriately signified by change of mind, but not by repentance. The same remarks apply to the preaching of Christ. Many of his sermons are reported by this evangelist, and many specific duties mentioned in them, and urged on the attention of men ; but he never describes him as once mentioning repentance, either in his public preaching or private conversations. This is very strange, on the supposition that he preached repentance chiefly. But he did no such thing ; he preached righteousness chiefly ; and in the case of sinners, this commences with a radical change of mind in regard to its customary judgments and affections generally.

21. Mark uses these words three times : (1.) Mark 1 : 4. John baptized in the wilderness, preaching the baptism of a change of mind for the forgiveness of sins. (2.) verses 14, 15. And after he was cast into prison, Jesus came into Galilee preaching the gospel of God,

saying, The time has fully come, and the kingdom of God is at, hand : change your minds, and believe the good news. (3.) 6 : 12. And they went out, and preached that they should change their minds.

There is nothing here, any more than in Matthew, to indicate a departure from common usage ; none, therefore, can be allowed.

22. Luke uses these words in his Gospel 7 times, and in Acts 10 times, — in all, 17 times. They are favorite words with him, and found more frequently in his writings than in all the other books of the New Testament. (1.) Luke 3 : 3. And the word of God came to John, the son of Zachariah, in the wilderness ; and he went into all the region around the Jordan, preaching the baptism of a change of mind for the forgiveness of sins. (2.) verse 8. Bear, therefore, fruits worthy of a change of mind. (3.) 13 : 2–5. And he said to them, Do you think that those Galileans were sinners above all the Galileans, because they suffered such things ? I tell you, No ; but unless you change your minds, you shall all be destroyed in like manner. (4.) Or those 18, on whom the tower in Siloam fell, and killed them ; do you think that they were sinners above all men that dwelt at Jerusalem ? I tell you, No ; but unless you change your minds, you shall all be destroyed in like manner. (5, 6.) 15 : 7. I tell you there shall be joy in heaven over one sinner that changes his mind, more than over 99 righteous persons who have no need of a change of mind. Change of mind is here, as elsewhere, the equivalent of conversion. (7.) So in verse 10.

23. (8.) 16 : 30, 31. But he said, Father Abraham, if one should go from the dead to them, they would change their minds. But he said to him, If they hear not Moses and the prophets, neither would they be persuaded if one rose from the dead. Hearing Moses and the prophets, and being persuaded, are here the equivalent of the change of mind. Moses and the prophets preached holiness, and persuaded to holiness, but never preached repentance.

24. (9.) 24 : 46, 47. And he said to them, Thus it is written, that the Christ should suffer, and be raised from the dead on the third day, and that there should be preached in his name a change of mind, and forgiveness of sins. (10.) Acts 2 : 37, 38. And when they heard [that], they were distressed in mind, and said both to Peter and the rest of the apostles, Men and brothers, what shall we do ? Then Peter said to them, Change your minds, and be baptized, every one of you, in the name of Jesus Christ, for the for-

giveness of sins, and you shall receive the gift of the Holy Spirit. (11.) 3 : 19. Change your minds, therefore, and be converted, that your sins may be blotted out, that times of refreshing may come from the presence of the Lord, and he may send Jesus Christ to us, the before-appointed. (12.) 5 : 31. This man has God exalted a chief Leader and Saviour at his right hand, to give a change of mind to Israel, and forgiveness of sins.

25. (13.) 11 : 18. And when they heard these things, they were silent, and glorified God, saying, Then indeed has God given the Gentiles a change of mind to life. (14.) 13 : 24. John having preached, before his coming, the baptism of a change of mind to all the people of Israel. (15.) 17 : 30. God, therefore, having overlooked these times of ignorance, now commands men that all, every where, should change their minds.

26. (16.) 19 : 4. But Paul said, John indeed baptized with the baptism of a change of mind, telling the people to believe on one that was to come after him. (17.) 20 : 21. Testifying to both Jews and Greeks a change of mind to God, and faith in the Lord Jesus Christ. (18, 19.) 18 : 20. But to those in Damascus first, and also at Jerusalem, and in all the region of Judea, and to the Gentiles, I preached that they should change their minds, and turn to God, doing works worthy of a change of mind. None of these passages require repenting, but all look to conversion.

27. The verb in question is not found in the Epistles. The noun is found in the following passages : (1.) Rom. 2 : 4. Not knowing that the goodness of God leads you to a change of mind. (2, 3.) 2 Cor. 7 : 9, 10. Now I rejoice, not that you were sorry, but that you were led by sorrow to a change of mind ; for you were sorry in a godly manner, that you should suffer injury from us in nothing. For godly sorrow produces a change of mind to salvation, not *to be repented of*. In this passage the change of mind is contrasted with regret as something different from it. It is also described as not to be repented of, and is thus clearly discriminated from repentance.

28. (4.) Heb. 6 : 4–6. For it is impossible to renew the once enlightened again to a change of mind. (5.) 12 : 17. For you know that also, afterwards, wishing to inherit the blessing, he was rejected ; for he found no place for a change of mind, though he sought it with tears.

29. John the evangelist does not use these words either in his Gospel or Epistles. This is one of the peculiarities of his style,

and separates him widely from the other evangelists, and also from the author of Revelation. John the evangelist has another uniform title of conversion, which is peculiar to him. He calls it regeneration, being born again, born of God, etc. This new term marks a different mode of thinking, and is an advance on the other. It is one of several circumstances which indicate a composition of this Gospel as late as 90 or 95 A. D. It wants time for him to get away from the others to some of its peculiarities, and this among the rest.

30. The author of Revelation uses the verb 7 times: (1, 2.) Rev. 2: 5. Remember, therefore, whence you have fallen, and change your minds, and do the first works. But if not, I will come and remove your candlestick out of its place, unless you change your minds. (3, 4, 5.) verses 21, 22. And I gave her time to change her mind, and she will not change her mind from her fornication. Behold, I will cast her on a bed, and those that commit adultery with her into great affliction, unless they change their minds from her works. (6, 7.) 9: 20, 21. And the rest of men who were not killed with these plagues, changed not their minds from the works of their hands, that they should not worship demons, etc.; and changed not their minds from their murders, nor from their sorceries, nor from their fornications, nor from their thefts.

31. In none of these instances is there any departure from classic and Septuagint usage. The preposition signifying *from*, which follows the verb, and governs the object changed from, is a direct collateral evidence in favor of the previous usage, and is incompatible with the other supposition. Repentance is not *from* its object, but *of* it. We repent *of* misdeeds, and change *from* them. Repentance is retrospective; change from misdoing is prospective.

32. There is a reason for this use of change of mind to denote conversion, and the adoption of Christianity, by all the first teachers, which did not exist afterwards. In those times, Christianity was entirely revolutionary. It required the abandonment of all the cherished traditionary opinions of the Jews respecting the excellence and permanence of their polity, and turned their hopes to righteousness alone as of value in the sight of God. To become Christians, men had to change their minds, and embrace a system of ideas fundamentally different from their traditionary ones. This was the state of things when the first three Gospels were written. Christianity was upsetting an old faith, and introducing a new one. Then change of mind was the first thing to be contended for. But

when men's minds had become generally changed, then another term, taken from a still higher principle in the system of Christianity, naturally superseded the original one with which the first preachers started. Then it was mainly important to represent the adoption of Christianity, and becoming pious and good, by regeneration, and being born again. This peculiarity of the Gospel of John is of great significance, and deserves more attention than it has yet received.

33. This view is sustained by the Peshito, the old Syriac version, both the oldest and most accurate of all the ancient versions, belonging, perhaps, to the close of the second century. The testimony of this version is the more important, because the Syriac was the common language of Palestine in the time of our Lord, his own vernacular tongue, as well as that of John the Baptist, and of all the apostles, with the exception, perhaps, of Paul. This is the Hebrew language of our Lord's time, and is so called in the New Testament. John and Christ preached, and held all their recorded conversations, not in Greek, the language in which they are narrated to us, nor in the Hebrew of the Old Testament, but in Syriac, the vernacular language of Syria, to which Palestine belonged, and which then bore the name of Hebrew because the Hebrew had gradually been changed into it. The old Syriac version probably gives us, in many cases, the original words which were used by John the Baptist and Christ, and by the apostles, in their preaching. In this most venerable of the ancient versions, the verb for change your minds, and the noun for change of mind, are represented by the Syriac words corresponding to the Hebrew for turn and turning, making John and Christ preach that men should turn, and making John's preaching and baptism not the preaching and baptism of repentance, but the preaching and baptism of turning, or conversion. Modern scholars have translated the old Syriac, in these passages, to agree with the Vulgate, and with the common English version; but that is incorrect. The words mean only turn and turning, and are not only of the same stock as the Hebrew words which express these objects, but are the same words, with the slight modifications peculiar to the Syriac, and distinguishing it from the Hebrew.

34. Let us now inquire into the origin of the repentance mode of translation, and the repentance theory of Christianity. This leads us first to the Vulgate, from which it has been adopted into most modern translations.

35. The Vulgate renders μετανοέω *pœnitentiam agere*, to exercise penitence, and the noun *pœnitentia*. This mode of rendering, however, did not originate with Jerome. It appears in the writings of Tertullian, a presbyter at Carthage, in Africa, who died about 220, at the age of 60. Among his works is an article on penitence, in which he describes John's baptism as the baptism of penitence ; and for repent, of the common English version, Tertullian says, enter on penitence. He renders Ezekiel 18 : 21, 23, 33 : 11, (where the common version has, correctly, turn,) be penitent, and I will save you ; I live, and I prefer penitence rather than death. He also teaches that, in Rev. 2 : 5, pardon is, by implication, promised to the penitent. Cyprian calls the way of life the way of penitence. Cyprian was converted A. D. 245, and suffered martyrdom A. D. 258, and received many of his religious opinions from Tertullian. But we cannot stop with Cyprian and Tertullian. Where did they get these views ? They received them from the ascetics.

36. The ascetics arose in the second century, and began to attract general attention to their severe discipline about 171, when Montanus commenced his movement in that direction. Montanus claimed to be the Paraclete, or Comforter, promised John 14 : 16, and proposed to improve Christianity by multiplying and extending fasts, forbidding second marriages, refusing pardon to such Christians as had fallen into greater sins, rejecting all personal decorations of dress, banishing polite learning and philosophy, and insisting on other austerities and superstitions.

37. The claims of Montanus to be the Paraclete were not admitted ; but many of his principles were adopted, and other similar austerities were received from other quarters ; and from this time we may date the penitential system of Christianity. Tertullian was a Montanist. Christians of the second century thus received from enthusiasts, some of whom were little better than monomaniacs, new views of religion, inducing erroneous interpretations of the Scriptures. Jerome, the author of the Vulgate, was a devoted monachist, and deeply imbued with the prevailing superstitions. He misunderstood the words under consideration, and translated them incorrectly, in conformity with the prevailing superstitions. The severities of the monastic system would have found no shadow of support in the Scriptures without this perversion.

38. Has the error never been observed before ? Yes, once and again ; but it has proved a monster hard to kill. It bears decapita-

tion, and lives still. Beza, the successor of Calvin, at Geneva, and one of the most eminent scholars of his age, saw the error of the Vulgate in respect to these words, and corrected it in his Latin version of the New Testament, published in 1565, 46 years before the publication of King James's Bible. He rendered the Greek words by *resipisco*, to return to one's right mind, to recover one's reason, to return to wisdom, and *resipiscentia*, a return to one's right mind, change of mind, a return to wisdom. This was the best translation which the Latin language admits by the use of single words for single words ; and if the English had corresponding words, we should well represent the Greek by using them ; but it has not.

39. Beza's rendering makes religion consist essentially in attaining a right, wise, and discreet mind. This is essentially correct, and a great improvement on the method of the Vulgate. But it made little impression on the popular mind of Europe. Indeed, it hardly reached the popular mind, and was little attended to by scholars. Certainly it did not reach with effect King James's translators, though many of them acknowledged Beza, after Calvin, as their religious leader, and probably translated with his Latin version before them. It can hardly be supposed that they would neglect such a help, furnished by an authority which they so highly respected.

40. Beza's improvement had the effect, however, of calling some attention to the subject ; and it has generally been observed by English scholars, that the common version of these words does not fully express the sense of the originals. The error is often pointed out as a deficiency, in not representing the original fully, but has seldom been attempted to be exposed as a radical departure from the truth, and the inculcation of a positive and hurtful error. Almost all respectable Protestant commentators recognize change of mind as the exact sense of the original, or as a sense comprehended under it ; but they generally allow repentance to be an approximation to the same thing, and to be entitled to its place in the Scriptures, in dogmatic theology, and in the science of Christian morals.

41. But some have dissented from this. George Campbell, of the Church of Scotland, the great champion of Christianity against Hume and other distinguished infidels of his day, for a time head of Mareschal College, and in 1771 made Professor of Divinity, is the most distinguished of these dissenters. He viewed the error of the common version as somewhat serious, and demanding correction ; and in a version of the Gospels made by himself, substituted

reform and reformation for repent and repentance. This improvement was proposed nearly 100 years ago, and has been before the people to some extent. Campbell's translation is a standard work, and has been extensively read; but his correction has not been generally approved. Alexander Campbell, of Virginia, declared in favor of it many years ago, and it has recently been adopted in a portion of the translations of the American Bible Union, said to have been made by him.

42. Campbell's rendering is a great improvement on the common version; but it does not represent the original with exactness; it represents the less general by the more general. Campbell himself did not appreciate its importance; and in his dissertation on the subject, makes μετάνοια reformation, a species of repentance. This error is very surprising in a Greek scholar who is generally so accurate; and in one of the most accomplished reasoners of modern times. The μετάνοια is neither repentance nor a species of repentance. Repentance is an affection; the μετάνοια is not an affection; repentance is retrospective; the μετάνοια is prospective; repentance denotes a state of affection; μετάνοια change of mind in respect to its faiths, judgments, affections, and purposes. Μετάνοια and repentance have nothing in common, except that the former embraces the latter in all appropriate conditions as one of the objects of its changes. It is not strange, therefore, that with so fundamental misapprehensions in his arguments for it, Campbell's improvement did not obtain general favor. It did not deserve it. If the μετάνοια is only a species of repentance, then it is properly called repentance, and that title may be continued without prejudice to truth.

43. It has been proposed to improve my rendering by substituting heart for mind, and making it change of heart. We have an example of this mode of expression in Ezek. 18 : 31. Make you a new heart and a new spirit, for why will you die, house of Israel? The Hebrews often use the word heart for mind; they do so in this case. The change of heart in Ezekiel is the same thing as the change of mind in portions of the New Testament; and heart in Ezek. 18 : 31, and often elsewhere, signifies mind. But that is not its usual signification, nor is it generally understood as being synonymous with mind. Most understand it erroneously, in a more limited sense, as not comprehending the intellectual powers, but only the affections. That is not the sense intended in Ezekiel, nor

is it the sense in which mind is used in the New Testament. Change of heart, therefore, can not in this case be admitted as the better translation. It is less admissible than it would otherwise be, because mental philosophy ignores the term heart, and recognizes only mind and its exercises. This circumstance creates a necessity for keeping to the term mind to express the sense intended, in the current language of the times.

44. The different modes of representing a change of moral character from sin to holiness in the Scriptures are as follows : —

(1.) Conversion, in both Testaments.

(2.) Change of heart, in the Old Testament.

(3.) Change of mind, in portions of the New Testament.

(4.) New creation, in Paul's writings.

(5.) New birth, and being born again, in John's Gospel and Epistles.

In our writings we may take our choice of these terms, or use different terms to signify the same thing ; but in translating the Sacred Scriptures the terms of the writers ought to be carefully preserved. We want them all, and all in their places ; neither is it right to drop or change them, or to substitute one for another.

45. Christianity displayed its greatest power under the apostles and their successors, before the introduction of the penitential system. When penitence came to lead the van of the Christian virtues, then their prosperity declined ; and instead of reaching a millennium of universal knowledge and holiness, and of unexampled prosperity and happiness, the hope of the first Christians, the world, after some ineffectual struggles, fell into the dreary superstitions of the dark ages, and there remained for centuries. To use a favorite Hebrew figure, the sun withdrew its light, and the stars fell from heaven. The adoption of the penitential system was the virtual abrogation of the system of righteousness with which Christianity commenced. From this time practical righteousness ceased to be the supreme object of moral culture. Instead of loving and hoping, men busied themselves with sorrowing and regretting, and what was, if possible, still worse, they made this a satisfaction for not doing. It was not the great thing with religious men to *do right*, but to repent of doing wrong.

46. Righteousness was still inculcated and pressed on the attention and practice of men ; and not a few pursued it, together with their superstitions. But they pursued it at a disadvantage, and many

religious men made less progress in it than they would have done with a more scriptural and correct theory of its value and importance ; and thousands and tens of thousands, being put on the penitential road to righteousness, never attained it at all, but rested in perpetual sinning and perpetual repenting. Tears and cries, fastings and prayers, self-inflicted flagellations, and weary pilgrimages attested the sincerity and earnestness of their search ; but they were on the wrong track ; they sought the Lord in the sepulcher, and did not find him. How much better to have sought him on the throne, where he was !

47. The introduction of this error in the church of Christ is one of the greatest calamities which has attended its progress. The ancient persecutions, cruel and bloody as they were, are not to be compared with it. But it came in by stealth ; it was the devil in the garb of an angel ; it had an appearance of superior sanctity, and men were deceived by it. Our Lord's most solemn warnings are recorded against deceivers and deceptions, and the history of his community shows how correctly he judged in respect to the danger from that quarter.

48. The prevalence of the penitential system has been long and mournful. Unhappily it still continues. But a better day is at hand ; truth must rise and live ; delusion must fall and pass away. Who can say that a return to the genuine doctrines of Christ and the apostles on this subject, would not be accompanied with a recovery of the primitive power of Christianity, so long and so strangely lost ?

49. Many object that change of mind does not express as much as the common words. The difference is not one of quantity ; it is one of quality. The two renderings represent different moral and ethical systems. The common rendering represents the penitential system ingrafted on Christianity by the ascetics of the second century ; my rendering represents the system of Christ and of John the Baptist, as reported by the first three evangelists and as preached by Paul.

50. If any suppose that length of time has made these words any less unsuitable for the places which they occupy in the common Bible than they originally were, he is greatly mistaken. The corresponding mistranslation of the Vulgate has continued 14 centuries, and reckoning its use from the time of Tertullian, 16 centuries ; but it represents the original Greek no better to-day than

it did when first introduced. Neither is the common version of these words improved in a period of 336 years since it was first proposed by Tindal. It was erroneous then, and it is erroneous now. It put repentance in the foreground of all the virtues then; it does the same now.

51. I am well aware that repentance is defined and preached as including much more than repentance — as including faith, love, all holy obedience. To omit these altogether from the objects of moral culture, has been impossible. In the darkest periods of the dark ages they claimed their place as objects of human pursuit, and heaven's genial light was not altogether darkened then. It could not be. Penitence was connected with holiness, and was made a schoolmaster to lead men to Christ, as it now is. How poorly the learners advanced with such leading, time has shown. The preaching of repentance is the same now, and, according to the common Bible, demands instant and universal attention as an effectual commencement of a religious life. It is no such thing. Repentance does not comprehend holiness, and is not the beginning of it. Holiness is far above and far beyond it in active obedience.

52. The words repent and repentance have a constitutional inability to signify the same things as the Greek words for which they stand. Repentance is derived from the verb repent, and takes its meaning from it; repent is derived, through the French, from the Latin *pœniteo*, to make repent, to displease, and *pœniteo* is derived ultimately from the Greek ποινή, and the Greek ποινή from the Greek verb φένω, to kill. In agreement with its derivation it signifies kill-money, kill-punishment, or punishment for killing, satisfaction, retribution, punishment, pain. The Latin *punio* and the English punish and pain are from the same theme, and have similar meanings. Repentances, penitences, and penances are species of pains and punishments. The Roman Catholic doctrine of penances is a legitimate portion of the common system, and ought not to be abandoned if the other is retained. The Protestant reformers abandoned the system of penances, as a great perversion of Christianity, and a wide deviation from the most effective methods of moral culture. It is next in order to abandon the system of repentances, and put moral culture on the scriptural basis of faith, holy affections, and holy actions. Then men will easily be made to know what they have to *do* to be holy, and moral culture will be prosecuted to much greater advantage than it now is, from being better understood.

30 *

53. Christianity does not ignore the affections ; it fully recognizes their existence and importance, and has many lessons for their due regulation. It makes the love of God and the love of man first principles of practical holiness. It insists much on hopes and fears ; encourages courage, and nerves the good to suffer and die for the right, if need be, without fear and without regret. It recognizes punishments also, and often adverts to them as objects to be feared and shunned. To divinely appointed punishments belong repentances and every species of regrets. They are the worm that dies not and the fire that is never quenched. Repentance without hope is remorse, and is in some of its manifestations the most terrific and overwhelming of all human passions. It occupies the gate to madness and lunacy, and passes many miserable convicts through it to despair and death.

54. Repentance is the most inevitable of all known punishments of sin, and is that in which all others meet and unite. It is a species of pain, and in the form of remorse, where it exists without being tempered and modified by milder and pleasurable affections, rises to the keenest and most insupportable anguish. What an amazing blunder, to put the highest class of punishments inflicted on sinners in the front rank of virtues which characterize the reformation of the offender ? Punishment may lead to reformation ; it is inflicted with that design, and adapted to that purpose. But it is no part of reformation, and its greatest possible bitterness is without an element of moral virtue. Bodily pains are not to be pursued as an object, and just as little are they to be nursed and cherished. Who would think of basing a system of cure for diseases on headaches, and putting patients to nursing their pains as a means of getting on to health ? Repentances occupy the same place in the moral system which pains occupy in the material. Both are divine warnings and divine punishments, and the man that does not heed them is a dead man ; as much so in respect to the soul-pains of repentances as bodily pains. It is the part of wisdom not to seek them nor cherish them, but to note their slightest monitions and improve from them. As soon as the monition is received, the pain may be dismissed, if it will leave ; but it will not always do this ; the cessation of the punishment is not submitted to the discretion of the criminal ; it rests with the court. God's arrangements, however, in this respect as in others, are tempered with mercy. He allows the reformed sinner to forget in a measure his sins, and cease from fruitless regrets as

soon as they become unnecessary. What an instance of the divine compassion! and what an encouragement to desist from evil doing!

55. Repentance is not a good *per se*, but an evil. It is no part of human blessedness and glory, but belongs to the family of pains and sorrows, and is the sister of shame and despair; no better entitled to a place among the virtues than either of them. Its sole use is like that of the prison and the scaffold, to punish sin and discourage its commission. Like other punishments it has no direct relations to well doing or well being; its direct relations are to ill doing and ill being; these it repels.

56. The present argument is not meant to depreciate the value of repentances. They are invaluable; they are an absolute necessity, and can not be dispensed with. But they have their place, and there is the field of their usefulness, and not among the virtues. Loves and hates, affections for present objects, hopes and fears, affections for future objects, and approbations and repentances, affections for past objects, all have an appointment from the kind Father to serve us; and all sustain relations to our holiness and happiness. Of these, loves and hates are first, hopes and fears next, and approbations and regrets last. The remembrances of the past, with all their just and reasonable affections, whether of pain or pleasure, have their uses; but our possible good and evil at every stage of our existence, all lies in the future. The past is gone and lost; we never can recall it, nor go back to it. It has left us forever, and is continually receding further and further from us, till the gulf of separation, which is from the first bottomless and bridgeless, widens to infinity. The present is an instant; it is a dividing line between the two eternities, of no breadth whatever. The possibilities of the past are lost; those of the present are joined to the past the next instant; and all the objects of our labor are in the future. There is our battle field, and there our harvest field; and we are approaching every point in it to which the line of our existence can come with the ceaseless progress of the ages. Loves and hates, hopes and fears, all find their objects in the future, near and remote; repentances and approbations find their objects in the past, and they are receding every instant further and still further from us. Surely then we ought not, in our systems of moral culture, to give any of the retrospective affections the preëminence over the present and prospective.

57. Still less ought the affections to take the precedence of ideas.

The eye of the mind is its faculty of ideas ; all the objects of our affections are first objects of our knowledge and faith. It is the policy of Christianity to increase and exalt our knowledge, and perfect our faith, and thereby develop our affections. This is the order of the Scriptures, and it is equally the order of reason and sound philosophy, and can not be reversed. Right doing is conditioned mainly on right knowing and believing, involving right judging. For all our knowledges and faiths are judgments in which we infer objects from evidences, and conclusions from premises. Faith is a judgment ; all believing is judging, and all right believing is right judging, inferring from the evidence what it shows and all it shows. To judge and believe thus is to perceive the truth, and the truth perceived and acted on conducts to holiness and happiness. To believe without evidence, or in opposition to it, or differently from what it shows, is to believe wrong, and peril all the interests involved in such faith. Correct faith is a virtue, and leads to all virtue ; incorrect faith is a sin, and leads to all sin.

NOTE II.

THE LATER PROPHETS AND THEIR ARRANGEMENT — JONAH, ISAIAH, JEREMIAH, ETC.

1. THE third division of the Hebrew sacred books consists of 15 Hebrew prophets, arranged in two series. (1.) The major prophets, Isaiah, Jeremiah, and Ezekiel ; (2.) The minor prophets, Hosea, Joel, Amos, Obadiah, Jonah, Micah, Nahum, Habakkuk, Zephaniah, Haggai, Zechariah, and Malachi. These books, in the Hebrew arrangement, are placed next after Kings, and followed by the fourth and last division of the Hebrew sacred books — an arrangement entitled to be continued in the English Bible, and on no account to be abandoned. Daniel belongs to the next division, and will appear in its place.

2. The Hebrew arrangement of the major prophets is in chronological order ; Isaiah first, then Jeremiah, and last Ezekiel. The impropriety of a different order is manifest ; but in the minor prophets, while a chronological arrangement is observed in the collocation of the last three books, and to some extent in that of the others, it is in several instances departed from, showing that the true order of the books was not known to the compiler. In the

present work, I have abandoned the division of major and minor prophets, as of no advantage in the study of the sacred books, but an injury ; and arranged all the books in a single series, according to their supposed times. This is not always according to the probable date of their composition. Jonah, first on the list, may have been latest written. The affinities of its style are with the later Hebrew books ; it is not attributed to Jonah as its author, and has every mark of being a parable, and not a strict literal history. The Old and New Testaments abound in parables, and the oriental and ancient taste inclined strongly that way ; with what reason, the universal popularity of our Lord's parables and other ancient writings of the kind clearly shows. The absurdity of Jonah's conduct as a prophet of Jehovah, and its inconsistency with that sacred office, and the extravagance of making *animals fast, clothing them with sackcloth, and prohibiting them from eating and drinking*, to avert the divine anger, are not unsuitable to an eastern parable, but do not comport with strict and literal history. As a history, the book is embarrassed with great difficulties ; as a parable, its exposition is easy, and its lessons weighty and powerful.

3. The earliest date in Isaiah is the last year of Uzziah, (6 : 1,) 759 B. C. ; another date occurs in the time of Hezekiah's sickness and recovery, 15 years before his death, 711 B. C., including an interval of 48 years. This is a long public life. But few clergymen preach their half-century sermons. The labors of Isaiah are here represented for nearly half a century in the first 39 chapters of his book. The names of then living persons are often mentioned, and specific dates are sometimes given. The different poems are independent of each other, and some differ widely from the rest, but most of them are directed to the men of those times, and interspersed with notices and incidents, giving occasion for the advice of the prophet, and creating a demand for his messages. At the 40th chapter the style and structure of the book are entirely changed. The language bears marks of a later date than most of the poems which precede. There is no allusion to any living man of the age of Hezekiah, or to any contemporary incident or event of that period ; but the people addressed as contemporaries are the Jews of the Babylonian exile. The great contemporary sovereign referred to, the Hezekiah of the age, is Cyrus ; the great blessing proclaimed is the return from the exile, and the latter-day glories to follow, and the great duties, the abandonment of idolatry, the worship of Jeho-

vah, and the practice of righteousness. Other representations and peculiarities concur to define this portion of the book as belonging to the close of the Babylonian exile, and not to the period of Hezekiah, 170 years earlier. If no express date had accompanied the song of Moses at the passage of the Red Sea, who would think of ascribing it to Joseph, or Jacob, or some other Jewish patriarch, who lived previous to the Egyptian oppression? The position of this part of the book next after the poems of Isaiah, with some slight historical notices only intervening, would create a presumption in favor of its earlier date, if the contents were consistent with such a conclusion. Against the indications of the contents, it proves nothing. I have therefore not ventured to give the chronology of this part of Isaiah at the head of my pages. Its most probable date is B. C. 536, a period of excitement well adapted to furnish the conditions for such a composition, and apparently well entitled to have its own contemporary prophet and poet.

4. The following are some passages in the latter part of Isaiah which sustain the above views: Isa. 40: 1, 2. Comfort, comfort my people, says your God; speak kindly to Jerusalem, and cry to her, that her warfare is accomplished, that her wickedness is forgiven, that she has received from the hand of Jehovah double punishments for all her sins. This is a message of consolation to the Jews, at the close of the Babylonian exile. It is not the method of God to comfort men before he has afflicted them. With this date the whole chapter agrees. The voice crying in the wilderness implies that the return was already proclaimed; and the admonition to Zion, as a news-bearer, to lift up her voice with strength, and publish her news aloud, implies that the decree permitting their return was then published. The connection of predictions with this reference to passing events is in order.

5. 41: 25, 26. I have raised up one from the north, and he shall come from the rising of the sun, he shall call on my name; and he shall come on princes like mortar, and like a potter tread the clay. Who declared [this] from the beginning, that we may know [him], and from before, that we may say, He is righteous? Indeed, none declared it; indeed, none published it; indeed, none hears your words. I first gave to Zion, Behold, behold, and to Jerusalem, the bearer of good news. The sense of the latter part of this passage is misapprehended in the common version, but correctly translated it refers to Cyrus as having come, and the good news of the return as being already proclaimed.

6. 44 : 27, 28 ; 45 : 1.   I am Jehovah that says to the deep, Be dry ; and I will dry up all your rivers ; that says to Cyrus, He is my shepherd [king], and shall fully do all my pleasure, saying to Jerusalem, You shall be builded, and the temple shall be founded. ˙ Thus says Jehovah to his anointed, to Cyrus, whom I have taken by his right hand, to subdue nations before him : And I will ungird the loins of kings, to open before him the folding doors, and the gates shall not be shut, etc.   This is precisely the style in which the prophets refer to contemporaries, and must be understood as referring to Cyrus as a contemporary.   It recognizes Cyrus as having already appeared and commenced the execution of his office, and refers to the decree concerning the rebuilding of Jerusalem and the temple, in a way that is natural on the supposition that it is already published.   But however that may be, the allusion to Cyrus contemplates him as a contemporary, and not as a monarch who was to arise after more than a century and a half.   Is. 46 : 1, 2.   Bel has bowed down ; Nebo bows down.   Their idols were a burden to the beasts and to the cattle ; your burdens were taken up, a load for the weary [beasts].   They stooped, they bowed down together, they were unable to deliver the burden, and went into captivity. This describes Babylon as not only to fall, but as having fallen, and her idols as prostrate in the dust.   47 : 1–15, predicts the fall of Babylon as an event at hand, and not as several generations distant.

7. Isa. 51 : 14.   The bent captive hastens to be released, that he may not die in the pit, and his food not fail.   Verse 17.   Awake, awake, stand up, Jerusalem, who has drunk from the hand of Jehovah the cup of his indignation, she has drunk the goblet-cup of trembling, [and] sucked it out.   This refers to Jerusalem after the destruction of the city, and not before.   So also verses 21, 22. Hear, therefore, now, afflicted one, and drunk, but not with wine. Thus says your Lord Jehovah and your God : I have taken from your hand the cup of trembling, the goblet-cup, and you shall drink it no more ; and I have put it into the hand of your oppressors, who said to you, Bow down, that we may go over ; and you made your back like the earth, like the street to them that went over. Before the destruction of Jerusalem, this would have been entirely inappropriate and untrue.   It was only late in the Babylonian exile that the cup of trembling was taken out of the hands of the Jewish nation.

8. 52 : 1–15, refers to the return from Babylon as at hand, and
already taking place, and not in the distant future, to be preceded
by the whole period of the exile, and many years previous. It is
the language of a living ministry to a living people. So is 60 : 1.
Arise, shine, for your light has come, and the glory of Jehovah has
arisen on you. Then follow predictions of great blessings to come,
which are yet deferred. Promises and threatenings in the prophecies are alike conditional. If a nation turns from its evil doings,
threatenings are averted, and if a nation falls into sin, blessings
promised are not conferred. This appears from the case of Nineveh, as represented in Jonah ; and is conformable to Ezek. 18 : 1–
30, etc.

9. 64 : 10, 11, belongs to the time of the exile. Thy holy cities
are a wilderness, Zion is a wilderness, Jerusalem is a desolation ;
our holy and beautiful house, where our fathers praised thee, is
burned with fire, and all our desirable possessions are laid waste.
How absurd and false these would have been in the times of
Hezekiah !

10. The first part of Isaiah has some prophecies that seem to belong to the period of the latter part. Of this description is prophecy
9 (13 : 14 : 1–23), the title of which is therefore erroneous in ascribing it to Isaiah ; and prophecy 20, (34, 35). Some others are
doubtful. Each prophecy is an independent production, the date
of which must be determined from its contents, and not from its
position in the series merely. When the contents do not determine
the dates, they are indeterminate. A determination of them from
other sources of evidence is impossible. No other reliable evidence
on the subject has been preserved.

11. In Jeremiah the collocation of the prophecies is exceedingly
irregular. The first 39 prophecies extend to the destruction of
Jerusalem ; 40–43, relate to the flight to Egypt, etc. ; and 44–50,
to foreign nations ; and the whole is concluded with an account
of the destruction of Jerusalem.

12. The Hebrew prophets are generally independent poems, interspersed with passages and sometimes extended narratives in prose ;
and a considerable part of Ezekiel is prosaic. I have therefore
resolved these books into prophecies, and omitted the division of
chapters, as not suitable for poems. This will be found a great
improvement, and one that is imperatively demanded. I have not
deemed it expedient to adopt the line-divisions which some have

adopted and many approved. The Hebrews did not divide these poems into lines, in the manner of the Greeks and of modern poetry. They wrote them continuously, the same as prose. The Hebrew line-division of poetry is restricted to Psalms, the prayers of Jonah, and Habakkuk, and a few lyric odes found elsewhere, and was introduced in them probably for the convenience of music. The best modern translations of the Greek poets abandon the line-divisions, and print them continuously, like prose. I can not think, therefore, that these divisions are called for in a version of the Hebrew prophets designed for common use ; it certainly is not to represent the originals, for in them it has never been used.

13. The later prophets are not the only poets of the Hebrews ; but they are poets of a certain class, different from others. Job is a Hebrew poem, but not a prophecy. So are the Song of Songs and Proverbs. Several of the Psalms are supposed to be prophecies. The three greater prophetic books are remarkable examples of different styles of poetic composition. Isaiah is the hopeful poet, anticipating future good, and painting, with inimitable beauty and sublimity, scenes of joy and peace. Jeremiah is the weeping poet, depicting, with matchless power, scenes of distress, desolation, and misery ; himself an example of great suffering. Ezekiel is the transcendental poet, the author of visions, and the painter of the invisible and ideal. God in his flaming cherubic chariot, with the burning glories and rainbow brilliancy and beauty of his person ; angels ; a resurrection of the Jews, and restoration to their land with David as their king ; the post-resurrectionary war which follows, with the congregated hosts of the wicked ; the post-resurrectionary temple and its ordinances, with every door and chamber of the holy edifice ; the post-resurrectionary division of the land ; the river of life, and the trees of life, and the final reign and residence of God on earth, are among the themes of his graphic pen.

14. He sketches with the hand of a master. His creations are perfect ; they live, they breathe, they strike the reader with all the force of absolute realities. It is no small compliment to his genius and skill as a poet, that his most refined and unquestionable idealities have generally been mistaken for realities — a similar compliment to that which is paid to the painter when the visitor mistakes the picture for the object represented. In an artistic point of view, Ezekiel has his faults, and there is no poet of any language or nation that has not. Some of his figures are low and mean, and

some of his illustrations require illustrating. But on the whole, modern criticism has done him great injustice, mainly from not understanding him. He is different from Isaiah and Jeremiah; Zechariah alone resembles him, among the minor prophets; but the creative power of his genius has never been excelled, and he has contributed as large a number of sublime and beautiful conceptions to the poetic treasures of the Scriptures as Isaiah, Jeremiah, or David.

NOTE III.

CONTEMPORARY TRANSLATIONS AND THE TRANSLATION CAUSE.

1. It is not a new thing to translate after King James. The subject has engaged the attention of learned and good men for the last 100 years, and the attempts made in this direction hitherto have not been entirely unproductive. Many valuable improvements have been made by different translators, and though they have received less attention from the people than they deserved, they have not been in vain. Most great battles begin with preliminary skirmishes, in which the advantage may sometimes appear to be with the weaker party; it is not the preliminary skirmish, but the completed conflict, that determines the day. The master of the field is the party that holds it when the battle is over. So in regard to the progress of knowledge. Old opinions do not retreat the moment new-born knowledge, child of God, claims their position and demands their surrender. They stand their ground, and are dislodged with difficulty. Their early skirmishes with the truth seem often to leave them with the advantage; but sooner or later the conflict deepens, and truth gains the deserved mastery. It has been so in other sciences besides religion, and it has been so in religion from the earliest times. The Latin Vulgate was frowned on at its first appearance as an unwelcome intruder. It was not deemed comparable to the old and less perfect version, as a book of instruction for the people, and some of the lights of the age, including the great Augustine, extremely regretted its publication, and thought its learned author might have been better employed. But it took the field, and held it. Its victory was not completed in a day, nor in a year, nor in a century, so great was the dominion of prejudice; but it went on, gradually extending its circulation and multiplying its friends, till in about two centuries it remained sole

master of the field, and its rival was gone. So complete was the final victory of the Vulgate, that its illustrious predecessor, with all his sacred associations going back nearly to the times of the apostles, was not only driven entirely from the field of common use, but actually destroyed and lost ; and now, when it would be deemed of almost infinite value as a historical monument, it can not as yet be found. It is to be hoped that some future Tischendorf will yet penetrate its tomb, and call it forth to light and life ; but its prospects of resurrection are very faint, and the resumption of the place it once occupied as the last and most perfect dispensation of the Jewish and Christian Sacred Scriptures, is impossible. We trust a better destiny awaits the version of King James.

2. Many circumstances conspire to give the common version a degree of credit for accuracy and perfection which do not belong to it. Among these may be reckoned the fame of its translators, their number, the testimonials of their contemporaries in its favor, and the general method of interpreting the originals in conformity with it, and with the ancient versions, with great ignorance both in England and America of the vast and valuable results of German criticism, both on the text of the New Testament and in the interpretation of both Testaments. Conservatism in knowledge has characterized men in all ages. With many, progress is a mortal sin. That it is not still punished with the cross, as in the case of our Lord, and with the scaffold and burning, as in the case of the bones of Wickliffe and the persons of William Tindal and John Rogers, those immortal translators, is not the fault of the spirit of this conservatism, but of the times which prohibit such injustice. The religious conservatist wishes to keep us to King James, first as right, and deludes himself with the idea that nothing valuable or important has been learned in biblical science since King James's time. Secondly he wishes us to keep to King James, even if wrong, because he imagines that his truths contain all that men need to know, and his errors do not entirely block up the way of salvation and the temple of religious knowledge. Admirable philosophy! Anticipated by those scourges and terrors of Christians in past ages, the successors of Mohammed, who consigned other books to indiscriminate destruction because the Koran contained all that was necessary for man to know.

3. Several able translations of the New Testament have appeared in England since the time of King James, some of which have been

republished and circulated in this country.   G. R. Noyes, a distinguished Professor in' Harvard College, published his new translation of the Hebrew prophets, in 3 volumes, in 1833–37.   Prof. M. Stuart, one of the fathers of sacred learning in America, published translations of select portions of the Sacred Scriptures, with elaborate notes, many years since.   Rev. Albert Barnes is also before the community, both as an elaborate commentator on the common version, and a translator of some portions of the Sacred Scriptures from the originals.   The day is not sufficiently dark for the wholesale condemnation of independent versions, even by the most conservative.   They *have* come, and they *must* come ; and they will ere long take the field with the common version, and hold it, and command the general respect and attention of mankind.   They claim it now, and past infelicities are no evidence that they will not hold it.

4. The contemporary version which is now in progress under the direction of the American Bible Union, conspires with different independent translation and revision movements in England, and some others in America, to show that a new era is dawning on this subject, and that the demand for 'improvement is earnest and determined.   I also infer the same, from the success of my New Testament thus far, under great disadvantages.   Blind devotion to King James, right or wrong, and King James forever, against the Hebrew, against the Greek, against all the improvements in biblical science since his time, is the sentiment of some', declared on the occasion of great religious anniversaries, published and circulated through the press, set forth in public lectures, and preached from the pulpit, as a part of the everlasting gospel of salvation.   Shocking profanation !   But a mighty under-current is setting in the other way, and will soon be at the surface, if it has not already reached it.

5. I give honor to King James's version, and to the other able versions that preceded it.   But King James's is not the last successful translation of the Bible that is to be.   It attained many different versions before King James's time, with successive improvements, and must go on to different and improved versions still, while time shall last.   It is sometimes objected that it is a bad precedent for an individual to translate the Scriptures ; it should be done by ecclesiastical authority.   So thought the Church of Rome, and so it decreed previous to the time of Wickliffe ; so

thought the persecutors of Tindal, and brought him to the stake. Impartial history and the order of divine Providence teach no such thing, but the contrary. If religion is a science, it may be left to the laws of the sciences for the perfection of its books, as well as for other improvements. If it is an erroneous system of imposition, the freedom of the sciences will ruin it, and it had better be rescued as soon as possible from the perils of free inquiry and fearless discussion. All special arrangements to uphold the truth of Christianity imply an apprehension of its weakness, which is disgraceful to honest Christians. Christianity is truth, built on truth; it fears not the storm; it lives not by authority, nor by sufferance, but by right and necessity, because, as a system of truth, it is in its nature immortal.

6. It is not Christianity that cries for safe quarters and ecclesiastical protection, but the false interpretations that have mixed themselves with it. These are vulnerable and mortal, and need protection. True Christianity scorns it. Protection, earnest and zealous as it may be, can not keep deceptions in credit forever. It is happy for the race that it can not, and indicates on the part of the Creator a direct partisanship in favor of the true, and against the false.

7. Translating the Bible is no more the business of ecclesiastical tribunals than deciphering the heavens, resolving the mysteries of the earth, or the principles of chemistry. The Bible is the book of the world, not of ecclesiastical authorities; and every human being has a divine and *inalienable* right to translate and publish it according to the best of his ability. To interdict or restrict this right is an act of oppression and wickedness which God can never sanction nor bless. When this restriction has been attempted to be enforced, it has not prospered, but has proved a curse. Truth's first utterances are always from individuals. Their acceptance by ecclesiastical tribunals follows their acceptance elsewhere, never introduces it.

8. 250 years ago King James's Bible represented the originals in the main, according to the best knowledge of the times; now it is left far behind the more advanced state of biblical science. 250 years ago the English language was very different from what it now is, and far less refined and less copious, as well as less exact and discriminating. We owe it to the people and to the cause of religious knowledge to furnish a translation for general use, as a contem-

31 *

porary version with the common one, and with all others to appear, that shall be as correct as possible, and bear the impress of the language and learning of the times.

NOTE IV.

THE LORD'S PRAYER.

1. THE Lord's Prayer is in common use according to the common version, and also according to a previous version preserved in the Episcopal Prayer Book, which substitutes *trespasses* for *sins*. The prayer in Matthew differs from that in Luke by having the doxology appended to it, and by some other diversities of expression; but both have the same number of petitions. In my version these prayers stand as follows : —

Our Father in heaven, hallowed be thy name, thy kingdom come, thy will be done as in heaven so on earth; give us to-day our essential bread, and forgive us our debts, as we forgive our debtors ; and bring us not into trial, but deliver us from evil.

Father, hallowed be thy name, thy kingdom come ; give us daily our essential bread, and forgive us our sins, for we also forgive every one who is indebted to us, and bring us not into trial.

2. My principal corrections of these prayers are the following : — Representing an improved text which omits the doxology in Matthew, and those interpolations in Luke taken from Matthew. (1.) Our, before Father, and, which art in heaven, after it ; leaving the address simply, Father — that which Christ is reported to have used in his prayers, and one preeminently consonant with the principles of Christianity, which make God a spirit, and on earth equally as in heaven ; and which also make him the common Father of all men.   (2.) Thy will be done as in heaven, so on earth, which is comprehended in the previous petition, Thy kingdom come.   (3.) But deliver us from evil, which is comprehended in the previous petition, Bring us not into trial.   These prayers are not injured by being freed from interpolations, but improved ; and however suitable the doxology may be for church or private use, it ought neither to be taught nor used as a part of the Lord's Prayer.   What would

we think of interpolating the Ten Commandments. Represented correctly, each of these prayers has its peculiar beauties ; Matthew's is the more full and Hebraic; Luke's more condensed and classical.

3. My translations of the Lord's Prayer differ from those of the common version in several particulars. I omit which art, in the address in Matthew, making it, Our Father in heaven, instead of Our Father which art in heaven. The interpolation of the relative in this case adds nothing to the sense, and if admitted at all it ought to be who, and not which.

4. For Give us this day our daily bread, in Matthew, I substitute, Give us to-day our essential bread. Σήμερον properly signifies to-day, in opposition to αὔριον, which signifies to-morrow. Considered in this view, to-day is its most exact and appropriate rendering, and is preferable to this day, the antithesis of which is not to-morrow, but another day. For daily I substitute essential; the original word is ἐπιούσιον, not ἐφήμερον. The latter word is appropriately used in agreement with its derivation from the Greek ἡμέρα, day, to signify daily, in James 2: 15, If a brother or sister is naked, or destitute of daily food, and any one of you says to them, Go in peace, be warmed and be filled, but you give them not the necessaries for the body, what is the use ? So elsewhere. If the Evangelist had wished to signify daily, this word would have been the natural and proper one by which to express it. Instead of that, he has taken a word nowhere else used by Greek authors, and as far as we know, coined for the express purpose of defining this bread. Words are the offspring of ideas, and a new word implies a new idea. The introduction, therefore, of a new word in the Lord's Prayer, both in Matthew and Luke, is very significant, and creates a presumption in favor of something peculiar and important as being expressed by it.

5. Ἐπιούσιος can not mean daily, and we have no certain evidence to show its meaning but its derivation and its position. These were deemed sufficient by the sacred writers. Its position shows that it is a definitive term, and means some kind of bread. Its derivation is also significant. It is from οὐσία, entity, essence, nature, property, and is formed by dropping the noun termination, annexing that of the adjective, and receiving an intensive prefix. It means, therefore, according to its derivation, pertaining to one's nature, natural, essential, pertaining to property. Taking it in the sense of natural it signifies bread suited to our nature, our higher nature as well as our lower, and the higher especially, as the more

important; in the sense of essential it signifies the same thing, the bread of our being, of our entire being, and of our necessity. The latter is the view of the old Syriac version. In the sense of pertaining to property, it signifies the property that we require. I do not apprehend that any single word can express the original perfectly, but I have adopted essential as corresponding with it in derivation, and the most exact single word representation that the language admits. It can not fail to be accepted as a valuable improvement on King James's version. Jerome, in the Vulgate, in one of the prayers renders this word by the Latin for daily, and in the other for super-substantial, which bears the sense of super-material. I judge that the bread of life, the bread of divine grace and knowledge, is principally intended. This is conformable to our Lord's common method of representing the spiritual by the material, and also agrees with the context, in which we are admonished not to be anxious as to what we shall eat or drink, or with what we shall be clothed, but to seek first righteousness and God's kingdom, and all these things will be added.

6. For Lead us not into temptation, I substitute, Bring us not into trial. Εἰσενέγκῃς, the verb, never signifies to lead, but always to bring, bear, carry; and there is no necessity in this case, as some have supposed, for departing from the uniform meaning of the word elsewhere. The common version of that word, therefore, is wrong. Πειρασμός, which the common version renders temptation, has the generic sense of trial, and in some cases the specific sense of temptation. It is used extensively in both of these senses in Acts 2 : 19, Gal. 4 : 14, etc. When a word admits of different senses, the more generic sense naturally prevails, unless there is evidence from the nature of the subject or the context of the more restricted sense. In this case such evidence is entirely wanting. The general sense of trial must therefore prevail, and not the restricted sense of temptation. The correctness of this interpretation is confirmed in Matthew by the supplementary clause, But deliver us from evil.

7. With these improvements I propose the Lord's Prayers, as rendered in my version, to the earnest consideration of the people. I do not expect them to come into general use immediately, and perhaps not into exclusive use in a long period; but they have just claims to attention as the genuine Lord's Prayers of Matthew and Luke respectively, without addition or interpolation, and as renderings of them somewhat more exact and perfect than those of the common version, or of other previous versions.

NOTE V.

THE SUBSTITUTION OF POISONOUS DARNEL FOR TARES.

1. Ζιζάνια (Matt. 13 : 24–30 ; 36–43), poisonous darnel, is rendered in the common version, tares. Tares are a species of vetches. Vetches belong to the magnificent order of leguminous plants, which contains, according to an estimate in 1845, 467 genera and 6500 species. No family of the vegetable kingdom has a higher claim to respect, both as objects of ornament and utility. The acacias, sweet pea, etc., are cultivated for their flowers ; beans, peas, etc., for their fruit ; and among trees which belong to this order are the rosewood, the laburnum, and the locust ; in medicines, liquorice, senna, tamarind, gums Senegal and Arabic, balsams of copaiva and tolu, indigo, Brazil wood, logwood, and red sandal wood.

2. Tares belong to the first sub-order of these plants, to the 2d genus, the vetch, and is the 5th species, the common vetch. They are slender plants, found in the cultivated fields of Europe, with stems from two to three feet long, decumbent or climbing. The tare entirely fails to answer the description in the parable, and the whole order protests against such dishonorable imputations as the parable makes.

3. The ζιζάνιον is described by some as a species of bastard wheat. Bastard wheat is a grass of the 34th genus and 1st species. It is a handsome grass, resembling wheat, and often found in it. It is commonly called chess. This grass infests wheat, and is difficult to be separated entirely from it. Many suppose that wheat is deteriorated into chess, but the most eminent botanists hold the contrary, and consider chess to be propagated in all cases from its own seeds, like the other grasses. Chess agree with the design of the parable much better than tares. The ζιζάνια, however, were not tares nor chess, but a species of darnel grass called poisonous darnel. The grasses consist of 291 genera and 3800 species, diffused universally through the world to the utmost limits of vegetation, and contribute more to the support of man and beast than all other plants. To this order belong the grains wheat, rye, barley, oats, rice, etc.

4. One sub-order of the grasses is the lolium. Of this there are

two species: (1.) The perennial lolium or darnel grass, which grows from one to two feet high, naturalized in meadows and cultivated grounds. (2.) The lolium tumulentum, intoxicating lolium, or poisonous darnel. The poisonous darnel grows 2 feet high, and is distinguished from all other grasses by its poisonous seeds.

5. This grass was sometimes found among wheat and other grains in ancient times, both in the East and elsewhere, and still infests the grain fields of Palestine and other parts of Asia. It was also sometimes sown maliciously by personal enemies, after good seed, to injure the crop and make it worthless. Chess and other grasses which infest grain, could be eaten by cattle, and turned to some valuable account, but the poisonous darnel was required to be burned, and was unfit either for the use of man or beast. The injurious effects of the poison are referred to by the Latin poets, and agree with the design of the parable.

6. Poisonous darnel, when sown with wheat, or immediately after it, comes up at the same time, resembles it in its leaf and stalk, and can not be distinguished from it till it heads out. Then the poisonous darnel appears, and the work of the enemy, if it is sown by an enemy, shows itself. There are two ways of disposing of it: the first is to pull it up and throw it away before the seed ripens; but the other and more usual method is, to select it out from the wheat at the harvest, and burn it to destroy the seeds. All this is conformable to the description in the parable, and shows clearly that the poisonous darnel is meant, and not the bastard wheat or chess, and still less tares.

NOTE VL

THE SUBSTITUTION OF ASSEMBLY FOR CHURCH IN MATTHEW.

1. In Matt. 16 : 18 it is said, And I tell you that you are Peter [a rock], and upon this rock will I build my assembly, and the gates of hades shall not prevail against it. 18 : 17. And if he will not hear them, tell the assembly, and if he will not hear the assembly, let him be to you as a gentile and a publican. Acts 2 : 47. And the Lord added the saved day by day to the assembly [church]. After the latter passage I always translate ἐκκλησία church, when the Christian organic body is referred to. In the two instances in Matthew the common version renders the original church.

2. The same words have different meanings in different ages.

The Greek word meant assembly in our Lord's time, and his church was his assembly ; *ecclesia* was its name, and assembly was the definition of it. The same name was transferred into Latin, and is used both in Greek and Latin still, retaining in Greek also its primitive signification of assembly.

3. The English word church, derived from kirk, which is still retained in Scotland, is derived ultimately from the Greek κυριάκος, that is, Lord's, and was applied first to denote the Lord's house, the place of Christian worship ; secondly, the assembly of his worshipers ; and lastly, the organic Christian body worshiping in the house, in distinction from other attendants.

4. Church is in no case a perfect translation of ἐκκλησία. It is its equivalent as a name, but has not a corresponding signification. In both passages in Matthew the word is reported as supposed to be used by our Lord, and in the sense which belonged to it in his time. It is not therefore to be interpreted in these cases by later usage, but by contemporary usage. Contemporary usage restricts it to the sense which I have given it, and the common rendering in these cases is erroneous. Christ's churches in his lifetime were his assemblies only. After his death indications appear of a separate, independent organization, and the common name of *ecclesia*, assembly, is still applied to denote it ; but then it denotes it in a more specific sense than before. I have, therefore, translated this word according to its meaning. As long as it was a common name, though applied to a specific community, I translate it assembly ; and when it became appropriated, and virtually changed from a common name of the Christian body to a proper name distinguishing it from other assemblies, then I translate it church. Several other improvements appear in these passages. My usage in this respect is not arbitrary or without reason.

NOTE VII.

THE SUBSTITUTION OF CRANIUM FOR CALVARY.

IT is not an exact translation of ancient names to represent them in all cases by the modern ones which have succeeded them, and especially when the names are significant. The ancient name of the hill on which our Lord suffered, has been superseded since the time of Jerome, and perhaps still earlier, by Calvary and its Latin original. But its ancient name was not Calvary, nor any thing like it. It was Κρανίον, Cranium, head or hill top, bearing probably some fancied resemblance to the human head. Names are among the monuments of history, and are not to be changed arbitrarily. The name of this hill at a later period was not its name in our Lord's time. I have deemed it proper to give the hill its true name, as reported by all the four Evangelists. The common version gives its later name, as rendered by Jerome in the Vulgate. If I had translated from the Vulgate, I should have rendered the name of this hill Calvary, as is commonly done; but translating from the Greek, I considered myself bound to translate according to the Greek, and not according to later authorities. Even the correct reporting of a name may have some importance; and the correct rendering of it involves a principle of accuracy which is all-important.

NOTE VIII.

THE SUBSTITUTION OF JUSTIFYING ORDINANCE FOR JUSTIFICATION AND RIGHTEOUSNESS IN ROM. 5 : 16, 18.

1. THE original word in both cases is δικαίωμα, which neither signifies righteousness nor justification. The word for righteousness is δικαιοσύνη, and the correspondence between this and its English representative is nearly perfect. Paul uses this word for righteousness as constantly as we use the corresponding English word to denote the same thing. He uses it in this paragraph, at verses 17, 21. Righteousness is the opposite of sin, and the synonym of holiness; it is a quality of moral agents and moral actions. This clearly distinguishes its meaning and that of the original both from δικαίωμα, which does not signify righteousness nor any quality of moral agents or moral actions, but things done or made; and from δικαίωσις, justification, which signifies the doing of something not the object of an action, or a thing done.

2. Δικαίωμα signifies, (1.) The rectification of a wrong; (2.) An ordinance, law, or precept; both of which are not the doing of something, but things made, the object of some action pertaining to righteousness. This word is constantly used in the Septuagint in the latter of the above senses, as signifying an ordinance or statute, and in the plural, ordinances or statutes. It is the common Greek title for ordinances and statutes in Psalms and elsewhere.

The translators of the common Bible deviated from what they probably knew to be the common meaning of this word in both the instances under consideration. Commentators have followed them in this deviation, knowing that such usage is without a parallel elsewhere. They have done it, therefore, from a supposed necessity; and if there is no such necessity, they have done wrong. The whole question involves two points. (1.) Whether the common meaning of the word must be abandoned; (2.) What other meaning must be assumed. If the common meaning of the word is not *required* to be abandoned, it must be retained; and if it is required to be abandoned, the meanings assumed by the common version may not be the right ones; very different ones may be required. A common meaning of a word is never to be abandoned when it makes good sense, and is suitable to the context.

3. Let us try the common meaning, with no change whatever, and see what we get. Verse 16. And not as by one that sinned is the gift, for the judgment was from one to a condemnation; but the gift is from many sins to an ordinance [the ordinance of Christianity]. This certainly does not make a bad sense. Still, it is somewhat improved, perhaps, by being changed to the form in which it stands in my version. For the judgment was from one to a sentence of condemnation, but the gift is from many sins to a justifying ordinance, meaning, as before, the gospel. The common version departs from the usual meaning of δικαίωμα, ordinance, and takes that of its correlative, δικαίωσις, justification, thus confounding these two words, when the apostle clearly distinguishes them by using them both in the same paragraph. This can not be right; and whether my version is correct or not, the common version of this word must be wrong. It is not the method of Paul to use words so loosely and improperly as such a rendering assumes. But my version is not wrong; it adheres to the constant usage of the Septuagint and Greek Testament, and agrees perfectly with all the requisitions of the subject treated of and the context. It was Paul's professed object to magnify the gospel, and demonstrate its excellence and necessity; and this rendering agrees with that object. It magnifies the gospel, and asserts its excellence and necessity.

4. Let us now examine verse 18, and try the word δικαίωμα with its common signification there : Therefore, as by one sin [judgment] came on all men to condemnation, so by one ordinance, [it] comes on all men to justification of life. The word which is here rendered

justification both in my version and in the common one, means justification, the act, not the object on which it terminates; and the word which in King James's version is rendered righteousness, is the same that in verse 16 is rendered justification.   That version commits one error there, and another here.   In this passage justification is opposed to condemnation, and ordinance to sin.   In verse 16, ordinance is opposed to condemnation, and gift to judgment.   It is not necessary that objects contrasted or compared should disagree or agree in all respects; it is enough if they disagree or agree in the respects required by the argument.   The supposition of any thing more is not a legitimate hypothesis, but an unauthorized assumption.

5. In both these passages the contrasts are duly preserved, and the demands of the argument fully met, without imposing any unusual meaning on δικαίωμα; no such meaning is therefore to be imposed, and the common rendering is erroneous in verse 18, as well as the different rendering of the same word in verse 16.   The sense of the original, however, is given with some additional clearness in the slightly altered form of my New Testament, which in verse 18 is as follows : So then, as by one sin judgment came on all men to condemnation, so also by one justifying ordinance it comes on all men to justification of life.   Justification of life is here the same as a sentence of life, or judgment declaring for life.   I conclude, therefore, that the common version is erroneous in these two passages, and that their true sense is given in my version.

6. This improvement is the more valuable because the error of the common and other versions of this passage has extended to dogmatic theology, and transferred salvation from Christ and the gospel of Christ as its instrumental cause, to the righteousness of Christ, introducing a theory of salvation unknown to the Old Testament, unknown to the four Gospels, and unknown to all the Scriptures, both earlier and later, by Paul and by others.   Paul argues salvation by Christ and by the gospel, and there stops.   The whole theory of forensic justification and salvation by Christ's righteousness, is an addition which Paul never taught, and which is not to be found in his writings, when correctly interpreted.   It is a great sin to abridge the instructions of the apostles, and not allow them to teach what they actually do teach; and it is as great a sin to extend them, and make them teach more than they really teach. The business of the translator and of the interpreter is to find in their writings what they say, without adding to it or detracting from it.

7. This is a point to which Christendom is destined to come. Our opinions as to what is true are one thing, but the teachings of the sacred books are another. It is important to observe where these teachings end, and where the additions made to them in later times begin; and this we can only do by a strict application of the principles of interpretation.

8. To put on the Scriptures more than they express, is to treat them with disrespect; and if done intentionally, is an act of dishonesty and wickedness. It has been, however, a common error in the interpretation of both Testaments, and cries aloud for correction. Christendom has not till now, arrived at a point of improvement, since the days of the apostles, at which this correction was practicable. It was not possible to Origen, nor in his day; it was not possible to Jerome; the Protestant reformers made considerable advances in that direction, but stopped far short of the goal. Little has been done since but to prepare for another movement that shall accomplish the work.

NOTE IX.

THE SUBSTITUTION OF ACCOUNT FOR IMPUTE IN ROM. 4: 6, ETC.

1. WE hear nothing of imputed righteousness or sins in the Old Testament, nor in the New, till we come to Romans. In this book, according to the common version, imputation occupies a prominent place in the Pauline theology. Is this correct? Was Paul the author of this doctrine? or has it a different and later origin? The question is solely one of interpretation; and in my version both the word *impute* and the idea expressed by it, are ruled out of the Scriptures. Which is correct? Let us look at the facts. Rom. 4: 6, reads in the common version, Even as David describeth the blessedness of the man unto whom God imputeth righteousness without works, saying, Blessed are they whose iniquities are forgiven, and whose sins are covered, etc. My version is thus: 3: 3, As David describes the blessedness of the man to whom the Lord accounts righteousness without works; blessed are they whose transgressions are forgiven, and whose sins are covered; blessed is the man to whom the Lord does not account sin.

2. In these cases the verb which the common version renders impute, and mine account, is λογίζεται, the proper meaning of which

is to account, and not to impute. It has some diversity of meanings, and signifies to think, consider, judge, reckon, suppose, but never to impute. The common version, therefore, is incorrect in these and all similar cases. Paul never mentions impute or imputation, and wherever the common version represents him as doing so, it is erroneous. Instances of this: In verse 11, That he might be the father of all them that believe, though they be not circumcised, that righteousness might be imputed to them also. Here, as before, it should be, accounted to them. Verse 22, And therefore it [his faith] was imputed to him for righteousness. This, too, should be, accounted. So in verse 23. The verb, in all these cases, is the same, and is the same which in verse 4 is rendered reckoned, in verse 5 counted, and in verses 9 and 10 reckoned. These latter renderings are essentially correct, though the term account suits all the passages, and expresses the sense of the original more appropriately. In chapter 5: 13, *ἐλλογεῖται* is used and mistranslated impute in the expression, Sin is not imputed where there is no law. It should be, Sin is not accounted, or, No account is made of sin, where there is no law.

3. The imputation, therefore, supposed to be taught in Romans, is a mistake; properly rendered, there is none in the book, but only God's having an account with men, and making account of their doings. The objects of this supposed imputation are in every case the doings of the person whose account is referred to. Abraham's faith is put to his account as righteous, and to him that works not, but believes on him that justifies the wicked, his faith is accounted to him, that is, set to his account as righteous; and the fact that Abraham's faith was set to his account as righteous, is recorded for our benefit, to whose account a like faith shall also be set, if we believe on him that raised up Jesus our Lord from the dead, who was delivered up for our offenses, and raised up for our justification.

4. God has been represented from the earliest times as keeping an account with men, as men keep accounts with their servants, and certain things go into the account as righteous or righteousness. The Jews of Paul's time supposed the observance of the Mosaic institutions were the exclusive matters of that account. Every work of obedience prescribed by them, was, in their estimation, an act of righteousness, and procured favor; nothing else did. Contrary to this, Paul maintains and proves that righteousness was older than the law of Moses, and did not depend on it; that God kept accounts with

Abraham, in whom they gloried, and admitted his faith as righteous; and that David dissents from them, when he declares, Ps. 32 : 1, 2, Blessed are they whose wickedness is forgiven, and whose sins are covered. Blessed is the man to whom the Lord accounts not sin.

5. According to the Jews of Paul's time, Abraham ought to have had account made of nothing in his favor but his circumcision, when he was 100 years old, and his sacrifices. These were his [legal] works in the Jewish sense. According to them David ought to have said, Blessed is the man that keeps the law of Moses; and should never have gone beyond that.

6. There is no doctrine of imputation found, therefore, in these words of Paul, and none demanded by the context. All the demands of the context are to disparage works of the law of Moses, and exalt the law of Christ. This does not require imputation, nor the imputation scheme. It only requires that the gospel of Christ should be maintained as a genuine law of righteousness, prescribing what God prescribes, commanding what God commands, and correctly setting forth the principles of righteousness in the sight of God. This is what Paul claims for the gospel; and he ably sustains this claim.

7. Paul's doctrine of righteousness and justification, as taught in other parts of this Epistle, agrees with the above views. His δικαιωσύνη, righteousness, corresponds to the Hebrew צֶדֶק, rectitude, justice; and צְדָקָה, rectitude, justice, righteousness; and denotes the character of a moral agent. Character is personal and inalienable; the most sacred of all human properties. Paul's righteousness of God which is revealed in the gospel; Rom. 1 : 17, which is made manifest without the law, and testified to, by the law and the prophets, and which is by the faith of Jesus Christ to all and on all that believe; 3 : 21, 22, which is fully exhibited by Christ Jesus after long endurance of men's sins by the forbearance of God; verses 25, 26, which God approves and requires, and by which alone true happiness is attained, is not an imputed but a personal righteousness according to the law of Christ. Such is the teaching of Paul. Nothing beyond this is found in his words, and to make him say more is to interpret him in conformity with later traditionary opinions which he entirely ignores. This is not to take opinions from him, but to impose opinions on him; to pervert his testimony, and interpolate matters into it of which he says nothing. If the sin was not committed ignorantly, like the crucifixion of our

32 *

Lord, it would be one of the most enormous acts of wickedness possible, analogous to corrupting testimony designed for judicial tribunals, and poisoning fountains from which men take their common drink.

NOTE X.

THE SUBSTITUTION OF COVENANT FOR TESTAMENT.

1. THE word Testament occurs several times in the common version of the New Testament: in Matt. 26 : 28, For this is my blood of the New Testament, which is shed for many for the remission of sins.   Luke 22 : 20, Likewise, also, the cup after supper, saying, This cup is the New Testament in my blood, which is shed for you. 1 Cor. 11 : 25, After the same manner, also, he took the cup when he had supped, saying, This cup is the New Testament in my blood ; this do ye, as oft as ye drink it, in remembrance of me.   Heb. 9 : 15–20, And for this cause he is the mediator of the New Testament, that by means of death, for the redemption of the transgressions which were under the first testament, they which are called might receive the promise of eternal inheritance.   For where a testament is, there must also of necessity be the death of the testator.   For a testament is of force after men are dead, otherwise it is of no strength at all while the testator liveth.   Whereupon neither the first testament was dedicated without blood.   For when Moses had spoken every precept to all the people, according to the law, he took the blood of calves and of goats, with water and scarlet wool and hyssop, and sprinkled both the book and all the people, saying, This is the blood of the testament which God hath enjoined unto you.

2. The Greek word translated testament in all these passages is διαθήκη, which in the Septuagint uniformly answers to the Hebrew בְּרִית, covenant arrangement.   It is derived from διατίθημι, to set in order, to dispose, to arrange, to make an arrangement or covenant.   Any arrangement for the government of men, and any disposition of property whatever, is a διαθήκη, whether donative or testamentary.

3. A διαθήκη does not necessarily require the consent of a second party ; it may be completed by the first.   This word and the corresponding Hebrew one are rendered generally in the Old Testament and New, covenant ; and that word is applied to denote

God's arrangements with men, and the constitutions of society which are attributed to him. There is not a perfect propriety in this application of the word. Arrangement, or constitution, would represent the original more exactly. But the word has long been so used, and this usage is adopted in King James's translation, and carried through it every where, except in the passages above quoted.

4. The instances in which the word is translated testament are few, in comparison with the whole number of instances in which it occurs ; and its meaning is the same in these cases as in the others. Here and elsewhere it signifies God's arrangements with men. (1.) The arrangement with Abraham, which is called God's covenant with that patriarch, as in Luke 1 : 72, 73, To perform his mercy with our fathers, and to remember his holy covenant, the oath which he swore to Abraham our father, to grant us to serve him without fear. So in Acts 3 : 25 ; 7 : 8 ; Gal. 3 : 17. (2.) The arrangement made with the Israelites by Moses. This is every where called by the Hebrew בְּרִית, translated in the Septuagint, διαθήκη. The Mosaic covenant was the Mosaic body of laws or constitution. (3.) Last of all follow the Christian laws or constitution, which are also called by the same title. In Gal. 4 : 2, the laws of Moses and of Christ are described as two covenants ; one from Sinai, which produces children for servitude, and the other the Jerusalem above, which is the mother of us. The law of Christ is called the new covenant, predicted Jer. 31 : 31–34, different from the covenant which God made with their fathers. This word, therefore, means an arrangement, constitution, or body of laws imposed on men, and denotes the different constitutions and bodies of laws established at different times ; (1.) The Abrahamic laws ; (2.) The Mosaic laws ; (3.) Lastly, the laws of Christ. In the several passages at the head of this note, the common Greek title of all these laws is rendered in the common version, testament. The same objects are expressed as in other cases. It is manifest, therefore, that one of the renderings is erroneous. If διαθήκη is rightly rendered covenant every where else, it ought to be so rendered here ; and if these passages are rightly rendered testament, the others ought to be so rendered ; if neither is right, then we ought to adopt what is right.

5. Testament does not represent these constitutions correctly ; they are not wills, disposing of property and privileges after one has died ; God never dies ; but they are laws. They are not covenants in the sense of mutual contracts, which require the consent of the

second party for their validity and binding force; they are simply constitutions and bodies of laws, imposed by authority; and if called covenants, must be so called in this peculiar limited sense. Thus defined, and explained by the objects to which it is applied, covenant may perhaps be continued with propriety, though the more general term of arrangement answers most exactly to the original Greek and Hebrew, and constitution is most conformable to modern usage in respect to fundamental organic laws. Schemes of government in modern times are generally called constitutions. The passages under consideration, therefore, all require correction, by the substitution of covenant for testament.

6. With this correction and others, the passages read as follows: Matt. 26 : 28, This is my blood of the covenant which is poured out for many, for the forgiveness of sins. Luke 22 : 20, And the cup in like manner, after supper, saying, This cup is the new covenant by my blood, which is poured out for you. 1 Cor. 11 : 25, In like manner the cup, after supper, saying, This cup is the new covenant by my blood; this do as often as you drink, in remembrance of me. Heb. 9 : 15–20, And for this reason he is the mediator of the new covenant, that [his] death having been for redemption from transgressions over the first covenant, the called might take the promise of the eternal inheritance. For where there is a covenant, there must necessarily be brought the death of the covenanter; for a covenant is strong over the dead; since it is [otherwise] never strong when the covenant maker lives. Whence the first covenant was not dedicated without blood; for every commandment having been spoken according to the law by Moses to all the people, taking the blood of bullocks and goats, with water and scarlet wool and hyssop, he sprinkled both the book itself and all the people, saying, This is the blood of the covenant which God has commanded you.

7. The Mosaic law was not a testament, made valid by the death of the testator, but a constitution dedicated and ratified with the blood of sacrificial victims. Just as little is the law of Christ a testament. That, too, is a body of ordinances and instructions, not ratified by the death of Christ as a testator, but by the blood of Christ as a sacrifice. Christianity, therefore, is not a testament or will, nor are its sacred books testamentary documents. The name testament, applied to them in English, and the corresponding *testamentum* in Latin, do not agree with the facts. A more proper name would be covenant or constitution.

NOTE XI.

THE SUBSTITUTION OF BROTHERS FOR BRETHREN.

BROTHER originally formed its plural by the addition of *en*, and all brothers were brethren. In the process of time the ancient plural was abandoned, and brothers used for brethren, in respect to relations by blood ; but the old form, being in the Scriptures, has caused it to be retained with the other, as the form appropriated to members of the same churches, crafts, and societies. This is a departure from ancient usage, which applied the same forms to denote religious and society brothers as others. Besides the old form is less eligible than its successor in consequence of its adding a syllable to the singular, and otherwise changing the word, while the modern term only changes the final syllable. My version follows the original writers closely ; who represented religious and society brothers by the same term as others. The method of the common version is a departure from their usage which requires correction ; besides misrepresenting the originals, it contributes to form a religious dialect different from the secular one. This is not the policy of Christianity, and can only injure it. On every account, therefore, my improvement ought to be sustained. It adds both to the beauty of the style and the exactness of the translation ; and is intrinsically a better form for practical use, giving to the language of religion an improvement which belongs to the common language, and which constitutes one of its graces.

NOTE XII.

TABLE OF CHAPTERS

IN THE NEW TESTAMENT OF THIS VERSION, AND IN THE COMMON VERSION, IN PARALLEL COLUMNS.

MATTHEW.

CHAP.		CHAP.
1	corresponds to	1.
2	"	2.
3	"	3, 4, 1–11.
4	"	4, 12–25.
5	"	5, 6, 7.
6	"	8, 9.
7	"	10, 11, 1.
8	"	11, 2–30.
9	"	12, 1–21.
10	"	12, 22–50.
11	"	13.
12	"	14.
13	"	15.
14	"	16.
15	"	17.
16	"	18.
17	"	19, 20, 1–28.
18	"	20, 29–34; 21, 1–22.
19	"	21, 23–46.
20	"	22.
21	"	23.
22	"	24, 25.
23	"	26, 1–35.
24	"	26, 36–75.
25	"	27, 1–26.
26	"	27, 27–61.
27	"	27, 62–66; 28.

MARK.

1	corresponds to	1.
2	"	2, 3, 1–12.
3	"	3, 13–35.
4	"	4.
5	"	5.

CHAP.		CHAP.
6	corresponds to	6.
7	"	7.
8	"	8.
9	"	9.
10	"	10.
11	"	11, 12.
12	"	13.
13	"	14, 1–26.
14	"	14, 27–52.
15	"	14, 53–72; 15, 1–15.
16	"	15, 16–47.
17	"	16, 1–8.
18	"	16, 9–20.

LUKE.

1	corresponds to	1, 1–38.
2	"	1, 39–80.
3	"	2.
4	"	3.
5	"	4, 1–30.
6	"	4, 31–44; 5, 1–16.
7	"	5, 17–39; 6, 1–11.
8	"	6, 12–49.
9	"	7, 1–35.
10	"	7, 36–50; 8, 1–21.
11	"	8, 22–56.
12	"	9, 1–27.
13	"	9, 28–50.
14	"	9, 51–62; 10, 1–24.
15	"	10, 25–42; 11, 1–13.
16	"	11, 14–54.
17	"	12.
18	"	13.
19	"	14.
20	"	15.

(382)

CHAP.   CHAP.
3 corresponds to 3, 21–31; **4, 5.**
4   "   **6.**
5   "   **7.**
6   "   **8.**
7   "   **9, 10.**
8   "   **11.**
9   "   **12, 13.**
10   "   **14, 15.**
11   "   **16.**

PHILEMON.

COLOSSIANS.
1 corresponds to **1, 2.**
2   "   **3, 4.**

EPHESIANS (*Laodiceans*).
1 corresponds to **1, 2, 3.**
2   "   **4, 5, 6.**

PHILIPPIANS.
1 corresponds to **1, 2.**
2   "   **3, 4.**

TITUS.

1 TIMOTHY.
1 corresponds to **1, 2.**
2   "   **3, 4, 5, 6.**

2 TIMOTHY.
1 corresponds to **1, 2.**
2   "   **3, 4.**

THE CATHOLIC EPISTLES.

JAMES.
1 corresponds to **1, 2.**
2   "   **3, 4, 5.**

1 PETER.
CHAP.   CHAP.
1 corresponds to **1, 2,** 1–10.
2   "   **2,** 11–25 ; **3, 4,** 1–11.
3   "   **4,** 12–19; **5.**

2 PETER.
1 corresponds to **1, 2.**
2   "   **3.**

JUDAS.

1 JOHN.
1 corresponds to **1, 2, 3.**
2   "   **4, 5.**

2 JOHN.

3 JOHN.

HEBREWS.
1 corresponds to **1, 2, 3, 4,** 1–13.
2   "   **4,** 14–16; **5, 6, 7.**
3   "   **8, 9, 10,** 1–18.
4   "   **10,** 19–39; **11.**
5   "   **12, 13.**

REVELATION.

1 corresponds to **1.**
2   "   **2, 3.**
3   "   **4, 5.**
4   "   **6, 7.**
5   "   **8, 9.**
6   "   **10, 11,** 1–14.
7   "   **11,** 15–19; **12, 13.**
8   "   **14.**
9   "   **15, 16.**
10   "   **17, 18.**
11   "   **19, 20,** 1–10.
12   "   **20,** 11–15; **21, 22.**

CPSIA information can be obtained
at www.ICGtesting.com
Printed in the USA
BVHW081806220819
556561BV00019B/4304/P